DATE DUE

Management Essentials
for
Christian Ministries

Management Essentials
for
Christian Ministries

Edited by
Michael J. Anthony and James Estep, Jr.

BROADMAN
&HOLMAN
PUBLISHERS

Nashville, Tennessee

Published by Broadman & Holman Publishers
Nashville, Tennessee

Dewey Decimal Classification: 254
Subject Heading: MANAGEMENT \
CHURCH ADMINISTRATION \
LEADERSHIP

3 4 5 6 7 8 9 10 11 10 09 08 07 06 05

*We would like to dedicate this book to
those who have given us their unconditional love
and support over many years—
our families.*

To Michelle
and our children Chantel and Brenon Anthony

To Karen Lynn
and our children Budd, Dovie, and Dylan Estep

Contents

Contributors   ix

Introduction   1

PART 1: INTEGRATION / 9
1. Biblical Perspectives of Christian Management   13
2. A Theology of Administration   35

PART 2: PLANNING / 53
3. Building Mission and Vision   59
4. Developing Goals and Objectives   76
5. Developing a Strategic Ministry Plan   87
6. Policies and Procedures as Planning Tools   101
7. Preparing and Reading a Budget   115
8. Ministry by Objectives   133

PART 3: ORGANIZING / 155
9. Organizational Structures   158
10. Preparing Job Descriptions   174
11. Conducting Effective Meetings   190
12. Ministry Leaders as Change Agents   201
13. Decision Making and Communication
within the Organization   222

PART 4: STAFFING / 240
14. Recruiting and Screening Volunteers   244
15. Developing Staff Members   258
16. Legal and Ethical Considerations in Ministry   274

PART 5: DIRECTING / 293
17. Developing Leaders   297
18. Mentoring in Ministry   313

19. Transforming Groups into Teams   333
20. Leadership Strategies   349
21. Working with Boards and Committees   365

PART 6: EVALUATING / 383
22. Conducting Performance Reviews   387
23. Evaluating the Effectiveness of Programs   411

Notes   427
Index   451

Contributors

Michael Anthony, Professor of Christian Education, Talbot School of Theology, Biola University

Michelle Anthony, Pastor of New Generation Ministries, Coast Hills Community Church, Aliso Viejo, CA

Gary Bredfelt, Professor of Christian Education, Moody Bible Institute

J. R. "Tony" Buchanan, Executive Vice President, Florida Christian College

Gordon Coulter, Director of Field Education, Professor of Christian Education, Haggard School of Theology, Azusa Pacific University

Jane Carr, Associate Professor of Christian Education, Talbot School of Theology, Biola University

James Estep Jr., Professor of Christian Education, Lincoln Christian College and Seminary

Mark Henze, Attorney at Law, Ph.D. student, Talbot School of Theology, Biola University

Richard Leyda, Associate Professor of Christian Education, Talbot School of Theology, Biola University

Larry Purcell, Associate Professor of Christian Education, Southern Baptist Theological Seminary

Mark Simpson, Professor of Christian Education, Southern Baptist Theological Seminary

Dennis Williams, Dean of Institutional Research, Professor of Christian Education, Southern Baptist Theological Seminary

Introduction

Management Origins in Perspective

THERE ARE THOSE WHO OPPOSE any form of management or administration in the local church and other religious nonprofit ministries. They view such efforts as secular and see their contributions as tantamount to accepting the methods of the devil. These believers have little understanding of the biblical basis and theological foundation of management. They are simply uninformed about what the Bible teaches about organizing the affairs of ministry. As stewards, we are expected to administrate God's work in a wise and efficient manner. In fact, as ministry leaders we will one day give an account for our oversight when we stand before our Master. A good steward is one who recognizes his responsibility to oversee the affairs of his master and focuses his efforts toward that end.

New reflections and considerations of administrative theory and practice are essential for the Christian community if it is to remain relevant. However, we need to resist the impulse-shopping approach that characterizes our age. Managing God's ministry requires serious biblical examination and focused thinking. Providing oversight and management for God's work must depend on more than fads and three-step methods. Digging deeper into the biblical, theological, and theoretical foundations of biblical stewardship of ministry is what this book is all about.

Management theory has changed a great deal over the past fifty years. Methods of management and administration have made significant improvements in business, education, health care services, and the military. Yet the churches have failed to keep abreast with these new insights and have fallen far behind. The result is mismanagement and confusion. When congregational members, many of whom are trained in these fields, observe the ineffective ways church leaders manage

1

ministry resources, they lose trust and view these leaders with suspicion and contempt. Since many of these management principles have their origins in Scripture, what is needed is a foundation of biblical teaching regarding the concepts of management, organization, and administrative practice.

Past Paradigms: Fads and Fantasies

Few books on ministry management are based on a comprehensive theory of management or a theological integration of teachings on administration. Rather, they focus on individual tasks, narrowly focused principles, or even endeavor to provide *a* solution to an administrative setting requiring more than *one* response, resulting in the formation of a new administrative fad. Complex ministry problems are not solved with a three-step seven-laws formula. This may sell books, but it doesn't solve the real problem. These books lack an overriding paradigm in which to conceptualize administration. Instead, they focus on a management technique or gimmicks to solve a problem. They result in a plethora of contemporary fads and fantasies for quick-fix solutions. Without meaningful discussion of the theoretical basis for the solution, the problem comes back in a slightly different form—much like a bacteria that has grown resistant to antibiotics.

This text delves below the surface of nonprofit management problems to explore possible solutions from a more systematic perspective. This systems approach to management is certainly not new but is somewhat unique to nonprofit contexts. It is based upon the work of R. Alec Mackenzie, who first published his paradigm in the *Harvard Business Review* in its November-December 1969 issue. It has served as the basis for the structure of business administration texts for decades. Graduate degree programs in business, education, and nursing were designed around its rubric. Our figure represents a significant modification from the original model due to the addition of a biblical worldview and twenty-first-century content updates. Figure 0.1 illustrates this paradigm.

This diagram illustrates an ongoing cycle of institutional recreation. It is not a stagnant portrait of administration today but rather a *process* of administrative design. It is not a snapshot but a movie. The paradigm is based on a fourfold focus: Scripture, Ideas, Things, and People. These four elements are necessary; without any one of the four basic elements, Christian administration lacks a comprehensive perspective. From these four elements arise further management tasks. Each task is necessary for conceptualizing management in the community of faith. Each task plays a vital role in the ongoing process.

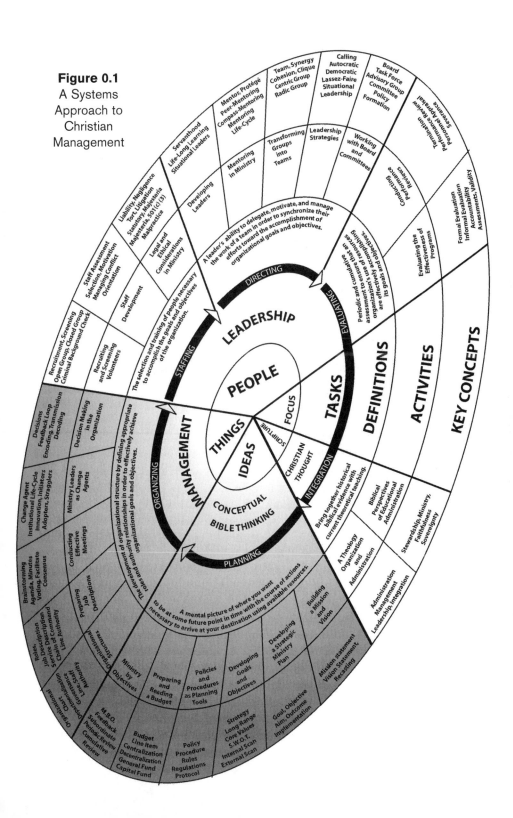

Figure 0.1
A Systems
Approach to
Christian
Management

- *Christian thought* calls for a process of *integrating* Scripture and theology into what we do as administrators, reflecting on the foundational assumptions of administration that is Christian.
- *Conceptual Bible thinking* calls for a process of *planning* in administration with Scripture and theology in mind, putting to paper the "ideas" of the organization.
- *Management* calls us to commit to *organizing* the institution to achieve its plans, focusing on the proper utilization of resources, "things."
- *Leadership* calls us to a multiphased process of *staffing, directing,* and *evaluating,* while focusing on the "people," not as resources but as participants in our ministry endeavor.

Six functions of management flow out of these conceptual tasks. These six functions are integration, planning, organizing, staffing, directing, and evaluating. Each is critical to the success of Christian management theory and practice. Eliminate any one and the entire institution collapses into disarray and confusion. The activities associated with each of these functions become the practical out-flowing of the theory. In this way practice is always connected to theory and vice versa. Each depends on the other for validity and meaningful purpose.

Once the content of the cycle has been incorporated into the life of the institution, the cycle repeats itself. A reintegration of theological thinking based on the evaluation of present conditions gives rise to a new look at the functions of planning, organizing, staffing, directing, and evaluating. In short, the paradigm recreates itself, maintaining not only a contemporary approach to administration, but ensuring its compatibility with the Christian community of faith because of its commitment to continual integration and conceptual Bible thinking.

Design of the Text

In order to provide a comprehensive application of this theory, this text is designed around the twenty-three components of this systematic paradigm. Once we affirmed the major tasks and functions and updated for twenty-first century application to religious nonprofits, we assigned individual chapters to authors who had achieved national recognition for expertise in these respective areas. Figure 0.2 illustrates how the chapters address the key concepts of this systems approach to Christian management paradigm.

Chapters 1–2 address the process of integration, illustrating its presence in Scripture and providing a theological framework through which the Christian leader can approach administrative work. Chapters 3–8 provide insight into the management function of planning, including building mission and vision, developing a strategic plan, developing goals

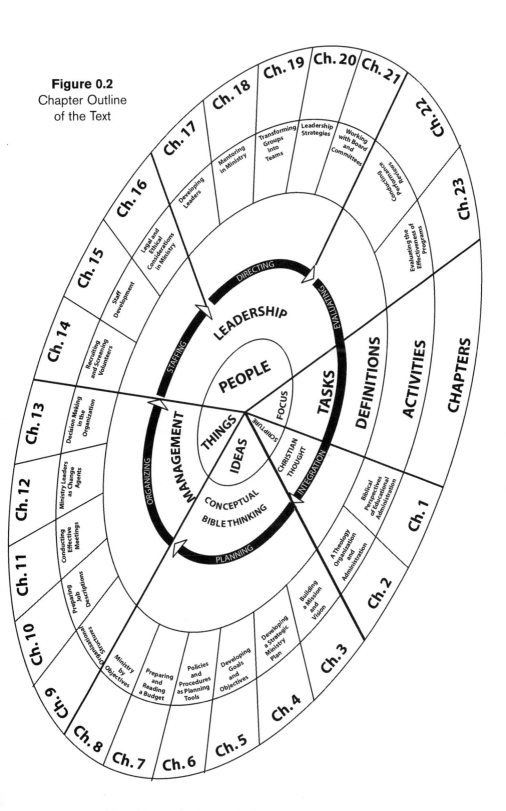

Figure 0.2
Chapter Outline
of the Text

Ch. 17
Ch. 16
Ch. 15
Ch. 14
Ch. 13
Ch. 12
Ch. 11
Ch. 10
Ch. 9
Ch. 8
Ch. 7
Ch. 6
Ch. 5
Ch. 4
Ch. 3
Ch. 2
Ch. 1
Ch. 23
Ch. 22
Ch. 21
Ch. 20
Ch. 19
Ch. 18

DIRECTING
EVALUATING
STAFFING
ORGANIZING
PLANNING
INTEGRATION

LEADERSHIP
MANAGEMENT

PEOPLE
THINGS
IDEAS

FOCUS
SCRIPTURE
CHRISTIAN THOUGHT

CONCEPTUAL
BIBLE THINKING

TASKS
DEFINITIONS
ACTIVITIES
CHAPTERS

Developing Leaders
Legal and Ethical Considerations in Ministry
Staff Development
Recruiting and Screening Volunteers
Decision Making in the Organization
Ministry Leaders as Change Agents
Conducting Effective Meetings
Preparing Job Descriptions
Organizational Structures
Ministry by Objectives
Preparing and Reading a Budget
Policies and Procedures as Planning Tools
Developing Goals and Objectives
Developing a Strategic Ministry Plan
Building a Mission and Vision
A Theology of Organization and Administration
Biblical Perspectives of Educational Administration

Mentoring in Ministry
Transforming Groups into Teams
Leadership Strategies
Working with Board and Committees
Conducting Performance Reviews
Evaluating the Effectiveness of Programs

and objectives for ministry, using policies and procedures in planning, preparing and reading budgets, and doing ministry with intentionality through a ministry-by-objectives approach. Chapters 9–13 outline the managerial function of organizing. This section details the activities of developing the organizational structure, preparing job descriptions, conducting effective meetings, implementing change and managing conflict, as well as the process of group decision making.

Chapters 14–23 detail the managerial functions associated with leading an organization: staffing, directing, and evaluating. Staffing is discussed in regard to recruiting, developing, and the fair treatment of volunteers and employees. Directing is presented in light of developing leaders, mentoring them, team building, leadership strategies, and working within a committee or board structure. Evaluating is focused on the assessment of individuals and programs. In short, the text divisions directly reflect the administrative paradigm for a comprehensive approach to the Christian management of a nonprofit ministry. Since religious nonprofit organizations encompass many avenues of service (e.g., Christian schools and camps, parachurch agencies, etc.), a wider application to these functions is encompassed beyond church application. However, since church application is its primary focus, ample material will be directed toward this perspective.

Each chapter was written by an individual who has not only academic training in the specialized subject area but also practical ministry experience in congregations and Christian organizations; hence, the text is pastorally friendly to the reader.

Bridging Theory and Practice

When we began this project, it started with a conversation in 2002 at the annual conference of the North American Professors of Christian Education. However, it was not an academic objective we pursued, but rather a pastoral one. From the time of our initial discussions until we outlined the text, recruited contributors, and published the book, we have had one desire. We desire that this text will provide Christian leaders in congregations and Christian organizations with a resource for improving their efficiency and effectiveness for Christ's kingdom. It is not designed to be one more book of administrative theory or another textbook used once and discarded; rather, it is intended to be an ongoing resource to help those in Christ's service to fulfill their calling in the community of faith. Bridging the gap between theory and practice has been a major focus of this book. Theory is essential, for it provides us with the rationale behind our actions. However, theory disconnected from practice results in ignorance and stagnant ideas. It was critical that we blend theory with contemporary practice to make this book a valuable resource for decades to come. We pray that the material in this text will serve the ultimate purpose of building up the kingdom by training and equipping God's leaders for effective service.

Michael J. Anthony
Talbot School of Theology, La Mirada, California

James Riley Estep Jr.
Lincoln Christian Seminary, Lincoln, Illinois

PART 1

INTEGRATION

As we read through the pages of Scripture we find that God cares a great deal about how we represent him before the eyes of an unbelieving world. He is also deeply concerned with the manner in which his people use the gifts and talents he has provided. When a servant misuses a resource or doesn't take his responsibilities seriously, as in the case of the parable of the unjust servant (Matt. 24:45–51), God is quick to judge that servant with harsh treatment. Likewise we see in the parable of the talents that God gives to his servants a certain number of talents and responsibilities and expects that they will be busy doing the work of their eternal Master until he returns (Matt. 25:14–30).

The lesson in these stories is that if we are careless in the administration of our duties, we will be the recipient of God's discipline. These passages, and many more that could be related, speak of God's concern for the proper use of his resources. As his servants we are responsible for the care and proper distribution of his material, financial, human, and spiritual resources. This stewardship role is not one that should be entered into lightly, because it comes with high expectations of honest and ethical behavior.

The Bible has a great deal to say about stewardship and the proper use of God's possessions. The biblical perspective on stewardship is that God's resources are not our own. They are his, and he has entrusted them to our safe keeping until he feels it appropriate to have them returned. For this reason, a Christian manager should view himself or herself first and foremost as a servant of God's resources. Whether our ministry happens to be the care and feeding of a local church congregation, the distribution of food and shelter to homeless individuals, directing a camp or conference center, the administration of a private Christian school, or perhaps serving on an international mission board, the same realization is needed that we are just passing through, and God has given the supervision of his ministry into our hands for a prescribed time.

There is an expectation that a future accounting will be required of us, and this accounting should include some degree of spiritual dividend. In short, God is expecting an increase as a result of his investment. Christian leaders, regardless of the ministry organization in which they serve, have a profound responsibility to administrate God's organizations within specified boundaries. These boundaries are clearly laid out for us in his Word. However, some degree of hermeneutical skill is required to interpret his Word correctly. Without an accurate interpretation there is no hope for a correct application. History has shown us that the end does not justify the means. Just because we are busy building the kingdom doesn't mean God is not concerned with the ethical and moral treatment of his leaders. Indeed, he is very concerned about proper management because when one of his organizations becomes the focus of a legal or ethical probe in the national newspapers, God's reputation is soiled as a result.

That's why this book is so important. It isn't just another book about how to manage a business. If it were, it would be redundant, for there are already plenty of good books on the market to serve that purpose. This book's unique contribution is the integration of solid biblical teaching about stewardship with sound practices of business management. It isn't a stretch to bring the two entities together, for both are concerned with stewardship. As one Lutheran executive writes, "Administration and theology are contextually supportive and consistent, reflecting a church that is undivided and whole—human and divine, secular and sacred, present minded and future minded."[1]

Many local church pastors lament and scorn the need for church administration. They speak of long hours spent in committees trying to make decisions about matters which have far less importance than preaching or counseling. "Seminary just didn't prepare me for this," said one senior pastor. The problem isn't so much that administration or management is an alien language; the problem is that seminary curriculum is generally devoid of instruction in this most important of pastoral responsibilities. Since more senior pastors are removed from office over matters of mismanagement than doctrine, you would think that seminaries would be more attentive to this important topic.

Management of ministry is necessary for a variety of reasons.[2] First, because ministry is all about people, not programs. Individuals have strengths, weaknesses, gifts, and desires. They hurt and need our attention. Their lives are fragmented and torn apart by their human condition. We do not provide ministry in a vacuum but within the context of people. For this reason we need to remember that management is the means to the end, never the end by itself. Christian management allows us to serve people more efficiently.

The second reason for the need of management in Christian ministry is because the body of Christ is a corporate entity. It's not an organization but rather an *organism*, living and breathing as the body of Christ incarnate in this world. The church is a community of people who have come together out of their own volition to function as a group. As such believers are members "one of another" of the same spiritual body, members of God's family. The management functions of planning, organizing, staffing, directing, and evaluating are critical for ministry operation because Christian ministries are part of the corporate body with a corporate life and mission. The Bible is clear about communicating this corporate reality by conveying images such as the family, the body of Christ, the household of God, people of God, nation of God, holy nation, and royal priesthood. Without Christian management the corporate life of the church is compromised and negated.

The third reason for management in Christian ministries is because the church has a mission and cannot accomplish that mission apart from coordinated effort. Regardless of the metaphor that is used—the military in battle, the football team on the field, or the orchestra in the chamber hall—nothing is accomplished apart from preparation and planning. Support lines need to be established and defended. Materials need to be acquired, and people need to be selected and trained. All of these activities are at the heart of sound management.

Though the mission may be described differently depending on the organization's context and audience, it is still concerned with the overall goal of bringing people into a relationship with God through salvation and spiritual formation. These two primary activities are the thrust of the Great Commission. As summarized by one senior pastor, "Administration is not peripheral to the life and work of the church. It is necessary because the church is people—corporate people with a mission."[3]

Administration and *management*, terms used synonymously within this text, are clearly demonstrated throughout the pages of Scripture by those who were used by the Lord to accomplish his purposes (e.g., Moses, Joseph, Nehemiah, Jesus, Paul, Peter, etc.). In addition, administration is offered as a divine gift to the church for the express purpose of helping Christian ministries function effectively and efficiently. First Corinthians 12:28 states that "God has appointed in the church first apostles, second prophets, third teachers, then miracles, then gifts of healings, helps, administrations, various kinds of tongues" (NASB). It is of note that the Greek word for administrator is *kubernesis*. This word is used to describe the role of the ship's helmsman. A description of this gift and its possible use in the early church is found in *The Theological Dictionary of the New Testament.*

The reference can only be to the specific gifts which qualify a Christian to be a helmsman to his congregation, i.e. a true director of its order and therewith of its life. What was the scope of this directive activity in the time of Paul we do not know. This was a period of fluid development. The importance of the helmsman increases in times of storm. The office of directing the congregation may well have developed especially in emergencies both within and without. The proclamation of the Word was not originally this. . . . No society can exist without some order and direction. It is the grace of God to give gifts which equip for government. The striking point is that when in verse 29 Paul asks whether all are apostles, whether all are prophets, or whether all have gifts of healing, there are no corresponding questions in respect to *antilenpseis* and *kupernesis.* The congregation may step in to serve as *deacon* or *ruler.* Hence these offices, as distinct from those mentioned in verse 29, may be elective. But this does not alter the fact that for their proper discharge the charisma of God is indispensable.[4]

There clearly was a spiritual gift of administration provided for the early church that continues to serve a critical role for the body of Christ today. This unit is designed to provide a biblical basis for Christian management (chapter 1) and also a summarized perspective which pulls the various passages together into a coherent theology (chapter 2). The reader will note that these chapters are a bit longer than most of the remaining chapters, since they lay a critical foundation for all of the material which follows. Indeed, there is a biblical theology of management for Christian ministries, and it is necessary for all ministry leaders to understand it and to be able to articulate it to members of their congregations and ministry audiences.

BY
MICHAEL ANTHONY

Chapter 1

Biblical Perspectives of Christian Management

ONE OF THE GREATEST OBSTACLES we face in managing the resources of ministry is our misunderstanding about the origins of management—both in terms of principles and practice. Many well-meaning Christians mistakenly believe that since businesses have incorporated and promoted popular methods of management in order to produce financial profit, then there must be something inherently wrong with integrating these same principles into the way we organize and administrate the affairs of the church. The problem with this faulty reasoning, however, is that many of the principles found in secular organization and administration textbooks used in MBA programs across North America did not originate in corporate America. Most of these principles of management originated more than four thousand years ago and are recorded in the pages of Scripture.

The Old and New Testaments are replete with examples of planning, organizing, staffing, directing, and evaluating long before North America began using them in their business ventures. This chapter will provide the reader with biblical examples and theological principles of organization and administration which have their origins in the Bible. Each of the five managerial functions will be surveyed and explored through the lens of the Old and New Testaments with the hope that the reader will come to a realization that God is the ultimate author of sound principles of management.[1]

Planning

Planning is defined as a process which starts with a mental picture of where you want to be at some future point in time (goal). It then lays out a course of action (strategy) in measurable steps (objectives) following the correct road signs (policies and procedures) so you can arrive at your destination using the resources available (personnel, budget, facilities, etc.). Effective leaders are able to articulate their destination in words that captivate and inspire others to follow. This is often referred to as a mission statement. This statement allows others who may not be able to foresee the future as clearly to have an idea about where the leader intends to take them.

Planning is not mystical or magical. Some people equate it with conjuring up the unknown like false prophets using a crystal ball. This, however, is not planning. Planning sees into the future and hopes for what can become, but it is not a blind leap into the dark. Once grabbing hold of a vision, a leader begins to build that future in a detailed, step-by-step process. It involves a great deal of effort and tenacity. For those who see dimly into the lens of the future, it also involves a degree of faith. There are plenty of examples of planning recorded in the Bible. Time doesn't allow an exhaustive account of all the accounts of planning, but a brief survey of the more prominent examples might be helpful.

Genesis records the creation of the universe in such a manner as to leave no doubt that God had a plan. He established the order of events from the smallest details of the atom to the limitless expanse of space. Each of the days of creation is marked with purposeful activity and design. Nothing is left to chance or random accident. Each day contains specific direction spoken by God about what should be established. From the creation of the stars and planets in our galaxies to the formation of life in the seas and on dry land, nothing is overlooked. All the details of God's created order are set in motion and held under his control. At the end of God's work, Genesis 2:1–2 records, "Thus the heavens and the earth were completed, and all their hosts. And by the seventh day God completed His work which He had done; and He rested on the seventh day from all His work which He had done" (NASB).

This sequence of events in creation demonstrates forethought and planning. God created plants for the dry land only after establishing water and sunlight to provide them with nourishment. Once this was done he created animals with this established source of food. Each of these events testify of God's created order and planning.

The story of Noah found in Genesis 6–9 also speaks of God's planning. Having become disappointed by man's sinful lifestyle, God establishes a plan for a new beginning. God chose to send a flood to remove this destructive influence from his creation but only after he developed a plan to save a small remnant of faithful followers. God spoke to Noah and gave him a set of plans for the construction of the ark. With this blueprint of dimensions, required building materials, and the supplies that would be needed for the duration of his trip, Noah prepared for the coming flood. Without God's plans and Noah's obedience, humanity would surely have had a short-lived existence on this planet.

Soon after the flood God revealed additional plans by selecting a man by the name of Abraham to establish a relationship which would have eternal consequences. God revealed his long-range plans by declaring: "Go forth from your country, and from your relatives and from your father's house, to the land which I will show you; and I will make you a great nation, and I will bless you, and make your name great; and so you shall be a blessing; and I will bless those who bless you, and the one who curses you I will curse. And in you all the families of the earth shall be blessed" (Gen. 12:1–3 NASB).

God later revealed to Abraham that his descendants would subsequently number more than the dust of the earth (Gen. 13:16), the stars of the sky (Gen. 15:5), or the sand of the sea (Gen. 22:17). Such forethought and advanced planning provided Abraham with the assurance that God could be trusted to keep his promises and not forget his plans.

The bondage and subsequent departure of God's chosen people from the land of Egypt reveal his sovereign planning. Having selected and trained Moses to lead his people out of bondage after eighty years of preparation (forty years in the courts of Pharaoh and forty years as a shepherd), Moses came on the scene at just the moment of God's choosing. During the journey God delivered his laws to Moses who in turn presented them to God's people. These laws revealed God's prescribed order for maintaining a pure and holy relationship with the Lord and instructions on how to live in proper relationship with those in one's community.

In addition to these laws, God also provided Moses with instructions about the building of the tabernacle. This tent would be the focal point of worship and would come with detailed instructions about its construction. The plans and blueprints once again revealed God's exacting nature. Every detail, from the color of the covering skins to the size and dimensions of the beams, walls, and rods was carefully crafted and installed. The type of furniture, each piece's dimensions, and their location within the tabernacle compound were carefully prescribed by God. Descriptions of the priest's robes, their ritual washings and preparations, as well as instructions for packing and unpacking the tabernacle were given by God to his people.

Before Israel entered Canaan, God presented Joshua with his plans for the destruction of those who inhabited the land. The conquest of the land was prescribed by God with the purpose of purifying it for his people (Num. 33:50–56).

During the period of the Kings, God revealed his plans for the construction of the temple. In 1 Kings 5 God revealed his plans for Solomon to build a magnificent structure with the resources that King David had been told to lay aside in reserve. Solomon conscripted laborers at God's command to cut the stones, hew the beams, and sew the veils. Nothing was left to chance. Everything was carefully planned by God and revealed to Solomon.

Many years later God appointed Nehemiah to rebuild the walls of Jerusalem and Ezra to rebuild the temple after they had been destroyed during the conquest of King Nebuchadnezzar. Both Ezra's and Nehemiah's plans and preparations reveal their careful insights and planning. Perhaps the most notable for our purposes is found in Nehemiah. Examples of his careful planning include gaining permission from King Artaxerxes to lead the pilgrimage (Neh. 2:1–6); his requisition of construction supplies (Neh. 2:7–9); his assessment of the conditions of the wall and the development of an accurate building estimate (Neh. 2:15); and the distribution of labor and the creation of a construction timetable (Neh. 4:15–23). Indeed, Nehemiah was able to overcome many obstacles because of his foresight and detailed planning.

The New Testament likewise reveals many examples of planning. Obviously God was at work in the lives of his people in the New Testament to reveal his many sovereign plans. Ephesians 1:4–5 reveals that before the foundations of the earth were laid God chose who would be followers of Christ. Now that is an example of long-range planning!

As a result of God's divine plans, Mary and Joseph traveled to Bethlehem where Jesus was born at just the right moment in time. Numerous fulfillments of prophecy took place at the precise moment of time, revealing God's divine planning and preparation for the birth of his Son.

Clearly Jesus was a planner. The Gospel of Luke repeats a phrase that organized and divided the periods of Jesus' earthly ministry. The phrase "that He resolutely set His face to go to Jerusalem" (NASB), or similar derivations, appears in Luke 9:51, 53; 13:22, 33; 17:11; 18:31; 19:11; and 19:28. What is interesting to note is that after each time this phrase occurs you would expect to see Jesus making his way south to Jerusalem. There were times, however, when Jesus actually went in a different direction. He experienced a season of ministry with his disciples, the phrase was repeated again, and he moved on to the next phase of his earthly ministry. If you didn't know what Jesus was doing, you would think he was lost and didn't know how to find Jerusalem.

But the Creator of the universe knew full well where Jerusalem was. He simply had other things to accomplish before he arrived at the cross. He had an appointment to keep in Jerusalem, but before he got there he had to be sure his disciples were trained and prepared to assume the mantle of ministry leadership in his absence. In essence, Jesus' ministry was following prescribed plans. He needed to reveal the Father's character to a lost and needy world, while at the same time it was necessary to train and equip a small group of men to transform the world in his name.

One of Jesus' most penetrating parables was on the theme of planning. He declared: "For which one of you, when he wants to build a tower, does not first sit down and calculate the cost, to see if he has enough to complete it? Otherwise, when he has laid a foundation, and is not able to finish, all who observe it begin to ridicule him, saying, 'This man began to build and was not able to finish.' Or what king, when he sets out to meet another king in battle, will not first sit down and take counsel whether he is strong enough with ten thousand men to encounter the one coming against him with twenty thousand? Or else, while the other is still far away, he sends a delegation and asks terms of peace" (Luke 14:28–32 NASB).

Although the theme of this passage is the cost of discipleship, the underlying issue is that a person must make plans for the future, especially as it relates to his spiritual condition.

The apostle Paul was a man of action and persistence. If ever there was a man prepared to step onto the stage of eternity and fulfill the divine plans of God, it was this apostle to the Gentiles. Having been prepared to enter into a challenging field of missionary expansion, Paul revealed his plans for accomplishing his goal of reaching the world for Christ. Though a number of passages could be used to articulate his mission statement, perhaps the one most indicative of his personal passion is Romans 1:16, where we read, "For I am not ashamed of the gospel, for it is the power of God for salvation to everyone who believes, to the Jew first and also to the Greek."

Throughout Paul's epistles we see evidence of his planning efforts. For example, we find instructions for orderly worship services (1 Cor. 11; 14); methods for building up the body of Christ (Rom. 12; 1 Cor. 12; Eph. 4); qualifications for church leaders (1 Tim. 3); prescribed methods of church discipline (1 Cor. 5; 2 Cor. 6); his plans to travel to Rome and eventually on to Spain to preach the gospel (Rom. 15); and of his careful efforts to leave trained men in the churches to carry on his work after his departure.

Despite these obvious evidences of planning found in Scripture, it needs to be stated that although planning is an important aspect of ministry stewardship, it must not take the place of seeking God's guidance or following the influence of the Holy Spirit. Detailed plans are not a substitute for prayer. Neither is planning a formula that God always follows. God seems to revel in circumventing the plans of man with his own. He states, "Many are the plans in a man's heart, but the counsel of the LORD, it will stand" (Prov. 19:21 NASB). The Bible teaches that God delights in doing what is unexpected and unplanned from our perspective. His ways are not our ways, and his plans are not always ours. But God can be trusted to bring to pass what he has planned. The end result of those plans will be glorious and worth the wait.

Organizing

The Scripture teaches that God is not the author of confusion but of peaceful order (1 Cor. 14:33) and that he desires for all things to be done properly and in an orderly manner (1 Cor. 14:40). Organization can be defined as doing things in an orderly manner. In an organizational context, this involves two primary activities. First, developing an organizational structure which depicts the relationships between each of the members of the organization and, second, preparing job descriptions so those who serve will know what is expected of them in terms of qualifications and responsibilities.

The Old Testament begins with God's created order, which was described in the previous section. God is the supreme head of the universe. Man is his creation and is given authority and dominion over the environment. Humanity has authority over the plants and animals and must act as stewards of this trust. It is not an authority that allows us to abuse or waste these resources. With this responsibility comes accountability.

The family unit was the first institution fashioned by God when Adam and Eve were joined together as husband and wife. From the first days of their relationship God sets forth his expectations about family structure. He states, "For this cause a man shall leave his father and his mother, and shall cleave to his wife; and they shall become one flesh" (Gen. 2:24 NASB). Speaking of this dynamic the apostle Paul wrote, "For the husband is the head of the wife, as Christ also is the head of the church, He Himself being the Savior of the body. But as the church is subject to Christ, so also the wives ought to be to their husbands in everything" (Eph. 5:23–24 NASB).

Likewise regarding children Paul states, "Children, obey your parents in the Lord, for this is right" (Eph. 6:1 NASB). These passages reveal God's organizational structure for the home. Much has been said about how this working relationship between husband and wife, parents and children gets worked out in daily living. Such discussions go beyond the purposes of this text, but suffice it to say that God designed the family unit to function under clearly delineated expectations of organizational structure.

Other books in the Pentateuch give evidence of God's desire for organizational structure and specifications about job responsibilities. For example, the nation of Israel was divided into twelve tribes with each given a responsibility during the journey through the desert. They were told what order to march in and where to pitch their tents in relationship to the tabernacle. The tribes of Judah, Issachar, and Zebulun camped on the east side of the tent of meeting. The tribes of Reuben, Simeon, and Gad pitched their tents south of the tabernacle. The half tribes of Ephraim and Manasseh along with the tribe of Benjamin, set their tents to the west. The tribes of Dan, Asher, and Naphtali set their tents north of the sanctuary (Num. 2). The Levites were given the responsibility of carrying the tabernacle and all its components. The Gershonites carried the tent itself while the Kohathites carried the ark, the table, the lampstand, the altars, and the articles which were used in the sanctuary worship. Finally, the Merarites carried the frames of the tent, its crossbars, beams, bases, and corresponding pieces of equipment (Num. 3).

The books of Exodus and Leviticus spell out the job description of the priests, how they were to wash before putting on their robes (Exod. 28–29), how to prepare and offer the sacrifices (Lev. 1–6), and also how they were to dispose of the remains (Exod. 29). Along the way Moses was met by his father-in-law, Jethro, who upon seeing the burden of his daily workload admonished him to create some form of organizational structure to distribute the workload among seventy elders (Exod. 18:17–18). The books of Leviticus, Numbers, and Deuteronomy are accounts of various policies and procedures for healthy living—both in relationship to God and also in relationship to those in our communities.

Eventually the people arrived in the promised land and began the process of taking possession through numerous military conquests. The end of the Book of Joshua records his final days, when the land was apportioned among the people and they were charged with completing the task of taking ownership (Josh. 12–20). The Levites were not given a portion of land. It was God's desire to see their influence spread throughout the country. They were, however, given a number of towns where they could reside (Josh. 21).

The historical and prophetical books provide us with a glimpse of order from a national perspective. National leaders such as judges and kings were vested with authority over the people, but this was an authority which came with specific expectations and high levels of accountability. Those who abused these expectations were severely punished by God directly or through his designated vessels such as neighboring kingdoms.

At times the kings developed highly refined organizational structures when it met their needs. King Solomon had numerous officials who worked for him. Their responsibilities were divided into departments. He designated a department for priestly work. The priests offered the daily offerings and animal sacrifices at the temple. Other Levites were also given responsibilities according to their family of origin. These included such things as serving as gatekeepers, treasurers, singers, etc. The second department was for ministry within the district in and around Jerusalem. Since there were twelve tribes the king structured his kingdom around twelve district governors who reported to him. The third department was responsible for the stewardship of the king's property and material resources. The final department was responsible for managing the affairs of the military.

David had scribes, prophets, and counselors under his employ (2 Sam. 20:23–26). David also had three mighty men who were particularly victorious in battle (2 Sam. 23:8–39) along with an additional thirty men who were charged with organizational leadership over the remaining ranks of men. Solomon also continued this practice of designating district governors (1 Kings 4:7–28).

The use of organizational structure does not end with the closing of the Old Testament. We see ample evidence in the New Testament of organization in the earthly ministry of Jesus. He selected from among hundreds of followers just twelve men who were entrusted with the responsibility of ministry preparation. He further designated three of these disciples to form an inner circle of confidants (Luke 9). Some were given specific job descriptions such as Judas serving as group treasurer (John 13). During his ministry training Jesus organized his followers into groups of two and sent seventy-two of them out for a form of internship training. By the time Jesus departed his earthly ministry, he had established an organizational structure consisting of himself, three inner-core devotees, twelve apostles, seventy disciples, 120 ardent supporters, and thousands who were actively following in his steps.

Very early in the Book of Acts we see evidence of organizational structure with the designation of Matthias as a replacement for Judas (Acts 1:24–26). Peter, James, and John assumed the leadership of the church (Acts 1–3). In chapter 6 of Acts the first deacons were selected to assist the apostles in the ministry of the church. Qualifications of these men were clearly spelled out in terms of their moral character and in their work responsibilities. Paul's writings to the church he had established give evidence of his expectations for church organizational structure. Though there is no prescribed structure that must be incorporated into every church, the qualifications for those serving as overseers or elders are unequivocal (1 Tim. 3:1–13). There are two categories of elders: teaching and ruling (1 Tim. 4:14; 1 Pet. 5:2). The ruling elders managed the business of the church, while the teaching elders focused on the instruction and application of God's Word in the lives of the believers.

Paul provided additional insights into the organization of the church by giving policies pertaining to its decorum (1 Cor. 11), worship service (1 Cor. 11), use of spiritual gifts (Rom. 12; 1 Cor. 12; Eph. 4:11–16), corporate discipline (1 Cor. 5), the Lord's Supper (1 Cor. 11), and how to resolve conflicts between members (1 Cor. 6:1–7; Phil. 2:14).

Organizational structure and design are evidence of sound planning. The two functions of planning and organizing are difficult to separate. Each is dependent on the other for harmony and effective service. If the planning process is done thoroughly, correctly, and with forethought, it will make organizing that much easier. Fewer things are less likely to "drop through the cracks," and people will not be hurt through the mismanagement of resources. Those who serve in positions of church leadership should make a periodic inventory of the positions their church offers—both paid employees and volunteers—and determine if their organizational chart is up to date and accurately reflects lines of authority. They should also review job descriptions to be sure they are brought up to current expectations. Gaps which could lead to misunderstanding and mismanagement should be closed. It is much easier to do this organizational appraisal before problems arise rather than after they occur.

Staffing

Staffing is a relatively straightforward process of selecting, orienting, training, and developing the competent people who are needed to accomplish the goals and objectives of the ministry. One of the greatest challenges that church leaders face today is recruiting enough volunteers to staff the various departments in the church. Nowhere is this more acute than in the children's department, which requires the lion's share of the volunteers. Church ministry leaders during the past couple of decades have found themselves the target of lawsuits when they failed to follow a series of prescribed steps in the selection, orientation, and training of volunteer workers. Staffing is critical to the success of a church ministry, but the days of standing in the pulpit and declaring "Whosoever will, come on down!" are over. Staffing must be done with wisdom and discernment. It was no less important in the days of the Old and New Testaments. God placed a great deal of emphasis on the selection, orientation, training, and development of those whom he called into ministry service. There are some important principles we can learn from how it was done in biblical days.

The Old Testament provides numerous examples of men and women being called into God's service. This selection process sometimes involved miraculous calls into service such as that experienced by Abraham, Moses, Gideon, and many of the prophets. Although it may seem commonplace for the selection of ministry leaders to be accompanied by miraculous signs and wonders, it is certainly not the norm. Mediators were often chosen on the basis of their heart condition, not formal education or previous experience. Patriarchs such as Abraham, Isaac, and Jacob were certainly called into a special relationship with God based on little more than the condition of their hearts and the sovereignty of God. Yet there were times when ministry leaders were chosen because of their skills and abilities.

An example of this is the selection of Bezalel and Oholiab. They were chosen by Moses to lead the building of the tabernacle because they had hearts that sought after God, but they also possessed a superior skill in various arts and crafts such as weaving, woodworking, and embroidering (Exod. 36). Moses trained Joshua for the day when he would take over the leadership of the nation as they entered the land of Canaan.

When the Lord rejected King Saul as his national leader because he lacked obedience and sincerity, God commanded the prophet Samuel to anoint a young shepherd boy by the name of David. Samuel almost missed the opportunity to anoint David because he expected to find a strong, formidable warrior. Instead, he discovered a young shepherd boy with no military experience, little, if any, formal schooling, and no diplomatic training. God spoke to Samuel, "Do not look at his appearance or at the height of his stature, because I have rejected him [Eliab]; for God sees not as a man sees, for man looks at the outward appearance, but the LORD looks at the heart" (1 Sam. 16:7 NASB). Here we discover God's criteria for selection into service: the condition of a person's inward heart.

Other Old Testament examples of the selection and training of staff include Ezra's selection of Zerubbabel, Shealtiel, Jeshua, Kadmiel, Henadad, and other Levites to supervise and oversee the rebuilding of the temple (Ezra 3:8–9). Gideon likewise chose his warriors by using a highly selective process of drinking water from the river (Judg. 7). When Daniel was recruited to serve in a prominent position of national leadership, he selected three friends who were well qualified in character and ability to assist him in the task (Dan. 1:8–20).

In the New Testament we find Jesus beginning his selection process of the apostles as he went about his early days of ministry. The first disciples to be recruited were Simon Peter and his brother Andrew (Matt. 4:18–20). "Follow Me" was the simple appeal. They dropped their nets, and their lives were never the same again. In a similar vein, Matthew the tax collector was challenged to join Jesus' small group of faithful followers (Matt. 9:9). Although we do not know all of the details about the selection of many of the remaining disciples, we are told that it took place after an entire evening of prayer (Luke 6:12–16).

After selecting his disciples, Jesus began the arduous task of orienting and training them in the responsibilities of ministry leadership. This involved more than three years of discipline, confrontation, teaching, mentoring, prayer, and close association in order to transform this band of unlikely men into a formidable ministry team that eventually confounded the Jewish Sanhedrin (Acts 5:34–39). Jesus used teachable moments to present spiritual truth and often challenged them with questions to probe their critical thinking. He taught by using every available method of instruction. He used metaphors and parables, miracles and sermons to ensure their training was adequate for the task ahead.

The apostle Paul experienced a three-year orientation period prior to his engagement in the gospel ministry. His Arabian sabbatical was designed to train him in the true meaning behind the prophecies which he had come to know as a learned scholar of Judaism (Gal. 1:17). Barnabas was commissioned by the church in Jerusalem to travel to the newly founded church in Antioch. The apostles had heard reports of significant ministry events occurring in this church and wanted to ensure the authenticity of its doctrine and ministry practices. James asked Barnabas to represent the Jerusalem church, and after a brief visit to the church in Antioch he traveled to Tarsus looking for Saul (whose name was later changed to Paul). Barnabas brought Saul to Antioch, and there is strong evidence that he trained Saul in the methods of New Testament gospel ministry (Acts 11:19–26).

Eventually Paul became a trusted and renowned ministry leader in Antioch and also in Jerusalem. In this capacity he demonstrated the staffing process of selection, orientation, training, and development during his three missionary journeys. Prior to his second journey he removed John Mark from the ministry team and selected Silas as his partner. In many of the cities where he established churches, he selected, oriented, and trained the leadership to carry on after his departure. He gave them their charge and commissioned them for their responsibilities of ministry supervision and oversight. Paul was instrumental in training and developing countless ministry leaders. A brief list of these includes Timothy, Titus, Luke, Silas, Philemon, the elders in Ephesus, Corinth, Rome, and dozens of other leaders cited in Romans 16.

As we summarize this staffing function, it is interesting to note that God frequently selects and trains his servants regardless of their formal preparation and training. Those whom God chooses to use are generally qualified on the basis of their heart condition and spiritual sensitivity. This serves as a good lesson for those who desire a role in ministry leadership today as well. Being selected by God is the first important step in the process. Appointing yourself to ministry leadership is a journey down a painful road. God is jealous of his reputation and does not hesitate to intervene in the lives of those who are self-appointed prophets.

Today, just as in the days of the Old and New Testaments, God is searching the hearts of men and women to reveal his character and show himself strong (2 Chron. 16:9). Being chosen, however, does not guarantee service. The newly selected minister also requires sound training in biblical knowledge and interpretation. The spiritual gift that one receives at conversion is a first step of many along the road of ministry service. That gift must be developed, trained, and adapted for use within a particular context of application. One does not simply become a believer and immediately begin the gospel ministry without a season of preparation (i.e., orientation, training, and development).

Directing

The managerial function of directing is defined as a process where a supervisor leads subordinates to understand and contribute to the organization's objectives while at the same time allowing them to pursue their own personal objectives. In the context of a local church, a skillful supervisor (senior pastor, executive pastor, etc.) supervises his employees in such a way as to make being part of the church staff a win-win arrangement for both the church and the person being supervised. Directing is one of the most challenging of the five managerial functions because the supervisor is dealing with trying to figure out how to direct each staff member according to his own individual preferences since no two people respond to leadership in the same way. In essence, it is a complex interplay between individuals, attitudes, needs, desires, hopes, and dreams where the needs of the whole person must be taken into consideration, but not at the expense of the organization.

The activities associated with directing include delegating, motivating, coordinating, managing differences, and managing change. Another term for directing is *leading*. Anyone who has recently visited a bookstore realizes that there has been a virtual explosion of books on the subject of leadership. From both a secular and a Christian perspective, the subject of leadership is popular and widely circulated. However, this is not to say that it is a new topic for those involved in ministry leadership. Indeed, the activities associated with directing are demonstrated throughout the pages of Scripture. God is deeply concerned about who directs his ministry endeavors and how these efforts are conducted.

Space does not allow a detailed analysis of each activity, but a couple of examples in each category may prove helpful.

Delegating

The Book of Genesis begins with God delegating the stewardship of his creation to Adam (Gen. 1:28–30). In chapter 24 we have the unusual account of Abraham delegating the important responsibility of finding a wife for his son Isaac. Abraham gave his chief servant the responsibility of traveling back to Abraham's homeland to select a wife for Isaac from among his relatives. Additional examples of delegation in the Old Testament include Moses delegating judicial responsibilities to the seventy elders (Exod. 18:17–27) and later delegating the responsibility of military leadership to Joshua.

In the New Testament we read of Jesus' delegation of ministry responsibilities to seventy disciples (Luke 10:1–20), and also his twelve apostles (Mark 6:7–13). The Great Commission found in Matthew 28:19–20 and repeated again in Acts 1:8 is another example of Jesus delegating his ministry to his followers. The apostle Paul delegated ministry responsibilities to the elders in each of the churches he established and commissioned them for the work of service (Acts 14:23). He delegated the responsibility of overseeing the ministry in Crete to Titus and encouraged him to be faithful in his work (Titus 1:5–9).

Motivating

God uses unique methods for motivating humanity. At times he uses strong and forceful methods, such as when he motivated Lot and his family to leave Sodom (Gen. 19) or in getting Jonah to go to Nineveh (Jon. 1). In the Old Testament we see countless examples of people being motivated to action based on desires for power, sex, greed, money, or selfish ambition.

In the New Testament Jesus serves as an example of how to motivate people to respond based upon the virtues of love, selfless service, commitment, faithfulness, and humility. It is a stark contrast to the methods of motivation used by humanity that we saw earlier in the Scriptures. Jesus motivates his followers to ministry service out of a heart filled with appreciation for all that God has done for us. In essence, since God has demonstrated his love for us by sending Jesus to die on the cross, how could we possibly hold back our service to him? Jesus sought to motivate his disciples by using intrinsic motivators as opposed to those of an external origin. His paradoxical teaching through the use of parables and stories revealed a different approach to motivating workers. Chief among them was the condition of the heart.

The apostle Paul continued this theme in his reflections about dedicated service. We get a glimpse of what motivated Paul in his account about his personal sufferings recorded in 2 Corinthians 11. In spite of all his hardships, chief among his concerns was not his own survival but the condition of the churches that he had started and nurtured (2 Cor. 11:28). As his life began to draw to a close, he revealed his motivation for service: "I have fought the good fight, I have finished the course, I have kept the faith; in the future there is laid up for me the crown of righteousness, which the Lord, the righteous Judge, will award to me on that day; and not only to me, but also to all who have loved His appearing" (2 Tim. 4:7–8 NASB). Paul was motivated to serve Christ because he saw himself as a sinner in need of forgiveness. Once having received that gift, he expressed his sacrificial service not for fame, recognition, or material gain, but for the eternal reward of hearing his Lord declare, "Well done."

Coordinating

One does not have to look far to see the coordinating work of God in creation, Joseph's coordination of the material resources during the seven years of plenty as preparation for the upcoming seven years of famine in Egypt, Moses' coordination of the twelve tribes during the wilderness years, Joshua's coordination of Israel's army throughout the military conquest of Canaan, David's coordination of the division of labor among his governors, Solomon's coordinated efforts to build the temple, Ezra and Nehemiah's coordinated efforts to rebuild the temple and walls of Jerusalem, and the coordination involved in the many Old Testament prophets who preached the message of repentance to the nation of Israel.

In the New Testament we see evidence of coordination in the training of the disciples which we have already mentioned. Likewise, we see coordination in the early church in the selection of Matthias as a replacement for Judas (Acts 1:15–26), in the selection of the seven deacons (Acts 6:1–6), in Paul and Barnabas being set apart by the church in Antioch for missionary service (Acts 13:1–3), and in Paul's efforts to receive an offering for the troubled church in Jerusalem. These ministry ventures, and many others that could also be cited, did not occur haphazardly but involved coordinated effort between churches and various ministry leaders.

Managing Differences

God is a God of creativity. We see it in his creation. The unique patterns of colors, textures, shapes, sizes, and designs reveal God's propensity for creation. Chief among God's unique creation is humanity. We see a great diversity in humanity's origins, personalities, and compositions. Naturally, with all of this diversity we will have individual differences. When these differences come into the church, we should not be surprised that they bring tension as well. Most people dislike change and don't readily accommodate these differences.

In the Old Testament we see the management of differences from the first chapters of Genesis, where we discover that there is a significant difference between the children of Adam and Eve. We read that Cain was a farmer while Abel was a hunter. These uniquenesses required different parenting methods for Adam and Eve. This difference among siblings occurred again in the offspring of Isaac: Jacob and Esau. If ever there were two different children whose parents needed to learn to manage differently, it was these two sons. What is of note in each of these examples is that God related to each of these individuals differently. God directed Abraham differently from Jacob. God managed the judges, the kings, and each of the prophets differently as he took into consideration their unique differences and contextual conditions.

A great example of managing difference is found in 1 Samuel 25, where we read the account of Nabal and his wife Abigail. It seems Nabal had insulted king David and was about to pay with his life. While David was en route to punish him, Abigail, his wife, came with food and provisions for David and his men. The Bible states that Abigail was "an intelligent and beautiful woman" (1 Sam. 25:3 NIV). She evidently used that intelligence to manage the differences between her husband and King David. It resulted in her life being spared and—after the death of her husband from a heart attack—her subsequent marriage to David.

In the New Testament we see Jesus responding to people differently as well. At times he confronted the religious leaders with scathing rebuke (Matt. 23), while at other times he brought them into his confidence and addressed them with respect (John 3:1–21). At times Jesus was forceful and confronting with his disciples (Mark 8:33) while at other times he was affirming and congratulatory (Matt. 16:13–19). At one point as he entered Jerusalem he wept for the inhabitants (Luke 19:41). But just a few minutes later we see him kicking over their tables in disgust (Matt. 21:12). Jesus took into consideration the individual needs of those who came to him and did not treat everyone the same. Managing individual differences requires great insight and discernment and generally takes a lot of time to develop.

Managing Change

If there is one thing that can be said with certainty about ministry service, it is that when dealing with people, expect the unexpected. Rarely does a ministry plan run from start to finish without some form of unplanned change. With this change comes conflict. Observing nature reveals the truth that where there is life there is change. Nothing that is alive remains static. Ministry generally involves change in one capacity or another. In the Old Testament we find God approving a change from a theocentric model of governance to a monarchial model. This represented a significant change from God's original plan. We move from a system where one chosen leader mediated between God and man (i.e., Abraham, Isaac, or Jacob) to one where an entire nation was chosen to be the recipient of God's special relationship. When we progress into the New Testament, we discover that every believer has the privilege of entering into this special relationship with God through the atoning work of Christ.

God is always at work conforming us to the image of his Son, and this must be a life-long process of change and transformation (2 Cor. 5:17). This process of spiritual formation is one of the central themes of the New Testament. The maturation process requires a constant transition from old nature to new, from taking off our corruptible flesh to the taking on of our new incorruptible nature in Christ. As Paul stated to the believers in Philippi, "I am confident of this very thing, that He who began a good work in you will perfect it until the day of Christ Jesus" (Phil. 1:6 NASB). Spiritual formation is a long-term process of dying to the self and remaining alive to the work of the Holy Spirit in our lives.

Evaluating

Controlling is the most popular term used in secular texts in the field of management to refer to this last managerial function. Controlling is defined as the process which ensures that progress is being made toward the accomplishment of the organization's objectives. Controls can take a variety of forms such as a simple budget or a more complex PERT chart. The term *control* has not always received a positive response from members of a church congregation since it sounds too much like manipulation or coercion. We prefer to use the concept of *evaluation* instead. Evaluation is certainly a biblical concept because of its close alignment with the concept of stewardship. We know, for instance, that God has called us to be faithful stewards of his ministry resources and that one day we will be called to give an account of our use of these resources. This is evaluation pure and simple.

Evaluation in the context of ministry can be defined as the process by which we provide an accounting for the manner in which we administrated the resources entrusted to us by God. It may involve evaluating the use of facilities, finances, personnel, and a host of other entities. Evaluation is a four-step process: It requires (1) some form of reporting system, (2) a set of standards by which the criteria for evaluation is compared, (3) a corrective action plan where deviations are discovered, and (4) a reward system for those who have faithfully discharged their responsibilities. Each of these steps in the process has clear biblical evidence.

Reporting Systems

The Old Testament records a variety of reporting systems in effect. Obviously we begin with God having direct feedback and dialogue with Adam and Eve in the Garden of Eden. He was aware of their status and living conditions and immediately confronted them once he was aware of their fallen state. They recognized that they were accountable to God for their actions. In spite of their efforts to pass the blame on to others, they had to accept the consequences of their actions (Gen. 3). Soon after, Cain was held to account for the dysfunction of his interpersonal relations with his brother Abel (Gen. 4).

Throughout the Old Testament God maintained a system of evaluation that involved personal accountability. We see it in his dealings with Moses, Joshua, and the judges who followed. Kings Saul, David, Solomon, and others after the kingdom was divided were held to account for their actions. Being in a leadership role did not release them from the need to act within God's moral standards and remain accountable for their motives and actions. God used the prophets as a means of keeping accounts with the nation of Israel. God did not simply establish the nation and then walk away. He provided a means for constant feedback and direction through the ministry of the prophets.

In the New Testament the primary reporting system is the unique role and ministry of the Holy Spirit. Jesus revealed part of this supervisory role when he stated, "I will ask the Father, and He will give you another Helper, that He may be with you forever; that is the Spirit of truth, whom the world cannot receive, because it does not behold Him or know Him, but you know Him because He abides with you, and will be in you" (John 14:16–17 NASB). "But when He, the Spirit of truth, comes, He will guide you into all the truth; for He will not speak on His own initiative, but whatever He hears, He will speak; and He will disclose to you what is to come. He shall glorify Me; for He shall take of Mine, and shall disclose it to you" (John 16:13–14 NASB).

Later in the Book of Acts the disciples give us clear evidence of the reporting relationship they had to the Holy Spirit when they revealed the method by which they made ministry decisions: "And while they were ministering to the Lord and fasting, the Holy Spirit said, 'Set apart for Me Barnabas and Saul for the work to which I have called them.' Then, when they had fasted and prayed and laid their hands on them, they sent them away. So, being sent out by the Holy Spirit, they went down to Seleucia and from there sailed to Cyprus" (Acts 13:2–4 NASB). It is obvious from these passages and countless others that church leaders had a clearly defined reporting system established between God and themselves through the ministry of the Holy Spirit. Prayer was the conduit of dialogue and communication. The church was admonished to bring all of their needs and concerns to God through prayer in order to maintain vitality in their ministry pursuits.

Establishing Performance Standards

We have already identified the many standards that God had prescribed for his people. In both the Old and New Testaments, we find evidence of God's commands and directives about qualifications for ministry service. The Ten Commandments are probably the most noteworthy of God's performance standards for his people. In addition, there are numerous other laws in the books of the Pentateuch which serve as standards of performance for those who desire to have a relationship with God. Other standards are established for those who aspire to leadership, and strict criteria is used when determining a person's competence.

A willing spirit is not sufficient for service. Other factors such as a lifestyle of purity, personal discipline, and humility are also required. Requirements for becoming a ministry leader were strict and specific in both the Old and New Testaments. How worship should be conducted is also prescribed. In many respects, God allows a good deal of freedom in the application of ministry principles. But where there are prescribed standards, these should be closely followed.

In the context of most ministries today, there are job descriptions which set forth the expectations of ministry leaders. There should be no excuse for a ministry leader entering a position of service and not knowing what is required of him. It should be clearly stated in his job description what the expectations of the church are in relation to his job. These performance standards should clearly express the expectations of those in charge.

Beyond the more obvious expectations stated in the job description, most ministries have policies and procedures manuals to ensure that performance standards are clearly communicated. For example, many churches today require pastors to leave their office doors open when counseling members of the opposite sex. Likewise, male youth pastors should not be allowed to transport young girls home after a church event. Due to recent litigation, additional performance standards exist in many churches about the use of church vehicles, who can drive for youth events, and under what restrictions. These performance standards should be written down to eliminate confusion.

Developing Corrective Action Plans

The Old Testament mandated a variety of ways to take corrective action. Leviticus 4–6 gives detailed instructions for those who desire to offer a sacrifice to God and thereby receive his forgiveness. Numbers 5:5–7 gives instruction about a person who has wronged another and desires to seek reconciliation. The person who has committed the offense is to seek restitution plus add one-fifth to his settlement. In the same way, Leviticus 6 states that when someone lies, steals, or cheats another, "He must return what he has stolen or taken by extortion, or what was entrusted to him, or the property he found, or whatever it was he swore falsely about. He must make restitution in full, add a fifth of the value to it and give it all to the owner on the day he presents his guilt offering" (Lev. 6:4–5 NIV).

Sometimes the corrective action in the Old Testament was severe, such as stoning someone who offered their child to a false god. In such cases the individual was to be stoned to death by the members of the community (Lev. 20:2). Similarly, anyone who cursed his parents or committed adultery was to receive capital punishment. Harsh corrective punishment was intended to serve as a deterrent to others: "Then all Israel will hear and be afraid, and no one among you will do such an evil thing again" (Deut. 13:11 NIV).

Examples of correction abound in the New Testament as well. Jesus sought to correct the faulty theology of the religious leaders of his day. He admonished them with God's Word and demonstrated a life of personal discipline. He was gentle in his approach to most people but was not afraid to stand firm when corrective action was needed and the attitude of the person receiving it was closed to critique. Jesus provided us with a model for church discipline in Matthew 18. The church is admonished to use this form of corrective action where appropriate and with the right attitude.

We see examples of stern correction when Peter confronted Ananias and his wife Sapphira for lying about the amount of their land sale (Acts 5:1–11). We also see it in Paul's confrontation of Peter (Gal. 2:11) and again in his handling of church discipline in the Corinthian church. The apostle John wrote a letter to the seven churches evaluating their work and ministry success. Although the letter had an element of praise for some of the churches, others received a stern rebuke for their lack of faithful service. At the end of the correction John wrote, "He who has an ear, let him hear what the Spirit says to the churches. To him who overcomes, I will give the right to eat from the tree of life, which is in the paradise of God" (Rev. 2:7 NIV).

It is interesting to note that the New Testament admonishes believers to evaluate themselves. We are challenged to administer our own corrective action plan and to look for ways to evaluate our own actions. If we will correct our own behavior once it goes astray, then we will not be in need of receiving it from the hands of others (1 Cor. 11:28; 2 Cor. 13:5). The apostle Paul spoke of the need to live a life of personal restraint and self-discipline so as not to become disqualified for ministry service (1 Cor. 9:26–27).

Providing Rewards

The Bible speaks of rewards on many occasions. God lavished rewards on those who faithfully and obediently followed his commands. When the nation of Israel lived in obedience to God's laws, he blessed them and rewarded them abundantly. Deuteronomy 7 cites a number of rewards that would be given those who obeyed God's commands. They included a large family, healthy crops, fruitful cattle, and protection from famine, plagues, and one's enemies. Even life itself was seen as a reward from God (Deut. 8:1).

The New Testament testifies to God's rewards. Those who enter into a personal relationship with God through Christ become recipients of eternal life (John 3:16). They are taken into God's family as his adopted children (Eph. 1:5) and given an inheritance (Eph. 1:11). We are given every spiritual blessing in the heavenly places in Christ (Eph. 1:3). Those who serve with faithfulness will receive rewards in heaven (1 Cor. 3:11–15). Perhaps the greatest reward believers will receive is a return to that special relationship that Adam and Eve once held in the Garden of Eden when God walked among them. There will be no more tears, death, mourning, crying, or pain (Rev. 21:4).

In summary, we see that many of the principles which are being used in secular systems of management are not new. Most of these principles of business management had their origins in the days of the Old and New Testaments. God laid out an orderly universe and provided clear direction about maintaining that order. So with this in mind, let's summarize these managerial functions in relation to biblical teaching.

Axioms of Theological Integration

1. **God Is a God of Purposeful Planning.** From his revealed character to the works of his hands as demonstrated in creation, God is actively engaged in the planning process. From the first pages of the Scriptures he forms the world with purposeful order and structure. The universe did not evolve from a cosmic collision of random atoms in some kind of big bang. God planned it, formed it, and now maintains it according to select laws of governance. Replenishing the world with

water each day through a complex process of evaporation, condensation, and precipitation reveals his careful planning. Space does not allow the multitude of examples that could be given to remind us of his careful planning. To believe God is anything other than a master of planning is an insult to God's character and to the amount of careful planning that he has done on our behalf.

As God created the universe through careful planning, so he also maintains it. He chooses his methods with care and governs his creation with purpose and sovereign direction. It should come as no surprise to us that he prefers to see humanity live in the same manner. Some believers view their relationship with God as a blind leap of faith with no thought about purposeful direction. God desires for us to live a life of faith, but it is one that is maximized through careful planning and direction. Our choice of a life's mate, a major in college, the career for our vocation, and the number of children we have should reveal some degree of planning rather than haphazard and random activity. It should be no less in the way we manage his ministry. Our ministry programs should reveal careful planning and design. We will accomplish the Great Commission as an army strategizes a military campaign, taking one mountaintop after another until all of the enemy's ground has been captured. This requires careful planning.

2. **God Prefers to Operate with Clearly Established Patterns of Organizational Structure.** We see this in creation (i.e., hierarchy of God, man, environment), the establishment of the family (i.e., Christ, husband, wife, and children), and the church (i.e., Christ, elders, deacons, congregation). God gives to humanity an organizational structure for the family, society, and the church. He desires this prescribed structure. Without it we end up in anarchy and confusion.

3. **God Established Specific Qualifications for Those Who Desired to Serve Him.** We see this in the office of the high priest, the roles of the Levites, and in leadership positions of the church (e.g., elders, deacons, etc.). These leadership qualifications were nonnegotiable and not open to debate or compromise. God has high standards and is worthy of our best efforts to represent him and serve him.

4. **God Selects Those Whom He Desires to Use.** It is not always according to man-made preparation because he also takes into consideration the heart condition of the servant. Motives are difficult to judge because we can only see the evidence of motives in one's outward activities and behaviors. We are limited in our ability to see the inward thoughts of man, but God is not so constrained. He judges the thoughts of man and is able to determine our motives before they are manifest in our behavior. God examines the heart and provides correction and reward based on man's heart condition.

5. **Those Whom God Selects He Trains for Ministry Service.** This will come about through a variety of means such as formal training, teachable moments, personal crises, and unplanned opportunities that come our way. God expects his servants to maintain an attitude of lifelong learning for continuous personal spiritual development. God is not always predictable, and his ways are certainly not always ours. God's methods frequently go outside the bounds of our understanding. Degrees earned in formal instruction can be very beneficial for ministry service, but God is certainly not limited to them when choosing his servants. They have their place and serve an important purpose, but they can also serve as a stumbling block because of pride or lack of willingness to try something new.

6. **God Doesn't Let Go.** It is apparent from the section on directing that God did not simply create the world and walk away. He maintains his control over the sovereign events of our lives and desires to play a role in our ongoing spiritual transformation. His goal is to see us grow into conformity with the character of his Son. For most of us, that will be a significant lifelong process of supernatural intervention and direction.

7. **The Ministry Is Not to Be Taken Lightly.** God has expectations of service and of those who represent him. He has prescribed standards of conduct for godly living and is jealous of those standards. Those who do not live up to these expectations are put on a spiritual corrective action plan and judged accordingly. Those with humility and a teachable spirit can expedite the process by constantly evaluating their lifestyle in relationship to God's Word. If we would judge ourselves we will not be the recipient of as much corrective action on the part of others. Spiritual discipline in the church is a form of corrective action, and God expects his church to exercise it when needed. For those who are faithful to the cause of Christ, there will be abundant rewards and blessings.

BY
JAMES ESTEP

Chapter 2

A Theology of Administration

TRYING TO DEFINE AND UNDERSTAND the concept of administration has been the focus of research for countless decades. Many have sought to define the term, explain the theory, and provide a rationale for the activities involved. A few Christian authors have tried to determine whether or not administration was a value-neutral concept, or one that must be contextualized theologically and institutionally. For example, is there a difference between the way non-Christians and Christians perform the functions of administration? Should there be? They have made every effort to determine whether or not a theology of administration exists, and if so, how such a theology should be articulated. Answering these questions will be the focus of this chapter.

Contemporary Approaches to Administration

There are a number of ways to examine and explore the fundamental issues involved in administration. Each approach brings a little different perspective and combines together to give the serious student a comprehensive overview of the field of administration. Six major administrative paradigms are present in the public realm. These six paradigms reflect differing approaches to administration, particularly in regard to management's role in increasing workers' effectiveness, efficiency, and/or productivity. A summary of these administrative paradigms is as follows:[1]

Classical. A hierarchical approach to administration that adheres to a one-way-only style to work as determined by an expert or authority; workers are expected to simply adhere to the instructions given by the expert. This view is espoused by Fredrick W. Taylor.

Behavioral. A psychological approach to administration that seeks to improve workers' efficiency by better understanding the worker, rather than better defining the task, so as to better motivate workers. This view is espoused by Elton Mayo.

Management Science. A scientific or mathematical approach to administration advanced after World War II that sought to increase workers' productivity by using scientific and mathematical methodologies to better understand the task and efficiency (also known as Operations Research). This view is espoused by Herbert Simon.

Contingency. A situational approach to administration which suggests that maximizing efficiency and productivity is a process of applying the correct leadership style to a given situation; i.e., leadership is contingent on the situation. This view is espoused by Fred Fiedler.

Theory X and Theory Y. Made popular by Douglas M. MacGregor, this view is a human-nature approach to administration that states administrative decisions and initiatives are based on assumptions about the work ethic of humans. Theory X asserts that workers are generally lazy, apathetic, and irresponsible—responding to discipline. Inversely, Theory Y maintains that people are energetic, participatory, and responsible—responding favorably to rewards.

Theory Z. This is a participative approach to administration that emphasizes consensus decision making and achievement among groups, not individuals. Although this view of administration originated in Japan, it recently became popular in the United States, where it is expressed in two administrative models—Quality of Work Life and Quality Circles. This view is espoused by William G. Ouchi.

As we can see, the study of administration has been applied in the corporate arena for many years, but what about in the church? Do any of these approaches and definitions have application in the context of a nonprofit organization such as a church, camp, or mission agency? The community of faith provides a distinctive context in which administration occurs, but do any of these theories readily apply given the unique nature of the church? For example, the church depends almost exclusively on volunteer participation; do any of these administrative approaches reflect the climate of a volunteer-based organization? Similarly, these approaches assume the administration's primary purpose is to increase workers' efficiency, effectiveness, and/or productivity; whereas in the church the "workers" themselves are the subject of its ministry, not their efficiency, effectiveness, and/or productivity. In the context of a church the individuals themselves are the focus of administration and are not viewed as the means to accomplishing an end.

For evangelicals, simply redefining *administration* by recontextualizing it into a congregational body is insufficient. While administration, to be effective, must be institutionally defined, something more influential and critical is needed to shape both the institution and the position. This something is a theological paradigm based upon a comprehensive understanding of Scripture.

Necessity of a Theological Approach to Administration

The place of theology in the discussion of administration has always been debated.[2] In reality, the pragmatic or business models of administration dominate the church's approach to ministry, even in Christian education. Poling and Miller observed that "most planning and administrative theories represent a more pragmatic approach to practical theology."[3] This is primarily due to the lack of a theologically informed approach to administration. In the absence of a distinctively Christian concept of administration, many ministry leaders have simply accepted the theories and practices of their secular counterparts without theological forethought. For example, in the mid-1970s Johnson notes that "the church has bought into the 'process movement' [of management] . . . and has done so in an uncritical way, without the foggiest notion of the movement's theological implications."[4]

The absence of a theologically informed approach to administration results in a dichotomy, characterized by a lack of integration between the congregation's theological culture and administrative culture. An example of this may be seen in fund-raising campaigns which use secular-driven methods and gimmicks to motivate giving. How are these methods integrated with the apostle Paul's admonition to give joyfully? Is there such a thing as a theologically informed view of fund-raising? How would George Muller's philosophy of simply praying and waiting for the movement of the Holy Spirit to stimulate giving be viewed today?

Paul's concern for integrity in the ministry is given in 2 Corinthians 6:1, 14: "And working together with Him, we also urge you not to receive the grace of God in vain. . . . Do not be bound together with unbelievers; for what partnership have righteousness and lawlessness, or what fellowship has light with darkness?" (NASB).

Administration from a Christian perspective is not value-neutral, but it is a practical expression of one's theological and philosophical viewpoints. For this reason, it is essential that ministry leaders develop sound theological convictions at the core of the administrative ideal and find ways of integrating biblical theology with administrative theory. As Myron Rush comments, "It is tragic that so many Christian organizations have accepted the world's philosophy of management. They attempt to accomplish God's work using a management philosophy diametrically opposed to biblical principles."[5] This concern for theological integrity is not simply institutional, but personal and pastoral. If ministry leaders (whether paid or volunteer) conduct their administrative duties in contradiction to their theological convictions, they appear to be duplicitous and hypocritical. Obviously, this does not foster a beneficial environment for ministry. As Broadus observed, a pastor's "leadership style communicates his theology; his theology dictates the way he leads with people."[6] One's theology cannot be held in one hand and administration in the other; the two must be clasped together, integrated into a consistent approach to conducting ministry.

The desire for an integrated, holistic approach to administration in the congregation rests on "a strong conviction that business decisions and spiritual awareness belong to one another in the life of the church, and especially with those who are charged with leadership."[7] In the absence of such integration, the congregation functions in two distinctly separate spheres of influence rather than having a consistent response to congregational needs that is sound both theologically and administratively. Poling and Miller comment that "too frequently, church leaders attempt to give spiritual answers to organizational problems and organizational answers to spiritual problems. This often leads to the idea that administration is nonessential, uninteresting, and that it is not spiritual."[8] Theological and organizational aspects of ministry should not contradict one another but symbiotically coincide in harmony with one another.

Toward a Theological Framework
for Educational Administration

Just as the Christian education community has advocated the necessity for a theological approach to education, it must likewise advance a theologically informed administration for education that is Christian. A basic theological rubric for ministry has acknowledged the simple paradigm that God reveals himself to humanity, and humanity, both individually and corporately as the church, responds to God in faith for reconciliation. This view is depicted in Figure 2.1.[9] In it, humanity lives in response to God's self-initiated revelation so as to have a restored relationship with God—redemption. As this paradigm suggests, ministry begins with God's revelatory and redemptive activity in response to the needs of humanity (individually and corporately). Hence, it introduces the five principle elements of a theology of administration. A Christian approach to administration must be first and foremost centered on God. Second, it should be responsive to humanity's condition, and third, be based on his revelation. Fourth, it should be redemptive in nature, and finally, it must contribute to the formation of a distinctive community.

Figure 2.1
Schema of Ministry

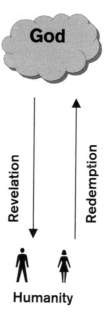

What is needed is a systematic theology of education that can be related to the subject of educational administration in the church.[10] Figure 2.2 illustrates just such a theological framework of Christian education and ultimately its administration. It is an administrative expression of theological concerns which includes several essential components:

- Centered on God: God as Leader
- Responsive to His Revelation: Scripture as Core Document
- Formation of a Distinctive Community: Congregation as Institutional Context
- Redemptive in Purpose: Transformation as Mission and Motive
- Responsive to Humanity's Need: Humanity as Valued Participant

This following section will address each of these elements in a systematic theology of administration.

Centered on God: God as Leader

As with anything Christian, our discussion must begin with God, including both education and administration that is Christian. "Then Jesus came to them and said, 'All authority in heaven and on earth has been given to me'" (Matt. 28:18 NIV). At the risk of stating the obvious, the ultimate power and authority in the church is God. Any authority or

Figure 2.2: A Systematic Theology of Administration

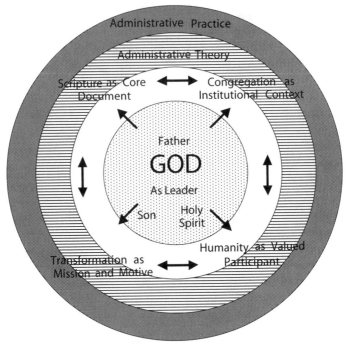

power that may be present in the church was given by him and extends from him. Paul wrote about the problem that plagued the Corinthian congregation: "For this reason I am writing these things while absent, in order that when present I may not use severity, in accordance with the authority which the Lord gave me, for building up and not for tearing down" (2 Cor. 13:10 NASB). He emphasized God's authority and Paul's redemptive rather than punitive use of it in his ministry.

Ultimately, God is the sole authority in the church. We are simply stewards of his ministry, not the authority within it. Hence, the other elements of this theological framework gain their purpose and power from him—Scripture as God's Word, the church as his people, transformation as God's salvation, and humanity as the *imago dei*. A Christian approach to administration must be God-centered. Just as Christian education is God-centered, so must be the administration of the congregation's ministry.

All of the evidence of administrative activity must ultimately bring glory to God. This places a unique requirement on Christian administrators, particularly those in leadership roles since they must manifest humility and servitude. Christian administrators stand humbly before the Lord, their leader, and with a servant's attitude before him and those who serve with them. As such, we are called to a higher standard, ultimately owing our allegiance to God. "And whatever you do, whether in word or deed, do it all in the name of the Lord Jesus, giving thanks to God the Father through him" (Col. 3:17 NIV). If the classical model of administration calls one to a hierarchical structure with an expert as an authority, for the Christian administrator God is the head of the church and the authority in all things. In the pyramid of administrative hierarchy, God is at the peak. This is a position reserved only for him, unattainable by any human administrator.

Responsive to His Revelation: Scripture as Core Document

Every institution, even the church, has a core document. It serves as a foundational statement for establishing their mission, vision, purpose, and core values. These values guide the institution through the changes of time and culture. For the ministry leader, the Bible is the institution's core document. The reason for regarding Scripture as foundational to Christian administration is its affirmation of divine authorship (1 Cor. 2:10–13; 2 Tim. 3:15–17; 1 Pet. 1:10–12, 21; 2 Pet. 1:20–21, 3:2, 15–16). As a special revelation of God, to which all of us must respond, the Christian leader is compelled to formulate a model of administration that is consistent with God's expressed design. The apostle Paul contends that the Scriptures were given "for our instruction" (Rom. 15:4; 1 Cor. 10:5–11; 2 Tim. 3:15–17). The Bible's influence on Christian education is not limited to supplying the content of our instruction, but extends to providing direction, models of education, and values for decision making, as well as administrative and instructional methodologies.

Scripture serves as the plumb line for administrative decisions and functions. Perhaps one of the best illustrations of this in the New Testament is the Jerusalem Council of A.D. 50/51. In Acts 15 the apostles, elders, and other church leaders gather to discuss the question of admitting the Gentiles directly into the church, rather than requiring them to first become Jewish, or submitting to circumcision and acknowledging the Law of Moses. After Paul and Barnabas shared their experiences of their first missionary journey (Acts 15:12), highlighting the faithful response of the Gentiles to Christ, James entered the discussion and asserted, "With this the words of the Prophets agree, just as it is written" (Acts 15:15 NASB, citing Amos 9:11–12). James then concluded, "Therefore it is my judgment that we do not trouble those who are turning to God from among the Gentiles" (Acts 15:19 NASB).

Once a decision was rendered and accepted by those gathered in Jerusalem, a written statement of the decision was prepared and provided to the Gentile congregations, much like the establishment of an organizational policy (Acts 15:22–30). In fact, Acts 16:4 uses the term *dogma* (δόγμα), here translated *decision* (NIV) but elsewhere translated as *decree* (especially in regard to decisions of the emperor; Luke 2:1; Acts 17:7), to describe the decision and written document. It signifies a formal decision and implies a degree of authority. As such, Scripture is the primary lens through which the ministry leader derives administrative principles and practices for the church's activities.

Formative of a Distinctive Community: Congregation as Institutional Context

Administration implies an institutional context. The size, character, and commitments of the community shape the formation of administration, just as the administration shapes the community. Congregations as organizations have structures (both formal and informal), relationships, prescribed roles and functions, procedures and policies (either stated or implied), and yet congregations are *not* simply institutions. What the church *is* by nature cannot be contradicted by what the church *does*; it must be consistent in its *being* and its *doing*.

In Scripture, the church is rarely described with an institutionally driven image, favoring more qualitative images such as body of Christ (Eph. 4:12), bride of Christ (Eph. 5:22–32), flock of God (1 Pet. 5:2), or household of God (Eph. 2:19). These images emphasize the aspect of individuals in community with God, not an organizational structure. Hence, Christian administration should not contradict or minimize the church as a body. In *A Theology of Church Leadership*, Larry Richards argues that the church is an organic body, not an institution, and that confusing of the two has created difficulties for the community of faith. However, even he affirms that administration is essential to preserving and advancing the organic health and growth of the institution, limiting it to those "tasks absolutely necessary for the body to gather as an organism."[11]

The need to integrate what Richards identifies as the organic as opposed to the institutional dimensions of the church is obvious. The administrative infrastructure of the church must not interfere with or replace the ultimate identity of the church as Christ's body. Organisms, such as the human body, are very highly organized and orchestrated in their functioning; hence the concept of organism and organization are not necessarily contradictory.

In fact, the administrative service of the congregation exists to preserve the unity that exists within it because of Christ, preserving and facilitating the qualitative maturing of the congregation: "It was he [Christ] who gave some to be apostles, some to be prophets, some to be evangelists, and some to be pastors and teachers, to prepare God's people for works of service, so that the body of Christ may be built up until we all reach unity in the faith and in the knowledge of the Son of God and become mature, attaining to the whole measure of the fullness of Christ" (Eph. 4:11–13 NIV).

Organization and administration can never substitute for the spiritual dimension of the church. It preserves and builds upon the spiritual oneness of Christians as Christ's body. The business aspect of the congregation is in service and support of the congregation as Christ's body.

Redemptive in Purpose: Transformation as Mission and Motive

The ultimate purpose of ministry is spiritual maturation, both of the individual and the corporate body, in Christ. Paul wrote, "We proclaim him, admonishing and teaching everyone with all wisdom, so that we may present everyone perfect in Christ" (Col. 1:28 NIV). The transformation toward Christlikeness is a gradual process, not completed by the event of conversion. This process is reflected in Scripture in terms of our deepening relationship with God (particularly Eph. 2:1–10 and 1 Cor. 2).[12] The transformative process can be described in four spiritual statuses:

- *Natural Status*: Humanity's sinful status, separated from God, in need of conversion (cf. 1 Cor. 2:6–8, 14; Eph. 2:1–3).
- *Immature Status*: Humanity's redeemed status, but immature, infantile in faith (1 Cor. 3:1–3; Eph. 2:4–9).
- *Spiritual Status*: Humanity's redeemed status, but mature in Christ (1 Cor. 2:10–13, 15–16; Eph. 2:10).
- *Eternal Status*: Humanity's eternal status with God in heaven.

Hence, spiritual maturation is a gradual process of transformation, stemming from our conversion. As Peter writes, "Like newborn babies, crave pure spiritual milk, so that by it you *may grow up in your salvation*" (1 Pet. 2:2 NIV, emphasis added). Christian transformation is both punctiliar (conversion) and process (sanctification) in nature.

Christian administration must understand that its ultimate mission is to aid in the transformation of individuals within the church as well as in the community. As previously mentioned, the purpose of Christian administration is *not* the increase of workers' efficiency, effectiveness, and/or productivity (viewing workers as a means to an ends) but rather, the transformation of individuals as the end, aiding them in personal growth in the community of faith. Ministry leaders administrate for a spiritual reason and for a spiritual purpose, not for bureaucratic or mere institutional necessities. Transformation not only becomes our mission but our motive, as we are progressing toward spiritual maturity in Christ and desire others to mature. The purpose of Christian administration is to aid the process of transformation, the growth of the individual, who ultimately will desire to serve in the congregation as a valued participant in ministry.

Response to Human Needs: Humanity as Valued Participant

All the contemporary administrative paradigms make assumptions about human nature and/or the administrative response to workers, each with their own bias about human nature: negative and positive, individual and corporate. Christian administrators place a high value on humanity. It is unique among the creative acts of God because we are the *imago dei*, the image of God, which is equally shared by both male and female (Gen. 1:27). While this image may be described in a multitude of dimensions, it obviously includes that humanity was created to be in communion with God as its Creator. In Genesis 1–3 this image was created innocent, was broken by freewill sin, and was given the promise of restoration in a coming Savior, Jesus Christ.

Since human nature itself is not rigid, humans are in a constant state of transition. A fundamental assumption of evangelical theology about human nature is that it can be transformed. This is based on Romans 12:2: "Do not conform any longer to the pattern of this world, but be transformed by the renewing of your mind. Then you will be able to test and approve what God's will is—his good, pleasing and perfect will" (NIV). Christian administrators require a more pliable approach to humanity than is offered by many of the secular approaches to administration. However, the contingency paradigm of administration offers a more applicable model for the Christian administrator, since it rests on the premise that differing styles of leadership should be used in response to various levels of worker maturity, readiness, or ability.

Ronald Habermas identifies three "practical dimensions" of the *imago dei*: (1) "transformed attitude" toward others, (2) "transformed behaviors," and (3) "greater appreciation for diversity" among humanity.[13] For Christian administrators, regardless of the individuals' spiritual status (natural/unsaved, carnal/immature Christian, or spiritual/mature Christian), or their position within the organization, or their level of performance, they are possessors of the *imago dei* and hence deserving of a respectful relationship and to be treated with dignity by the administrator. James notes the contradiction of doing otherwise: "With the tongue we praise our Lord and Father, and with it we curse men, who have been made in God's likeness" (James 3:9 NIV). The affirmation of Christian theology is that all people are of innate value to God and hence should be valued by us as Christian administrators.

A Christian Perspective of Administration

If it is true that Christians ought to operate in the world in a distinctive manner, then this new paradigm should be evident in the way we administrate what we view to be God's resources. It stands to reason that a Christian will perform the activities associated with administration somewhat differently because of this new perspective. The following section will serve to illustrate just how a Christian perspective of administration should influence the way it is conducted in the context of ministry.

Administration as Ministry

One of the first realizations about a Christian perspective of administration is the awareness that administration is a ministry in and of itself. It is more than a method of operation or a means to an end. In a very real sense it is also an end in and of itself. Scripture teaches that "each one should use whatever gift he has received to serve others, faithfully administering God's grace in its various forms" (1 Pet. 4:10 NIV). Administration is ministry. Administration in the New Testament was not related to a business or corporate structure, but primarily for the redemptive ministry of the faith community. In fact, a survey of words translated *minister* or *ministry* in the New Testament could readily be rendered in terms of an administrator or administration.

"Surely you have heard about the administration of God's grace that was given to me for you . . . to make plain to everyone the administration of this mystery, which for ages past was kept hidden in God, who created all things" (Eph. 3:2, 9 NIV).

The emphasis on God's grace in this passage almost supplies a sacramental tone to the work of administration within the church, implying that our administrative work should serve others in the congregation, not simply the institution itself. It is a response to God's revelation ("mystery") and redemption ("God's grace"). In our twenty-first-century setting, one can easily be inclined to conceive of administration as business, but for the Christian educator it is ministry, used in the service and encouragement of others.

Administration as Servanthood

Servant leadership is intrinsic to the scriptural concept of administration. On two occasions in Mark's Gospel, Jesus reminded the Twelve of the cardinal principle of Christian service, "If anyone wants to be first, he must be the very last, and the servant of all" (Mark 9:35b NIV). In a later passage he is quoted as saying, "Whoever wants to become great among you must be your servant, and whoever wants to be first must be slave of all" (Mark 10:43b–44 NIV). In this latter passage, Jesus explained to the twelve disciples that "you know that those who are regarded as rulers of the Gentiles lord it over them, and their high officials exercise authority over them" (Mark 10:42 NIV). He then gives them an injunction, "Not so with you" (Mark 10:43a NIV), advocating servanthood as the attitudinal focus of ministry leaders. Figure 2.3 illustrates this principle.

Figure 2.3
Servant Vs.
Hierarchical
Leadership

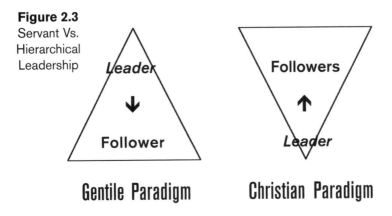

Leader

Follower

Gentile Paradigm

Followers

Leader

Christian Paradigm

In the Gentile paradigm, leadership is suppressive, with authority at the top of the hierarchy and followers being lorded over and dictated to by those in authority. In Jesus' paradigm, leadership is supportive, with authority at the bottom of the pyramid and followers being served by the leader and subject to the nurturing oversight of the leader.

The Christian administrator views his authority as coming from God. He serves as a steward of that authority and understands that he is to perform the duties of his office with an attitude of humility and service. We are not to use our position to *lord* or *exercise authority over* our partners in ministry. Servanthood leads from relationship, not position. It leads by example, not edict. Servanthood leads by providing pastoral ministry, not by being served. It leads in a spirit of humility, not through power. Leading as a servant invites others to join in the ministry as servants.

Administration as Spiritual Gift

When Paul wrote to the Corinthian church, he discussed God's approach to conducting ministry. It would be inherently different from approaches used in the past. Rather than restricting God's movement to a limited number of patriarchal leaders or members of one tribe, God would now distribute his resources among all of those who had surrendered their lives to him. The concept of the priesthood of all believers was born. Each member of the body of Christ would be a priest and would assume the responsibility for serving as a minister of God's grace and mercy to the world around him. In order to accomplish this ministry, God chose to give each believer an area of giftedness which would empower him to serve the extended body of Christ.

Since no one believer possesses all of the gifts, Jesus admonishes them to come together in unity and share in the work of the ministry. There are four lists in the New Testament which identify most of the spiritual gifts given to the body. They are found in Romans 12:6–8; 1 Corinthians 12:7–11; 27–30, and Ephesians 4:11–16. One of the gifts he identifies in these sections is the spiritual gift of administration. The purpose of the gifts was not merely for demonstration of the miraculous or to signify God's presence, but to fulfill a pastoral function within the congregation.[14]

What exactly did Paul mean by "administration"? The term used in 1 Corinthians 12:28 is *kubernēsis* (κυβέρνησις), denoting the function of providing guidance or more literally steering. The word is related to *kubernētēs* (κυβερνήτης), denoting a ship's master or helmsman (cf. Acts 27:11; Rev. 18:17, and in the Septuagint Ezek. 27:8). The term does not necessarily denote the owner of the vessel, but rather the function of determining its destination and the necessary passage to reach it. Gangel comments that this concept is tied to wisdom in the Old Testament, when reflecting on Proverbs 1:5; 11:14; 24:6, and hence noting an essential quality of a gifted leader.[15] Rienecker and Rogers comment that in the New Testament the plural form of the word denotes the ability of a person to hold a leadership position within the church.[16]

Administration is a gift of God given to individuals to equip them to serve in a leadership role. While it may be a temptation to rely upon our own abilities and talents to provide leadership, the Christian administrator must always remember that our capacity for leadership is in fact a God-given gift for use in his service. In 1 Corinthians 12, Paul emphasizes three times that God is the giver of the gifts and that the gifts were meant not for personal benefit or betterment, but for the ministry of his people.

Administration as Stewardship

Stewardship is another dimension of the broader concept of Christian administration. Paul writes, "Let a man regard us in this manner, as servants of Christ, and stewards of the mysteries of God. In this case, moreover, it is required of stewards that one be found trustworthy" (1 Cor. 4:1–2 NASB). Paul describes the pastor as a steward, or *oikonomos* (οἰκονόμος), denoting a steward or manager of a household, often a trusted slave. "The word emphasized that one is entrusted w[ith] great responsibility and accountability."[17] In the New Testament this term is used of the work of the elder/bishop (Titus 1:7), ministry within the church (1 Pet. 4:10), and of the care of a child (Gal. 4:2); and hence it signifies a general quality of trustworthiness, selflessness, and dependability.

The term signifies being a steward of something not our own, but God's. Christian administrators must be impressed by the awesome responsibility with which they have been entrusted as stewards of God's revelation and redemption. Christian administrators are called to lay aside personal agendas and concerns in light of the value of that which has been entrusted to us. This is the case in the parable of Jesus about the unfaithful servants.

In the parable of the talents Jesus presents the account of a master who "entrusted his property" to three servants, each a different amount, "each according to his ability" (Matt. 25:14–15 NIV). Hence, no one was burdened or called to perform above a reasonable level of expectation. Upon the return of the master, each servant's stewardship of the property entrusted to him was assessed. The first two doubled the number of talents. The one given five talents increased it by five. The one given two increased it by two (Matt. 25:19–20; 22). In both instances the master declared, "Well done, good and faithful servant! You have been faithful with a few things; I will put you in charge of many things. Come and share your master's happiness!" (Matt. 25:23 NIV).

However, the third servant was not a good steward. He allowed personal agendas and concerns to overshadow the property entrusted to him by his master: "I knew that you are a hard man, harvesting where you have not sown and gathering where you have not scattered seed. So I was afraid and went out and hid your talent in the ground. See, here is what belongs to you" (Matt. 25:24–27 NIV). His master declared the servant to be "wicked," "lazy," and later "worthless" based on his poor administration of the resources placed at his disposal (Matt. 25:26–27, 30), failing even to produce a minimal return on the investment with little effort (Matt. 25:27). He removed the entrusted property, giving it to the ten-talent servant, and pronounced, "For everyone who has will be given more, and he will have an abundance. Whoever does not have, even what he has will be taken from him. And throw that worthless servant outside, into the darkness, where there will be weeping and gnashing of teeth" (Matt. 25:29–30 NIV).

Being an *oikonomos*, a steward, is not an entitlement; it is God entrusting to us the administration of his people, ministry, message, and mission, all of which requires our full attention, devotion, and service.

Administration as Spritual

At first, it may be difficult to conceive of administrative tasks and practices as being spiritual. So much of administrative work seems routine or businesslike that it appears to function counter to—even at times contradictory to—the spiritual nature of the church. Perhaps the reason we do not perceive it as being spiritual is the lack of integration between the pastoral nature of the congregation and the more business side of running the ministry.

However, it should be regarded as spiritual for several reasons. First, administration is a spiritual gift given to the church by the Holy Spirit. Second, it is part of the pastoral role of ministry oversight. Third, it is part of the transformative mission of the church to its community and also to the world. Fourth, administration that is Christian leads through servitude, humility, relationship, and trust, all of which are values reflective of Christian character. Finally, Jesus serves as a model for our administrative activities in ministry. Jesus has been described as an *administrator* and *supervisor*, noting the practical implications for the organization and administration of ministry oversight today.[18] In short, we need not regard administration in the congregation as a necessary evil, nor as the disconnected or separate business aspect of the ministry, but as part of our spiritual service to God as ministry leaders.

Implications for Christian Administration

As this chapter draws to a close, it might be helpful to the reader to see a more summative listing of how one's Christian worldview impacts the manner in which administration is expressed. Five implications for a theologically informed perspective of administration are readily evident. A theological framework can influence the following five administrative dimensions: (1) administrative tasks, (2) values in the institution and decision making, (3) metaphors to describe the administrative function and position, (4) relationships within the institution, and (5) role of administration in Christian education. All of these in concert with one another provide lenses through which ministry leaders can view their administrative roles.[19]

Administrative Tasks

Some administrative tasks are theologically unique to the Christian leader. Tasks such as praying for volunteers and teachers or providing pastoral care and counsel are *direct* means of integrating one's Christian worldview into the administrative functions of the ministry leader. Next, the Christian educator's *rationale* to the general tasks should be motivated and understood in a theological context. For example, while something as simple as sending a memo or writing a newsletter column may not be *innately* theological, the reason for performing these tasks may be theologically motivated, such as building a sense of acceptance and belonging within the Christian community. Finally, some administrative tasks may be *redefined* in a theologically informed context. For example, providing correction/discipline to a volunteer or teacher should be done in a manner described in Scripture and with Christian grace and familial concern, not simply with businesslike politeness or procedural adherence. In short, the actual work of ministry leaders can and should reflect their theological convictions.

Administrative Metaphors

Metaphors are used to define concepts which are difficult to describe or grasp. Sometimes they are simply a complex description and add meaning to what has not been part of someone's personal experience. They are useful in capturing the essence of an idea rather than the mere concrete appearance of it. "Metaphors create ways of seeing and shaping organizational life."[20] Hence, how one chooses to describe himself in ministry is a reflection on his assumptions, expectations, and preferences. Metaphors influence how we conceive our ministries. They pose limiting factors and defining features. Metaphors tend to define relationships, placement within the institution, educational purposes, or the functional aspects of the position.

While one may be tempted to simply borrow business or educational metaphors for congregational ministry leaders (e.g., senior pastor as CEO, etc.), more theologically appropriate metaphors provide a pastoral understanding of the position being discussed. Perhaps recapturing the New Testament imagery of a ministry leader as pastor-shepherd, elder, overseer, slave-servant, helmsman, or steward should orient the younger members toward a more theologically informed understanding of the ministry. The titles and metaphors we choose to use in describing ourselves, personally and professionally, reflect our own understanding and expectations, hopefully with a recognizably theological orientation.

Administrative Values

Values, whether stated or implied, shape the institution and the administrative theory and practice managing it. The values that shape and direct the contemporary world of business are the result of a different worldview than that of ministry leaders. Values ultimately designed to entice customers, increase profit margins, and enhance workers' efficiency and productivity simply do not lend themselves to a Christian view of administration. Similarly, many modern values within contemporary ministry settings appear to be more consistent with the philosophy of pragmatism than with an evangelical, theologically informed viewpoint. The mantra "If it works, do it" has become an alarmingly popular voice heard at ministry development conferences this past decade. Some critical thinking about the integration of secular methods into ministry application is long overdue.

As with any Christian endeavor, ethical and spiritual values govern administrative theory and practices. Articulating such values in a statement of purpose and vision, using Scripture and theological tradition to guide in their formation and facilitates the theological informing of administrative values. Likewise, it serves as a theological expression of our core convictions as Christian leaders. A core value which is expressed as "We value Christians as the priesthood of believers" illustrates a biblical paradigm based more on the biblical teaching of spiritual giftedness and mutual ministry participation than on a hierarchical or corporate model. Christian administration that is consistently Christian in its approach to ministry is accomplished by advocating theologically informed values.

Administrative Relationships

Relationships are implicit to the Christian life and ministry. Relationships that are Christian in character maintain the presence of a qualitative difference within the administration. Such relationships place a priority on the spiritual dimension of Christian relationships. For example, institutional relationships can exist on multiple levels (supervisor-worker, teacher-student, generational, gender-related), but the prime relationship between Christians is that of brother-sister in Christ. Regardless of what other relational levels or bonds may be present, this one is core. Hence, for the Christian, relationships extend beyond the institution or task at hand, resting in something more substantial—Jesus Christ.

Another aspect of Christian relationships is that they are developmental. The notion of mentoring or discipling implies the presence of a positive relationship, aiding in the maturing and encouragement of fellow Christians. "But encourage one another daily, as long as it is called Today, so that none of you may be hardened by sin's deceitfulness" (Heb. 3:13 NIV). While relationships within any administrative structure may differ depending on one's particular place within the organization— e.g., peer relations, leader-subordinate relations—the presence of the qualitative concern for Christian relationship is always necessary. The spiritual and familial relationship we share as Christians must underlie, and on occasion supersede, the institutional necessities of relationship within the Christian institution.

Administrative Roles

A role refers to the actual function within the institution, the part played in the performance of ministry. Our role as Christian administrators is determined by our theological convictions, practical necessities within the context of the ministry (e.g., church, parachurch, mission, etc.), individual giftedness, and our own level of spiritual maturity. The administrative role is the amalgamation of the items previously mentioned: tasks, values, metaphors, and relationships. Our role as administrators must be theologically defined at the center. Other factors contribute to incarnate the position's expectations and responsibilities.

What is the role of a Christian administrator in the context of the local church? This role can be characterized by four properties: pastoral, educational, communal, and institutional. First and foremost, the Christian administrator is a pastor-shepherd of a spiritual flock. Second, the pastor is an educator, the means by which pastors fulfill their ministerial role. As such, their role is communal, meaning it is done within the context of the faith community and performed for its maturation as the people of God. Finally, their role is institutional, which need not be considered nontheological or contradictory to the life of the congregation, with the specific responsibilities of the role being described by the congregation's mission, ministry, and programs.

A Christian approach to administration is a spiritual approach that endeavors to mature employees and volunteers toward Christlikeness through pastoral service and relationships which enrich their personal lives and increase their participation in ministry. In this more theological context, administration can be a God-given pastoral function within the community of faith wherein Christians participate in maintaining (managing) and advancing (leading) the transformative mission of the church, in accordance with the Scriptures, while endeavoring to preserve the qualitative nature and function of the church as Christ's body. Hence, administration is a practical expression of our theological convictions and a vital part of our education ministry.

PART 2

PLANNING

The managerial function of planning is simple to define but challenging to execute. As definitions go, it could be described as the process of taking a look back at where the organization came from in terms of its initial mission statement, examining the current context of its existence, and then seeking to proactively anticipate the future and making preparations to meet it. There are many textbook definitions of planning, but for the most part, they all expand on the basic concept of what has just been presented. For example, Peterson (1980) defines planning as "a conscious process by which an institution assesses its current state and the likely future condition of its environment, identifies possible future states for itself, and then develops organizational strategies, policies and procedures for selecting and getting to one or more of them."[1] Simply stated, planning is trying to predict the future and then to project what resources will be necessary to function successfully when that future becomes a reality.

MacKinney states with bold assurance that "in every organization—and I believe the point to be universal—some kind of planning takes place."[2] Planning is challenging because if it is done right, it involves a great many people functioning together with a specific goal in mind. The first of five managerial functions, planning is the starting point for institutional success or failure. It is critical to the life of the enterprise that effective planning take place. Done right, it is intentional and developed into a comprehensive working document which guides the organization into the future.

The activities involved in the planning process comprise the substance of this second unit of the text. Each element is developed in more detail as a separate chapter.

Chapter 3 provides a detailed discussion about the development of a mission and vision statement because planning starts with these important activities. This _raison d'etre_ provides a clear understanding for why the organization was created.

It should be stated up front that there is ample disagreement within both corporate and nonprofit settings about the semantics of these two terms. Some prefer to use the term _mission_ to describe the big picture and _vision_ to describe the more specific interpretation of that plan. Others prefer to see _vision_ coming first, followed by the organization's _mission_. There is credible evidence for arguments on either side of the debate. The important issue for our purposes is to understand that the big picture comes first and is followed by a more specific plan to accomplish that picture. Each should be clearly articulated in a statement and made available for both members of the organization and for society in general. In essence, first _why,_ then _what._

Chapter 4 provides the reader with an understanding about how one writes and incorporates goals and objectives into the planning process. Once again, some authors use the term _goal_ to describe the more general plan and _objective_ to describe more specific application. Other authors reverse this terminology. What is important is not so much the definition of each term as the concepts that each term represents. A plan must be spelled out in writing and stated in such a way as to provide for specificity and measurement. Without this there can be no eventual accountability and evaluation. Goals and objectives commit the organization to direction and ensure that the resources are available to accomplish its intended direction.

Chapter 5 takes what is the natural next step in the process and develops it in such a way as to package the mission, vision, goals, and objectives into a strategic plan. This strategic plan becomes the master plan upon which all institutional activity is coordinated and guided. Many churches and other ministry organizations fail at this point because they lack coordinated effort. What is taking place in the children's ministry seems to have little, if any, bearing on the youth department. When each area fails to coordinate with what the senior pastor and church board envision for the future, conflict and strife are the natural outcomes. Proper strategic planning prevents this from occurring. It also ensures that adequate resources (human, financial, facility, etc.) are assigned to each of the goals and objectives that have been documented in the preceding step.

Chapter 6 presents the reader with the value and contributions that policies and procedures make to ministry. Policies and procedures are types of plans in that they are general statements or understandings which guide and channel thinking toward the accomplishment of the organization's mission and vision.[3] In essence, they help those involved in the ministry stay on track and remain focused on accomplishing the goals and objectives. Many ministry leaders don't like policies and procedures because they view them as restrictive and confining. Policies are necessary statements which guide behavior and decision making. Ideally, they help decide issues before they arise and become problems.[4]

For example, it is a policy in many churches that those who drive vehicles for youth activities be licensed drivers with current registration and insurance coverage. In addition, they must be at least twenty-one years of age and have had no major accidents within the past three years. Such a policy helps guarantee a certain level of maturity on the part of those who are assigned the task of transporting the young people of the church. Such a policy will also have a beneficial influence on the insurance rates paid by the church.

Procedures, on the other hand, go beyond policies in that they establish the method by which the policies are to be implemented. They build upon policies and make them more complete and functional. Using the above policy as an example, the procedures that all church drivers must follow may be stated as: *"Before anyone can drive minors for a church function, they must provide a photocopy of their driver's license to be kept on file, proof of insurance in effect, a copy of their driving record from the state's department of motor vehicles, and sign a statement that they agree to comply with all existing laws of the state while transporting church minors."* Procedures bring specificity to policies and go hand-in-hand in guiding the organization toward its stated goals and objectives. Chapter 6 presents the reader with the value and contributions that policies and procedures make to ministry and provides a template that can be used to establish both types of plans.

Chapter 7 documents the simplest form of plans: the budget. Stated in financial terms, a budget is a plan stated in numerical terms. It allocates financial resources and directs them toward the accomplishment of the goals and objectives agreed upon in the strategic plan.

One of the greatest mistakes made in churches today is the sequence of budgeting in relation to the other elements discussed thus far. When budgeting is allowed to drive the development of the goals and objectives (and therefore the strategic plan and program), the church is characterized by shortsightedness and an overemphasis on money. When a decision needs to be made, the final outcome will be based on how much money is available rather than on mission or vision. Evidence of this spiritually dysfunctional thinking is seen when the church's finance committee (comprised of ministry volunteers) develops the church budget and presents it to the church staff (professionally trained ministry leaders) and then allows them to envision their future based on the financial resources which are being allocated to them. This approach demonstrates no faith because money rather than the Holy Spirit drives all decision making.

Admittedly, some ministry leaders strike out into such grandiose realms of faith that the reality of funding receives little, if any, consideration. This has led to heavily mortgaged buildings, manipulative fundraising practices, feelings of betrayal and deception, and significant power struggles between ministry leaders and church members. A reasonable compromise between faith-reaching and reality-funding is possible and presented in this chapter.

The final chapter in this section does not appear in many ministry-oriented management texts or planning flow charts. This is unfortunate because management by objectives (MBO) has been available as a planning tool for corporate organizations since the 1950s. Chapter 8 provides the reader with the knowledge and background necessary to develop a management-by-objectives program for ministry application. Such a program has been revolutionary for many churches, camps, mission organizations, schools, and other nonprofit agencies. Though some texts include this concept under *directing* or *evaluating*, we feel it is best included as a planning tool, though indeed it is an effective means of directing and/or evaluating staff.

This hierarchy of planning pyramid presented on page 57 allows the reader to see the relationship of each element to the whole.[5] No one piece is independent of the others since they all flow out of an ordered priority. When all the elements of the planning process come together, they allow the ministry organization to function with effectiveness and satisfaction. The end result is that the ministry comes that much closer to fulfilling its part in the Great Commission.

Though the flow of these elements may appear to be sequential, and in most cases they are, it is important to realize that management is by nature a dynamic phenomenon. Rarely, if ever, does an organization stand still long enough for its managers to arrange all the elements of management in their proper order. The organization is usually in the middle of a myriad of activities while stretching its resources to the limit. Yet it is in the midst of such movement that managers are called to exercise their expertise and to bring order to the enterprise. In reality there is overlap, while the ministry ebbs and flows through their efforts. So as you examine the chapters throughout this section, remember that although there is a sequential ideal, ministries rarely operate in the ideal for prolonged periods of time. The elements on the hierarchy may look great on the chart, but usually they are all in movement simultaneously. That's why it takes a gifted managerial leader to bring coordination to the process.

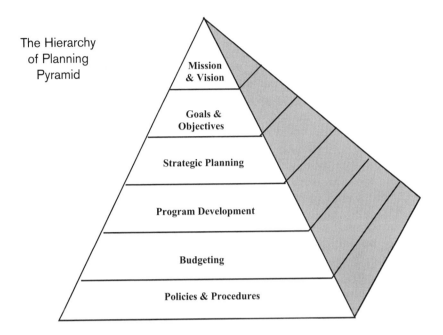

The Hierarchy of Planning Pyramid

Mission & Vision

Goals & Objectives

Strategic Planning

Program Development

Budgeting

Policies & Procedures

We have chosen not to include a separate chapter in this text on program development because ministry organizations using this book have such a diverse array of programs to develop, and no one program will meet the needs of all ministries. For example, the kind of program that is developed to meet the needs of inner-city youth will be inadequate to reach suburban kids in a different part of the country. Likewise, a program for children will not be applicable for adults. Parachurch programs will look different from those in churches even though both may focus on the same demographic group. Rather than trying to create a "one size fits all" program, we felt it best to incorporate the material of this planning element throughout the chapters of the book to allow for a more integrated approach to programmatic design.

As you read through the chapters in this unit, remember that planning is a process, not a destination per se. It is much more than a document labeled "ministry plan." The planning process involves many people coming from different perspectives if it is going to be done right. It takes time and requires a commitment from all members of the ministry team. When done correctly, planning yields many obvious benefits. First, it provides a conceptual framework for organizational direction. Second, it minimizes the impact of any one person by allowing input from multiple sources. Third, planning reduces the detrimental influences brought about by hidden agendas since it brings all of the important information out in the open for everyone to see. Fourth, planning allows more *buy in* on the part of those members of the ministry team who have a vested interest in supporting it.[6] In short, planning is a critical component of successful ministry. Although it requires a good deal of effort if done well, the benefits derived from effective planning are worth the energies expended.

BY
GORDON COULTER

Chapter 3

Building Mission and Vision

THE PURPOSE OF THIS CHAPTER is to explore some practical ways of establishing a mission and vision for your ministry. Over the course of your life you may assume a variety of career-oriented roles such as visionary leader, manager, staff developer, or mentor, but the passion and dynamic of one's mission and vision will most likely remain constant. One's mission and vision flow out of a personal philosophy of ministry. They answer the questions of "why," "who," "what," and "how" as they pertain to ministry programming. They provide the ministry leader with direction, focus, and life-transforming power, especially when difficult life circumstances come along to threaten one's peace and stability. They also allow the leader to say *no* to what may seem like wonderful opportunities at the time. A clearly defined mission and vision not only releases and empowers you for ministry but also protects and defends you from making untimely mistakes.

Understanding and Defining Mission

The terms *mission* and *vision* should be used with precision. Barna states, "Sadly, the majority of churches I've studied have confused mission and vision. For some reason, most pastors equate the two. They believe that the two terms are interchangeable. They're not."[1] Understanding these concepts is critical to the successful implementation of a ministry's subsequent strategic plan. "The mission of a church must be clearly defined and members of the body must be led to understand and accept the mission. There needs to be a basic understanding of the essential character of a church before its mission can be described."[2] That basic understanding of the church's essential character must be founded on a strong biblical understanding of the nature of

59

the church. Perhaps the best New Testament example of a mission is provided with the Great Commission from Jesus in Matthew 28:18–20: "All authority in heaven and on earth has been given to me. Therefore go and make disciples of all nations, baptizing them in the name of the Father and of the Son and of the Holy Spirit, and teaching them to obey everything I have commanded you. And surely I am with you always, to the very end of the age" (NIV).

Defining the substance of a mission statement is essential for successful ministry. It allows the ministry leader to differentiate it from the vision statement. Simply defined, the mission of the ministry "is a broad, general statement about who you wish to reach and what the church hopes to accomplish. It is very likely that many churches share the same mission and could even use the same wording of that mission. Why? Because the mission is basically a definition of ministry. It is not geared to uniqueness or distinctives or direction. It is designed to reflect a heart turned to God in service and obedience in which the church is a vehicle used to unite people to do His will."[3]

In many ministries across North America, mission statements are tied to a particular passage of Scripture. Often they are reduced to a short phrase or brief narrative statement. They might read something short and to the point such as "To know Him and make Him known" or "Reaching the unreached in the name of Christ." Those that tie themselves to a passage of Scripture may read like a precursor to the verse itself. "The Mission of New Harvest Church is to make disciples of all nations, baptizing them in the name of the Father, Son and Holy Spirit" [based on Matt. 28:19–20]. Another example might be: "The mission of First Baptist Church is to proclaim Christ, admonishing everyone and teaching them with all wisdom, that we may present each one complete in Christ" [based on Col. 1:28].

There is a good deal of confusion today between what differentiates a mission statement from a vision statement, for they are clearly not the same. A mission statement paints the general and broad stroke of the ministry. In a real sense it is a statement of philosophy with theological underpinnings. It provides the audience with the reason *why* the ministry is in existence. The vision statement, on the other hand, is far more precise, detailed, customized, and distinctive to each ministry. It provides the audience with the *who, what,* and *how* of its efforts.[4]

Barna provides a set of guidelines to help ministry leaders determine whether what they have is more of a mission statement or a vision statement. Using the set of questions cited below, if you can respond with a no to most of them, then what you have is a statement of mission rather than vision.

1. If someone contacted your church regarding involvement in what seemed like a reasonable ministry opportunity, is the statement specific enough to permit you to have a ministry-oriented reason to reject that opportunity and explain the reasoning for the rejection?
2. Does the statement include information which, when compared to the vision statements of other nearby churches, clearly sets your church apart in a significant manner?
3. Does the statement identify a target audience whom you hope to impact through the church's ministry?
4. Is the statement one that points the church in a clear and unique direction for the future?
5. Does the statement lead to a precise understanding of the strategies and tactics that are permissible in ministry?
6. Does the statement provide focus for the ministry so people are excited about being involved in the work of the church?
7. Does the statement prevent the church from seeking to be all things to all people?
8. Have any inactive Christians who regularly attend the church become excited about the prospects for ministry after being exposed to the statement?[5]

The Biblical Basis of Mission

In Genesis 12, Abram accepted a mission from God, not knowing how it was to be accomplished. In verse 1, the Lord says to Abram, "Leave your country, your people and your father's household and go to the land I will show you" (NIV). Abram only had the mission, but the specifics of where and what was to happen had not yet been revealed. The penetrating truth here is that Abram accepted the mission to "go." Mission is an action word. It requires movement, change, and a willingness to move to the next important step, which will be finding, identifying, and implementing a specific vision derived from the broader mission. Both the mission of the church and the personal mission of each follower have much to do with engaging ourselves and others in a life transformation that will change individuals as well as communities into Christlikeness. In order to stay true to the biblical mandate of Christ's mission, we must guard against compromising to fit our own view rather than following a clear biblical path.

Rick Warren puts it this way: "Nothing precedes purpose. The starting point for every church should be the question, '*Why* do we exist?'"[6] By understanding the mission of the church from a biblical basis, you have this question answered.

Paul tells us that in order for something to last, it must be built on the right foundation: "But each one should be careful how he builds. For no one can lay any foundation other than the one already laid, which is Jesus Christ" (1 Cor. 3:10–11 NIV). Jesus also stated this in the parable of the house in Matthew 7:24: "Therefore everyone who hears these words of mine and puts them into practice is like a wise man who built his house on the rock" (NIV). Our ministry's mission is that solid foundation.

In summary, a mission statement is a general statement about what the church and Christ's followers hope to accomplish in broader terms. In aligns closely with Scripture and answers the question of *why* a particular ministry is in existence. Stated another way, the mission statement is mostly philosophical while the vision statement is strategic in character.[7] Here are a few examples of how various ministries have chosen to articulate their mission.

Churches

At First Baptist Church of Los Altos, we believe that Jesus Christ died on the cross for sin, to purchase a unique people of His own, from all nations, and to make them holy like Him. He is working today, by the Holy Spirit, to accomplish just that. Through the making known of the gospel, He is forming the church, His bride, and making her pure by His Word and Spirit.

The mission of the First Baptist Church of Euless is to reach our region, impact our nation, and touch our world.

It is the mission of First Baptist Church of Davenport to be a living expression of God's love in the world by inviting people to a saving relationship with God through faith in his Son, Jesus Christ, and by nurturing each other in Christ-like living.

Insitutions of Higher Education

The mission of Biola University is biblically centered education, scholarship and service, equipping men and women in mind and character to impact the world for the Lord Jesus Christ.

Under the lordship of Jesus Christ, the mission of The Southern Baptist Theological Seminary is to be totally committed to the Word of God and to be a servant of the churches of the Southern Baptist Convention by training, educating and preparing ministers of the gospel for more faithful service.

The mission of Dallas Theological Seminary as a professional, graduate-level school is to prepare men and women for ministry as godly servant-leaders in the body of Christ worldwide. By blending instruction in the Scriptures from our doctrinal perspective with training in ministry skills, the Seminary seeks to produce graduates who do the work of evangelism, edify believers, and equip others by proclaiming and applying God's Word in the power of the Holy Spirit.

Parachurch Organizations

The mission of Peace Officers for Christ International is to bring peace officers and their families to a saving knowledge of, and close personal relationship with, our Lord Jesus Christ.

The mission of Youth for Christ is to participate in the body of Christ in responsible evangelism of youth, presenting them with the person, work and teachings of Christ and discipling them into the local church.

As you can see from the examples given above, they don't all look alike. Some emphasize more of a narrative approach to stating their mission while others prefer to highlight a set of essential qualities. The particular format is not really that important. What counts is the substance of the mission and how well it communicates the heart of the ministry as a whole.

Differentiating Between Mission and Vision

In obedience to the mission, the ministry's leaders and volunteers will need a means of carrying out the mission. Throughout the Bible, God often made known his will through visions. Psalm 89:19 refers to God speaking in a vision to his people. God spoke through the visions of the prophets (Num. 12:6). Sometimes his vision came through an audible voice, as in Genesis 15:1 or 1 Samuel 3:4–5. He also used angels to communicate his vision (Luke 1:11, 22; 24:23; Acts 10:3).

Another notable example of God providing a vision is seen in Paul's conversion on the road to Damascus. After Paul was blinded and had fallen down in the road in front of his fellow travelers, the Lord spoke and told him to go into the city where he would be told what to do. Now the Pharisee and persecutor of Christians was being led as a blind man into the city. The Lord called to another man, named Ananias, in a vision. Acts 9:12 tells us that Saul also had seen Ananias in a vision restoring his sight.

Peter's vision in Acts 10 helps us understand a vision from God's perspective. During prayer, Peter fell into a trance. He saw heaven open and a sheet that contained all kinds of four-footed animals, as well as reptiles and birds. The voice said, "Get up, Peter. Kill and eat" (Acts 10:13 NIV). We must understand the background of the Jews to understand how radical this vision was. The dietary restrictions of the Jews that were sacred were now being abandoned. The Jewish and the Gentile believers would no longer be separated by the centuries-old .

rules. This vision was so dramatic that Peter argued with God, but three times God restated his vision to Peter. This vision was intertwined with the story of Cornelius, a centurion in the Italian Regiment. As the story unfolds, this vision of banning the dietary laws was a clear mandate for Peter to associate with Gentiles. Peter now was able to speak the gospel message to Cornelius, his relatives, and friends. The gospel was now being spread throughout the area to those who were previously considered "unclean" by Jewish law.

God's visions are often very specific, as illustrated by these biblical accounts. One of the most quoted and perhaps most misunderstood statements in the Bible about vision is Proverbs 29:18, which reads in the King James, "Where there is no vision, the people perish." The NIV translation says, "Where there is no revelation, the people cast off restraint." Too few Christian educators spend enough time in developing vision in their regular teaching. Not having a vision is not an option for the Christian leader. God has a very clear vision for our ministries and your life. It is an adventure to discover what that is and trust him to bring it to fullness.

Barna defines vision as "a clear mental image of a preferable future imparted by God to His chosen servants, based upon an accurate understanding of God, self, and circumstances."[8] Martin Luther King Jr. put it this way: "If a man hasn't discovered something he will die for, he isn't fit to live." Dr. King's vision led to one of the most significant social movements of the last century.

To further unpack the notion of vision, some have described it as *foresight.* It means seeing that which is yet to be and putting a plan together to make it a reality. Joel Hunter talks about how most of us deal with getting a group focused, but sometimes the focus is on the wrong things. He states, "Vision is critical to any ministry. Ministry without vision is like a ship without a compass, a surgeon without a scalpel, a writer without a pen."[9]

God is calling out leaders to fulfill the great "mission" as well as to implement visions that will bring this mission to reality. One of the greatest leaders of recent history was Dr. Bill Bright. In a recent *Christianity Today* article, Josh McDowell, Dave Hannah, and Rick Warren wrote of Dr. Bright's legacy. McDowell met Dr. Bright at Wheaton College in 1961. After Dr. Bright spoke in chapel, McDowell and a few other students met with him in the coffee shop. During that time, Dr. Bright shared his vision of how to be filled with the Holy Spirit by faith as well as his passion for evangelism. Dr. Bright had a passion for evangelism, and he was so "captivated by his calling to reach others for Christ that it became contagious. You simply couldn't be around Bill without walking away with a greater desire to share Christ. To Bill, evangelism was just a way of life."[10]

Warren comments that Billy Graham is gifted to speak to hundreds of thousands at one time, but Bill Bright spoke to hundreds of thousands one at a time—two different visions of carrying out the same mission. Warren states that Campus Crusade for Christ is the largest ministry in the world, yet the legacy of Bill Bright is the millions he either personally or corporately led to faith in Jesus Christ. Dr. Bright's vision for evangelism led him to develop the Four Spiritual Laws, the most widely distributed religious pamphlet in history. It has been translated into two hundred languages and read by an estimated two and one-half billion people. Bill Bright's vision started as a personal one—to reach the unreached—and developed into one of the most significant Christian ministries of all time.[11] This tool, among many developed by Bright, was his vision for accomplishing God's mission of the Great Commission.

Taking hold of a mission given by God and implementing a vision to accomplish that mission can be life-changing. It can be empowering because the disciple realizes God is on his side and desires to partner with him to accomplish that ministry venture. Hybels speaks of this transforming power when he says: "You don't have to be a cynic to feel a little skeptical when someone starts talking about changing the world. Even if you agree that the world is due for some major reconstruction, you probably consider the chances of such change to be slim. But when God fuels a dream, and a leader becomes inspired—well, who knows what might happen?"[12]

Every great work for God starts with a dream that becomes more; after a long night's tossing and turning, the dream becomes action. Hybels says that "when a church needs a God-honoring, kingdom-advancing, heart-thumping vision, it turns to its leaders. That is why God put in the leader's arsenal the potent offensive weapon called vision."[13]

Imagine what would happen if every ministry would take their vision seriously and give all they had to accomplish that vision. Infuse your vision with passion and commit to staying with it. What if each one of us at the local ministries or worldwide mission organization level would keep on visioning the impossible biblical mandate to reach out to every living person on earth starting with our own neighborhoods? Nothing could stop such a movement.

Recasting the Vision

There are times when one is given a vision by God to venture into a particular area of ministry. For a season of time that only God knows, that individual perseveres through the challenges and difficulties of accomplishing that vision. This does not mean, however, that God is not able to change the vision according to his sovereign plan. People change as a result of the natural progression of life development. Demographics of a community change as well. Sometimes God just seems to want to make a change that is not as clearly foreseeable as we would like. When this occurs we must be willing to change as well. This is particularly true when God's methods of reaching a generation change as a result of the different issues facing that generation. A classic example of this is Calvary Chapel in Costa Mesa, California, which recast its vision of ministry and reached an entire generation for Christ. This renewed vision led the charge for beginning the Jesus People movement of the 1960s.

Sometimes an entire church can go through this vision recasting as a result of the changes that take place within the demographics of the surrounding neighborhood. Other times a ministry such as a camp or mission enterprise may need to recast its vision as a result of leadership transitions, financial setbacks, or unforeseen occurrences. When a ministry refuses to recast its vision, it remains stymied in the past, refusing to retool and refocus its vision. History is replete with examples of ministries that refused to keep their vision updated and current and remained stuck in tradition. They refused to change because "they had always done it that way before," and those who had received the original vision found it impossible to change with the times.

A wise leader and ministry board will periodically ask themselves if the vision they received at the beginning of the venture still remains the same or if changes need to occur. In many cases, the vision may remain the same, but the methods may need to be updated. In some instances, the vision itself needs to be reexamined. When this happens, a season of prayer is warranted to wait upon God's guidance for a new and revised vision for the future of the ministry. Perhaps a personal example of this process of vision recasting will help illustrate my point.

The church where I currently serve as senior pastor has been located at its present address for forty-two years. The founding pastor had a vision to reach out to the children and families of this new community being developed where orange groves once covered the area of Covina, California. Over time a shift in demographics within the community occurred, resulting in a majority population of ethnic groups. The church leadership struggled with trying to decide whether to sell the church and move into the suburbs or remain and reach the new community. After waiting upon God for his guidance, the leadership took on the challenge of staying and refocusing their efforts on reaching a different ethnic group from their own for Christ.

This recasting of vision did not come without some fallout and tension. Several of the most faithful members were not comfortable with the new emphasis of reaching out to our immediate community. Many left to serve in other churches, some taking groups with them. However, because those in leadership felt this new vision directive had come from God himself, they were willing to ride out the storms and remain focused on the vision they had received.

By the time I came as their senior pastor the church had gone through several leadership transitions but had remained steadfast in maintaining its renewed vision for reaching a changing community for Christ. Because of my friendship with the previous pastor I was well aware of the cost it would take to rebuild this small, declining urban church into a dynamic, seven-day-a-week ministry center. Soon we wrote a revised vision statement that would allow us to fulfill the passion that God had given the church's leadership to reach out to all within a three-mile radius. Our vision statement defines our church as a "neighborhood church." This gives us the focus. Our core values come out of John 1:14: "The Word became flesh and moved into the neighborhood."[14] The application for us was to become an incarnational church for the many ethnic and socioeconomic groups in our community.

We began a twenty-four-hour prayer meeting and spent two years in study. Out of all these efforts we were able to write our vision statement in such a way that it would give us the lens to keep our focus without giving up the passion for undertaking new things. Our new vision statement reads: "We are a Christian Community called to worship God by impacting our neighborhood through meeting physical, educational and spiritual needs, resulting in devoted followers of Jesus Christ."[15]

Over time we have blended three distinct congregations into one membership. The church's motto is "Three Congregations . . . One Church." There are English, Spanish, and Filipino congregations. All the congregations cooperate in various aspects of Christian education and fellowship but keep their cultural distinctions for the worship service, having separate services simultaneously.

Because we believe our vision is from God, we did not limit him in finding the resources to meet these ministry needs. Currently on our property, Youth for Christ pays rent for its offices and offers classes, training, and ministry to students. Another ministry is Stepping Stones for Women, a ministry to single mothers who desire to get off welfare and develop a career. This ministry also has its offices at the church and uses the facilities. We started a skate park, and now three times a week it is open and full of students skating. But more important, these students are in the process of seeing Jesus through our leaders and several are now attending the youth group. In addition, we have a linen closet for Love Inc, a ministry of World Vision, which supplies quilts for the Lives ministry. Our women make over one hundred quilts annually for orphanages all over the world.

Just last month, we opened a computer lab, which serves those who are unable to pay for tutoring and computer training. In a room with eight new computers, several volunteers managess this important ministry. Our newest ministry is a bread giveaway that came through the vision of one of our newest members. In hindsight, we have seen God recast our vision as a church and have witnessed his life-transforming power at work in the lives of those within our community.

Communicating the Revised Ministry Vision

Once a renewed vision has been developed, there are some keys to effectively communicating it to your audience. Terry Wardle suggests the following: "Be clear and concise. Communicate comprehensively. Identify those people who are most essential for translating the vision into reality. Communicate as creatively as possible. To capture the future, a vision must be continually before the people."[16]

Ministries that are able to successfully transition their vision have learned that it is not possible to overcommunicate their outcome. They look for ways to be in contact with their constituents and realize that people need to hear the new vision time and time again before it sinks into their psyche. Putting the revised vision statement on the organization's letterhead is one method that some ministries have found effective. Obviously, putting it in the weekly bulletin, monthly newsletter, and web page helps as well. It should also be the focus of an annual sermon. Look for creative ways to communicate this revised statement and allow people time to take hold of the new direction. In the long run, the effort will pay dividends of eternal rewards.

Team Building and Vision Casting

Larson and LaFasto reported on a three-year study of secular teams in widely differing workplaces. They wanted to answer the important question: "What are the secrets of successful teams?" The researchers interviewed the leaders and members of thirty-two real-life management teams. In preparation for this study, the authors developed two sets of core questions that were asked in each interview. Interviewees were asked to describe a situation when they were involved in an "unusually effectively functioning team" and an "unusually poorly functioning team," identifying what they thought were factors contributing to the respective levels of effectiveness. From this study, Larson and LaFasto discovered eight characteristics that explain how and why effective teams develop. Topping the list as the highest value was a clear and elevating goal.[17] In other words, each member of the team could articulate the vision of the organization and understood the part he or she played in its accomplishment.

In every case when an effectively functioning team was identified, it had a clear understanding of its vision and a high value on meeting it. Whenever the researchers found an ineffectively functioning team, the "goal had become unfocused . . . politicized; the team had lost a sense of urgency or significance about its objective . . . and individual goals had taken priority over team goals."[18]

Bennis and Nanus conducted an extensive study of those who were deemed to be effective leaders in their organizations. Seeking to determine what common characteristics might be evident among the high achievers, the researchers discovered at the top of the list was an impassioned leader who had a clear understanding of where the organization should be headed. They knew their vision and were committed to taking the organization in that direction. In the summary of their findings they stated, "All ninety people interviewed had an *agenda,* an unparalleled concern with outcome. . . . Intensity coupled with commitment is magnetic . . . [the] intense personalities do not have to coerce people to pay attention; they are so intent on what they are doing that, like a child completely absorbed with creating a sand castle in a sand box, they draw others in."[19]

A clear and compelling vision should have a profound impact on the direction and focus of the ministry. It helps shape the budget, determine personnel placements, and provides focus on setting goals and objectives for activity. There are few things as transforming to an organization as seeing it catch hold of a vision and harnessing its energy in making progress toward its reason for being in existence.

Integrating a Department Vision into Corporate Vision

One of the least understood areas about vision is how to integrate a department's vision within the context of an organization's vision. Various programs within a church's ministry go through changes over time. The rate of change within a particular program may vary from the church as a whole, resulting in a department having a vision that may not be congruent with the rest of the church. This occurs as a result of a variety of factors.

Demographic Transition

Not all departments within an organization change at the same rate. For example, young married couples in a church may decline while the older members of the church remain relatively fixed. These demographic changes can produce a department that has a different vision from the main congregation.

Personnel Changeover

Another reason this discrepancy between department vision and organizational vision may occur is personnel change. For example, a youth pastor may remain in his position for ten years while during that same time the church may go through several senior pastors. This personnel change may result in the senior pastor coming in with a particular vision which is not necessarily consistent with the youth pastor's.

Political Entities

It would be nice to state that ministries are exempt from personal politics, but such a statement would not be honest or realistic. The reality is that organizations, including most ministries, are comprised of people who sometimes insist on having their own way in spite of the greater good of the organization. When this happens there can be a discrepancy between the vision of the organization and particular departments within that organization. It depends to some degree on where this political power exists and the degree to which it manifests itself. For example, the chairman of the finance committee may have a personal vision for the development of a ministry to homeless people within the community. Since this church leader controls the financial resources of the organization, he may insist on creating a department with a vision that is not necessarily consistent with the church as a whole.

Budgetary Crises

A final reason why departments within an organization may have a different vision from the host organization is budgetary changes that may occur. When the organization undergoes a significant financial crisis, it may respond to that crisis by cutting back in a programmatic focus. Departments may be eliminated or merged in order to weather the financial storm. What was once a particular passion or vision of those within one department must now become subsumed within another department. Sometimes these adjustments result in mismatched visions between departments and the main organization. For example, a church going through financial crisis may decide to merge the junior high program with the senior high program and thereby eliminate one pastoral salary. If the selection of which pastor remains is due more to salary scale than ministry philosophy, a discrepancy between department vision and church vision may result.

Researcher Kevin Lawson conducted a national survey of church associate staff members who reported unusually high levels of personal and job-related satisfaction. These staff members who were thriving in their particular ministry contexts had some things in common. Chief among them was a department vision that was consistent with that of the host congregation. In essence, there was congruence between where the church body wanted to go (congregational vision) and where the associate staff members wanted to go (departmental vision). In essence, they were on the same page going the same direction.

A healthy church is characterized by a sense of unity in Christ (John 17:20–21), an evident love for God and for others, especially for fellow disciples of Jesus Christ (Luke 10:25–28), and the opportunity for all to exercise their gifts in ministry, building up the body of Christ (Ephes. 4:11–14). A healthy church is characterized by unity in ministry vision and church members who use their gifts to strengthen the body in its pursuit of that vision.[20]

If you are an associate staff member, let me suggest a few important steps to take in developing a vision for your specific area of ministry. First, research and know how the ministry organization's vision was developed. You will need to understand the history, something about the founders, and critical times in the ministry's life span. Often some of the older members can give you information that will help in this research. Second, listen to the pastor's or director's personal vision for the ministry. Whether by listening to a sermon or through a personal meeting, understand where this leader wants the organization to go. Third, talk to other staff members who are familiar with this ministry. They can be most helpful in telling you the strengths, the best ways to make progress, and, most importantly, those with hidden political agendas which may pose a hazard to you. Fourth, after thinking and praying about your department's vision, ask for some time with the senior pastor or ministry director so you can share your vision in person.

This would be a good time to get off the campus so you can get their undivided attention. Know this leader's style; some prefer to see things in writing while others prefer to hear it with feeling and inflection. During this time you will want to illustrate how your department's vision integrates with the host ministry's vision. Make the connection obvious and without conflict. Be willing to let him critique your vision without becoming defensive or offensive.

Lawson says that when you give input into other ministries, you will be encouraged in your own area. Your pastor will see you as a team player, not a lone ranger.[21] The goal, of course, is what Lawson calls a sense of unity in the church regarding its purpose and ministry vision.[22] One of the greatest benefits of this unity of staff and purpose is that the team will stay together far longer than is normally the case, and each member will experience a more lasting satisfaction both personally as well as in terms of ministry performance.

Losing Ministry Vision

One area that is often overlooked in church ministry is "how vision is lost." Barna writes about reasons why a church slowly loses its strength, focus, and then its purpose. Perhaps a summary of these would be beneficial.

1. *Being out of touch with God.* The visionary leader must stay in close communication with God. If we depart from God's presence, the vision he gave us will depart as well. We have found that having several twenty-four-hour prayer vigils during the year has helped us stay in touch as leaders and as a congregation.

2. *Burnout.* We live in a driven culture that feeds into our accomplishments rather than our relationship with God. Our primary service to God needs to be in our gifted area so that we are continually inspired and fueled to continue growing. Burnout occurs when we operate outside of our gifts for an extended period of time.

3. *Poor leadership.* When the vision is not nurtured properly, often people will give up. Visionaries need to be around other visionaries to stay inspired and effective.

4. *Absence of accountability.* Make a pact with a respected mentor that will keep you on target and focused. It is suggested that this pact consist of two mentors, one who is in a similar role to yours but who is at a different ministry location than yours and a second mentor who is older and more experienced in ministry.

5. *Impatience.* It takes time to build an effective ministry. Clearly the evidence shows that those who remain in their ministries for extended periods experience higher levels of happiness in their lives. Constant job transition takes its toll emotionally, physically, and spiritually on you and your family. Don't run from every storm that comes along.

6. *A broadened focus.* Church growth experts believe that a church of any size can do about eight ministries well. Beyond that, we spread ourselves too thin.

7. *Egocentricity.* When we begin to read our own press and believe that we are the secret to God's success, then we are misguided and have become an obstacle to God's work. Never forget that we exist to bring glory to God, who gave the vision in the first place. Any notoriety that comes from ministry success belongs to God alone.

8. *Ignoring values.* Ethics and integrity in ministry must never be compromised. History is replete with examples of people who lost sight

of their values and began to believe the ends justified any means. They don't!

9. *Another vision or other interests.* If God gave your congregation a vision, then to pursue another, even if it seems good, is one way the enemy tries to defeat you.

10. *Ministry becomes tedious.* Faithfulness is not always fun. It requires a consistency that withstands time. So often in Scriptures and in our lives, we see that staying the course has a great payoff, even though the tedium of the day-to-day matters must be endured.

11. *Lack of evaluation.* From time to time, there must be evaluation of the vision and a means to measure its progress. These can be painful times that may result in the changing of staff or leadership or redistributing dollars to be more effective in reaching the desired outcomes.

12. *Inappropriate lifestyles and structures.* We must have a consistent personal lifestyle that includes our personal finances, families, and spiritual disciplines. For vision to turn into action, we must stay true to the disciplines that keep us growing and being examples to others. Sometimes new structures in an organization can assist in implementing the vision or possibly revitalizing a system that is already in place.

13. *Extreme conflict.* When this occurs, prayerfully deal with it sooner than later. Too often, a pastor or ministry leader's heart does not deal well with conflict. However, failing to address important issues can often derail the vision. Discernment is needed to determine what is worth confronting and what is not.

14. *In search of a new vision (the vision becomes outdated).* This may be appropriate when the old vision has been fulfilled, there is a new pastor, there is a dying church that must be renewed, or the demographics of the community have changed significantly over time.[23]

Crafting a Personal Ministry Vision

You may be reading this wondering "What is my personal vision for ministry" or "How does God want to use me over the course of my life?" Someone may be reading this who is destined to become the next Bill Bright or Lottie Moon. Men and women who are capable of shaking the foundations of the earth for Christ always start with a vision from God. But how does one receive that vision, and how do you know it is authentic and not comprised of your own selfish ambitions?

One thing is obvious from reading Scripture: when it comes to delivering a personal ministry vision to his followers, God is never predictable. Sometimes the vision comes in a dream while at other times it is accompanied by a miracle. Occasionally it comes after a season of prayer and fasting while at other times it arrives much to the surprise of a person and as an interruption to the person's life. At times God speaks through an individual to deliver his message while on other occasions he speaks directly and audibly to the messenger. Rarely can it be said that God is predictable. For this reason it must be stated that there is no definitive means by which God delivers a personal ministry vision. It is highly personal and unique for each person. Much like the call to ministry, it comes from God's heart to the leader's, and it may be different from one individual to another.

Bill Hybels captures the power of vision when he says, "When God brings clarity of vision to a leader's life, everything changes. The dominoes start to fall."[24] He then gives the following progression as one possible scenario for how God delivers a personal ministry vision.

1. First, the leader sees the vision, a life-changing image of the future that makes the pulse quicken. The leader then knows deep down in his or her spirit that there is a capacity to give his or her life to this cause: "For this I was born." It might have come as an epiphany or gradually over time, but the conviction is there.

2. Second, almost immediately comes the feeling. The picture of the future produces a passion and that gives power to the vision. That is Holy Spirit-induced power. Is the vision you are living out one about which you can say, "For this cause I was born"? If you can, you have found the answer that will keep your life focused until you meet Jesus face to face.

3. Finally, the leader must take responsibility for the vision. In Acts 20:24, Paul says, "I consider my life worth nothing to me, if only I may finish the race and complete the task the Lord Jesus has given me" (NIV). Your vision must be your priority in life. It will impact who you marry, how you invest in your education, the place you serve. and, most of all, it will impact heaven's population. Hybels says, "To squander a vision is an unthinkable sin."[25]

Dale Galloway captures the idea of vision out of Acts 2:17: "And it shall come to pass in the last days, saith God, I will pour out of my Spirit upon all flesh: and your sons and your daughters shall prophesy, and your young men shall see visions, and your old men shall dream dreams" (KJV). The author continues by describing what happens when you live in the land of visions and dreams with God. Your life moves from the ordinary to the extraordinary: (1) Men and women of vision and dreams have no trouble tithing because they believe in it wholeheartedly. (2) Men and women of vision and dreams have no trouble believing God for big things because they know that God can do the impossible. (3) Men and women of vision and dreams have no trouble with drifting and laziness because they know where they're going and they're turned on for Jesus. (4) Men and women of vision and dreams find themselves setting measurable, realistic, motivating, and attainable goals, though not easy ones that don't challenge their faith.

A Personal Application of Mission and Vision

As of this writing, I have survived two bone marrow transplants and am currently a seven-year cancer survivor. During the many weeks I spent in the hospital, nearly dying from the side effects of the treatment, I experienced an epiphany. I heard from the Lord about my personal vision for the rest of my life. This included teaching at Azusa Pacific University as a professor of Christian education in the Graduate School of Theology and remaining the pastor of a local church I serve. Both ministry organizations profess an institutional mission that I love and respect. My heart resonates with each, and I admire their commitment to evangelism and discipleship. Through this ordeal I received a renewed vision for developing the next generation of leaders and continuing to lead our multiethnic church into an exciting future.

The other part of God's vision for me is my life as a godly husband to my wife Lindy, a loving father to my daughter Kimi, a caring father-in-law to Bobby, and "Papa" to my grandchildren Madison Pearl and Morgan Lee. My life seems far less complicated. With the renewing of my personal ministry vision, I have been able to focus my energies on the essential aspects of my life while letting go of that which is of less importance. Life is extremely fulfilling as I wake up each day with a desire to serve the Lord, his church, and my family with the vision he has given me.

BY
GARY BREDFELT

Chapter 4

Developing Goals and Objectives

"WHAT ARE WE TRYING to accomplish here?" "What exactly are we trying to do?" If we cannot respond to these two simple questions, we probably are not doing anything, and we'll probably end up accomplishing nothing. Goals in the context of church and other nonprofit ministries are not simply limited to lesson plans or learning outcomes, but to the administration and leadership of an institution. By their very nature, they are statements of faith in where God is leading individuals and congregations. "Now faith is the assurance of things hoped for, the conviction of things not seen" (Heb. 11:1 RSV). Goals are about the future, "things hoped for," and the drive to accomplish something new, "the conviction of things not seen." As Dayton and Engstrom said, "Goals lie in the future. Christians should be people who live in the present *and* the future."[1]

Goals have power! Goals have the power to unify a group, establish direction, propel a project, and create a sense of achievement. Goals have the power to motivate, generate passion, and move people to action. That's why it is critical for the effective Christian leader to understand how to formulate goals and craft objectives so as to maximize their value both personally and for the ministry.

Motivation and Goals

"A goal is a target to be strived for and, one hopes, attained."[2] It is in both the striving and the attainment that motivation is fostered and the power of goals is clearly seen. Goals establish direction and, in doing so, they focus the energy and efforts of the individual or an organization toward a worthwhile end. Goals, whether organizational or individual, provide a means by which the organization or the individual can

76

systematically accomplish something that appears at first to be too big or too difficult to achieve. Through the use of goal setting, people are motivated and progress occurs. Likewise, churches, Christian organizations, and even individual believers will discover that goal setting will bring unexpected beneficial results.

Goals Raise Expectation Levels

"Aim low; you'll never miss." True, but by aiming low, you never truly achieve anything either. Achieving goals and objectives that are attainable yet just beyond our normal reach raises the level of expectation for the individual, congregation, and organization. Goals can motivate us toward a higher level of participation, commitment, attention to ministry, and achievement.

Often our goals are too low, calling for underachievement or simply completing a routine ambition. Goals call us to "look carefully then how you walk, not as unwise men but as wise, making the most of the time, because the days are evil" (Eph. 5:15–16 RSV). Bolman and Deal note that the presence of authentic goals within an institution can reduce the hierarchical or unilateral politicizing of its decision making: "The final opposition for the political frame emphasizes that organizational goals are set not by fiat at the top but through an ongoing process of negotiation and interaction among the key players."[3] In so doing, the institution is called to higher levels of participation through the development of goals.

Individual and Team Goals

A goal is defined in management literature as "a specific commitment to achieve a measurable result within a given time frame."[4] This definition can apply to a personal goal or a team/organizational goal. For example, if I want to lose weight I can set the goal to lose twenty pounds before Christmas. This goal is specific, measurable, and time-frame oriented. To achieve this goal, I still will need a plan of action, but it does serve to set out a defined target. Likewise, teams can develop goals that also give direction and unity to a cooperative effort. For example, a new church plant can set the goal to grow the morning service attendance to two hundred before the church's first anniversary Sunday.Again, this goal is specific, it is measurable, and it establishes a defined time frame for achievement. Such a goal can serve as a motivational force toward a greater end.

Goals should point us toward something bigger than the goal itself. Why do I want to lose twenty pounds in the first place? What is the objective that lies behind my weight-loss goal? Is it to reduce my blood pressure or cholesterol? Is it to get into my wardrobe again? That's why behind every goal should also be an objective. Why does our church want to have two hundred in attendance by the end of its first year? Is it because we need two hundred people to meet our budget? Maybe it is because we desire to be a church that is reaching people for Christ. In that case, we might want to clarify the goal. We might want to reflect our objective in the goal. Rephrasing the goal, "to grow the morning service to two hundred in attendance by the church's first anniversary Sunday by reaching unreached families with the gospel" would give greater clarification and measurability to the goal.

Ministry has moved from being pastor-based to "team-based" in the last few decades. Because of this, it is vitally important for Christian leaders to understand the role of goals in both the organizational setting and in the lives of individual organizational members. Effective leadership demands the development of goal-setting skills. Leaders must be able to guide ministry team members in establishing team goals and in forming and reaching personal goals. Group goals give ministry efforts direction toward a unified mission. Personal goals foster motivation, a sense of achievement, and a means of improvement for each team participant.

The process of goal setting used by a congregation or Christian organization reflects the leadership paradigm within which the institution operates.[5]

Structural Frame: Keep organization headed in right direction

Human Resource Frame: Keep people involved and communication open

Political Frame: Provide opportunity for individuals and groups to make interests known

Symbolic: Develop symbols and shared values

Real leadership operates on two levels simultaneously. It must operate on the team level and the individual level. On the team level, leaders must foster unity, a sense of common purpose, and measurable team achievement. At the same time leaders must be committed to affirming, motivating, and developing the individual team member. In the establishment of goals and objectives for ministry, both individual and team goals are intertwined.

Goals and Objectives: What's the Difference?

Business administration literature frequently addresses the subject of goals and objectives, but these terms are not always used with consistency in either corporate or nonprofit settings. To make matters even more confusing, the field of education adds additional terms to the mix. Educators use the terms "goals," "objectives," "outcomes," and "aims." Here too, authors are inconsistent in their use of these terms, though most use "outcomes" to describe the measurable results of any educational experience or transaction.

Goals are considered the larger more general concept, with objectives providing support for their measurement and accountability. Objectives are short-term, measurable steps designed to move the organization toward the achievement of long-term goals. For example, in a business setting a goal may be *to increase market share by 10 percent.* This goal is accomplished by meeting several short-term objectives. These may include *being first to market with our new product* or *increasing customer satisfaction ratings from 3.5 to 3.7 on service calls by the end of the current quarter.*

So what are we going to agree upon? What terms should we use in ministry management? Figure 4.1 illustrates the relationship of purpose, goals, objectives, and implementation.[6]

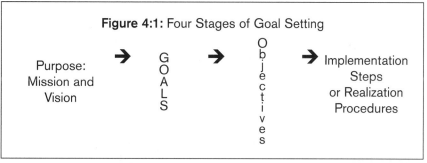

Figure 4:1: Four Stages of Goal Setting

Purpose: Mission and Vision ➔ GOALS ➔ Objectives ➔ Implementation Steps or Realization Procedures

The mission and vision of a ministry must be achieved by identifying a few key result areas and then writing a goal for each key result area. In order to reach each goal, specific and measurable objectives must be established. Finally, these are combined into a strategic plan where specific individuals, budgetary resources, and time expectations are assigned to each objective.

Mission/Vision: What does God want us to do?

Goals: What needs to happen for the vision to be realized?

Objectives: What do we need to do to achieve each goal?

Strategic Plan: Who is accountable and with what resources to accomplish each objective?[7]

In reality, most Christian management and leadership authors tend to use these terms without precision. Many authors use them interchangeably or without much consistency. Given the growing focus on a "team" model of ministry management, it could be argued that sports terminology should prevail. Frankly, whether one uses the term *goal* or *objective, aim* or *outcome,* the important and universally agreed upon point is that Christian leaders must take the time to set specific, measurable, and motivating goals. Figure 4.2 demonstrates the difference between goals and objectives.

Figure 4.2 Goals and Objectives

Goals	Objectives
Directly dependent on purpose	Directly dependent on goals
General	Specific
Indeterminate	Measurable
Usually long-term	Usually short-term
Broader statement	More narrow statement

Goal-Setting Theory

Think of three or four people who are successful. Think of a business that has risen from little to become significant. Now reflect on the most effective church ministries in your town. In all likelihood, you will discover that their success and effectiveness has come because of a commitment to setting and achieving goals. In business, the military, ministry, politics, athletics, and community service, goal orientation plays a fundamental and indisputable role. Goal-setting theory recognizes this role and seeks to develop applicable goal-setting principles for the improvement of individual and organizational performance. Setting objectives is likewise contingent on goal-setting processes. Hence, goals are inclusive of objectives.

Bolman and Deal speak of various forms of goals common to institutions, noting several forms of goals that are *not* beneficial but highly debilitating to the institution.[8]

Honorific Goals: Fictitious goals that credit the organization with desirable qualities

Taboo Goals: Actual goals not talked about

Stereotypical Goals: Goals that any reputable organization should have

Existing Goals: Goals quietly pursued even though inconsistent with the organization's stated value and self-image.

Goal-Setting Process

Goal setting is the process of (1) formally defining a performance target, (2) creating standards to measure accuracy in hitting the defined target, and (3) establishing the outcomes of success or failure in goal achievement in order to improve individual, group, and organizational job performance.

Goal-setting theory is a rigorously researched branch of management theory from which several principles of motivation and organizational development have been derived. Edwin A. Locke and Gary P. Latham articulate these principles in *Goal Setting: A Motivational Technique That Works!* Locke and Latham suggest that effective goals must be specific, difficult, and participant-owned. Given these three characteristics, Locke and Latham believe that goals can have an enormous motivational power for both the individual and the organization.

Objectives, or specific goals, provide more exacting targets. For example, when a parent tells a child to "just do your best," he or she is establishing a goal that lacks motivational power because it lacks specificity. Instead, a goal like, "You need to achieve B's or better if you plan to drive the car" is far more specific and therefore motivational.

Objectives begin with a focus on a clearly defined result. The more unambiguous one can be in setting the goal, the more likely it will be accomplished. Objectives that are too broad—lacking the critical quality of measurability—lack direction and have little ability to lead or motivate action. If you have read *Alice in Wonderland,* you may remember Alice's encounter with the Cheshire Cat. Their dialogue points to the importance of specificity in goal setting: "Would you tell me, please, which way I ought to go from here?" asked Alice. "That depends a good deal on where you want to get to," said the Cat. "I don't much care where—" said Alice. "Then it doesn't matter which way you go," said the Cat.[9]

The following chart contrasts well-written objectives with poorly written ones.[10]

Figure 4.3 Statements of Objectives

Good Statements of Objectives	Poor Statements of Objectives
• Stated in terms of end results	• Stated in terms of process or activity
• Achievable in definite time	• Are never fully achievable: No specific target dates
• Definite as to what is expected	• Ambiguous about what is expected
• Practical and feasible	• Theoretical or idealistic
• Precisely stated in terms of quantities, where applicable	• Too brief and indefinite or too long and complex
• Limited to one important item	• Written with two or more items per statement

How might this principle of goal setting be applied to the church and its ministry? Let's assume, for purpose of illustration, that you are developing goals for a worship team ministry in your church. You begin by writing the goal: *To lead worship effectively.* While this is a worthy desire, as a goal it lacks the power to motive because it lacks definition and a precise outcome. A specific goal might be stated something like this: *To provide quality contemporary music that actively engages the congregation in worship.* By developing the more focused goal, the worship team can sense the importance of their ministry. Based on this specific goal, the team can determine direction as well. The team knows the nature, purpose, and performance expectations of their ministry task.

Specificity in goal setting can be taken a step further by making the goal measurable. This is the formation of multiple objectives for each of the goals set. Typically, the most powerfully motivational goals can be measured in some way. It is important in goal setting to establish concrete criteria for measuring progress toward the attainment of the goal. When progress is measured, teams stay on track and experience the exhilaration of achievement that spurs on continued effort.

Many teams exert great effort but fail in their task because they lack a specific, measurable goal. In his 1961 state of the union address, John F. Kennedy said, "Efforts and courage are not enough without purpose and direction." Specific, measurable goals give that purpose and direction. Later that year in a special, joint session of Congress, President Kennedy cast the vision of space exploration. He gave that vision direction by proposing a goal that had enormous motivation power: *"First, I believe that this nation should commit itself to achieving the goal, before this decade is out, of landing a man on the moon and returning him safely to the earth."*[11]

This goal had motivational power because it was specific and measurable. The goal required that (1) America would land a man on the moon, (2) return him safely to earth, and (3) achieve it by the end of the decade. The criteria for measuring the goal was found in its specificity. A measurable goal sets a benchmark to evaluate progress. This goal does that by clearly defining the final state and by identifying the time frame in which that goal must be accomplished.

Here is an example of how adding the elements of specificity and measurability to a goal can enhance its power to motivate results. Rick Copperman, an associate pastor of worship and music at Green Valley Community Church, formulated the following goal: *To develop, before the end of the current year, three highly dedicated worship teams that are trained, musically competent, and effective in worship leadership.* This goal can be measured. Were three teams developed? Are they dedicated to their ministry? Was the goal achieved by the end of the year? Are the teams adequately trained for their task? Does the quality of the music demonstrate musical competency? By being specific and establishing time frame-based criteria for measurement, motivation and direction result.

Difficult goals are more powerful than easy goals. While a goal must be reasonable, goals that are too easily accomplished have little impact. To tell a son that he needs to get a C on a test when he is more than capable of getting a B will do little to improve long-term performance.

John F. Kennedy's goal to send a man to the moon and return him safely within a decade was ambitious. It was difficult. But that was part of the power of the goal. Goals must challenge. Goals that are too easily achieved have no power to motivate people. Goals must be lofty yet reasonable and realistic. Setting a realistic goal is fundamental to goal-setting theory. Goals must be attainable. Difficult goals are more motivational than goals where the outcome is a sure thing. But unattainable goals will discourage team members.

Motivational goals balance the reality with vision. Goals must be difficult to reach but not so difficult that they are discouraging. Micheal Kay suggests that goals be written to produce what he calls that "Everest feeling." Team members need to feel they are part of a demanding endeavor and are embarking on an adventure. But they must believe that they can reach the mountaintop.[12] As Hersey and Blanchard put it, "Goals should be set high enough so that a person has to stretch to reach them, but low enough so that they can be attained."[13]

Finally, *participation* is important in goal setting. Rather than define performance for someone else, it is best to let them participate in defining the goal. A wise parent will say, "Let's set a target for your grade in science this fall. What is a reasonable yet challenging goal you can set this year?" The parent must guide goal setting while making sure the child is a participant in the process. Participation gives the individual a sense of *goal ownership,* an aspect of goal setting essential to sustained performance.[14]

In church ministry that means we must take the time to work through group goal-setting processes. It is tempting for leaders to set the goals for the group. But in volunteer organizations, goal ownership is essential. For this reason some means by which group participants can become involved in goal setting is important. Ivan Scheier, author of *When Everyone Is a Volunteer* (1992), suggests that participation in goal development is the key to the success or failure of volunteer-based organizations. Scheier believes that when group goals are not owned by members of an organization, a few faithful core group members will pursue the goals to the point of burnout.

In response, Scheier suggests that a process he calls the "member input process" be used to get participants involved in goal setting for larger organizations. The process begins with the organization's leadership, such as the senior pastor or church board, sharing the vision and mission of the organization in an enthusiastic manner. This step is followed by a clear statement from the leadership that the leaders do have goals, but that they are seeking "input" from the members in shaping those goals. A survey is then conducted asking three open-ended questions:

1. What are the three top subjects, projects, or goals on which our group should be working over the next year? Be as specific as you can.
2. For each goal, list at least three doable steps to implement achievement of the goal. These must be things which are realistically within the capabilities of our organization.
3. Put a check mark next to any doable step in which you are personally willing to invest significant amounts of time and effort.[15]

The final step in this process is to form a goal review committee. Their task is to correlate and analyze the goal suggestions of all participants and to develop a set of recommendations to be brought back to the leadership and the group as a whole for adoption. Scheier believes that this process promotes active participation in the establishment of goals, increases ownership of the goals, motivates volunteer involvement in achieving the goals, and builds a sense of responsibility for the results.

Why Do We Resist Goal Setting?

Though goals seem to be a natural part of an individual or institution's existence, resistance to the idea of goal setting is somewhat common. Perhaps the most common reason for failing to set goals is the *fear of failure*. With failure comes a diminished level of self-worth and the fear of public humiliation or stigmatization that may accompany it. If it is announced, "We're going to average 400 in Sunday school this year," where in previous years we've had an average of 375, what if we fail? The failure will be obvious! Teachers may be demoralized. The congregation's leaders will hold me accountable for the failure. Other congregations may find out, and our whole congregation will be disgraced. Not really. First, if you don't set a goal, then the program in question will simply continue to degrade. That's humiliating. Second, what if you don't achieve the 400 average, but a 390 average? That's still an improvement. In short, fear of failure, while human, should not be avoided but confronted by individuals and congregations.

A second general cause of failing to set goals is couched in *spiritual openness*. Individuals may appeal to such passages as James 4:13–14 to object to goal setting: "Come now, you who say, 'Today or tomorrow we will go into such and such a town and spend a year there and trade and get gain'; whereas you do not know about tomorrow. What is your life? For you are a mist that appears for a little time and then vanishes" (RSV). Hence, *our* setting of goals is perceived as an affront or obstacle to God's setting of goals. However, this is an unfair and unnecessary dichotomy. James 4:15 concludes with the admonition to set goals in light of the Lord's leading, a harmonizing of God's leading and our setting of goals to achieve it: "Instead you ought to say, 'If the Lord wills, we shall live and we shall do this or that'" (RSV). In short, goal setting *without* God is "arrogance" and "boasting" (James 4:16 RSV), but the passage encourage us to establish goals that rest on God's will (Figure 4.4).

Figure 4.4
Christian Vs. Non-Christian Goal Setting

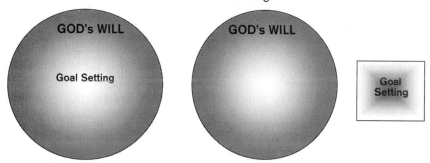

Perhaps a scriptural example of this is the second missionary journey of Paul. He obviously had a planned path for his travels, as indicated in Acts 16:1–5, but then we read of the Holy Spirit's intervention in his plans:

> They went through the region of Phrygia and Galatia, *having been forbidden by the Holy Spirit to speak the word in Asia.* And when they had come opposite Mysia, they attempted to go into Bithynia, *but the Spirit of Jesus did not allow them;* so, passing by Mysia, they went down to Troas. During the night Paul had a vision. . . . When he had seen the vision, we immediately tried to cross over to Macedonia, being *convinced that God had called us to proclaim the good news to them* (Acts 16:6–10 RSV, emphasis added).

Conclusion

Christian leaders must take the time to establish organizational goals and objectives. According to Kreitner, the establishment of well-devised goals and objectives has a fourfold benefit. He writes, "From the standpoint of planning, carefully prepared objectives benefit managers by serving as targets and measuring sticks, fostering commitment, and enhancing motivation."[16] Each of these benefits is crucial to the work of the church. Without a target, we lack direction for our efforts. Without a measuring stick, we lack a means of knowing our progress. Without commitment, we lack the involvement and partnership of others. Without motivation, we lack the will to do great things for God.

A study of Harvard graduates found that only 3 percent had written goals for their future. Twenty years later, a follow-up study discovered that the 3 percent who had developed personal and career goals for themselves had earned more money than the other 97 percent combined.[17] Clearly, goals have power to transform. They can change lives and renovate ministries. Writing goals and objectives is a vital step in the planning process and should be part of every ministries' annual practice.

BY
MICHELLE ANTHONY

Chapter 5

Developing a Strategic Ministry Plan

IN 1933, A YOUNG MAN ROSE to power as the result of a promise to implement a plan to ensure that his people would be renowned throughout the world and bring back the prosperity and honor that had once been a part of Germany's heritage. Yet this plan, when implemented, led to the slaughter of twenty million people and the ultimate destruction of his country. Unlike Adolf Hitler, we find another leader who had a "dream" that all people should be treated equal regardless of their race. His strategy was to bring about racial reconciliation through nonviolent, peaceful means. Although violence was widespread during Martin Luther King's years of influence, the effect of his plan initiated the Civil Rights Act of 1964 which helped end segregation.

While highlighting these two examples from the twentieth century, we further recognize that the *Strategic Plan* has been utilized for thousands of years, at least in concept. We see a strategy for building the world's greatest empires in Egypt, Greece, and Rome. At closer look, we begin to understand that these world powers didn't simply arise through happenstance, but rather the leaders of these empires had clearly defined goals and objectives that would be implemented at all cost.

These plans (whether altruistic or self-serving) were articulated, documented, communicated, and executed in every effective acquisition or battle. As these plans were realized, so were the desired results. Today, we discover the plans of great emperors who sought to overtake cities, to build the great pyramids or coliseums, to amass enormous armies or riches and, in doing so, we can analyze what they did right and, to their eventual downfall, what they did wrong. We learn from both their victories and their defeats, but more importantly we learn that no elevated plan is accomplished without the clear strategies of process and implementation.

The word *strategy* derives its meaning from the Greek *strategos*, which is literally translated "general of the army." Back in the days of ancient Greece, each of the ten ancient Greek tribes annually selected a *strategos* to head its regiment. These key leaders gave "strategic" advice about managing the various battles and skirmishes involved in their warfare rather than "tactical" advice about managing troops or material resources. From these military roots, strategic planning has always been concerned with the "big picture." The focus was on the results or final outcomes, rather than resources or outputs. With this in mind, it should be understood that strategic planning is less concerned with *how* to achieve outcomes than with defining *what* those outcomes should be.[1]

The Biblical Basis of Strategic Planning

Scripture tells us that the next great empire after Rome will be an empire that never ends. Upon that throne will sit the King of kings and the Lord of lords. In this dynasty, Christ himself will rule with power and authority through love and truth (Mic. 5:2–5). Unique to his leadership, God has developed a strategic plan in advance and has enlisted the service of each of his followers to begin the process of implementation. First, let's take a look at this biblical strategic plan and then at what principles can be gleaned for today's church and Christian organizations that share in his mission.

Immediately after the fall of humanity in the Garden of Eden, God himself promised that a redeemer would come to reconcile sinful man back to a sinless God (Gen. 3:14–15). This redeemer would be victorious over evil once and for all, and men and women would again enjoy a pure and undefiled love relationship with God. The prophets and New Testament writers went on to explain that this "Messiah" or Savior would be the perfect sacrifice to pay the penalty for the sin of every human being who would die to himself and accept God's provision (Isa. 53:10–12; Rom. 3:20–24). *This is the strategic plan of God.* God embarks on the ultimate mission to enjoy communion with his most prized creation, you and me.

From this position, God set forth the most wondrous strategic plan that transcends time, language, culture, sin, Satan, and human understanding. He assembled a nation and set it apart as the chosen race (Gen. 12:1–3). He instituted laws and leaders to enforce those laws (Exod. 20). Then when the time had been fulfilled he came to us in human form (Phil. 2:5–8), grew and taught us about the Father and repentance (John 14:1–6), and then left his Spirit among us (John 14:15–18). We know that the final chapter of this strategic plan has yet to take place, but when it is finished it will have accomplished what God set out to do. The God of this universe will commune in harmony with his beloved creation, free from the restraints of sin (Rev. 21:1–4).

Upon leaving this earth, Christ himself gave us our "marching orders." He gave us the Great Commission. The disciples who were living, as well as those who would follow, were charged to make disciples through repentance, baptism, and the teaching of the Scriptures (Matt. 28:19–20). This is the same global mission that we as Christians embrace today even though our own specific vision may differ in just how we go about accomplishing this goal.

In writing a strategic plan for any church or ministry organization, one must first understand the plan of God: *reconciling humanity to himself.* Next, the question needs to be asked, "What part does my church or organization play in accomplishing this plan?" and finally, "What part do I, as a disciple, play in this plan"? Only when these questions are answered can any church or Christian organization begin the process of developing an effectual strategic plan.

Strategic Planning and Long-Range Planning

Leaders often blur the line between long-range and strategic planning. Nevertheless, there are distinctions between the two that are important to note. For example, long-range planning covers a period of ten to twenty years and assumes that the environment will remain somewhat constant for at least that long. On the other hand, the strategic plan covers a period of three to five years and assumes that the environment is likely to change.[2]

While these two strategies may seem to be in conflict, they actually work together to serve the function of planning for a variety of futures. One major advantage of the strategic plan is that it is far more flexible and revisited at shorter intervals to deal effectively with creating solutions to problems as they occur.

A Model for Strategic Planning

Although the models of strategic planning may vary, the basic framework or concept is the same. By definition, the strategic plan is a written agenda that embraces both mission and vision while setting forth a series of goals and objectives that propels the church or organization toward the desired and envisioned future. It should be specific and measurable and yet high and elevating in its inspiration. The strategic plan is the impetus for the members of any organization to rise up and say, "Now that's something worth being a part of!" Lumpkin defines it this way:

Strategic planning is a formal, continuous process of making organizational decisions based on internal and external assessments. It involves the organization of people and tasks to execute the decisions and to measure achievement and performance. Strategic planning also consists of asking and answering four critical questions: How did we get here? Where are we going? How will we get there? How will we make it all work? In sum, strategic planning is an interactive, unending, and iterative process comprising mission, vision, situational analysis, and long-range objectives, strategies and measurements.[3]

There are two parts in the strategic model provided in Figure 5.1 below. Part one guides an organization to analyze the church or organization by asking questions from key individuals to determine the starting point of this strategic endeavor. Linked with this step is the process of prayer and seeking God's guidance during this season of planning. "Unless the LORD builds the house, its builders labor in vain" (Ps. 127:1 NIV), we are reminded in Scripture. The next three stages help the leaders to determine three guiding principles: their mission, their vision, and their core values. Once these are determined, the unique shape of their future begins to emerge.

Part two consists of executing an internal and external scan, followed by a strategy development, a strategy implementation, and finally, ongoing evaluation. Often evaluation brings the necessity of doing more internal and external scanning which then leads to revised strategy development and revision. While part one is constant and relatively unchanging, part two of this strategic model is revisited often and is open for revision as deemed necessary.

Part One

Analysis and Prayer. The analysis of any church or organization begins with questions such as: "How are we doing?" "What kind of church are we?" "Are we happy with who we are and where we're going?" It forces the community to take an honest look at themselves and to pull the proverbial ostrich head out of the sand.[4]

At this stage it is important to receive input from a variety of sources with an open mind and heart. One may utilize a variety of audits to glean information about the life cycle of the church or organization, the pulse of the stakeholders, as well as performance audits that measure productivity and effectiveness.

With this information in hand, it behooves the ministry leaders to dedicate themselves to the discipline and privilege of prayer. Prayer is the means by which we align our efforts with God's will. It is at this

Figure 5.1
Strategic Planning Model

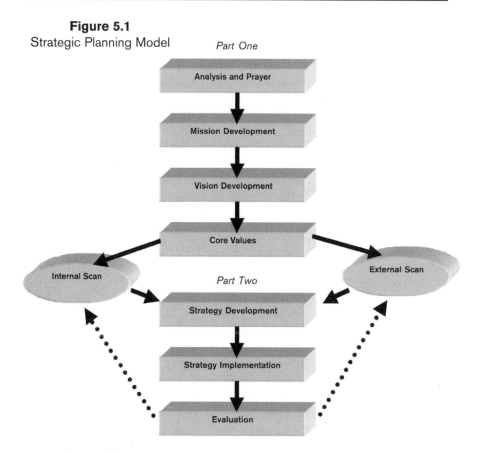

point that God's Spirit guides the spiritual leaders to decisions that can transcend the temporal into the eternal.

Nehemiah is a great example of a godly person who followed a strategic plan with God's will at its core. It broke his heart to see the city of Jerusalem in such ruin, and he began to beseech God about the problem: "They said to me, 'Those who survived the exile and are back in the province are in great trouble and disgrace. The wall of Jerusalem is broken down, and its gates have been burned with fire.' When I [Nehemiah] heard these things, I sat down and wept. For some days I mourned and fasted and prayed before the God of heaven" (Neh. 1:3–4 NIV).

After this time of mourning, personal prayer, and fasting, Nehemiah understood what his role might be in this terrible distress. He was given a mission from God to go to the king and ask to lead a group of people back to Jerusalem to rebuild the city and its walls. As we read on further in the story, Nehemiah understood his own personal vision of how this would be accomplished, set the values that would be implemented, and began a process of measurable goals and objectives which would one day be used for future evaluation. He was strategic in his plan of action and relied completely on the Lord and his strength to bring about the desired results. At no point did Nehemiah begin to believe that the mission was about him or his personal success, but rather was tenacious about remembering that this plan was about the name and city of the Lord being high and lifted up.

Honest analysis and prayer are the two foundational pillars for the strength of the strategic plan. Without them or the insight that they bring, we toil uselessly about a list of ideas and plans that lack the anointing of a holy God. While prayer is utilized as a separate step in the beginning of a strategic process, it is prudent for each step to be prayerfully considered as well. After the proper time for analysis and prayer the leaders must answer the question of mission and create a concise and well-defined mission statement to launch the plan.

Mission Statement. This statement defines where the organization ultimately sees itself, in what ways it wants to fulfill the Great Commission, and what it is ultimately about. This statement should be short, memorable, and easy to understand without commentary. It dictates the ministry's direction, focuses the ministry's future, and shapes the strategy more than any other single element in planning.[5]

Vision Statement. The vision tells us what our community will look like as our mission is realized. The vision is more specific and communicates the heart of an organization, while clear and challenging in its message. It inspires and is caught more than taught.[6] Martin Luther King stated his vision when he declared, "I have a dream."

Core Values. What makes this organization or church unique? Just as personal values speak to what is most important in a person's life, so an organization's values speak to what is the soul of that community.[7] These defining values distinguish one organization from another and remain constant. They guide the decision-making process and the relevancy of goals and objectives.

After mission, vision, and core values are determined, the leaders of the organization begin to extract a specialized DNA for the direction of planning. This can be a very inspiring time in the life of any church or body. The outflow of this synergy is then processed through a grid of internal and external scans which set the stage for strategy development and implementation.

We have reviewed the stages of analysis/prayer, mission development, vision development, and core values (part one) and now are ready to embark on part two of strategic planning, which involves internal and external scanning, strategy development, strategy implementation, and evaluation.

Part Two

Internal Scan. An internal scan is, primarily, assessing your resources. These include but are not limited to:

- physical resources such as location or a building/facility;
- human resources such as staff and volunteers;
- financial resources such as cash flow, savings or investments, donations/gifts, and monetary reserves; and
- attitudinal resources such as the climate of the people, their morale, their cohesiveness, and their spirit or lack of enthusiasm.[8]

This scan should be done by the people who know the organization or institution the best and are privy to its latest data regarding resources. A "S.W.O.T." analysis is helpful at this point as the leaders assess the Strengths, Weakness, Opportunities, and Threats. While the strengths and weaknesses refer primarily to the internal issues and resources, the opportunities and threats are identified primarily from the external scan.[9] As the leaders take each unearthed resource in the internal scan, a categorization of each, with their current strengths and weaknesses, should be compiled. When completed, the organization is ready to analyze the external scan.

External Scan. An external scan is assessing your environment. This scan alerts the organization to what is going on around them in history, in the surrounding city or community, and in the economic and social events of people's lives. These issues are organized into one of two categories: opportunity or threat. Often because these deal with the external environment, the external scan is sometimes known as the environmental scan.[10]

Developing a larger strategic value for your church or organization means gathering information that looks beyond its immediate sector and toward the broader eternal, political, social, economic, and technological environment. As we allow these tidbits of information to be processed on a daily basis, they eventually add up to a greater understanding of emerging trends and tendencies.[11]

An opportunity is an instance or event that may enhance the direction of your organization to the extent that you would want to capitalize this prospect (for example, a prominent speaker might be in town and for a lesser charge would be willing to come and speak to your group). A threat can be antagonistic in nature and be a real or perceived danger (for example, an unsafe community that might put the youth at risk), or it could simply be a challenge that the team should be made aware of (for example, the lack of parking spaces available for the growing student population attending the university service).

By examining the diverse dimensions of the internal and external scans, one must consider that these factors will be dynamic and should be understood as changeable elements to the strategic plan. Once an organization has done an effective and thorough scan of both the internal and external environments and has documented the inherent strengths, weaknesses, opportunities, and threats, it is ready to begin putting together the strategy for development and implementation. This is the practical stage where most concrete thinkers begin to get their strategic juices flowing. The patient strategic planning committee or board will find these next few steps rather simple if the above steps are done capably.

Strategic Development. In order to fully develop a strategic plan that has action as its primary focus, goals and objectives must be developed based on the thought processes of step one (analysis/prayer, mission, vision, and values) and the tactical pieces gleaned from the internal and external scans. With this information in hand, the leadership of the church or organization begins to write out specific goals and objectives that will provide the framework for reaching the intended outcome. The reader is encouraged to review the development of goals and objectives discussed in more detail in chapters 5 and 8. For our purposes I will combine goals and objectives, but most times they will be split into separate entities.

Goals and Objectives. Goals and objectives are written as final outcomes. These statements are written with their completion in view. Goals and objectives should be specific, measurable, attainable, relevant, and trackable, or SMART, according to Ken Blanchard, a leading organizational management expert.[12] When these goals and objectives are visualized, each one should be held up and these questions asked:

- Is this goal and its corresponding objectives specific enough?
- Will I know when I have met them?
- Can I truly accomplish them with the time and resources allocated for them?
- Is this goal and objective relevant to my job or ministry?
- What tangible progress can be tracked along the way?

Most goals when first written fail to answer all of these questions adequately. That is why corresponding objectives may need to be added to provide specificity to the final statement. Often a team or committee can work with the concepts and wording to craft appropriate objectives that will actually produce the desired result. Without these more specific objective statements, goals can become little more than great ideas lacking momentum and meaning. Consider the following goal statement for a high school youth group:

> **Goal #1:** *To bring kids into relationship with Christ in our community and beyond through God's Word.*

Let's put this goal to the SMART test.

1. Is it *specific*? No, not really. What kids are we talking about? What age are they, where specifically do they live, what is their socio-economic background? What campus do they attend?

2. Is it *measurable*? No. When is this to be completed? How will I know when they are in relationship with Christ? Where is "beyond"?

3. Is it *attainable*? No. How can it be attainable without being specific or measurable? I can't attain something that I cannot determine if I have it or not.

4. Is it *relevant*? Possibly. I don't know the relevance of this goal until I have clear parameters.

5. Is it *trackable*? No. There are no clear marker points because there is no clearly defined finish line.

Take a look at how this same goal could be modified with a corresponding objective which addresses the SMART rules and makes it a clear statement which contributes to the formation of a strategic goal.

> **Goal #1:** *To bring kids into relationship with Christ in our community and beyond through God's Word.*
>
> **Objective #1:** *To design and implement quarterly outreach events for the high school students of Aliso Viejo by encouraging them to enter into a relationship with Christ through the teaching of God's Word.*
>
> **Objective #2:** *To incorporate the use of a contemporary music team, drama, and technology, and by make Bibles available to each student who attends.*

Let's put this goal and its corresponding objectives to the SMART test.

1. Are they *specific*? Yes. We know our audience is the high school population from the city of Aliso Viejo. We know that we are doing outreach events for the purpose of evangelism and outreach.

2. Are they *measurable*? Yes. We will know if we accomplish four of these events in the year. We will know if the Bible is taught, if music, drama, and technology are used in their services, and if Bibles are distributed to those who need them.

3. Are they *attainable?* Yes. This goal and its objectives are something that can be accomplished in the time frame and with the given parameters.

4. Are they *relevant?* Yes. High school students like to be where other students are, they traditionally like bands/music, and four events per year is a realistic number.

5. Are they *trackable?* Yes. We will be able to count the actual number of students who attend at the end of each quarter and reassess for the next event. In addition, we can tabulate the number of decisions made for Christ as well as the number of Bibles that we distributed and monitor progress against the total number of students in the area.

When each goal, paired with corresponding objectives, can meet these prescribed requirements, the organization is ready to ask the next question: "What needs to take place *specifically* to help make this a reality?" The answers to that question become the strategic plan's implementation phase.

Strategy Implementation. In this phase of implementation, every detail of the goals and objectives are thoroughly scrutinized to extract every imaginable element that might either assist or hinder the progress of these goals. It is the function of writing "next steps" that allows for people to take ownership in the strategy by either exploiting those things which enable success and/or eliminating those things which would impede progress.

Next Steps. These steps are actual to-do items. They are a checklist, so to speak, and can be entrusted to all levels of the organizational chart. The ability of an organization to enlist the gifts, talents, and passions of each person on the team is in direct relationship to the long-term success of the plan. As stated before, the strategic plan must be a vision that is caught at every level and becomes the heart and soul of the members. This is best done by spreading out the factors for the direct success of the ministry, in the form of next steps, to as many capable individuals as possible.

As the next steps are accomplished, the goals become within reach. As the goals are accomplished the vision is fulfilled, and thus the mission of the organization is realized. There is one more essential step that is often overlooked in the strategic planning process, and that is evaluation.

Evaluation. The step of evaluation is often overlooked because it was never woven into the planning process at its inception. Although it might occur to someone down the line to evaluate the past year's progress, it might be seen as superfluous or unimportant. Nothing could be further from the truth! Why, then, do so many churches and ministry organizations leave out this crucial step in progress?

Perhaps the daily grind of making deadlines, attending meetings, planning events, tending to interpersonal issues, putting out fires, and staffing and training squelches us from operating with the bigger picture in mind. In order to not get lost in the details, all activities and goals should be evaluated at predetermined intervals. Some activities are best evaluated weekly, some monthly or quarterly, while others may wait for an annual review.

Gene Mims states that "evaluations should be designed to fit the diversity of the specific ministry. It is not unspiritual to evaluate what God is doing, has done, and likely will do in our work for Him. In fact, proper evaluation will help us rejoice and celebrate the growth that He gives and help us to keep our focus to do the best things."[13]

William Shakespeare once said, "What is past is prologue." His insight proves true in the strategic planning process. The strategy cycle is not over once strategies and plans have been implemented. Strategies that work must be maintained and protected through vigilance, adaptability, and updated plans. Thus, Bryson notes in *Strategic Planning for Public and Non-Profit Organizations*, "Ironically, changes of some sort are probably in order if you want things to remain the same. Not all strategies continue to work as well as they should. These strategies must be bolstered with additional resources, significantly modified, or terminated."[14] Ongoing evaluation ultimately leads the team back to assessment of the internal and external scanning process to reevaluate the environments and make strategic changes as deemed necessary.

Arguments for Strategic Planning

Henry Klopp outlines six arguments for the advantages of implementing a strategic plan in his book, *The Ministry Playbook: Strategic Planning for Effective Churches*. They are paraphrased as follows:[15]

Argument 1: Because We Are Stewards. First Corinthians 4:2 says, "Now it is required that those who have been given a trust must prove faithful" (NIV). Luke 12:48 reminds us that "from everyone who has been given much, much will be demanded; and from the one who has been entrusted with much, much more will be asked" (NIV). The biblical ideas of effectiveness often parallel those of faithfulness and stewardship in the Bible. When God entrusts something to us, he expects us to manage it properly, and we are held accountable not only for maintaining what we have but also for increasing these resources creatively with the means given to us. While we are not solely responsible for the outcomes, we are expected to be committed to the process of biblical stewardship.

Argument 2: Because We Are Dealing with Limited Resources. Most would agree that if the church and other Christian organizations had unlimited resources, the overall planning process would not be as great. However, since our resources seem to always fall short of our great visions, the shotgun approach simply will not work. Most organizations need to spend critical time prioritizing to find the few things that they can do best with the limited resources available to them.

Argument 3: Because Failing to Plan Is Planning to Fail. There are those in the Christian community who believe that planning prevents God from working. I prefer to believe that planning displays God's creative sovereignty. The question is then simply, "What is your plan or system?" If you don't have one, that in itself is a plan. As the old saying goes, "If you aim at nothing, you will hit it every time."

Argument 4: Because of the Competing Agendas We Face. Most Christians probably assume that they are objective and that they do not carry biased agendas. But in reality, we all have differing opinions on how our organizations should run and what ministries should be funded on a higher level than others. Without a clearly defined plan, differing agendas can be in sharp contradiction to one another, allowing for destructive patterns of lobbying to get one's agenda accepted.

Argument 5: Because of the Need to Clarify Assumptions. One of the reasons why churches and organizations do a poor job of evaluating their ministry plans is because they make the assumption that true evaluation is impossible. With this assumption, members become cynical of the process and immediately discard the plan after it is drafted, leaving it to be little more than an "exercise" that is seldom brought up again. Clarifying this assumption by the effectual evaluation and implementation of a well-written strategic plan can reinstate the trust and eagerness with which people approach goals and objectives.

Argument 6: Because It Forces Churches (and Organizations) to Deal with the Issue of Change. For whatever reason the church and other Christian organizations seem to be resistant to change. It often takes serious intervention to make an organization change its habits, traditions, or even leadership. The strategic plan is one of the best tools to ensure this will happen more naturally.

These are just a few of the reasons for implementing a strategic plan in the Christian institution. However, just because there are numerous benefits to the church or Christian ministry that develops a strategic plan, it is not without its potential pitfalls and problems.

Pitfalls and Problems in Strategic Planning

Pitfall 1: Planning Is a Secular Tool. Many ministry leaders who have failed to consider carefully the biblical evidence draw the dichotomy of "Planning is secular but ministry is spiritual." Some even go to the extent of making a distinction between the spiritual and business affairs of the church. Biblically, there is no such distinction, for we are to view every aspect of our lives in Christ as spiritual.

Pitfall 2: Planning Eliminates or Reduces the Role of the Holy Spirit. Wanting to be free to be led by the promptings of the Holy Spirit, some organizations fail to plan at all. While we obviously need to seek the guidance of the Holy Spirit in all of our endeavors and decisions, his leading does not negate our responsibility in having a well-thought-out plan of action.

Pitfall 3: The Tyranny of the Urgent. Most staff and pastors find themselves under tremendous time constraints. There is never a lack of people who need care and counseling, programs that need our attention, or Bible studies that need preparing. In this time crunch, many leaders confuse the urgent with the essential. We can work hard, but not necessarily smart, without the aid of a clear plan that guides us from the urgent to the important.[16]

Pitfall 4: Preparing Objectives in Terms of Means, Not Results. Objectives tell us where to go and how to know when we have arrived. If we set our focus only on processes (acquiring the latest technologies) or resources (higher wages), we hinder the extent and meaning of those goals. We must complete the thought by asking, "If we use the latest technologies, what benefit will result in our organization?" Or, "If we receive higher wages, what benefit will that be to our organization or stakeholders?"

Pitfall 5: Selecting Solutions Before Identifying Destinations. Just about every activist group has a favorite solution or quick fix. It is prudent to resist picking a solution or resource until you know where you're headed and why. Without this insight we are not really solving problems; we are simply offering irrelevant options and opinions.

Pitfall 6: Skipping Some of the Steps in Strategic Planning. There are numerous steps in the strategic planning process. Omitting even one of them will diminish the quality and usefulness of the plan. If you look again at Figure 5.1, you will find that not even one of these steps can be deleted without seriously impacting the results of the entire plan.[17]

Conclusion

In conclusion, let's go back to Nehemiah for a moment. We learned that Nehemiah set out by analyzing the information that he was given and carefully and prayerfully bringing these burdens to the Lord. Next, we learned that he brought his basic mission or plan before the king and later enlisted the help of many people to carry out the personal vision that God had given him to bring honor back to Jerusalem.

Nehemiah led with the values of worship, integrity, and excellence and ensured that these values remained at the core of all the work that was done. Later, we find that he conducted internal and external scans to glean insights of his resources and environmental assets or threats. When fighting broke out against them, Nehemiah developed a plan to have teams that worked, rested, and fought and then rotated between these jobs. The implementation of this plan allowed them to fulfill the desired mission. We can learn several practical lessons from Nehemiah's planning efforts.

Ultimately, Nehemiah's efforts were effective not because of chance. He had a strategy . . . albeit God's. He was able to visualize how a massive project could be divided into manageable portions and then distributed to many capable individuals. In the end, the rebuilding of Jerusalem's walls was completed in just fifty-two days! Good kingdom planners today will take note of how strategic planning helps define the big picture, allows for a strategy for breaking it down into manageable pieces, and creates room for change and adaptability in a fluid and dynamic world.

BY
MARK SIMPSON

Chapter 6

Policies and Procedures as Planning Tools

IT WAS AN INNOCENT MISTAKE. Youth Director Dan had been on the job for six months and was doing a great job bringing youth into the church. A key ministry implemented shortly after his arrival was weekly Friday evening youth gatherings in the church's fellowship hall for a time of food, fun, and fellowship. The ministry was very successful, with the church's young people coming to the church on Friday nights rather than gathering around cars in local parking lots. It also provided the youth with an opportunity to reach out to their friends and invite them to church.

When Dan and his youth ministry team arrived to set up the fellowship hall for the Friday evening activities, they discovered the room was filled with empty tables and chairs set up as if for a banquet. In the kitchen, boxes of decorations were found perched on the food service counter. Inside were floral table centerpieces, pink and green crepe paper ribbon, and little decorated cups containing peanuts and pink and green candy mints. Within an hour the youth would be arriving to eat pizza and play games, so Dan moved the boxes into a corner while his ministry team took down several of the tables and chairs to create floor space for the evening's activities.

Later in the evening, a couple of the more inquisitive young people found the boxes Dan had placed in the kitchen corner. In short order, a couple of the little cups filled with peanuts and mints were passed around and consumed. By the end of the evening, most of the cups were empty. Given the number of young people in the fellowship hall, it was not surprising that Youth Director Dan was unaware the peanuts and mints were being consumed.

At the end of the meeting, as was their practice, Dan and the youth ministry team cleaned up the kitchen and took out the trash. Dan also put the boxes back on the food service counter where he had found them and took down all of the remaining tables and chairs to make it easier for the custodian to come in Saturday afternoon and set up fellowship hall for Sunday activities. It had been another successful Friday, especially since two young people had come to know Christ during the devotional time.

Early Saturday morning Dan got a call from Pastor Perry. Deacon Dave had called the pastor from the church kitchen, and Dave was furious. Someone had taken down all of the tables and chairs the custodian had set up for his daughter's wedding, and several of the decorations made for the reception were missing from the boxes on the kitchen counter. Dave wanted to know if the pastor knew who was responsible for this outrage. The pastor knew Dan's young people had used the church facilities the night before, and he asked Dan what he knew about this situation. Dan told Pastor Perry what he knew, and then immediately called Deacon Dave to apologize and volunteer to put things back in order. Unfortunately Dave was in no mood to hear Dan's explanation of what happened. The rest of the day Dan fielded phone calls from Dave's angry friends and family members, as well as words of encouragement from sympathetic and supportive parents who understood this was an error in communication.

Soon after the wedding, Deacon Dave introduced a policy to the deacons that prohibited the youth from using the fellowship hall except as approved by the deacons on a case-by-case basis. The argument was made that the church was a place for ministry, and other ministries of the church should be able to feel free to have exclusive use of the fellowship hall on Fridays and Saturdays without fear of interference from "parties and games" for young people. After much discussion, the deacons agreed that the use of fellowship hall on Sundays and Wednesday evening was sufficient for the youth, and the policy was passed and implemented. A few months later, Deacon Dave encouraged the church to recommend that Youth Director Dan resign, given the decreasing number of young people involved in the life of the church.

Dangerous assumptions, poor lines of communication, and the lack of a facility usage policy were ultimately responsible for the youth ministry and church wedding reception creating conflicting conditions. When this happens, tempers flare, and logic, reason, and common sense are often early casualties in the framing of policies and procedures to prevent the situation from recurring. But why were policies and procedures not in place to begin with? It may have just been an oversight. Sometimes tradition assumes the role of policy and procedure because "that's the way it's always been done." Churches and Christian organizations that experience a surge in growth often have trouble making the change from tradition to planning with policies and procedures. Sometimes, though, polices and procedures are not in place because of misunderstanding the theological relationship of ministry planning to following God's will.

Planning Is Not a Sin

In many churches and Christian organizations, planning with policies and procedures is akin to sin because of the belief that "planning prohibits moving in the Spirit." In James 4:13–17, James warns the church about making definitive plans in conducting daily business. Instead, he encourages believers to remember that all such planning should be made subservient to the Lord's will. Unfortunately many ministry leaders misinterpret what James was teaching. The example of the apostle Paul's ministry can help us understand the relationship of planning to following God's will.

The apostle Paul apparently did not find planning anathema. In Acts 16:6–10, we find Paul and his ministry partners on a second missionary journey planning to take the gospel to the north regions and then the south regions as they traveled through Asia. Instead, the Spirit prohibited them from doing so (Acts 16:7). As a result, Paul followed the unanticipated call to go to Macedonia and ended up in Philippi, causing the gospel to spread from Macedonia into Greece and finally Rome.

Paul did not let his ministry be tossed about upon the waves of fate and chance. Instead, he made plans that he changed as the Lord led him to make changes. It is a deadly mistake to interpret James's teaching on planning as meaning, "Don't do anything until the Spirit moves you." I know of one church where a well-meaning Christian education director refused to do any planning for the annual Christmas pageant because she believed in "moving in the Spirit." As a result, both children and parents alike were frustrated over what was supposed to be a happy family event. Young children were given Bible verses to memorize the night before the pageant and were expected to recite them in front of a room packed with people. No one knew what was going to happen next when the program was presented. You can image the stress this produced for both the children and the parents. The end result of the failure to plan ahead was that each year the congregation breathed a collective sigh of relief when the pageant was over, and the children despised what should have been a happy celebration.

If planning was truly unbiblical, then God would never have made administration one of the gifts of the Spirit. As we stated in chapter 2, the word translated as "administration" in the listing of spiritual gifts in

1 Corinthians 12:28 literally refers "to steering a ship."[1] The role of a helmsman is to steer the ship to the port of destination identified by the captain. As the helmsman steers the vessel, he does so in such a way that the ship avoids colliding with other craft and circumvents shoals and reefs that could cause a shipwreck. As any fisherman knows, just drifting with the current is not always smart. Swift currents sometimes lead boats to collide; others lead to river rapids and eventually to waterfalls. But when we follow Christ (the captain) and his leadership, charting a course (planning) to accomplish his will (port of destination) is not only appropriate but necessary and required.

Charles Haddon Spurgeon, the great evangelical Christian pastor of the nineteenth-century Metropolitan Tabernacle megachurch in London, believed that "planning was important but one must always recognize God's sovereign leading in any plans that one makes in this life. 'In his heart a man plans his course, but the LORD determines his steps' (Prov. 16:9 NIV). Once we know God's plan for us, we are then free to pursue His plan for action as we seek to accomplish His purpose."[2]

It may very well be that we sin when we claim poorly planned ministry and missed opportunities for ministry as "God's will." Take the candidate process for new pastors or Christian organization leaders as an example. Search committees often fail to respond in a reasonable amount of time to the résumés they receive, and then claim God's will when the most desirable candidates are no longer available. Then, when they finally do work down their list of candidates and call a new pastor or ministry leader, they claim it was God's will if the new hire leaves the next year. When we fail to plan for ministry and then claim the outcomes as God's will, we ascribe imperfection and possibly unrighteousness as actions of God's Holy Spirit. Jesus teaches us in Matthew 12:22–32 that this is to blaspheme the Holy Spirit. According to Jeremiah 29:11, God's plans for us are plans of prosperity and hope and a future filled with blessings if we seek his kingdom first.[3] Planning for purposes of seeking God's kingdom is not a sin; failing to plan to do so is.

Law, Grace, and Ministry Chaos

Even when "moving in the Spirit" is correctly interpreted and applied to the life of a church or Christian organization, other dimensions of planning can become problematic. Legalism and lawlessness toward following policies and procedures can inhibit ministry just as effectively as allowing ministry to be tossed about aimlessly by fate and chance. When policies and procedures become prohibitive to ministry, there is a tendency to view all such planning as suspect. When policies and procedures are all "negotiable," there is a tendency to view all such planning as inconsequential.

When legalism is the way policies and procedures are produced, implemented, and maintained, the "organizationally challenged" among us will be hard pressed to conduct ministry according to those rules and regulations. For these individuals, "grace" at times becomes necessary. The danger, though, is in allowing grace to be repeatedly exercised to excuse and accommodate poor planning. Once that precedent is set, grace no longer becomes requested but rather becomes expected, if not demanded. Grace has its place when errors are made in honestly attempting to follow policies and procedures, but it should not become the norm to ignore them and then ask for grace to cover the offense.

Sometimes policies and procedures are not communicated clearly, making it difficult for those conducting ministry to follow them. But when "it is easier to ask for forgiveness than permission" becomes the modus operandi of a church or Christian organization, the end result can be disastrous. Why? Because as ministry leaders see that policies and procedures can be ignored successfully by some, they expect the same treatment. To be fair, they should. After all, why should some ministries be exempt from following due process while others are compelled to comply? Under such inconsistent conditions, eventually no one will bother to follow policies and procedures intended to prevent ministry conflicts and abusive conduct (for example, overspending the budget). The end result is a waste of sometimes scarce resources and ministry chaos.

Planning ministry utilizing policies and procedures can help advance the kingdom of God all the while under the moving of his Spirit. These protocols, if used properly, will not "get ahead of God" or undermine his will for the church or Christian organization. Since God does all things decently and in order and expects us to do the same (1 Cor. 14:40), *not* deploying policies and procedures and allowing everyone to do what is right in their own eyes is contrary to the moving of the Spirit and contrary to God's will.

Policies, Procedures, and Protocols

The terms *policy, procedure,* and *protocol* can be easily misunderstood. The following definitions are provided to guide the reader when using these terms in the context of ministry. If we all operate from the same definitions, it minimizes the possibility of confusion and miscommunication.

- *Policy* is an explicit statement of a belief and/or attitude intended to shape and control ministry action.

- *Procedure* is an explicit statement of the appropriate and/or requisite progression of actions that must be taken in order to implement a stated policy.
- *Protocol* is an explicit statement of policy combined with an explicit statement of procedure.

Notice that each of these terms requires explicit documentation. Explicit statements are those that are clearly defined in writing. For example, explicit statements of policy and procedure are found in church constitutions, business meeting minutes, and Christian organizations' employee and ministry handbooks. Although it is possible to have an implicit policy or procedure (i.e., oral tradition), it is always best to have these statements written down for future reference. Implicit statements are those that are implied or assumed. Examples of these would include assumptions that policies for one ministry are applicable for all ministries or expectations of procedural conduct in ministry implementation without written guidelines or requisite permissions.

As we look at each of these terms carefully, we can begin to see how they can work together to aid in planning and administering ministry. Once we understand how policies relate to procedures, and how together they form protocols for ministry, we can then identify some key mechanisms that will enhance ministry growth and development.

Policies and Ministry Planning

A ministry policy has been defined as *an explicit statement of a belief and/or attitude intended to shape and control ministry action.* As such, ministry policies, when developed appropriately, can enable a Christian organization to be more effective in the development and implementation of ministries and more efficient in the use of the time, resources, and personnel. Unfortunately, ministry policies are often implemented as the result of negative experiences, rather than being created proactively to prevent them.

Take for example our opening case study of the youth ministry that collided with the preparations for a wedding. Because no policies were in place about the use of the church's facilities, Youth Director Dan had no way of knowing a wedding was taking place the next day. Granted, he could have known if the lines of communication in the church office were functioning appropriately, but apparently they were not. Because there was no policy in place that would have alerted Dan and the wedding party to conflicting ministries setting up to utilize the same space, Dan's ministry was ultimately dismantled in what appears to be a vengeful correction to that omission. Deacon Dave, while appropriately offended that his daughter's wedding reception had been compromised, failed to see that the deacons should have had a policy in place regarding the use of church facilities to prevent such conflicts from occurring.

When policies are implemented as a knee-jerk reaction to a problem, they often end up generating more problems. In the youth director's case, a successful youth ministry was disabled by a reactive policy preventing the youth from using the church's facilities on the weekends. A good policy enables ministry rather than disables it. When polices are created proactively to prevent ministry conflicts, reactive and punitive actions are more likely to be avoided.[4] Thus if the church had had a facility usage policy in place, Dan could have made other arrangements to conduct the regularly held youth fellowship, and the bridal party could have stored their reception supplies more carefully.

Knee-jerk reaction policies also often fail to take into account the domino effect that one policy can have on multiple ministries. When a policy is quickly framed to correct a problem area, ministry leaders must be careful to anticipate how the policy impacts other areas of ministry. For example, when the policy was implemented in our case study, the intent was to prevent youth ministries from interfering with the use of church facilities by other ministries. However, when the policy was implemented, other ministries accustomed to using church facilities with no advance notice suddenly found themselves prevented from doing so. The best policies are those that anticipate their impact as they are framed, rather than deal with the consequences after the fact.

A ministry policy is more effective when it is an explicit statement rather than being just an implicit expectation. When a policy is in writing (explicit), everyone hears the same thing. When church leaders change, the next generation of leaders has the written policies to guide them in framing ministry decisions. When a policy is simply tradition, by word of mouth alone, or assumed to be "the way things should be done" (implicit), the likelihood of ministry conflicts increases, especially as leadership changes occur. The same is true when a policy is framed arbitrarily and justified as "there's no reason for it; it's just our policy." A clearly written policy explains what must be done and provides to some degree a rationale about why the policy exists. Otherwise, in time the policy will fall into question, exceptions will be made to the policy, and ministry conflicts will occur all over again.

Ministry policies reflect both beliefs and attitudes about the overall ministry. The wording of policies—what they allow, disallow, encourage, require, discourage, and so on—are a form of decision making that reflects what a ministry believes it should be doing for Christ. One of the best ways to get a feel for the beliefs and attitudes that a Christian organization has about ministry is to look beyond its mission or vision statements to see how clearly its ministry policies are worded.[5] Even the absence of policies says something about an organization's intentions for growth!

Unfortunately, many Christian organizations spend hours creating mission and vision statements but fail to create compatible ministry policies to go with them. In such situations, the mission or vision statements end up becoming a nice slogan on a banner on a wall, but do little to enhance long-term ministry effectiveness.

A ministry policy is more effective when it is supported with written ministry procedures. Explicit procedures make a policy user-friendly in the sense that users are able to meet the expectations of the policy. An abstract policy without clear procedures of implementation encourages the policy to be ignored or circumvented.

Ministry Procedures for Ministry Policies

We defined a ministry procedure as an explicit statement of the appropriate and/or requisite progression of ministry actions that must be taken to implement a stated policy. As such, ministry procedures, when developed clearly and logically, can make adherence to the policies of a Christian organization more probable and possible. Efficient ministry procedures enable the work of ministry rather than disable it. Inefficient ministry procedures leave leaders guessing what they are supposed to do to conform to policy or make ministries jump through hoops that are not necessary or needlessly impede the work of the church. Procedures that consist of simple, specific, and measurable action steps are more likely to be followed than just leaving leaders to fend for themselves.

Combining Policies and Procedures
with Ministry Protocols

A ministry protocol has been defined as an explicit statement of policy combined with an explicit statement of procedure. As such, a ministry protocol attempts to combine policy and procedure in user-friendly ways. While it is true that sometimes you just have to follow the rules, understanding the reason for the rules increases the likelihood that each will be followed properly. In the context of ministry application, the term *protocol* can be used to describe proper implementation of the policy and procedure. A protocol refers to the means by which the policy and procedure are implemented.

In framing procedures in ministry protocols, the old adage "keep it simple" is sound advice. The best procedures are those that are step-by-step and as easy to follow as possible.[6] The more complicated and abstract the procedure, the more difficult it is for users to follow, and the easier it is for them to give up even attempting to do them. Step-by-step procedures make it easier for ministry leaders to know *who* to work with (persons and approval bodies), *what* has to be done (the flow of specific tasks), and *when* they must be completed (time frameworks). *Why* the procedures are necessary is the policy; *how* the policy is implemented is detailed through the procedures.

To assist Christian organizations in adhering to procedures in protocols, requisite forms to be completed in abiding by the related policy should be readily available. In our Internet-enhanced society, downloadable forms from the church or Christian organization's Web site can make it easier for ministry leaders to get forms quickly; this approach can also save on duplication costs and sometimes even postage. When the Internet is not readily available, copies of requisite forms should be easy to find in the main office of the church or Christian organization.

Procedures contained in ministry protocols do not need to be elaborate processes. For example, in our opening case study, both the youth director and the wedding party would have filled out a simple room request form. This form would have alerted the church office to the potential of a ministry conflict, allowing both ministries to be informed to make adjustments appropriately. The room request form could have included room set up instructions and a corresponding diagram that would have helped the custodial staff know how to prepare the room for ministry. Again, overly complex procedures would not have been required to implement a facility usage policy. Most of the time, simplest is best.

Every Christian organization will have different policies resulting in different procedures for ministry. Bruce Powers's foundational works *Church Administration Handbook*[7] and *Christian Education Handbook*[8] give excellent examples of procedures that can be easily implemented in protocols to enable common church policies. The formation of ministry protocols should include the following elements:

- title of the policy;
- statement of purpose for the policy;
- biblical-theological and practical rationale for the policy;
- statement of limitations of the policy (what it is intended to do) and delimitations of the policy (what it is not intended to do);
- bulleted list of the procedural steps to be taken in the implementation of the policy, including matters such as listing the resources available, listing resources required, etc.;
- identification of responsible parties in the administration of the policy and corresponding procedures; and
- inclusion of the date the policy was initiated and subsequent revisions to it (often as a footer or footnote to the document).[9]

There are five specific protocols that almost every church and certainly most Christian organizations seem to need in order to anticipate and/or accommodate policy concerns regarding ministry:
1. Master Calendar Planning Protocols
2. Transportation Protocols
3. Purchasing and Reimbursement Protocols
4. Facility Usage Protocols
5. Ministry Readiness Protocols

Master Calendar Planning Protocols

Master calendar planning allows many organizational policies and procedures to be addressed in one setting, reminding ministry leaders of the importance of following corresponding protocols. The process is simple and is also a time of fellowship for all participants. The main office of the organization creates a master calendar of twelve pages, one month per page, with weekly ministries already filled in, as well as any approved special ministries already in process. Following refreshments and a time of prayer and Bible study to get started with the right frame of mind, leaders from every ministry of the church or Christian organization walk through each month of the year together. Each leader identifies the dates and times of anticipated activities of their ministry for the month being discussed, which are then compiled on one calendar. Any ministry conflicts are immediately apparent, and changes in dates and times are negotiated or flagged for future discussion. The process is then repeated for each month of the planning year.

The calendar planning process has the added benefit of allowing the church or Christian organization to gauge the flow of ministries so that everything doesn't happen all at once. It also tends to generate a sense of excitement about what God will be doing through the church or Christian organization in the coming year.

Upon the completion of the planning meeting, all of the ministries are entered on a master calendar displayed prominently in the main office. Experience has indicated that this master calendar works best if only one person can write in or remove ministries from the calendar throughout the year. Having *one* point person in control of the calendar further avoids the potential of not-yet-approved activities being written in that create conflicts with ministries in progress. In my church experience, the best point person is the lead church secretary, not the pastor. Given electronic technologies, it is now easy to create and print a master calendar that can be distributed in hand-out form for boards and committees.

Transportation Protocols

An increasingly common purchase made by churches and Christian organizations is a bus or van. After the purchase the inevitable conflict arises of two ministry groups wanting to use the vehicle at the same time. A clear policy on how a bus or van is to be reserved, used, serviced, and returned eliminates a lot of dangerous assumptions, for example, there is a full tank of gas in the van. A reservation sheet in the main office is often sufficient to police the use of a bus or van, and a simple checklist that is returned upon completion of use of the vehicle helps insure that it is ready for the next ministry to use.[10] Groups or persons who choose not to follow the procedures in the protocol usually are restricted from using the vehicle for a period of time.

Purchasing and Reimbursement Protocols

The flow of financial resources is frequently a major concern for any organization. When ministry leaders can spend money without prior approval and then request reimbursement, governing bodies can quickly lose control of the budget. Often these expenditures are not inappropriate: Church school teachers frequently have to purchase supplies at the last minute when curriculum lessons involve resources currently out of stock in the church's resource center. However, sometimes well-meaning ministry leaders will buy supplies without checking current inventories carefully, resulting in a waste of financial resources. Then there is the issue of tax exemption. Unapproved purchases made without the benefit of using the church's or Christian organization's tax-exempt status waste money unnecessarily.

When the church or Christian organization protects the budget by following the protocol of requiring a purchase/reimbursement form to be submitted prior to making and reimbursing a purchase, ministry leaders quickly learn to comply. Duplicate expenditures are largely eliminated, purchases are made under tax-exempt status (if applicable), and the treasurer and trustees are able to better maintain the integrity of the budget. When ministry leaders choose not to follow the protocol, purchases made without prior approval may or may not be reimbursed at the discretion of the ruling bodies. Some churches and Christian organizations follow a policy of not reimbursing taxes paid on purchases when tax exemption was a possibility.

The key to making a purchase/reimbursement protocol successful is to make the process easy to follow and quickly processed. Most ministry leaders will agree with a policy to protect the financial resources from wasted expenditures, but if it takes weeks to get purchases approved, many will take the risk of not getting reimbursed in order to get ministry done. Others will just skip the whole process and "deduct"

Figure 6.1: Ministry Readiness Worksheet

MINISTRY NAME			LOCATION		
PRESENTATION DATE			TIME		
THEME/EMPHASIS					
AGE GROUPS INVOLVED EARLY CHILDHOOD CHILDREN YOUTH ADULT					

PUBLICITY				APPROVAL/NOTIFICATION		
NEED	HAVE	ITEM		NEED	HAVE	GROUP
		NEWSLETTER				CHURCH STAFF
		BULLETIN				CHURCH OFFICE
		FLYER(S)				DEACONS/NESSES
		POSTER(S)				CHRISTIAN ED.
		NEWSPAPER				TRUSTEES
		RADIO/TELEVISION				SELECT COMMITTEE(S)
		TELEPHONE				SOCIAL COMMITTEE
		PERSON-TO-PERSON				CLASSES/DEPTS.
		ANNOUNCEMENT(S)				

RESOURCES			
NEED	HAVE	ITEM	COMMENT
		REQUISITION(S)	
		SONG LEADER	
		ACCOMPANIST	
		MUSIC SHEET/HYMNAL	
		SPECIAL MUSIC	
		MEAL/REFRESHMENT	
		KITCHEN HELP	
		AUDIO/MEDIA HELP	
		AUDIO EQUIPMENT	
		VISUAL EQUIPMENT	
		SPECIAL LIGHTING	
		CUSTODIAN	
		ROOM LAYOUT/SETUP	
		PROGRAM/BULLETIN/SCHEDULE	
		DECORATIONS	
		USHERS/GUIDES	
		FACILITY MAP	

Continued on the next page

1

Continued from previous page

NEED	HAVE	ITEM	COMMENT
		NURSERY (AGES)	
		PARKING LOT ATTENDANT	
		MONEY BOX	

SCHEDULE	COMMENT

MINISTRY EVALUATION	
NUMBER ATTENDING	WEATHER

the expenditures from their tithe to the church or charitable contributions to the organization, ultimately distorting the true financial needs of the ministry they are supporting.

Facility Usage Protocols

The room sign-up and set-up policy used as an example to resolve our opening case study can prevent duplicate room usage and make it easier for custodial staff to set up a room appropriately. Rooms that are used consistently by the same ministry but change set up frequently to accommodate several ministries benefit from "standing reservations and set-up orders." Following a room sign-up and set-up protocol may not seem important at first, but custodial staff usually appreciate being able to prepare rooms for ministry without having to guess what is needed. This is especially true when chair and table sizes must accommodate younger or older participants.

Ministry Readiness Protocols

One major but by no means final protocol that is very useful for ministry planning is to deploy a ministry readiness worksheet (see Figure 6.1) for each educational activity of the church or Christian organization. This worksheet is a simple one-page, two-sided document that helps the leader of an educational activity follow through on all requisite policies and procedures so as not to miss an essential task along the way. The top of the worksheet records the theme, date, time, location, and anticipated number of participants by age group. Immediately following are "Need/Have" check boxes on:

1. forms of publicity needed for the activity,
2. approvals needed from church leaders and governing bodies, and
3. a universal roster of resources most commonly used across any ministry (such as musicians, audio-visual equipment and personnel, ushers, nursery personnel, kitchen help, monetary change, and so on).

These checklists are then followed by a working schedule of the activity. The form closes with a quick evaluation of the ministry, indicating the number attending, the weather during the event (which often influences attendance), and any notes about how to enhance the ministry in the future.

Conclusion

Ministry planning can be enhanced if policies and procedures work together in clearly stated protocols. Such an approach to ministry management is biblical when ministry remains subservient to the leadership of the Holy Spirit as ministry plans unfold. The challenge is to create policies that enable ministry rather than hinder it and to create procedures that are easily followed and profitable if observed rather than circumvented. The alternative is for ministry to proceed haphazardly and inconsistently, wasting time and resources and generating conflict along the way. That approach doesn't glorify God, advance his ministry, or faithfully use the gifts and talents he gives us to do his work decently and in order.

BY
TONY BUCHANAAN

Chapter 7

Preparing and Reading a Budget

IF YOU WANT TO KNOW a person's values, review his calendar and checkbook. Jesus' words resonate with this principle: "Where your treasure is, there your heart will be also" (Luke 12:34 NIV). This is also true of organizations, even the church or a ministry in the church. The Christian education ministry is one such ministry that underscores the importance of values assessment as a foundational activity to preparing a budget. This chapter will provide the reader with a basic understanding of the issues involved in preparing various kinds of budgets since most ministry leaders will be required to use them on a regular basis. It is not designed to provide a review of detailed accounting procedures.

Context of the Budget

An understanding of an organization's budget begins with an understanding of the church's culture and of the community in which it exists. Failing to know the culture or, worse, ignoring either the culture of the organization or the community in which it exists, sets up the ministry for failure in the budgeting process.

Organizational culture refers to the values and behaviors of the institution in the formal and informal context of leadership, addressing such issues as the trust level of leaders for leaders, leaders for the congregation or Christian organization, institution for leaders, the staff by leaders and corporate body. If there is a culture of distrust, the budget must be developed using a system and must be administrated using processes that permit those who distrust to see how money is received, counted, recorded, and disbursed. Refusing to recognize the distrust simply adds fuel for continued and increasing mistrust. Likewise, in a culture of high trust, it is not wise to develop systems that exploit the

115

trust culture by developing processes that ignore the good practice of checks and balances and accountability.

A significant issue involved in budget preparation and culture is the belief about centralization or decentralization. Centralization is easily described as a "mom-and-pop" setting, where dad and mom, being the highest leadership, make all decisions regarding approval of funds and policies and require that the children, those working in the ministries, seek permission from mom and dad before proceeding. The centralized structure is often a reaction to tight cash flow or a variety of problems in a congregation or organization. The culture also exists where there is a lack of trust, for whatever reason, between the highest leadership and those "in the trenches" of ministry.

If a centralization setting exists, the budget process in that organization may involve information from those "in the trenches," but the highest levels of leadership make the decisions regarding priorities for funds. A significant issue in centralized structures becomes the alignment of persons who do the work in the organization. They often feel a total lack of empowerment and that they are disenfranchised in the process of organizing for the ministry in which they work. The result is morale problems and heavy turnover in staff.

A culture of decentralization has its problems, but the culture must exist if the organization is to grow into a dynamic organization. Decentralization requires an increasing amount of work in alignment with the institution's mission, empowerment of leaders, organizational structures and processes for using financial resources to accomplish the work of ministry, moving the decision making as closely as possible to the place where the ministry is being accomplished and building appropriate accountability structures so that the organization is fiscally responsible.

Purpose of the Budget

In order to proceed with the budget process, one must understand the purpose of a budget and how it applies to one's organizational context. The discussion of budgets in this chapter will focus on budgets for a nonprofit organization, often referred to as "fund accounting" because it takes the total of anticipated income and distributes it into accounts or funds to be used by the leadership of the organization.

A budget will reflect the leadership's beliefs about the amount of money that will be received by the organization and how that money should be spent. Without a budget, the process of operating the organization becomes myopic, which results in expenditures based on who gets to the treasurer first and often reflecting only the values of the treasurer or a finance committee.

Gray states that "budgets are plans expressing in numerical terms anticipated future needs of the institution, covering requirements for a specific period of time. Budgeting in the church is normally expressed in terms of dollar and cents necessary to meet the cost of operations during the period of time, usually one year."[1] Figure 7.1 illustrates the theoretical link between budget and ministry.[2] Budget and financial resources are balanced with the current ministry plan. At some point a proposed plan for ministry is made that supersedes the present budget, creating an imbalance. At this point the leadership of the congregation or Christian organization has a decision—either reduce the proposed ministry plan to comply with the budget *or* expand the budget to affirm and support the proposed ministry, reestablishing the budget balance. While undoubtedly leadership has to both decline and affirm proposed ministry endeavors based on budget concerns, institutions in a progressive, growing, leading posture will typically favor the proposed ministry

Figure 7.1: Budget and Ministry

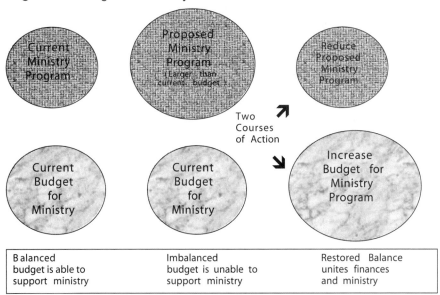

Balanced budget is able to support ministry	Imbalanced budget is unable to support ministry	Restored Balance unites finances and ministry

expansions. Institutions that favor reducing the ministry proposals are typically those in a maintenance mode.

A solid budget process includes people, reports, and equipment used to translate the organization's ministry plan into a dollar amount.

People

Persons involved in the budget process need time to call meetings to establish priorities, translate priorities into a budget, communicate the budget, meet the priorities, align leadership to the priorities and budget, create the final budget, and communicate this to the chief financial officer. In a congregation this individual may be the pastoral staff with the congregation's leadership, whereas in a parachurch organization it may be managers in cooperation with the business office. What skills are needed in order to formulate and administrate a budget? The budget process is based on some common-sense principles such as "don't spend more than you have," "money should be spent at about the same rate as it is received," and a few basic instructions regarding a spreadsheet.

A spreadsheet can be utilized as a ledger, and it contains horizontal lines and vertical columns (Figure 7.2). The point at which the horizontal and vertical lines come together creates a cell. That cell on a spreadsheet may be formatted to receive a number or perform a calculation. If you are not familiar with spreadsheets, please investigate some printed or on-line resources before attempting to create a budget using a spreadsheet. Computer spreadsheets are also helpful in running various budget scenarios, since they can be programmed to automatically recalculate data as it is changed.

Figure 7.2: Sample Spreadsheet/Ledger

Acct. #	Description	Budget	Actual for Month	Year to date	Difference
5101	Curriculum	15,400	1,280	2,400	13,000
5102	Library	6,000	500	2,500	3,500
5103	Activities	4,000	120	2,000	2,000
5104	Teacher Development	1,500	100	700	800
5105	Teaching Supplies	3000	250	496	2504

Some people have a gift for working numbers. Frequently they are called "bean counters." That gift may come wrapped in the body of a hard-nosed businessperson who lacks a good understanding of the difference between being a business and operating within good business principles. If so, care should be taken to make sure that teaching takes place. Even if a person has the basic talent, care should be taken to provide for development for those who are primarily responsible for budget formulation and administration. Many have said that it is a gift to work through a budget process in the church. I am not sure this is true, but I have witnessed financial leaders who did not appear to have a gift for it, and this is most often problematic to the financial stability of the Christian ministry.

Reports

A major learning curve for the common person trying to learn about budgeting is the understanding of tables, schedules, charts, and spreadsheets, most often collectively referred to as reports. Learning to make sense of financial reports is difficult for the most educated mind. The congregation or Christian organization should always seek to demonstrate financial stability by providing simple statements to leadership and the corporate body. However, this should never be used as an excuse for not providing the reports that minimize the financial picture to one page and make sure that persons participating in the financial ministry understand the more complicated reports to permit at least one body of people to have a thorough understanding of the organization's budget and expenditures.

Equipment

Computers play a large part in serving the needs of the budget process. While instruction in the use of financial management computer applications is typical for students in business programs, many seminaries do not provide this level of ministry training. Thankfully, more and more Christian colleges and seminaries are including instruction in how to use technology in the context of ministry settings. Most people in North America use a computer at home or in their workplace. This provides for a certain familiarity with basic functions of computer operations and spreadsheet programs such as Microsoft Excel or Quick Books. More complex accounting software programs exist, but either of these two provide the ministry leader with the basics for financial management.

The particular computer that manages the finances of the ministry should be used for the primary purpose of financial accounting and tracking. If it is used for other functions, it should be used only by those authorized to view financial information. The computer used to track budget details should not be used by anyone within the specific program that is included in the budget since the person would then not only see the information, but also be capable of changing it. Avoidance of such a situation will remove liability for that person and increase the integrity in the system.

Another issue is the important detail of backing up computer data. There are many backup programs available, and it is simply a matter of choosing one and using it. Some do this on an automatic and systematic basis while others have to be programmed to do backup. Either way, be sure that it happens at the end of every day in which financial transactions occur. Typically a three-backup system works fine: son, father, and grandfather. The backup closest to the current day is the son, the backup previous to the most current backup is the father, and the third backup out is the grandfather. It is wise to store one of the backups off the institution's site in the event of a cataclysmic event such as a fire.

Types of Budgets

There are three basic types of budgets used in congregations and Christian organizations: general fund, building or capital fund, and special fund. However, these terms are often labeled differently by each institution but serve the same functions.

General Fund

The general fund, sometimes called the annual fund or the operations budget, is the primary account of the organization. The money received each week is deposited into the general fund. The budget for the general fund typically includes all expenditures for annual costs of building repair and cleaning, utilities, personnel, program expenses, and accounting expenses, such as bank fees, etc. Generally when a person refers to the church checking account, the general fund is the desired account and budget.

Capital Fund

The capital fund is also called the building fund and is the account that usually pays for building construction, mortgage payments, and sometimes pays for the major renovation of the physical plant. In some settings, any piece of equipment purchased with a predetermined spending limit—for example, items priced over five hundred dollars—is considered to be a capital fund expenditure. The purchase of paper for the photocopy machine is a general fund expenditure, but the purchase of a new five-thousand-dollar copier would be a capital expenditure. The leadership should establish the maximum amount for purposes of determining what will be a general fund issue or a capital fund issue.

Designated Fund

Congregations and Christian organizations have several settings where the leadership chooses to establish this special fund. For a congregation, one very common special fund is the "missions" fund. Other examples may be a construction fund, or a fund for an auxiliary organization of the church, such as a Christian school. Whereas a designated fund serves a targeted purpose, the leadership should be very careful to restrict the use of this fund to save on bank charges, complexity of reporting, and the ease of creating a my-money mentality about various segments of the church. Additionally, in congregations some members will begin directing their contributions toward designated fund items rather than the general fund, sometimes innocently and other times as a means of voicing discontent over the general fund expenditures or the congregation's leadership.

If the leadership of a congregation or Christian organization determines to have a short-term special project, sometimes a separate account becomes the most effective way to manage the details of the account. Circumstances also arise where the nature of the special project would necessitate such a separate account, such as a special missions project. Good accounting can certainly handle the income and expenditures for special projects. However, having in a separate account the funds that are being used for one project or program is often a symbolic issue and has the positive benefit of showing clearly that the money being received and expended is going to the intended program. Never, under any circumstances, should the funds from a designated income source be used for anything other than their intended use. To do so is unethical and courts disaster with both the Internal Revenue Service and the ministry's constituents.

Accounting Can Be Complicated

On a general note, organizations with multiple special funds are often very trustworthy, with leadership being viewed as having integrity. Many times, however, the members establish special accounts because of a lack of trust of leadership. My experience is that there is a dramatic increase in designated funds or special accounts when members of the congregation do not trust leadership to account accurately for donated funds. Whereas this is not the intent of those who set up the accounts, many in ministry leadership have come to see that this is the rationale for the increase of such accounts.

Budget Models

Margaret Barr outlines five budget models often found in institutions of higher education: (1) incremental budgets; (2) zero-based budgets; (3) planning, programming, and budgeting systems (PPBS); (4) formula budgeting; and (5) cost or responsibility-centered management. Barr provides the pros and cons for each budget model in this unique nonprofit setting.[3] This section will examine these five budget models, with special consideration given to their applicability to congregations.

Incremental Budgets

Barr states that an incremental budget "assumes that the budget from the previous fiscal year is accurate and fairly reflects the expenditures of the unit."[4] This assumption is false in the higher education community where changes are often very slow because of the complexity of the institution and other external organizations. This assumption is also false in the church setting because it fails to recognize the sovereignty of God and the need for leadership to respond to the will of God as the needs of the congregation change, often rather quickly and drastically. This budget model is never appropriate for a congregation or Christian organization that is sensitive to the changing needs of the congregation and the ongoing challenges of making the ministry applicable to a changing society.

Zero-Based Budgets

The zero-based budget model is a budget where each item in the budget is justified and nothing is assumed to always be part of the budget process.[5] The name is used because each year every department begins at zero and builds all expenditures into the budget, providing a justification for each expenditure. This sounds good on the surface because of its close tie to demonstrating the need and justification for all expenditures. There are some problems, however.

The zero-based budgeting process requires significant time in order to process correctly. Many expenditures are appropriate each year. Spending time working through a complicated system to document each expenditure can be a waste of valuable time. For example, demonstrating that the mortgage must be paid makes no sense but is a necessity using this approach. It might if you were considering a change to a lower interest rate for the mortgage, different payment time frames, etc., but for the most part the church just pays the mortgage each month. The good qualities of zero-based budgeting are often used in a hybrid manner. Customary expenditures are relatively fixed, such as mortgage or utilities, often simply based on a schedule presented to the committee. New ministries or other budget areas that need attention are asked to justify the purchase that they have made. The strength of the system is its close connection to the planning process of the congregation.

Planning, Programming, and Budgeting Systems

The planning, programming, and budgeting systems (PPBS) model was popular in the 1980s and early 1990s in higher education.[6] The process is very intensive and focuses on budgeting as a function of a unit determining the cost effectiveness of each program. This reflected the intense focus of higher education on institutional effectiveness wherein the institution demonstrates that its programs are effective based upon research rather than merely asserting effectiveness because of the availability of resources. This simply means that just because a program has money does not mean that the program is functioning effectively. Therefore, the budget process was closely tied to the outcomes of a program, the documented effectiveness, so that the institution funded only those programs that had measurable outcomes and were meeting their objectives.

This budget model could be beneficial for congregations and Christian organizations, but only if they have engaged in an intensive level of assessment by researching their program's effectiveness. Because of the nature of church programs and their focus on spiritual development as well as cognitive development, the demonstration of effectiveness may be very difficult in a church setting. It is not easy to measure spiritual maturity or to prove that one particular program contributed to increased spiritual maturity compared to another. The result would be enormous frustration of the volunteer workers to produce a budget that would be accepted when measured by the PPBS model.

Formula Budgeting

The model of formula budgeting is used in the public school setting at all levels. The enrollment is established and submitted for an allotment of funds for each student. There are some exceptions to address students with special needs, but the basic approach is a formula. This model may be used in some church settings, specifically when planning the budget for the adult church choir. Simply choose the music for the year, determine the cost to purchase music for each choir member, and then multiply that by the number of choir members.

The problem with this model for establishing congregations and most Christian organizations is that the number of students in any given age group or class will change. New people come in and existing members stop coming or move to another congregation, or the number of campers subsequently fluctuates. This model is perhaps most applicable to a Christian school or institution of higher education where attendance figures are relatively set for a determined length of time (for example, quarter, semester, or academic term). The process of tracking these occurrences for budget purposes in other ministries can become labor-intensive and not worth the amount of assessment required.

Cost or Responsibility-Centered Management

The last of the five models presented by Barr is the cost or responsibility-centered management. This model is very similar to the business models of profit-centered or expense-centered budgeting. The idea is simple: each segment of the organization stands alone with the responsibility of raising the funds and paying expenses. "Although this works well for auxiliary enterprises, the model does not adapt itself easily to instruction and support units within the college or university,"[7] and congregations. A responsibility-centered budget may work well for special projects of the organization or for trips by departments within the church, but at a college or camp setting, the money comes into a general pool and is distributed based upon an approved budget. This may not be appropriate for a congregation or institution-wide budget process.

So which model should be used? Study your church culture, determine how you operate, and do what fits your organization. It may be a hybrid process, which is fine as long as the hybrid process addresses the total budgeting process needs. Regardless of the model used, plan to spend a good bit of time each year teaching the process to those who will be developing the budgets for the various departments in the church. No model is self-explanatory. When left to his or her own devices, the volunteer leader may simply create his or her own "customized" approach. When this occurs there is potential conflict with others on the team with regard to how the budget process works. Money is a topic of conflict even in churches!

If the group determines a change in process or procedure is required, the change process must include reasons why the change was necessary (i.e., what is wrong) before people in the organization will be open to hearing about another process, even if the new process suggests less work. It is recommended that a trained certified financial accountant (CFA) provide advice and consultation in the development of the appropriate policies and procedures for managing the finances of the ministry. They are well-equipped to provide the kind of direction that is needed for the ethical handling of ministry finances. Perhaps the best time to seek their advice for a ministry that has not considered their advice is after an annual audit has been conducted.

Budget Time Lines

The length of time for the budget process is dependent on many factors: size of organization, culture of participation in the organization, and the complexity of the organizational structure. The larger the organization and the more complex the institution, the longer it takes to work a grassroots budget process. The assumption that large organizations have more complex structures than small organizations is not always true. For example, if the budget approval process includes a committee and then the congregation, the time line may be adjusted to make the approval time shorter. On the flip side, organizations that require a multilayered approval process may need to expand the approval portion of the time line to permit more time to accomplish that process, for example, committee, ministry division, finance team, leadership, and corporate body.

Discerning the culture of the organization is also important. The caveat here is the more people involved in the budget process, the more time it takes to complete the process. This is an organizational structure issue in some ways because it all depends on the level of involvement that the average member of the congregation has in the development and/or approval of the budget. In some ministries, the budget is developed by seasoned professional and there is little room, if any, for the average person in the ministry to have any input. Other ministries prefer to have an extensive amount of lay leader involvement. The later approach will obviously require more time for planning and approving the final document.

Stages of the Budgeting Cycle

Budgets are perennial; they are developed in cycles. Understanding how these cycles work and the important functions of each stage can be beneficial for the novice ministry leader. The cycle typically consists of stages of planning, formulation, approval, administration, reporting, and approval.

Stage One: Planning

There are two general sections of the budget: income and disbursements. The goal is to have more income than disbursements. Cash flow and balance sheets are presented below. Income is the money received, regardless of source (e.g., tithes, special offerings, designated offerings, book store revenues, tickets sales, etc.). The church leadership establishes the anticipated income from the congregation. Disbursements are money paid to a person or organization, usually in exchange for services or a product.

Determining Organizational Goals. The budget process dovetails with the planning process. If the organization does not have a defined direction, the budget process becomes equally lacking in direction. This lack of direction has an increasing impact on the process because of the increase of demand on decision making as the organization gets closer to the final budget. The ideal approach in the budget-drafting process is for the initial draft to follow the goals-setting meeting (see chapter 11). Once the church leadership has determined what goals and objectives they are driving toward during the next year, it is time to fund those goals. Budgeting should never come before the goal-setting meeting. Remember: ministry drives budget formation, not the other way around, although understandably the two must work in a symbiotic relationship. You can't create a budget based on unrealistic dreams either.

Determining Available Resources. The budget committee of the church should establish a general percentage of growth based on anticipated income the organization may receive from general donations, ministry-specific income, grants, endowments, investment income, as well as wills and trusts. General donations are the primary source for the vast majority of income which congregations and Christian organizations receive. Donations generally serve as a very high percentage of the organization's income, and from a biblical perspective, this is fine.

Christian organizations that have other sources of income which significantly meet the general or annual fund needs often fail to challenge the membership to be good stewards of their time and finances. This happens when a church begins to develop its budget and addresses only the expenditures. Failing to evaluate the internal impact from the external environment can result in significant budget problems as the year progresses.

For example, I live in the Orlando area. Immediately following the tragedy of September 11, 2001, the number of people coming to Orlando on vacation dropped drastically. The income to hotels and major attractions dropped perilously low. Our local economy was devastated. The hotels and entertainment attractions responded by laying people off or reducing the hours of work for many of their employees. Many of these employees were members in the congregation I attended. When an individual's income declines, the tithe or offering he or she is able to provide also declines. That external environment impacted the church's budget (internal impact) rather seriously for that first year. The leadership of the church was aware of the economy and wisely revised spending habits to provide time to recover. This specific issue will be addressed more in budget administration later in the chapter.

Ministry-specific income is money that is generated by a ministry by requiring or requesting money in order to participate in an event. For example, youth groups often require payment of funds to finance such things as camps, mission trips, and other special events. In essence, the income derived from the trip will offset the total cost of the activity for the church. Care should be taken to make sure that if an individual receives something in return for the donation, the reporting of donation reflects the gift. Although this provision has been in the IRS rules for many years, it has been in recent years that organizations like churches and private colleges have been more closely monitored. There are guidelines, but again it is recommended that administrators seek advice from a lawyer or certified public accountant.

Grants from institutions or foundations are very popular in educational settings, but they are not as popular in church settings. A review of the funding patterns of some foundations suggests that there are elements of a church program that may be good candidates for grant funding. The issue usually centers on the question of advancing a particular faith or supporting the operating expenses of a church. It all depends on the intent of the foundation when it was established.

Investment income has the potential of providing stability to church budgets. For example, a congregation in Indiana decided after building a beautiful new sanctuary that it would endow the maintenance of the building so its upkeep would never negatively impact the annual fund of the church. The endowment has steadily grown and now provides more than adequate funding to maintain the facility. Investment income is one source of income often overlooked and very labor-intensive to get. Interest from endowments to pay for development of the volunteer teaching staff or persons going to college or seminary to prepare for ministry are a possible use for endowments in an educational ministry.

Wills and trusts are a great source of income; however, due to the nature of the time of the award (i.e., someone's death), this source of income is very difficult to plan for. People are increasingly including their church in their wills; however, building a budget using income from a will or trust is dangerous. There are some approaches used successfully in this aspect of the budgeting process.

One approach is to develop a list of major purchases that are in the long-range plan. If the church receives a disbursement from a will or trust, it can use the money to purchase these items at that time. A second approach is to move these funds directly into an endowment and to budget income from the earnings of the funds the second year. A third approach is worthy when the church is growing and there are increasing needs for new facilities. The funds are simply set aside until the building is ready to be built, at which time the funds are moved into the cash flow to pay the construction bills. Using the disbursement from a will or trust to meet budget deficits is not a good long-range plan for financing the programs of the local church, though it may be reasonable in times of unplanned economic crisis.

The ministry leadership may also have identified additional income sources for the ministry. These sources and the projected amount of income from each should be identified in the ministry budget presentation to the congregation's or organization's budget committee.

Stage Two: Formulation

The budget formulation stage has two parts: compiling the budget amounts from each aspect of the ministry and reviewing them for approval at the ministry level. In most instances an organization's budget committee does not require a specific approach to compiling the budget amounts requested by the various departments of the ministry. Therefore, the ministry leadership should agree on some standard approach to the work of translating the goals into budget numbers. This generally takes place in the strategic planning phase or during the ministry-by-objectives setting. In other words, each goal and objective needs to have a specific person and dollar amount associated with it. These dollar amounts must then be collected and assigned to a specific line item in the budget.

The second step in formulation is to review the compiled budget and address the following issues in the ministry setting:

1. Does the compiled budget in each ministry area accurately reflect the culture and ethos of the ministry? Is the ministry in harmony with the culture and values of the organization's leadership?

2. Is there a clear connection between the goals of the committee/ministry and their budget?

3. Is there adequate justification for each budget line? The ministry leadership's guidance here would be helpful to those working within the ministry. The degree of documentation required to justify budgets is a ministry culture issue.

4. How do the income and expenditures balance? Does the ministry budget stay within the allotment given to them by the budget committee? If not, is there additional income that is ministry specific to offset the difference?

5. Does the budget include everything? Are the amounts reasonable considering the description and justification for the expenditure?

6. Are there duplications? Have two ministry areas included the expense for the same item that is to be purchased or program to be funded?

Stage Three: Approval

The approval process should focus on two goals: alignment and permission. An approval process aimed at this two-pronged approach will take longer, involve more people, and establish a greater consensus on the budget.

The alignment involves all levels of those involved in the budget to give an opportunity to see how the budget reflects the values of the organization's leadership. Persons doing much of the work in the ministry appreciate seeing how their requests for funds have been addressed in the overall budget. When funds are not available, seeing the entire picture helps those people see that although their requests were not funded, the money is being spent wisely. So provide opportunities for review and responses from those who are within the ministry prior to that budget being moved farther into the process. Building alignment with the budget within the ministry will take additional time, but it should build a stronger team and provide for more understanding about expenditures.

The second is approval or permission. This will depend in part on the type of governance that is incorporated within the ministry. This budget process may have two levels of approval or permission: tentative and final. A tentative approval is simply an action of the approving body that states that pending confirmation and assurances regarding assumptions and factors: this budget is fine. Confirmations are important to the budget process. Much of the formulation process begins four to six months prior to the beginning of the next year. Issues may arise or factors present themselves in this time period that impact the budget positively or negatively.

Whereas having more money, a positive impact, is usually handled with relative ease, a negative impact that results in lessened income or higher expenditures is not always as easily handled. Leadership, providing tentative approval, signals to the ministry personnel that under the described circumstances the budget is appropriate for the coming year. This permits planning to begin (i.e., their goals and objectives have been funded). Waiting until much closer to the beginning of the year to give final approval on the budget lets those involved in the ministry know that there is a possibility of change.

Issues like personnel contracts and other issues that must be resolved prior to the actual budget year are often discussed individually by the leadership, and in some cases, that particular item is given approval to permit the ongoing work of the ministries.

Final approval comes when the issues or assumptions have been confirmed and the budget adjusted appropriately in view of the projected outcome of the present year and is ready for spending to be based on the budget.

The budget should be distributed at two points: tentative and final. Whether or not everyone sees the total budget is an issue of organizational culture. This is particularly true if salary amounts are a sensitive point for those in the ministry. If salaries are included in ministry department budgets, the parts of the budget may be distributed to each department separately. Many ministries prefer to combine all staff salaries as an aggregate figure in the administrative salaries line item. If salaries are not part of departmental budgets, the entire ministry budget may be distributed to those who are doing the work.

Stage Four: Administration

Robert Gray writes: "A primary principle of budgeting so often mis-construed in church management is that a budget is not an absolute, final, and unalterable guide. Frequently, the figures become obsolete when considered in the light of evolving conditions and need to be adjusted accordingly. The budget does not manage the church. It is not an end in itself. The budget is simply a tool to be used by the management and is a means to an end. When the budget becomes a 'straight jacket,' it loses its usefulness."[8] The previous discussion of external environment and internal implications should be, once again, applied. If the external conditions change, the internal implications change. For example, a budget is established and approved by the congregation or governing board at their meeting at the beginning of the fiscal year. Three months into the fiscal year, a major employer in the area moves away, leaving many church members without a job. The church leadership must move immediately to reevaluate the budget in view of the internal implications of the external environment. Simply put, they must adjust spending to reflect a lower income or identify additional income.

Stage Five: Reporting

This stage includes periodic and annual reporting. Periodic reporting may be weekly, monthly, and annually. Weekly reporting might include reports to the executive director/senior pastor and the finance committee. Monthly reporting might also include appropriate department heads and project leaders. Annual reporting might be to all persons in the church or ministry. All three reports have a different audience and should be customized to provide the information that is needed for those who are to receive the report. Hence, it is important to identify the audiences of a report. The total church membership does not need the level of detail that the staff would need. Therefore, the report for the audience of the church membership may be shorter and include only ministry totals with some comparative data. The staff may need significant detail, but may need it only in certain areas.

Make sure that the accounting software that you use has the option for customizing a number of reports. Meet with the different audiences and determine what is needed and what is reasonable for each audience. Sometimes the senior leadership may need to revise what is requested because it is not appropriate, in the leaders' view, that a person knows everything. The leadership should be the group that makes the final decisions about the level of detail that will be made available to the ministries and the total church.

Stage Six: Archival

Very little is stated in the literature about archiving budget information at the end of the fiscal year. The information that may be gleaned from making comparisons of past budgets is a valuable part of seeing how a ministry has grown and developed.

What information should be retained? The organization's treasurer or accounting office usually keeps the details of disbursements and what was part of each check. The office does not, however, usually keep the details of the creation of the budget when vision and goals are translated into actions. Records of meetings where the budget is developed should be retained with an end-of-the-year report of the ministry's budget. In addition to the files retained in the accounting office of the church, ministry leaders should retain information such as numbers used to calculate curriculum for a program and methods of calculating group activities. This information is valuable when it is once again time to plan a large function in the ministry.

Because of the diversity of programming in a church setting, perhaps begin by retaining the documentation you have for this year's budget for two or three years after the close of the fiscal year. Then next year make a note of what information you need from your budget archives and begin to establish what kinds of information you should retain in your files.

Budgeting Principles

Several principles of budgeting apply throughout the process of forming a budget and effectively utilizing it. First, *budgeting is a group process*. Budgets by individuals typically lack the eclectic perspective necessary to provide a viable plan for financial support for ministry. Input from those involved and approval by more than an individual is essential. Second, *ministry, then money!* People do not support budgets because of technical financial reasons (e.g., accuracy, balance, etc.), but because of the potential for a successful and impacting ministry. Establishing an account or budget line item will *never* replace action in ministry. Third, *spending controls enforce budgets*. Without controlled spending, such as purchase orders and authorizations for expenditures, the budget is a hollow document.

Fourth, *avoid debt-spending budget planning*. Budgets designed to send the congregation or organization into the red does the institution a disservice. This would include interfund borrowing—the proverbial "Robbing Peter to pay Paul." One budget item cannot be used to fund another. Similarly, the institutional debt should not exceed three times the annual income of the institution. If it does, the financial resources of the congregation or organization will be used for debt service rather than ministry. Fifth, *it is all a principle of stewardship*. Part of administration is being a good steward (see chapter 2), and this includes the financial resources of a congregation or organization.

Finance represents a critical issue in Christian ministries. Jesus was concerned with finances since nearly half of the parables he used in his teaching relate to the topic of stewardship. Finances can also be a highly explosive topic among members of churches and Christian organizations. Many ministry leaders have been surprised by the hidden agendas and level of politics associated with financial accounting. This chapter is designed to prepare the future ministry leader with the realities of life in the boardroom. Do your homework and take the time to learn how to manage the money of your ministry effectively. You may not enjoy it, and you may prefer to do other things with your time. But neglecting this important aspect of your stewardship responsibilities can get you fired faster than you thought possible.

The budget process should reflect the culture of the organization, must be derived from the results of a values-driven, broad-based participatory planning process and the wisdom of the ministry's leadership team. Such a process provides for spending that reflects the organization's values and plans and permits those carrying out the plans to be part of, and supportive of, the financial function of the organization. When this happens, the focus of finances is on the use of money to accomplish organizational purposes, rather than be a topic of conflict.

BY
MICHAEL ANTHONY

Chapter 8

Ministry
by Objectives

IT HAS LONG BEEN A CHALLENGE for those involved in the management of ministry to find a way to maintain progress toward accomplishing the church's goals while at the same time shepherding those whose passion is directed more toward the accomplishment of their own personal or ministry agenda. This is not an easy balance to achieve. Too much emphasis on either side of the equation leads to peril. With an overemphasis on accomplishing the church's goals, the ministry supervisor gets a reputation for not caring about those he or she manages. With too much emphasis on individuals or departments, the supervisor is labeled ineffective because he simply can't "get the job done."

Some of the most successful and effective ministry teams that we have seen over the years have been those staffed with passionate entrepreneurs. These ministry leaders (children's pastor, youth pastor, senior pastor, etc.) are characterized as operating with such a high level of personal drive and ambition that they need very little direct supervision or oversight. Their motto could be stated as, "Lead, follow, or get out of my way!" They don't require a great deal of oversight and control because they have within them a zeal for getting things done on their own.

However, where these ministry leaders get themselves into trouble is in the area of coordination. Each ministry department is actively achieving its own mission and vision, but without much coordination it eventually collides and self-destructs in conflict with other departments. In these high-achieving ministry settings, activity appears to be limitless, but not all the activity is purposeful. At the end of the year when each ministry director is held to account for his or her activities, it's discovered that they may have met their department's goals, but the church is no better off because their work lacked coordination and mutually

133

agreed-upon direction. What is needed to avoid this waste of human and material resources is a system of management that provides coordination toward agreed-upon objectives. That, in essence, is at the heart of ministry by objectives.

What Is MBO?

Management by objectives, or MBO as it came to be labeled, was developed as a result of the need to coordinate efforts toward the successful accomplishment of the organization's goals and objectives. The term *management by objectives* was first coined by Peter Drucker in 1954 when he wrote: "What the business enterprise needs is a principle of management that will give full scope to individual strength and responsibility, and at the same time give common direction of vision and effort, establish team work and harmonize the goals of the individuals with common weal. The only principle that can do all this is management by objectives and self-control."[1]

Although his approach to manager training was well received in the early fifties, it was the modifications and insights brought to bear by other management specialists that really helped integrate MBO into the way North America functioned in the workplace. About a decade after Drucker's initial ideas came to print, George Odiorne came out with a text entitled *Management by Objectives* which helped launch MBO into the commonly accepted system that it has become. Odiorne defines the MBO process as "the system of management whereby the superior and the subordinate managers of an organization jointly identify its common goals, define each individual's major areas of responsibility in terms of the results expected of him, and use these measures as guides for operating the unit and assessing the contributions of each of its members."[2]

Odiorne illustrated this MBO process as a cycle which begins with the goals of the organization and seeks to harmonize them with the interests of the subordinate. See Figure 8.1.

Since its inception it has been widely adapted into a variety of settings and contexts. For example, it has been applied to the fields of medicine,[3] government,[4] education,[5] camping,[6] churches,[7] and as a strategy for general life wellness.[8] The process of MBO lends itself to adaptation into a variety of settings because of its simplicity and ease of transferability. Various models have been formulated to depict the MBO format in graphic detail. Such models include Odiorne's MBO Cycle,[9] Morrisey's MOR Process,[10] Humble's MBO Cycle,[11] and Hillmar's MBO/R Operation System.[12] Each model has its own contribution to make, and each helps depict the MBO format as an ongoing process. Since we are emphasizing church ministry management in this text, we'll apply its merits to the context of the local church. Once broken

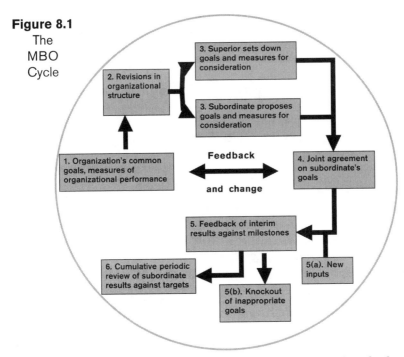

Figure 8.1
The MBO Cycle

down to its basic components, most church ministry leaders find MBO to be well worth the investment of their time and energy. For those reasons, we'll refer to it as *Ministry by Objectives.*

The Steps of Ministry by Objectives

Ministry by objectives starts with an understanding and appreciation for the stewardship of resources that we are given by God. Although it is true that God owns the cattle on a thousands hills, it is also equally true that few, if any, churches have all the cattle they can use. We must all make do with the resources that we are given. Since they are more limited than are dreams, we must make some difficult decisions about how they will be utilized. Setting priorities and then managing them wisely is at the heart of the ministry-by-objectives process. The process is broken down into three phases with corresponding steps within each phase. They are: the preparatory phase, the implementation phase, and the assessment phase.

The Preparatory Phase

This phase is a season of getting things ready. Some detailed analysis needs to be done, or the time invested in the ministry-by-objectives process will have been wasted. Most of the activity involved in this phase will already have been done at some point in the life of the church.

However, without periodic review and update, the benefits will be minimized. In this phase the church is basically reviewing and revising its mission and vision, deciding what it wants to accomplish in the next ministry season, and looking to see that it has the right staff in the right places to get things done. A more detailed explanation of each stage's contents will follow.

Step One. Revisit the mission and vision of the church and be sure that they are both up to date and relevant. You'll need to decide what your ministry focus and priorities will be for the coming year. This may change from time to time depending on variances in community-wide demographics, the availability of personnel (paid and volunteer), and the amount of material resources (facilities, vehicles, finances, etc.) which are available. Each must be taken into consideration.

As an example, let's assume your church's mission statement reads: "Reaching Beyond Barriers to Every Generation with God's Message of Love and Salvation." In order to accomplish that mission, you've developed a strategy or vision which is encapsulated in the phrase "Taking the Gospel to the Families of Lakeside County." Your church has revisited both the mission and vision and believe it accurately reflects where your church should put its emphasis for at least the next few years. If you've done all this, you're ready to move on to the next step.

If your church is not united on its mission or vision, you have some work to do before you can progress to the next step. Review chapters 2 and 3 and work the congregation through the process of developing updated mission and vision statements. These are critical to your future and will serve as boundaries for important decisions which will come up later in the ministry-by-objectives process.

Step Two. Those in leadership in the church must make some difficult decisions about what the church will and will not do in order to accomplish the mission and vision. No one church can do it all. Some priorities have to be set. This is not easy for some people because saying *yes* to one area of emphasis may require them to say *no* to another. To some the process may seem short-sighted and lacking in faith. To them it appears to be limiting God. In reality, we are not limiting God but rather asking God what he wants us to do with the finite resources he has entrusted to us. Through this prioritizing process we are becoming better stewards of God's ministry resources.

This is a time for the governing boards of the church to do some soul searching about where they sense God is taking them in this next ministry season. At this point some churches conduct an analysis of their strengths, weaknesses, opportunities, and threats. This SWOT analysis is a good place to start, but be sure that you query as many people as possible when you gather information. A mailed survey to the church members is a helpful piece for information gathering. Some churches hold an annual town hall meeting to request feedback from the congregation.

Form a few focus groups to request information that can't easily be written on a form. For example, an elder or deacon can meet with a half dozen members of the church choir after the Sunday service while another board member meets for lunch with a representative group of single adults. If each board member is given an assignment of leading a focus group, the board can get a finger on the pulse of the church in a relatively short time. It will also encourage the congregation to know that the board is concerned about their hopes, dreams, and aspirations about the future direction of the church. Once you receive this input from numerous sources, it is time to synthesize the information into a list of workable goals.

During this step in the ministry-by-objectives process you are developing a list of agreed-upon organization goals. You are encouraged to keep this list to a minimum—perhaps no more than ten goals. The temptation will be to appease as many people as possible and become hesitant to say *no*. Be advised, however, that it is better to say *no* now than it is to generate unrealized expectations.

The short list of desired organizational goals must be directly related to both the mission and vision of the church. For example, since we have clearly articulated mission and vision statements, we might have a short list of priorities such as these.

1. Begin a contemporary worship service for students in the new university extension campus that is being built in our section of the city.
2. Develop an integrated discipleship program in scope and sequence between the ages of birth through twenty-two years.
3. Support the addition of new missionaries in our missions budget.
4. Make initial inquiries with the city about the use of the vacant land adjacent to the church.
5. Create a small group leadership training program which provides a solid biblical foundation for the recovery ministries currently operating in the church.
6. Establish a new mothers of preschoolers program for young mothers and their children.
7. Refurbish the educational classroom facilities so each room can accommodate a higher level of instructional technology (TV, VCR, video data projector, etc.).
8. Increase the membership of the church by 7 percent through a more concerted effort of assimilation.

Obviously a few more could be added, but this short list will serve our purposes to illustrate this second step. Once the list is developed, it should have ownership or buy in by all the major staff members and lay leaders of the church. The elder board, deacon board, trustees, or any other form of organizational leadership, together with the senior pastor, must wholeheartedly support each of these goals. Some of these goals may be carried over from a previous year and some may be newly added. At any rate, they form the basis of the current year's ministry focus.

If you look at this step and realize that the future will involve serious negotiating and resolve, you're right. Progress never comes without a price. Busyness is no guarantee of success. One of Satan's best weapons is purposeless activity. Focusing on the essential activities is not easy, but it does prevent meaningless wandering.

Dale McConkey describes this process as renewal by objectives (RBO) because the identification of the essential activities of the church can become a renewing force within the ministry. He states: "An overwhelming reason for practicing renewal by objectives is to help us accomplish the most meaningful and rewarding results of the church by first determining the most important things we want to do, by directing all the individual efforts of our team toward the things we want to accomplish, and by avoiding spending our time and energy on efforts that are not needed. Emphasis is on the results we want to achieve, not on the unorganized efforts expended."[13]

Step Three. Conduct a structural analysis. It is time to review the church's organizational structure and make any necessary changes in order to achieve these goals. Eventually, an individual or department will be responsible for implementing and coordinating the successful accomplishment of these goals. Now is the time to make any changes in personnel, job descriptions, and/or reporting relationships before the plan gets launched.

Speaking of the need for organizational revision as an integral component of the MBO process, Odiorne writes: "The sketching out of the actual organization structure follows goal-setting, since if goals are changed then changes in organization may well be needed. Changes in organization will lead to changes in individual areas of responsibility and authority and should be clarified before subordinate managers are asked to work out their performance goals and measures for the coming year."[14]

This will involve an honest analysis about the giftedness and fit of each member of the church staff. In his book entitled *Good to Great*, Jim Collins uses the analogy of riding on a bus to describe the manner in which this organizational analysis takes place. In describing the characteristics of the most effective leaders in his nationwide study he writes: "We expected that good-to-great leaders would begin by setting a new vision and strategy. We found instead that they first got the right people on the bus, the wrong people off the bus, and the right people in the right seats—and then they figured out where to drive it. The old adage 'People are your most important asset' turns out to be wrong. People are not your most important asset. The right people are."[15]

Conducting this structural analysis is one of the most challenging parts of the process because it requires unbiased dedication to truth about personnel performance. When looking at the goals set out for the church, those in the highest level of leadership must ask, "Are we staffed to accomplish these goals?" If the answer is *no*, something needs to be done or the entire planning process is undermined.

Individuals may have been hired for a particular job years ago but no longer have the personal passion or commitment for the task today. For example, the youth pastor may have been hired right out of college when he was young, energetic, and eager to take on the challenges associated with youth ministry. However, ten years later, with a wife and three young children at home, he may lack the enthusiasm and conviction he once had for youth ministry. This doesn't mean he isn't a great Christian leader, and it doesn't devalue the many years of dedicated service he's made. However, the church can ill afford to keep him in that position indefinitely, particularly if he lacks drive, initiative, and passion from deep within his spirit.

Recognizing the changes that have occurred in the youth pastor, those in church leadership need to ask themselves some difficult questions about giftedness and fit. It's entirely possible (and actually quite probable) that the youth pastor himself realizes his own lack of enthusiasm for the ongoing demands of the church's youth ministry program. The senior pastor, or executive pastor if it's a large church, should meet individually with the youth pastor and decide if his gifts fit a different need in the church. Perhaps his years of leadership and ministry experience can be better utilized as the key leader in the church's new goal of establishing a college-oriented service. Or perhaps there is a different role for him as an associate pastor in a new avenue of ministry.

If no appropriate and legitimate place is found, then this person should be graciously told that the church no longer has need of his services and should be given a severance package which is generous and commensurate with his years of service. This process is what Collins means when he says it is time to assess if the right people are on the bus and if the right people are in the right seats. If not, then don't depart from the bus station!

Churches are notorious for failing to make the difficult decision of terminating the employment of someone for whom they no longer have need of their services. Desiring to be kind, gracious, and compassionate, the church instead wastes assets and becomes a poor steward of God's resources. The church does not do the youth pastor a favor in the long run by keeping him in a position that he neither enjoys nor appreciates. Further insights regarding this difficult decision can be found in chapter 22 entitled "Conducting Performance Reviews."

The Implementation Phase

Now that you have completed the steps associated with phase one, you're ready to begin the fruitful work of discussions between the supervisors (senior pastor, executive pastor, etc.) and the staff members (children's pastor, youth pastor, singles pastor, etc.) of the church. It is time for them to meet together and brainstorm ways to accomplish these goals. It should be an encouraging time as members of the church staff decide together what direction their efforts will take them during the months ahead.

Step Four. Managers and subordinates meet to translate each of these goals into measurable objectives. This involves determining what needs to be done to accomplish the goals, how the goal will be broken down into more manageable steps, who will be responsible for each of the steps, what resources will be needed, and a timetable for execution. This is a time for the manager to listen to the concerns and feelings of the subordinates. Now is the time to tie personnel, finances, and material resources together into one concise plan.

This can be done in any number of formats. Some managers prefer to draw up their list of how the goals will be measured while at the same time the subordinate draws up his or her list. Then they meet to share their objectives together. This allows the individual who will be ultimately responsible for accomplishing the goals and objectives to have the freedom of determining how he or she can best attain them. It also allows the subordinate to add individual goals which may have significant importance to the organization but were overlooked by those setting the larger goals. Some managers prefer to meet with their subordinates to draw up this mutually agreed-upon list together. Which alternative you select will depend on contextual factors such as the amount of time available, the working relationship between the manager and subordinate (i.e., does the subordinate feel the freedom to negotiate and speak freely?), the subordinate's ability to craft measurable objectives, whether the subordinate works well independently, etc.

To the list above will be added more specific examples. For example, Goal #1 may be made more specific by adding the following objectives:

Goal #1: Begin a contemporary worship service for students in the new university extension campus that is being built in our section of the city.

Objectives:

1. Identify and recruit four key individuals who will serve as a leadership team to provide direction in areas of worship, teaching, and tech support.
2. Develop a ministry plan that identifies the critical steps which need to be accomplished in order to begin this ministry.
3. Solicit the initial venture capital (finances) that will be necessary for this new ministry start-up. This form of funding prevents a strain from impacting other ongoing programs of the church.
4. Initiate an advertising plan on the university campus which includes newspaper, radio, flyers, and personal contacts.

Additional objectives may need to be added along with specific deadlines. The more specific and measurable you make these goals and objectives, the greater likelihood you will have of accomplishing them. The process of adding specific objectives to each of the goals is critical to the success of the end result because these objectives will serve as the basis for measuring future activity and in shaping decisions related to the allocation of ministry resources.

Writing objectives may appear to be deceptively simple to the inexperienced staff member. A number of guidelines will help identify important characteristics.

1. It should specify the action to be taken. The objective should clearly state what activity is to be performed.

2. It should focus on an identifiable target result. Each aspect of the objective should point toward the ability of measurement. The use of ambiguous generalities will only serve to nullify the objective.

3. It should be time limited. There should be a commitment to a completion date written into each objective. Target dates may be assumed as ending each quarter, semester, or period, but each objective should have a time frame attached to it.

4. It should be measurable, tangible, or verifiable. To the extent possible, each objective should be expressed in measurable terminology. This does not mean that every objective must be written in quantitative form. Some may be qualitative, but each should allow the reader to be able to determine whether or not it is accomplishable without doubt.

5. It should be challenging. This goes for both the organization and the individual. Without being stretched, the organization cannot grow.

6. It should be realistic and attainable. There is a balance between being a challenge and being realistic. A good objective is both.

7. It should be consistent with organizational goals. This is known as harmony of objectives. Each objective must be in harmony with and contribute to the organizational goals.[16]

Step Five. Communicate the plans and review them on a regular basis. At this point the church has a master list of goals to guide its activities for the upcoming year. In addition, each manager and subordinate have met together to draw up a set of agreed-upon objectives in relation to the church's goals. Each member of the ministry team understands the role he plays and should be empowered to action.

A good many people have invested sizable amounts of time in the crafting and development of these plans. They serve as boundaries to protect the church against unwarranted busyness. They guide decision makers in the allocation of critical resources, and they ultimately provide church members with markers along the road to arriving at the destination of their mission and vision. These are valuable documents and should be viewed as such by all concerned.

Now is the time to communicate these goals and objectives. The last thing you want to do is file them away and forget about their existence until it's time for their annual review. Some churches print their annual goals in the church bulletin as a reminder to the congregation. Some prefer to illustrate them in a place of prominence such as a major hallway intersection or monthly newsletter.

Step Six. The periodic review. These documents should serve as the basis for monthly progress reports and quarterly reviews between the managers and their subordinates. Whenever they sit down for a performance review, whether it's monthly or quarterly, these goals and objectives should be one of the first items on their agenda for discussion.

During this periodic review meeting, progress or the lack thereof should be ascertained. Taking stock of where we are compared to where we need to be allows us to take corrective action before it reaches a crisis stage. Where additional resources are needed, they should be identified and allocated. Where objectives were unrealistic or circumstances were unforeseen, some allowance can be made to adjust them. It is rarely advisable to amend the goals, however, because they were agreed upon by the governing board or congregation and their support would be needed before such a major step could be taken to significantly modify an annual goal.

This feedback of interim objectives against the annual goals is a valuable time of reflection and team building. It should be an open and honest assessment of current progress as opposed to wishful thinking or optimistic prophecies about the future. Remember, this is an assessment of past performance, not a musing about future possibilities.

Having conducted several periodic reviews, we now move into phase three of our process. In this phase we conduct assessments to measure our degree of effectiveness in accomplishing our goals and objectives. It is not a time for blame casting or excuses. It is a time to take an honest look at our progress, celebrate our achievements, and look for ways we can become even more effective in the future.

Step Seven. Department assessment. Each department in the church (children, youth, singles, music, etc.) takes out their list of goals and objectives and prepares a written summary of their accomplishments. Since each of the objectives was stated in a measurable fashion, there should be little doubt about the ability of the department leader to determine their degree of accomplishment. This report should briefly state the percentage of achievement using facts, figures, and data to support their findings. Where possible, this document should include charts and graphs which visually indicate progress and success.

Remember, 100 percent achievement of a department's objectives is not realistic, particularly if the objectives had a degree of challenge written into them. If they are all achieved, then either you have a high-achieving member of the team or the objectives were not challenging enough when they were drafted. There should be no surprises since you both have met to conduct monthly or quarterly reviews along the way. This is simply a time to bring all the pieces together into an annual cumulative report.

The role of the manager is to celebrate the accomplishments of the subordinate and/or to assess why the individual did not achieve the objectives he or she was working toward. Was the failure a lack of resources? Did they not predict circumstances that came along after the development of the objectives? Was there a personal issue which prevented them from achieving a higher level of success? What are the chances that this reason will be a factor for next year's goal-setting process? Were there important and unforeseen personnel changes that impacted the success rate? These and many other questions need to be addressed in order to have a meaningful and accurate cumulative document.

Once these annual department reviews have been conducted, it is the role of the senior pastor or executive pastor to assimilate them into a cumulative assessment report. This is the essence of the final step in the ministry-by-objectives process.

Step Eight. Cumulative assessment. This is an important step in the process, for it represents the summation of a year's worth of work on the part of numerous people and committees. This document should be prepared by the senior pastor and presented to the church's governing board. Taking each goal, the report focuses a specific response to identify the degree of success that has been achieved and where progress is still lacking. Emphasis should be on the successful achievements of the team and not on blame casting for nonachievement. Ultimately, the buck stops on the senior pastor's desk, and this report should reflect his analysis of events and activities during his watch. The report is presented to the board for its review and discussion.

Many churches choose to provide an executive summary of the progress toward the goals to the congregation in a "state of the church" address which is mailed to each member of the congregation. Colorful charts and diagrams provide helpful insights and allow a good deal of content to be synthesized and presented.

Management by objectives in its application to the local church can be a helpful means of strategic planning. It provides for goal setting and multiple sources of input from the boards, staff, and congregation. People take ownership for their areas of responsibility and are able to be held accountable for progress on the goals and objectives which they agreed to. It facilitates dialogue and discussion between a manager and his or her subordinates. It contributes to team building and allows people to have a sense of community while going through the process together.

Implementing Ministry by Objectives

There are basically four ways to approach the implementation of ministry by objectives in the local church. The first is the top-down approach whereby the church board initiates the process and then moves to the senior pastor, who then works the process with his staff. The second approach is the bottom-up approach whereby a manager implements the process in his or her department. Other departments incorporate it into their ministries, and it works its way up the organizational structure until it reaches the board. The third approach is a departmental implementation whereby several departments (children's ministry, adult ministry, etc.) utilize this approach, and it spreads out to all the other departments in time. The final method is the supervisory level approach whereby the process takes place solely between the senior pastor and his direct reports (supervisors) but the rest of the staff do not participate. In essence, only the top layer of managers use the system.

Which method is best? Most churches and other nonprofits that have integrated the MBO approach into their management have preferred the top-down approach. This method secures the highest degree of buy-in and gets all of the major players on the same team. It also leads to the greatest impact being felt throughout the church as a whole. Since long-range strategic planning is generally initiated by the church board and senior pastor, it stands to reason that their participation is critical to the most lasting benefits. Ministry by objectives functions better with church goals used as the basis for departmental objectives. Generally speaking, top management approval is usually needed for any large-scale permanent change if it is to be effective and sustainable.[17]

The following timetable is a suggested approach to integrating ministry by objectives into the annual calendar of the church. This timetable presupposes an annual budget cycle that starts with January 1 of each year. You will need to amend this timetable if your church's fiscal calendar begins on July 1. The important point is that MBO must take place before the allocation of resources in the budget. It is futile to allocate resources first and then begin the goals-setting process since the finances should be used to fund the church's goals and objectives.

November. Discussions take place between the church board, pastoral staff, and the congregation about hopes and dreams for future goal setting. The church board and ministry staff narrows this list to a manageable size.

December. The annual church budget is developed, allocating the resources necessary to financially support the goals of the church.

January. Within a two-week period each of the supervisors and managers meet to write and prepare their department objectives. Ministry by objectives is launched.

February. Each supervisor and manager is actively pursuing the accomplishment of his department's goals and objectives. Meetings take place between the supervisor and the manager to measure results against objectives at the end of this month.

March. At the end of this month the *first periodic review* is conducted which measures results against target expectations. A written report is filed, with each supervisor measuring current performance.

April. Each supervisor and manager is actively pursuing the accomplishment of his department's goals and objectives. Meetings take place between the supervisor and the manager to measure results against objectives at the end of this month.

May. Each supervisor and manager is actively pursuing the accomplishment of his department's goals and objectives. Meetings take place between the supervisor and the manager to measure results against objectives at the end of this month.

June. At the end of this month the *second periodic review* is conducted which measures results against target expectations. A written report is filed, with each supervisor measuring current performance.

July. Each supervisor and manager is actively pursuing the accomplishment of his department's goals and objectives. Meetings take place between the supervisor and the manager to measure results against objectives at the end of this month.

August. Each supervisor and manager is actively pursuing the accomplishment of his department's goals and objectives. Meetings take place between the supervisor and the manager to measure results against objectives at the end of this month.

September. At the end of this month the *third periodic review* is conducted which measures results against target expectations. A written report is filed, with each supervisor measuring current performance.

October. Each supervisor and manager is actively pursuing the accomplishment of his department's goals and objectives. Meetings take place between the supervisor and the manager to measure results against objectives at the end of this month. Brainstorming regarding next year's goals begins and should take into consideration the success and failures of this current cycle.

November. Each supervisor and manager is actively pursuing the accomplishment of his department's goals and objectives. Meetings take place between the supervisor and the manager to measure results against objectives at the end of this month. Simultaneous to this process each ministry director is anticipating the development of his cumulative report which will be due next month.

December. Early in the month the cumulative reports from the various ministry directors is submitted to their supervisors. They meet together to discuss the progress that has been made on the goals and finalize discussion about next year's goals. Finishing touches are made to the budget once that is completed. The "state of the church" report is written and distributed to the church congregation by the senior pastor at the end of the month as a celebration of all that has been accomplished to advance the kingdom.

Creating the Climate for Acceptance

Before a church can implement management by objectives, it needs to prepare the way. It would be naive to think that a managerial change of this nature would not be met with some degree of skepticism and resistance. It's only human nature to resist change, especially one that will hold staff members more accountable for their ministry activities. Both internal and external environmental changes will need to be considered when creating the climate for acceptance. An overview of these would include the following elements:[18]

1. **A Favorable Environment for Change.** Consider whether or not the climate of the church is open to change. Has the church experienced too much change over too short a period of time? Has the church had to undergo any significant change recently? How open to change is

the congregation as a whole as opposed to just a few select groupings of it? Have there been any recent programs which have not been successful that may influence how this approach to management might be viewed?

2. **A Relatively Open and Nonthreatening Environment.** Many churches have an aversion to change—in fact, most do. It has to be sold to them, and in many cases it has to be seen as the last resort as opposed to an enhancement. If the general attitude of the church is one of openness to new ideas and ways of doing things, then this approach will be received more readily.

3. **Willingness of Top-Level Staff (Senior Pastor, Executive Pastor, Associate Pastor, etc.) to Share Authority.** There are few secrets when operating under a ministry-by-objectives management system. Everyone knows the church's overall goals. Most staff are aware of the part they play, who gets what resources and why, as well as who is pulling their weight and who isn't. It becomes obvious soon after the first periodic review. Top-level managers must be willing to "reveal their cards" and have a willingness toward sharing both responsibility and authority with other members of the church staff. For some, it will require a shift in how they operate. They will need to approach other staff members as team players as opposed to pawns in the game of ministry.

4. **The Quality of Church Staff.** Once the senior staff have taken hold of the system, they will need to delegate the development of setting objectives to their department ministry directors. However, if those receiving this assignment are not sufficiently trained for the job, the entire system is threatened. Each link in the chain is critical to its overall success.

5. **Willingness of Ministry Directors to Accept Objective Measures of Their Ministry.** Some prefer the obscurity and vagueness of measuring their ministry. They figure if it can't be measured then they can't be held accountable. There must be a willingness on their part to accept objective measures as a basis of determining success. Some trust building may be necessary first between the senior pastor or executive pastor and subordinate managers.

6. **A Willingness to Comply with Procedural Requirements.** Most early entry members of the pastoral team have a difficult time complying with expectations on their time. Adhering to a budget, maintaining office hours, filing reports on time, attending committees meetings, and a host of other expectations do not come easily. These are things that are learned in time. Most people entering the ministry are oblivious about the myriad of expectations that are placed on them by members of the congregation and supervisory staff. However, it is a fact

of life and a reasonable request given our mandate for stewardship. Staff members who have a natural aversion to writing and submitting reports in a timely manner will need some extra guidance.

7. **An Environment That Is Predictable Enough to Make Planning Plausible.** Planning is more realistic at differing seasons in the life of the church. Soon after the new senior pastor arrives, people are anxious to voice new dreams and focus their energies on what the future may bring. However, if the church is currently going through a major crisis, or the senior pastor is laissez-faire in his management style or perhaps a couple of years from retirement, the church may find itself in a holding pattern in terms of planning for the future. In a setting like this, it is better to wait until after the leadership transition or crisis has been settled before initiating a ministry-by-objectives approach.

Critical Points to Consider

1. **Relate Goals to Mission and Vision.** This is not a question of what comes first, the chicken or the egg. There should be no doubt that the mission and vision of the church comes first and that any subsequent goals and objectives flow out of these statements. It is not uncommon for a church to receive what appears to be a "once-in-a-lifetime opportunity" from a wealthy developer or civic leader. But before accepting such an invitation be sure that it matches the mission and vision of the church. Countless churches, educational institutions, missions, and other religious nonprofit organizations began with a passion for Christ only to be taken off course by accepting great opportunities that were not related to their original mission or vision.

2. **Make the Objectives Specific and Measurable.** Remember that at the end of the process the department and cumulative reports depend on accurate assessment information. If you can't measure it, you will have a difficult time determining its degree of achievement. If a staff member's fate hinges on the success of a program and its effectiveness can't be measured, the ensuing personnel performance review will be equally difficult and vague.

We realize not all activities that take place in the local church can be measured and quantified. An overemphasis on number counting leads to a perilous conclusion. Even the Pharisees boasted of their measurable performance, but Jesus rebuked them for the condition of their hearts. One needs to find a balance between measuring what can be measured (attendance, baptisms, decisions for Christ, etc.) and what cannot (spiritual formation, recovery from addictions, restored relationships, etc.). Some things are best left to God for final assessment. What we are striving for is a more concerted effort at accountability and stewardship without going overboard on quantifiable verification.

Ministry by Objectives

STEP	ACTIVITY	WHO:		
1	Review and Revise the Church Mission and Vision Statements	Board & Sr. Pastor	PREPARATORY PHASE	
2	Develop and Prioritize Organizational Goals	Board & Sr. Pastor		
3	Review and Revise the Organizational Structure, Job Descriptions and Reporting Relationships	Sr. Pastor & Staff		
4	Negotiate Objectives Between Managers and Subordinate Staff Members	Manager & Subordinate	IMPLEMENTATION PHASE	
5	Communicate the Plan: Commit to It, Post It, and Fund It	Pastoral Staff		
6	Conduct Periodic Reviews	Manager & Subordinate		
7	Departmental Assessments	Manager & Subordinate	ASSESSMENT PHASE	
8	Conduct Cumulative Reviews and Write "State of the Church" Report	Board & Sr. Pastor		

3. Get Ownership from as Broad a Base as Possible. Ministry by objectives must be a team effort. It cannot be mandated from the top down of an organization without some degree of resentment and stonewalling. The church board, senior pastor, and critical lay leaders need to buy into the program and express their commitment to the process. Without these key players on board, it is still possible to implement MBO in just one ministry department, but it limits its ability to provide a benefit to the entire congregation.

4. **Communicate the Goals/Objectives and Keep Them Before the Congregation Throughout the Year.** Most planning breaks down after the plans are put in writing. Once the work is done and the plan is put in print, people go back to their homes and assume it will run on autopilot. The plans do not accomplish themselves. The goal setting and objective development steps are parts of the preparation phase. The real work comes after that happens. Advertise the plans, review them, and post them in prominent locations so people don't forget them. If they are shelved until the cumulative review, chances are very good that little will have been accomplished other than resentment for how much time was spent developing goals and objectives which were never achieved.

5. **Ministry by Objectives Is a Journey, Not a Destination.** Keep a long-term perspective on the process. It's true that many churches do this goal setting on an annual basis, but few accomplish everything they set their mind to. What doesn't get accomplished this year can be added to the list for next year. Some things that seemed so critical to the success of the mission back in January may not be as important in June, and that's OK. Remember, you own the plans; they don't own you. Plans and goals can be rewritten and revised. They are guidelines for future behavior and serve as means to ends, not ends in themselves. The end is always the same—moving people forward into Christlike character development (Eph. 4:15–16).

Benefits of Using Ministry by Objectives in the Local Church

Many churches have recorded an array of benefits from operating on a ministry-by-objectives approach to ministry management. A summary of these benefits includes the following.

1. It provides a systematic approach to the supervision and oversight of the church staff. MBO incorporates clearly established standards of performance measurement and reporting relationships which are agreed to by everyone involved. It employs a reporting mechanism which has a long history of success in the business world, and its terminology and process steps have enjoyed many years of successful implementation. This systematic approach to ministry management facilitates effective stewardship of resources.

2. Ministry by objectives provides guidance for the dilemma of trying to determine a supervisor's span of control. The span of control is

defined as the number of people who can effectively be managed by one individual. Some people can manage more than others for a variety of reasons, making the ability to standardize the number illusive. By incorporating MBO, the church can determine the number of reports any one manager can sustain by simply calculating how many subordinates a manager can meet with to prepare objectives and conduct periodic reviews.

3. Ministry by objectives gives clear evidence about where limited resources need to be directed. No longer are resources handed out on the basis of popularity, politics, and/or favoritism. The resources should be distributed on the basis of who needs what in order to accomplish the goals and objectives within their area(s) of responsibility. Clearly one cannot expect a staff member to accept a major area of responsibility without a corresponding degree of financial and material resources. That would be setting the staff member up for failure.

4. Another major benefit of using ministry by objectives relates to the managerial principle of parity. This principle states that a worker who is given a responsibility must also be given a commensurate degree of authority in order to fulfill that responsibility. Responsibility without authority is unacceptable and a clear violation of this principle. Staff members who have negotiated a set of objectives should be able to assume that they also have a corresponding degree of authority in order to achieve the objectives within their area of responsibility. This does not absolve staff members from accountability, but it should release them from constantly having to ask for permission to do things which have already been agreed to and put in writing.

5. Ministry by objectives benefits the church by revealing through a pattern of behavior (the best standard of proof) which staff members consistently accomplish their objectives and which ones do not. It takes much of the guesswork out of performance appraisal and reward systems since the rewards go to those who make the most significant progress toward the accomplishment of the church's mission and vision on a regular basis. "In this new approach, which encourages self-appraisal and self-development, the emphasis is where it ought to be: on performance rather than on personality. The active involvement of subordinates in the appraisal process leads to commitment and creates an environment for motivation."[19]

6. Ministry by objectives provides the staff member with performance appraisal information prior to the beginning of each ministry year. This takes the guesswork out of what will be required of them at the end of the year when it is time to review and assess each member's job-related performance. MBO gives each staff member a degree of security because the standards of performance measurement are already clearly

established and in writing. There are no surprises, and staff members can operate during the year with a level of confidence and trust in the appraisal system.

Dangers of Using Ministry by Objectives in the Local Church

This section could perhaps be labeled the dangers of the misuse of MBO, since it's really the misuse of the steps and principles that gets people into trouble.

1. Too much emphasis on measurable performance leads to a lack of risk taking and faith. Sometimes in ministry we have to be willing to live and lead by faith—by what we cannot see and therefore cannot measure. We are told that those who please God with their lives are people who are willing to act on the basis of what is not always seen (Heb. 11:6). That does not give staff members permission to act with reckless abandon, but living and leading by faith must be taken into consideration. It comes with the job. How can we expect members of our congregation to live by faith if we are not able to demonstrate it ourselves?

2. Another danger in using MBO is an overemphasis on reporting and meetings. Some organizations that have incorporated an MBO approach to ministry management require a weekly written report on progress toward the goals and objectives in their areas of control. This excessive volume of reporting leads to frustration, pessimism, and ultimately a sense of fatalism. Reports should never take the place of meeting face-to-face. The endless amount of paperwork that comes across the supervisor's desk is counterproductive to effective relationship and team building. The advent of e-mails has only served to increase the volume of information that comes at us from every angle. Reports for reporting's sake should be discouraged. Make them time- and cost-effective or their danger will outweigh their benefit. Weekly report writing is an overemphasis on measurement and accountability.

3. A third danger is in not providing the staff with the education and training they need in order to write measurable objectives. A well-written ministry objective looks simple to write until you take the time to write one yourself. The should provide a direct link to the church's goal and indicate the person, timetable, and criteria for determining successful achievement.

4. A final danger of MBO is a failure to allow the unexpected to influence legitimate opportunities. There is a tremendous value in putting our plans in writing. However, there are times (though rare) when these plans couldn't take into consideration all the possible contingencies along the way. People die, get married, accept job offers, have

babies, etc., and each of these significant life events alters our life direction. In addition, churches have similar milestones. Pastors have moral and ethical failures, they take opportunities elsewhere, finances aren't always as predictable as we prefer, and natural catastrophes such as fires, floods, and storms can alter the course of the church with little warning.

During these milestone events, and many others which could have been added to the list, we must not get so set in our ways and so locked into our goals that we prevent God from working in the life of the church. Goals may need to be rewritten, eliminated, or perhaps the time line needs to be extended. MBO should not produce a mind-set that locks all planning into fixed concrete. The purpose of planning is to guide and shape direction, not dictate it beyond reason.

Conclusion

Ministry by objectives is a planning system that encourages churches to coordinate their activities and resources. Busyness is no guarantee of progress, so some examination needs to occur on a regular basis to be sure that the activities are purposeful and contribute to the church's reason for being. The Scriptures teach us a great deal about stewardship of both human and material resources. God has gifted each of us, and he will one day hold us accountable for the use of our gifts. Likewise, God has given his church material resources for which its leaders must also give an account. Ministry by objectives is one method of coordinating this stewardship activity.

If there is any one evidence of God's hand upon an organization, it can be summarized by the word *change*. Change is a natural part of the growth cycle. When God is at work in the lives of his people, they are in a constant state of change and reformation. The old nature is ebbing away, and the new nature is emerging. With this change can come resistance. People, like churches, can get set in their comfort and security. They resist change because they are unsure of its ultimate destination. Ministry by objectives takes some of the fear out of the transformation process by making the change more intentional and controlled. In essence, you're saying to those around you, "Yes, our church will change as it responds to the changing community around us, but through MBO we get to set the rate of change and budget the cost we are willing to pay." Maybe not all change is desirable or avoidable, but MBO helps put some reasonable methods of control on it.

The benefits of using ministry by objectives far outweigh its dangers. A plan is a form of control, and some people prefer to live life and lead ministry with as few controls as possible. But that is certainly not the example given to us by Christ and the leaders of the early church.

Controls evidence maturity and intentionality. If the church is going to make a lasting impact on the world, it must recognize the value of planning and goal setting, not as a means of control but as a means of gaining freedom—freedom from random busyness and from responding to each new wave of popular methods that come along. Ministry by objectives gives church leaders freedom to set their own course and become intentional about achieving it.

PART 3

ORGANIZING

The act of bringing order out of chaos is often referred to as the managerial function of organization. Although it is clearly more than that, such a simple definition is not far off the mark, since organizing is concerned with proper order (authority, responsibility, and structure) and flow (communication, material resources, and personnel). Those who are skilled in this function are not intimidated by confusion. In fact, they revel in it because turmoil allows them to find the underlying meaning and purpose of institutional activity.

A more academic definition of organization is "a formalized intentional structure of roles or positions."[1] Some have argued for the merging of planning and organizing into the same category since both are concerned with the same fundamental activities. As one management expert put it, "Organizing is really planning applied to a department or function."[2] Those who hold to such a view are clearly mistaken because the activities associated with the function of organizing are qualitatively different from those of planning.

Organizing begins with the mission and vision of the organization which were articulated during the planning phase. It also takes into consideration the goals and objectives of the institution, since these provide direction and clarification. Organizing picks up where planning leaves off by answering the questions of *who* and *how* the organization will be managed. At some point a structural pattern needs to emerge, and clarifications regarding roles, responsibilities, authority relationships, qualifications, and position descriptions need to be established. Organizing naturally moves the ministry forward toward the accomplishment of its mission, vision, goals, and objectives that were developed during the planning function.

The starting point of bringing order out of chaos is to determine the best organizational structure around which the ministry will function best. Doing so is not always an easy task since no one organizational structure will fit every ministry context. For example, a church is structured differently from a camp or school. Likewise, a parachurch ministry like Youth For Christ or Young Life will be structured differently from an inner-city preschool for underprivileged children. Each needs to take into consideration its unique purpose as a ministry. Even in the realm of church ministry, there is no common agreement on how best to structure itself. Some denominations prefer to establish a hierarchical structure with bishops and archbishops while others prefer a more decentralized approach with congregational control. Such discussion is the focus of chapter 9, which seeks to help the reader understand all that goes into establishing the best organizational structure for the particular ministry involved. Since most of the readers using this book will be applying it to the context of the local church, a good deal of emphasis of this chapter centers around a local church application.

Chapter 10 is designed to help the reader understand how to develop position descriptions, also known as job descriptions, for those serving in Christian ministries. The church has long been guilty of neglecting this important administrative activity, and poor morale and disenfranchised members have been the result. Job descriptions for paid staff from those written for a volunteer. Each is essential to successful ministry operation, but they require different emphases.

Probably no complaint is as common among ministry leaders as the need to attend and coordinate meetings. Done without forethought, meetings can rob you of valuable time which could be better spent in other ministry-related activities. Since we are called to coordinate our efforts toward the goal of effective ministry service, conducting meetings with our staff, both paid and volunteer, is a necessary requirement. If we cannot avoid meetings, then it is incumbent upon us to make them worth the time spent planning and conducting them. How to conduct an effective meeting isn't rocket science. With the right elements included in the agenda, and a few guidelines for keeping things moving, the novice ministry leader can view meetings as part of ministry effectiveness rather than as an obstacle to it. Such is the thrust of chapter 11.

Someone once said that there are only two sure things in life: death and taxes. For those who operate in the realm of ministry, a third sure thing is change. The apostle Paul used the metaphor of the human body to describe the church. As the human body is constantly changing in response to its environment and health, so the church should also be in constant motion. Some of this change is positive and confirmation of spiritual health. Some of it, unfortunately, is evidence of the many destructive forces at work either inside the body or from a host of external factors. Chapter 12 discusses the positive and negative effects of change on the ministry organization with a view to helping the ministry leader understand how to facilitate change in a constructive manner.

Being a change agent in a Christian ministry is not for the faint of heart. Those who "move the cheese" in an organization had better have a clear strategy in mind and be prepared for misunderstanding and opposition. Yet as painful as institutional change can be, it is also the means by which long-term growth and development occur. Remaining static and stagnant in ministry leads to poor morale and purposeless activity. Simply stated, there can be no growth without change!

The final chapter in this unit discusses the issue of decision making within the context of the ministry organization. There are ways to make decisions that are constructive and lead to *esprit de corps*. There are also ways that result in misunderstanding and loss of trust. It can take years to build trust within a ministry team, yet it can be lost in one single act of decision making. It is the intention of the author to help the reader understand the basic factors associated with healthy decision making in a Christian ministry.

This unit is designed to equip the reader with the basic skills associated with the managerial function of organizing. Activities such as establishing structures, preparing effective job descriptions, learning how to conduct effective meetings with staff, guiding one's team through the minefield of institutional change, and making informed decisions are the focus of this important unit.

Chapter 9

Organizational Structures

YOU WILL RECALL from our discussions in chapter 1 that God is the author of order. Nothing happens in nature without some purpose or design. The manner in which the universe is held together reveals the character of God's incredible design. Likewise, Scripture clearly teaches that God intends for his people to be governed within a system of order and consistent coordination. This was seen by the way God organized the tribes of Israel and gave the priestly tribe of Levi specific responsibilities for moving and maintaining the tabernacle. In the New Testament, we saw abundant evidence of God's prescribed order in his selection of deacons and elders for leadership roles within the church. The giving of spiritual gifts for specific areas of service (evangelism, teaching, counseling, etc.) reveals God's desire for organization in ministry (Eph. 4:11–16; Rom. 12; 1 Cor. 14:26–39).

In essence, God desires to have ministry governed within prescribed patterns which contribute to an orderly assignment of duties, roles, and responsibilities. This is not to say, however, that all churches are to be identical in their organizational structure any more than all animals are identical in their design. Although God is the author of order, he is also the author of creative diversity.[1]

Designing organizational structures for church ministry may reflect this creative diversity as well. I do not believe that there is any one organizational structure that will work for all churches. There are simply too many variances which are reflected in the theology, geography, ethnography, and demographic distinctives of each local church. Even a cursory look at churches in the Book of Acts reveals differences among them. The church in Antioch did not replicate the structure of the Jerusalem church. The church in Ephesus did not pattern themselves after the church in Phillipi. The church in Corinth certainly had their own way of doing things which was unique to their fellowship! What is important about a church's structure is not whether it looks like another

158

church down the road, but whether the structure helps to facilitate ministry in their local community.

It may be important from the beginning of our discussion to draw a distinction between order and organization. From its earliest days the church has had to consider the question of order. It is still a vital issue of concern for the church today as well. Order is not the same as organization. Order is seen as an accepted plan, the agreed-upon guidelines that keep any group from chaos and set it free for growth. Order is accepted purpose, plus commonly accepted means toward recognized ends. Order both assigns and limits responsibility. It also defines and limits authority. Organization is the way that a particular group keeps its procedures orderly, for example, by selecting a chairperson, secretary, treasurer, etc.[2] The two are not the same, but both are needed if an organization is to function smoothly and effectively.

Since most organizations are too complex to be conveyed verbally, they are generally described in a schematic diagram called an organizational chart. This chart is a diagram of the various functions, divisions, departments, and/or positions which are to be found in the organization and how they relate to one another. Each unit is depicted as a box and is connected to other boxes through horizontal and vertical lines. These lines characterize authority relationships and communication between units.[3] Be careful, however, not to read into these charts more than is necessary. For example, just because an individual may not have a department (box on the chart) that is close to the top level (usually the church board or senior pastor) does not mean that it is an unimportant department. The church custodian may be several levels down on the chart, but without his/her effective service, visitors may never return to a church that has an unsafe or dirty nursery no matter how much they enjoyed the sermon. Every part of the organization is important and serves an essential purpose regardless of its location on a chart.

Formal and Informal Organizational Structure

Before we begin to survey the various organization charts that are common to churches, it might be helpful to take a moment and comment on the difference between a formal organizational structure and an informal structure. Many writers comment on formal and informal organizational structure because both are common in an organization, though generally speaking the formal structure is what you come to experience during your initial orientation. However, it won't be long before you soon discover that things don't always operate the way the chart says they do. Knowing this difference and why can save novice ministry leaders a great deal of frustration and disappointment.

Formal Structure

The formal organizational structure refers to the prescribed pattern or relationships which exist in order to accomplish the goals and objectives of the organization. These relationships describe authority and communication patterns. They let everyone know who is in charge of what resources and the degree of authority an individual has in order to do his or her job. This is not to say that there is no flexibility in the relationships described on the chart. However, in a formal description of organizational structure, patterns are usually set and have a limited degree of flexibility associated with them. To answer the question, "Who is in charge of the sound system in the auditorium?" you would look on the organizational chart and discover that the person in charge is the worship pastor.

Informal Structure

The problem that many ministry leaders face when they begin serving at a new church is discovering the discrepancies between what the chart says and the way things really work. For example, you might discover that the worship pastor is in charge of the sound system in the auditorium because he or she has authority over the worship service on the organizational chart. However, this does not always mean that the worship pastor actually has a key to the sound cabinet! Since politics can be a very strong force in churches, it may be more realistic to discover that the real person in charge of the sound system is a retired gentleman who designed and built the sound cabinet and treats it like his personal property. In essence, that is the difference between formal and informal organizational structure.

The informal structure of an organization describes who is in charge and how communication flows in the real world of ministry, not necessarily the way it's supposed to happen. An analysis of a church's informal organizational structure may reveal that the person who has the most power at the church is not the senior pastor but his administrative assistant because she controls who gets in to see the senior pastor, for how long, and what items get put on (or deleted from) the board's agenda. Knowing the difference between formal structure and informal structure can make a big difference in the early months of transitioning to a new job.

Common Organizational Structures

There are almost as many different ways to structure a church and its various ministries as there are churches themselves. Some denominations have their own preference for how churches in their fellowship ought to be structured. Other denominations allow churches within their fellowship to have autonomy and create their own structure. For some, tradition is strong and the way church ministries have been organized will continue for decades to come. There are obvious advantages and disadvantages to each approach. What follows is a brief overview of a few common ways that churches structure themselves. This chapter will discuss both the upper levels of church structure (denomination, congregation, board, and senior pastor) and its mid-range levels (children, youth, adults, etc.) since the educational ministries of a church do not operate within a vacuum but within the greater context of a church's overall organizational structure.

In addition, each structure will be critiqued in terms of its advantages and disadvantages. Contrary to what some conference speakers would have you believe, no one pattern is ideal for all churches. In fact, what works well in one location may be a disaster for a similar church in a different location.

Ecumenical Model

This approach to structuring a church has its origins in the early history of the church. Denominations such as the Catholics, Lutherans, Methodists, Episcopalians, etc. have an ecumenical approach to structuring their churches. "In its original form, it was a monarchial concentration of power in one bishop over a local church. Later it developed into the position of diocesan bishop who presided over a territory of a local church, called a diocese. It's based on the doctrine of apostolic succession (Catholic) or historical succession (Episcopalian)."[4]

Bishops are characteristic of Catholic, Orthodox, and also Episcopalian churches, but not necessarily descriptive of all Methodist or Lutheran bodies. That's part of what makes a "one style fits all" description so difficult in so short a chapter as this. Many Lutheran churches in North America may combine regional synods (see the next category) with a congregational structure. This allows them a greater degree of autonomy from denominational influence. And Methodists, at least those in the United Methodist Church, may have bishops, or superintendents, but this is not seen as a priestly office, as it may be in some other denominations found within this category.

Advantages of the ecumenical model are:

1. This approach allows for a greater degree of stability since change is seen within the context of a long historical perspective. In essence, the church does not easily fall prey to sudden shifts in leadership, doctrine, or methodology, etc.

2. There is a broad base of denominational support since the diocese or denominational body can provide resources in times of temporary need.

3. The bishop can place a ministry leader (pastor, rector, priest, etc.) in a church who can preach and lead according to the need of the community and local body without fear of being dismissed by the local congregation.

4. The ministry leader (pastor, rector, priest, etc.) is not likely to show partiality toward select individuals in the church since the diocese or bishops holds the ministry leader accountable, not the local church congregation.

Disadvantages of the ecumenical model are:

1. This approach is slow to change since new programs to meet changing community needs may not reflect the priorities of those in denominational leadership.

2. Those in denominational leadership make many of the critical decisions for the local congregation even though they may be far removed geographically or ethnically.

3. Due to large denominational governance structure, placing clergy in local churches can become highly political rather than based on local needs.

4. Many large denominations, in an effort to appease large sections of special interests, are forced to compromise their doctrinal distinctives. The result is a slow erosion toward biblical relativism.

Republican Model

This approach to church structure is demonstrated in the Presbyterian form of church organization. The Presbyterian denomination groups its churches (General Assembly) into what are called synods. A synod is a collection of churches within a specific geographical location (e.g., Southwest Synod). Each synod further divides itself into presbyteries. A presbytery is a local association of churches within a smaller geographical location (e.g., San Diego County). Within each presbytery are a number of churches. Obviously the number of churches within a presbytery will vary depending on the size of the district. For example, a rural presbytery may have fewer churches than a suburban presbytery, even though they may have a larger geographical area (see Figure 9.1).

Figure 9.1: Republican Model of Church Governance

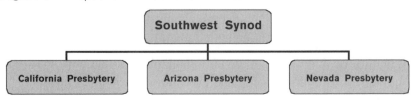

A Presbyterian church will have pastors, a board of elders, and a board of deacons. The latter boards may have both men and women in representation. The board of elders, sometimes referred to as "ruling elders," are laymen who are elected by the congregation. The "teaching elders" are usually ministers who preside over the presbytery.[5] The board of elders and the pastor work together to administrate the church. Together they form what is called the session. This assembly is comprised of the pastor, copastors, the board of elders, and a government of elected representatives from the congregation. Leaders from groups within the church, such as the men's group, women's group, worship committee, etc., will be the elected representatives of the session.

The senior pastor is the moderator of the session. There is also a clerk of the session, who, next to the pastor, holds the position of greatest responsibility. This church leader acts as the administrative officer of the church and the chairperson of the executive committee of the session.

In this form of church structure, the session is central. The pastor's position as moderator of the session provides one of the greatest opportunities for prophetic leadership. Pastors who have the session on their side—not by Machiavellian manipulation, but by genuine sharing of leadership through common study, candid discussion, and far-sighted policy making—are likely to enjoy a long season of fruitful church ministry.[6] For those who did not grow up in a Presbyterian church, this approach to organizational structure may seem foreign, so it may be helpful to illustrate this model with an organizational chart. It will not include all of the ministry programs commonly available at a Presbyterian church, but it will serve to illustrate the general consensus about how the educational ministries of the church are coordinated. An illustration of the structure of a local Presbyterian church with its associated ministries is shown in Figure 9.2.

Advantages of the republican model of church governance are:

1. This approach to church structure allows for a consistent philosophy to be directed through the church of a denomination. Church members who relocate can assume a similar approach to church ministry by remaining in the denomination.

2. In Presbyterian polity, pastors (teaching elders) are called by local congregations. Their call is subsequently confirmed by the presbytery. In this way there is shared governance between the church and the denomination based on mutual communication.

3. Denominational distinctives and publishing materials can be shared between churches, thereby keeping costs lower.

4. Denominational representatives can speak with some degree of certainty for their entire denomination. In matters of morality, social

Figure 9.2
Presbyterian Church
Organizational Structure

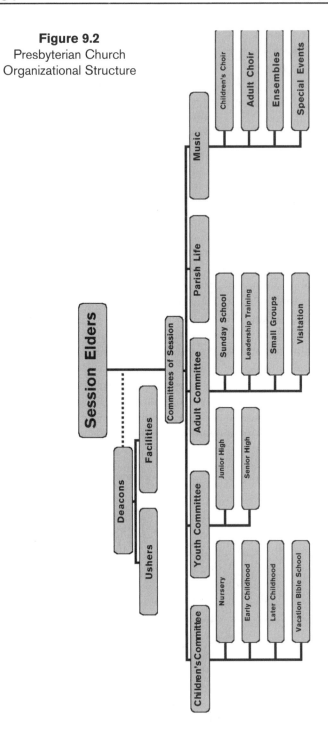

injustice, politics, etc., the denomination has a stronger voice than an individual church.

Disadvantages of the republican model are:

1. When the geographical distance for a presbytery is quite large, it can be difficult for the denominational representative to have an accurate knowledge of the needs of each church. Effective leadership requires the shepherd to be "in touch" with his people.

2. Pastors of a denomination can sometimes care more about pleasing denominational representatives than the members of their congregation. This is a danger found in any denominational setting.

3. Confirmation of a pastor to a particular local church can sometimes become political, particularly among denominational leadership.

4. Denominations, by their very nature, can become entangled in bureaucracy, making change very slow, if not impossible. This makes staying up to date on current trends very difficult.

Corporate Model

Sometimes referred to as the *board control model,* this corporate model is designed after the business approach to decision making. These boards use nomenclature and procedural operations associated with corporate settings. In the corporate model, members of the church board serve in the same way as members of a corporate board. They hire and fire the CEO (senior pastor) and decide the long- and short-range direction of the church. They set goals which the church staff is hired to execute and serve as policy makers for the church. In matters of financial, legal, or ethical decisions, the board decides and then communicates its decisions to the church staff and congregation. An example of this approach to church organizational structure in the upper level of management is depicted in Figure 9.3. Further application is demonstrated in Figure 9.4.

One problem that has arisen with this approach to church organizational structure warrants some discussion. If the pastor is controlled by the church board (by virtue of being hired and fired by them), there may come times when he does not feel the freedom to speak his mind about difficult matters of church discipline (especially if it involves a board member) for fear of losing his job. One denomination surveyed their pastors who left the ministry and discovered that 60 percent of them said unsatisfactory relationships with church board members was the reason. It was the opinion of one denominational leader that the authoritarian role assumed by elders to hire and fire ministers was the root problem.[7]

Advantages of the corporate model are:

1. It allows for quick decision making during times of crises and church conflict.

Figure 9.3: Corporate Model of Church Organizational Structure

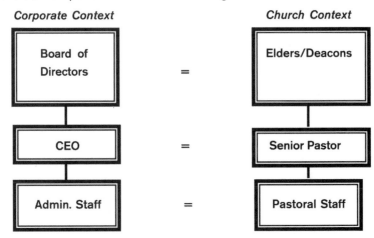

Figure 9.4

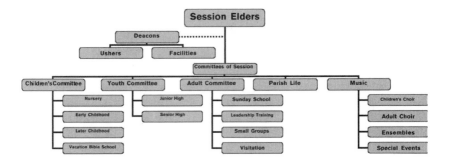

2. One body speaks for the entire congregation. In essence, there are fewer occasions for a breakdown in communication.

3. Authority and responsibility are clearly centralized in the board. There is parity between these two important management functions.

4. A senior pastor can be held accountable for matters of professional competency. In the event that termination is needed, this board can make the decision with a minimum amount of congregational influence.

Disadvantages of the corporate model are:

1. Although this form of governance works well in the business setting, it has little biblical support. In the Book of Acts the deacons were not elected to tell the apostles how to conduct their ministries.

2. The board can become entrenched with political power which determines the direction of the church apart from spiritual input.

3. This approach to church leadership does not allow for shared governance between the board and the pastoral staff.

4. The chairperson of the board controls the church and the members of the church staff in spite of the possibility that he or she may possess little, if any, formal theological training.

Entrepreneurial Model

In this model of church leadership, the pastor provides strong entrepreneurial leadership in the church. This approach is often seen in a new church plant where the founding pastor needs a strong presence to get things formed and functional during the early days of the ministry. As chief executive, he sets policy and procedures which the church board and pastoral staff implement. An entrepreneurial pastor is free to configure his own church staff team much like a president configures his cabinet. Cabinet members of a president would be analogous to the pastoral staff of a church. When existing churches operate using this approach, they allow the senior pastor, once selected, to fire all the staff which are currently serving at the church and replace them with his own team. Because it is stated in the church constitution that the pastor has such executive powers, any staff member who accepts a call to join this church staff team should be aware that his term of service may end when the pastor leaves. An example of this form of church model is depicted in Figure 9.5.

Figure 9.5
Entrepreneurial
Model of Church
Organizational
Structure

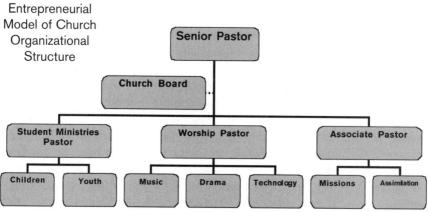

Advantages of the entrepreneurial model are:

1. Church board members have very little power or authority. Therefore, they do not need a great deal of training and leadership.

2. Churches that are very large and which have entrepreneurial pastors with a great deal of personal charisma can operate with this form of governance because the senior pastor "rules the roost."

3. Since the entrepreneurial pastor has such strong control over the church, one person can respond to demographic trends and changes with little effort. The church responds quickly to change.

4. The entrepreneurial pastor is able to build a team of staff around him that supports his own personal philosophy of ministry. Little time is wasted trying to convince staff members to join him in how things should be done.

Disadvantages of the entrepreneurial model are:

1. This approach to ministry is clearly not the servant-leader approach depicted by Jesus in the New Testament.

2. All the members of the church staff may be forced to resign when the entrepreneurial senior pastor leaves, thereby creating chaos and loss of momentum in ministry objectives.

3. There is very little accountability of the senior pastor in the entrepreneurial model. Since the board is seen as a "rubber stamp," it may not have the courage to confront the senior pastor during a crisis.

4. Entrepreneurial leadership demands a great deal of personal charisma from the senior pastor. Senior pastors with this personality quality are difficult to find. Continuity of leadership is broken when the senior pastor leaves.

Congregational Structure

This model views the congregation as the power base for the church. The congregational form of organizational structure has both Puritan and Baptist roots dating back to the colonists who separated themselves from the Church of England and sailed to America, where they could practice their own form of church structure without denominational control. In this organizational structure, the congregation selects the senior pastor, members of the pastoral staff team, and each board member. Decisions are made by vote in church business meetings. At these meetings, the church moderator, who usually serves as the chairman of the church board, directs the proceedings.

In this approach to church organizational structure, the board of elders/deacons take care of the administrative activities of the church such as budgeting, legal contracts, hiring and firing staff, maintenance of buildings and grounds, church equipment, etc. The pastoral staff takes care of the spiritual matters such as preaching, teaching, evangelism, counseling, etc. Staff members (who are usually not trained in administrative management) do not get sidetracked in their ministries by handling business matters. A diagram of this approach to church structure is seen in Figure 9.6.

Figure 9.6
Congregational
Organizational
Structure

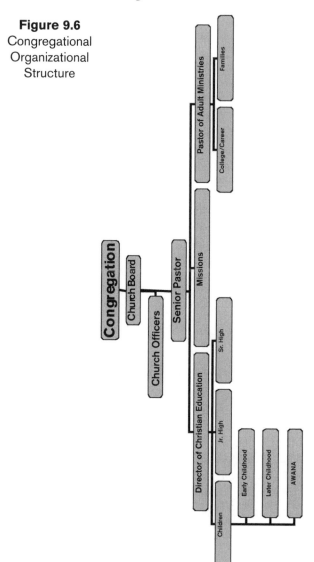

Advantages of the congregational approach are:

1. Each congregation can control its own destiny. It can select its own spiritual leaders and decide how long their term should last.

2. Free from denominational constraints, the church is able to select church curriculum which best meets its individual needs.

3. The congregation is given the authority to discipline its own members. It can follow the biblical patterns of church discipline without having to comply with any denominational procedures which may slow the process.

4. Each congregation has the ability to direct the affairs of the ministry in such a way as to reflect local resources, cultural patterns, and demographic trends.

Disadvantages of the congregational model are:

1. This approach assumes that administrative functions and spiritual matters are separate. Such a distinction is clearly not biblical. The effects of one greatly influences the plans of the other.

2. Sometimes a democratic vote in the congregation does not reflect the mind of God. The Spirit does not always abide by majority decisions of the congregation.

3. Some churches, reflecting a desire to support majority opinion, opt for consensus decision making in the church. Where this occurs, an entire congregation can depend on one person's vote. If that person is not being led by the Spirit of God, then the whole body suffers. Consensus voting becomes minority rule.

4. This approach to church structure assumes that the congregation is spiritually mature enough to make important decisions. It can negate the influence of the senior pastor and pastoral staff to direct the spiritual matters of the church.

Departmentalization

For many years there has been very little creativity about the manner in which departments were formed within the educational ministries of the church. The traditional approach involved standard age groups (children, youth, adults, etc.). These three divisions accommodated each individual, and it was up to each church to decide what programs would be included in each division. For example, with the children's division there would be individual departments such as cradle roll (birth to 1), toddlers (ages 2–3), preschoolers (ages 4–5), primary grades (K–3), and junior grades (4–6). The youth division would be subdivided into two departments (junior high and senior high). The adult division followed age categories of early adult (ages 21–35), middle adult (ages 36–50), and senior adults (ages 50+). Little, if any, distinction was made regarding marital status of adults. Never married, divorced, separated, widowed, and married adults were all grouped together. Although this may have worked in many North American churches for the past two hundred years, its appeal has long since been lost. Many modern churches have rejected this approach for more contemporary and culturally relevant models.

It has become rare to find churches with a full-time paid minister or director of Christian education who oversees the educational ministries of the church. It is far more common today to have specialized areas of ministry within the church with volunteer or professional staff members over each area. The variety of these educational ministries has virtually exploded over recent years. For example, where once a church may have had a general music program departmentalized according to children and adults, today there may be a creative arts department which coordinates numerous configurations of worship arts (e.g., multiple children's performance groups, youth worship teams, worship bands, adult ensembles, multiple choirs, performance teams, dance, drama, etc.).

Some churches have begun crossing generational lines in an effort to minimize the loss which takes place between these three major divisions. Many churches struggle with losing people as they transition between divisions. Children drop out after they graduate from the sixth grade and never transition well into the youth ministry programs of the church. Likewise, many churches have noticed that they lose young adults once they leave the youth program. Somewhere along the way they fail to transition into the adult ministry division until after they get married and have children. In an effort to close these gaps, a new paradigm of ministry called New Generation Ministries has emerged which has as its goal a coordinated ministry program between the ages of birth and twenty-one.

This creative approach to departmentalization seeks to coordinate all ministry resources around a coordinated theme. The pastor of New Generation Ministries will hire a staff (for children, junior high, senior high, and college) with an attitude of team participation. For example, the junior high worship leader may also lead a children's ministry worship team during a midweek program. The junior high pastor may speak at the children's winter camp, or the senior high pastor may conduct a special parenting series for those with new babies. It requires a consistent philosophy of ministry between each of the three divisions and a strong ethic of teamwork.

The rewards, however, have been significant for those churches that have persevered through the process. Children receive a consistent philosophy of ministry, they have already been introduced to their youth leaders so they make a smoother transition into the youth department, and the curriculum between each of the three divisions provides for a more comprehensive scope and sequence. Class content is less redundant, so students are not bored with the same old stories. Upper grades can focus more on developing critical thinking skills and ministry application rather than the acquisition of names, dates, facts, and figures.

Creating a Church Organizational Chart

The best way for a church to illustrate its organizational structure is by creating an organizational chart. This chart clearly depicts lines of authority and relationships. One glance at the chart and it is clear who has authority for what areas of responsibility and who does not have such authority. Such a chart helps to eliminate miscommunication and poor decision making.

If your church does not have such a chart already, it is best to draw up a chart which illustrates how the church is currently functioning in terms of working relationships. Each office or leader should be illustrated on the chart. If your church is associated with a denomination, then you will probably have some denominational preference about the grouping of your areas of ministry responsibilities. For example, you may prefer to classify groups as committees or commissions. Perhaps they will be called departments. The terms you use to depict the groups are not as important as getting each of the groups represented somewhere on the chart itself.

In his excellent book *Leadership for Church Education*, Ken Gangel provides four principles to help guide the church in the formation of an organizational chart and then presents four examples. The principles are as follows:[8]

- Chart the church as it presently exists.
- Circulate it among all the teachers and leaders.
- Construct another chart with suggested changes to improve the organization and administration.
- Continually update the chart.

To some people, the very nature of organization and administration is seen as contrary to the leading of the Holy Spirit. These people are uninformed about all that the Bible teaches on the subject of order and organization. Since God himself is the author of order, it seems only logical that he would desire his church to function in an orderly manner. In order to accomplish this, the leaders of the church together must decide which approach to organizational structure is in their best interest. Since the New Testament does not present a clearly defined pattern of church structure which is to be replicated throughout the history of the church, it seems God allows differing structures in different settings. There is great danger in demanding allegiance to only one way of organizing ministry when the New Testament does not teach such an approach.

The goal of organizational structure in the church is to help facilitate more effective distribution and stewardship of the resources which God has placed into our trust. The most critical factor in any structure is not the structure itself but the personalities represented. The right personalities can make almost any structure work efficiently. Likewise, a smooth and concise church structure can fall apart when the wrong leadership comes into the equation. It cannot be overstated that an emphasis on prayer is the essential component for any church structure to be effective.

Twenty-first-century ministry leaders also need to think creatively and outside the box in order to meet the changing needs of contemporary generations. Traditional approaches to organizational structure may have worked well for our parents and subsequent generations, but strategic thinking is needed to meet future needs. Where biblical roles, qualifications, and job descriptions have been provided (pastor, elder, deacon, etc.), these offices should be maintained according to the instructions that have been provided for us in Scripture.

However, for those offices which have been created over time in order to meet changing ministry needs (for example, children's pastor, youth pastor, minister of spiritual formation, small groups director, creative arts pastor, assimilation pastor, etc.), we are remiss as ministry leaders if we do not take the time periodically to assess the viability of these positions. Where changes need to be made in terms of roles and responsibilities or methods of operation, we have a responsibility as stewards of God's resources to make the necessary changes.

Organizing and structuring the ministries of the church is not rocket science, but it does require specific direction. It needs to integrate biblical teaching about prescribed church offices with an ability to exegete culture in order to apply these offices in an ever-changing ministry context. Those who are able to function in this difficult tension will experience a flourishing ministry for many years. Those who cannot will strive to maintain traditional patterns of ministry practice until these patterns become extinct. May God give us the courage to remain flexible in our organizational structures so that we may reach out to a lost and needy world for generations to come.

BY
MARK SIMPSON

Chapter 10

Preparing Job Descriptions

PASTOR BRENDON WAS COMING UP on his second quarter of service as the youth director of a midsized church in a small college community. All of his energies thus far had been devoted to developing ministries for junior high and senior high youth, and his efforts had been very successful. Brendon was loved by the youth for his creativeness and attentiveness to their needs. He was also respected by the parents and congregation at large for his sensitivity to church leadership concerns about the nature of youth programming, as well as doing ministry within the provided budget.

On the last Sunday of his first quarter of ministry, several Sunday school teachers approached Brendon and inquired where their Sunday school curriculum was for the next quarter. Pastor Brendon encouraged them to check with Chantel, the Sunday school superintendent, and thought nothing more about it. But later that afternoon Brendon received a heart-dropping call from the superintendent.

"Brendon, do you know where the Sunday school curriculum is for the new quarter that begins next week?" Superintendent Chantel asked frantically.

"No," Brendon replied. "I thought you had it. That's why I asked the teachers to check with you."

"But I don't have the curriculum!" Chantel said frantically. "I thought when you ordered it you would hand it out to the teachers!"

"But I didn't order the curriculum, Chantel," Brendon responded, fearful of what Chantel would say next. "I thought you placed the curriculum orders since you are the Sunday school superintendent." And Chantel's apologetic reply was just what Brendon feared.

"But I didn't order the curriculum either, Brendon. I thought that was your job now, since you work in the church office and are our youth director."

Obviously both Brendon and Chantel made assumptions that it was not their responsibility to order the Sunday school curriculum. Pastor Brendon innocently assumed the superintendent would order the curriculum since she had always done so in the past and also because his ministry was solely with the youth. Superintendent Chantel innocently assumed the youth director would now order the curriculum since he was on staff and worked in the church office as a ministry supervisor. Neither leader had a description of duties and responsibilities that would have alerted them to who was responsible for ordering the curriculum.

The opposite scenario can occur as well. Frank and Jonathon were serving as codevelopers of an annual Christian education conference sponsored by a nonprofit Christian organization. Both men had volunteered to lead the conference but agreed they should work together to plan the event rather than having just one of them take charge.

Frank and Jonathon were both very detail-oriented and made exhaustive checklists of everything needed for the conference. Unfortunately both men began working from the same checklists and unknowingly began duplicating efforts in several areas. Although the men had created the checklists together, they had not determined who was responsible for which tasks. Since neither one of them had a description of specific duties and responsibilities, the duplicated efforts in preparing for the conference did not become apparent until conflicting purchase orders and reservation forms were received. Fortunately, the duplications were caught in time to make cancellations and adjustments.

In both scenarios, the use of job descriptions could have prevented the embarrassing and costly mistakes made by these well-intentioned leaders and workers. In both cases, each party was simply trying to do his job as he understood it. That understanding, however, was based on assumptions made about duties and responsibilities associated with their ministry position. Job descriptions would have defined for both leaders what was actually expected of them and what general and specific tasks they were responsible for overseeing. "Job descriptions are not guarantees that your team will be a more solidified and prosperous team, but they can and have saved churches from crises. I've seen many beautiful, growing, and productive teams who never wrote a job description for anyone at their church, but I've also seen churches split and ruin the cause of Christ in a community for years, because they had no descriptions."[1]

Why Is a Job Description Valuable?

Job descriptions are a common part of business, nonprofit organizations, and higher education personnel management. A job description is usually presented as part of a job interview, even if only as a verbal explanation of duties and responsibilities. However, personnel offices almost always have on file an "official" job description for each position within the organization. These descriptions serve as a general guideline of what is expected of an employee, but by no means are the sum total of all the tasks that will be tackled in the performance of duties. Job descriptions also help employers set wage and salary scales, as well as identify key positions within the organization.

In churches, however, job descriptions have encountered varying levels of acceptance over the years. It is not uncommon for a church to not have job descriptions for pastoral staff. Usually if job descriptions do exist, they are developed for the hiring of support team members such as secretarial and janitorial staff. As with other organizations, these descriptions are then used to set wage and salary scales, define essential job positions, and outline typical job responsibilities.

The lack of job descriptions for pastoral staff is a sensitive issue for pastors as well as church leaders. For pastors, a job description can be a threatening document in that it can set boundaries that can prohibit the completion of pastoral duties. For example, if a pastor's job description *requires* home visitation of church members, other ministries may not receive the attention they need while the pastor attempts to do home visitation. For church leaders, a job description can be a plea for the pastor not to become overly focused on any one specific duty. If some pastoral duties are being neglected in favor of doing others, church leaders may see a job description as a way to control the job performance of the pastor. Unfortunately, both parties lose out on the value of having a job description when it is viewed as a threatening or controlling document.

Without a job description, an employee, no matter the level of a position within an organization, is forced to make assumptions about duties and responsibilities as well as lines of authority and lines of communication. These assumptions put the employee in the awkward position of having to guess what is appropriate to do and not do within the organization. Assumptions and guesswork can have unfortunate results, as occurred with Youth Pastor Brendon and Sunday School Superintendent Chantel, or financially disastrous results as was poised to occur with the duplicated plans made by Frank and Jonathon in the preparation of the education conference. The lack of a job description increases the probability that essential tasks will not be completed, and/or work efforts will be unnecessarily duplicated.

In some churches, an oral history of a ministry is often the "job description" given to volunteers recruited to lead ministries like Vacation Bible School, the annual Christmas pageant, or the youth Easter sunrise service. In a similar fashion, some business positions in Christian organizations are based on a verbal contract as the "job description" at the time of hire. Unfortunately for the church leader or the business employee, oral history and verbal contract "job descriptions" often lead to difficulties in the performance of duties, especially if others within the organization do not recognize or are not aware of a person's authority to do the job.[2]

"Job descriptions are wonderful tools. A document which is well-written and carefully conceived can clarify such things as responsibilities, authority, deadlines, lines of accountability, and a dozen other useful items."[3] Some additional values of having job descriptions include:

- elimination of conflict that can arise over unwritten expectations;[4]
- protection from role expansion (based on congregation/consumer expectations) or role contraction (based on employee interests and task preferences);[5]
- formation of performance standards for purposes of job appraisal;[6] and
- facilitation of strategic planning (enlisting new personnel on the basis of qualifications in meeting specific responsibilities and tasks).[7]

Job descriptions are invaluable to churches and religious organizations because they can facilitate the effectiveness of each member of a team and avoid the pitfalls of hidden agendas or misunderstood expectations. Rather than a team member being a "jack of all trades and a master of none," each one is recognized as a specialist with unique talents, gifts, and skills than can be deployed for the greater good of the team as a whole.[8] In circumstances where a generalist is needed, a job description can set predetermined boundaries in duties and responsibilities that help the volunteer or employee perform the job in a realistic manner. A job description can also help personnel avoid becoming overly focused on one duty or responsibility at the expense of other tasks.

One important value of having job descriptions becomes evident at the time of recruiting personnel to fill ministry employment positions or to perform volunteer services as ministry leaders or workers. When a potential hire or volunteer knows what to expect about a position, he can make a more informed choice as to whether or not he can take on the job or task. When recruitment efforts leave the potential hire or volunteer in the dark about duties and responsibilities, the position may get filled, but later the job may not get done if the person is incapable or unable to complete the task. For example, if "the church wishes its Sunday school teachers to attend prayer meeting, make a minimal number of calls each week, spend a certain amount of time in lesson preparation, and arrive at church at a given time on Sunday morning, all this should be specified in the job description or some similar document."[9]

I have generally found that volunteers are more likely to volunteer and do the job well with a sense of satisfaction when they have been given a job description that is honest about the tasks they are being asked to do. When the job description is missing or glossed over, the volunteer may do the job today, but not volunteer again tomorrow. Having served in several churches as a Christian education minister, I know how hard it is to find volunteers. Sometimes it's tempting to grab any warm body to fill the slate of positions and move on to the next task on your long list of things to do. Avoiding the use of accurate job descriptions might be a tempting immediate solution to recruitment needs, but in the long run it will come back to haunt you tenfold when you attempt to recruit volunteers in the future. Using job descriptions that provide an honest and accurate picture of what a job entails yields more positive results.

Job Descriptions or Service Descriptions: What's in a Name?

Once an organization recognizes the value of a job description, the next challenge is to develop descriptions appropriately. In order to do that, it is important to remember that there can be significant differences in expectations and work outcomes between an employer and a paid employee. While the term *job description* can be used for both employee and volunteer, a distinction in terminology can be made between the two so as to avoid expectations of volunteers that are more appropriate of paid employees. The following operational definitions are offered as a way to further clarify roles and relationships between employers/deployers and those working under their leadership:

A *job description* is a clearly defined and transcripted outline of the title, role, duties and responsibilities, lines of authority, and lines of communication mutually agreed upon between an employer and *an employee in a paid position*. A *service description* is a clearly defined and transcripted outline of the title, role, duties and responsibilities, lines of authority, and lines of communication mutually agreed upon between an employer and *a volunteer in a nonpaid position.*

Why are these distinctions important when the differences are so fine? A job description is appropriately a statement of performance expectations with concomitant performance assessments *in light of financial remuneration and promotion.* A service description, on the other hand, is a statement of performance expectations of volunteer personnel for *nonpaid services,* and thus performance assessments need to be made in light of that status. When the demands of ministry border on volunteers doing the work equivalent to that of a full-time or part-time staff position, it is too easy for a ministry leader to expect—if not demand—performance equivalent to that of paid personnel. If that happens, volunteers may be unfairly evaluated as failing in their duties, and their works of service unfairly criticized as a result.

One of the reasons I have heard volunteers give for not volunteering again is the way they were treated in their volunteer service. Some have felt that their work was not appreciated and was taken for granted. Others have felt that too many responsibilities were demanded of them without regard for family commitments and employment responsibilities. Granted, there are situations where volunteers drop the ball in developing and implementing ministry, and ministry leaders then have to make the unpleasant choice not to deploy these volunteers in future ministries. But too often ministry leaders expect volunteers to function like paid staff and thus end up evaluating volunteer acts of service as if they were performed by paid personnel. When that happens, volunteers can become frustrated, disillusioned, and/or angered about their role in the organization. Some will choose not to volunteer again; others will decrease their involvement or move on to other ministries (and in extreme cases, other churches or organizations).

When a service description is used for volunteers, it is a subtle but important reminder to ministry leaders that they are working with volunteers and should treat them as such. Service descriptions are also an important reminder to volunteers that their labors are not just a job but an act of service for the Lord Jesus Christ (Col. 3:24).

Who Needs a Job or Service Description?

Every paid person on a ministry team needs a job description; every volunteer on a ministry team needs a service description. "It is extremely important that every service opportunity include a written job [or service] description that can be given to the individual being considered."[10]

Each paid employee from the seniormost official to the juniormost team member needs a job description that establishes requisite skills for his or her position, delineates and assigns duties, defines lines of authority, identifies types of accountability, and indicates measures of support.[11] When every paid employee has a job description, all jobs in the organization can be coordinated to function together to complete all duties and responsibilities associated with the work of the organization. If only a handful of employees have job descriptions, errors and oversights can easily occur. "A clearly written job description will go a long way in lessening misunderstandings from people in various positions, whether full- or part-time, whether paid or volunteer. People have a clear understanding of what their job is, but more importantly they understand what their job is not."[12]

Creating and/or maintaining job or service descriptions for every employee or volunteer can be a daunting task. However, many positions within a church or Christian organization are duplicated among several individuals, such as Sunday school teachers, camp counselors, etc. One general description may be developed for these types of positions. However, it is recommended that each member of a board or committee not be given a *general* description of duties and responsibilities but rather be given a service description that identifies the *specific* functions the person will fill as a member of that governing body. Assigning specific duties and responsibilities to each person on a board and committee.

- mobilizes all members for active duty within the organization;
- insures every ministry area is managed appropriately;
- avoids omissions in the leadership and management of ministries that can occur when duties and responsibilities are randomly assigned; and
- diminishes participation on a board or committee as a spectator sport.

Job Descriptions for Senior Pastors

One of the hardest positions to create a job description for is the senior pastor of a local church. Although the New Testament gives explicit qualifications for the character of a pastor (1 Tim. 3:1–7), the primary duties of a senior pastor are (1) the devotion of time to continuous prayer and (2) the ministry of the Word (Acts 6:4). In addition to these duties, the contemporary senior pastor must also manage the operations of the local church that often vary according to the needs of the moment, and unfortunately, sometimes vary according to the whims of the congregation. Congregational expectations of pastoral duties and responsibilities need to appear in a job description for the senior pastor so that unwritten expectations and unfair performance evaluations do not occur.

Unfortunately, job descriptions for senior pastors are often created after the pastor leaves and before his successor arrives. These descriptions typically reflect the areas of frustration a congregation experienced in the performance of ministry duties by the outgoing pastor. The incoming pastor may then be encumbered by this new job description, especially if it was created to emphasize or deemphasize ministry activities neglected or favored by the previous pastor.[13] Ideally the senior pastor's job description should be developed and maintained with his specific gifts and talents in mind. This means creating or updating that description while the pastor is on the job. However, the most effective job description for a senior pastor is the one in which he has taken the lead or initiative in writing the initial draft.[14]

In my experience it is often easier said than done to get the senior pastor to write his own job description, or for the congregation to create one that is actually followed by the senior pastor. "Some persons in the congregation might use an antiquated job description, which they consider to be a legal document, as a means of destroying someone they want to see fired."[15] If this becomes the motive behind a job description for the senior pastor, the opportunity to coordinate all of the duties of the ministry team will be lost, and the document that is created will either be ignored or become a stumbling block to the advancement of ministry.

Service Descriptions for Ministry Volunteers

Like paid employees, every volunteer in a leadership or ongoing task position in a church or Christian organization should have a service description. Like job descriptions, a service description also establishes requisite skills needed for the area of service, delineates and assigns duties, defines lines of authority, identifies types of accountability, and indicates measures of support. When every volunteer position has a service description, the ministries of the church or Christian organization can be coordinated in such a way that duties and responsibilities are not overlooked and ministry efforts are not duplicated.

The idea of using service descriptions for volunteers came to my attention as a result of working for the first time on a board of Christian education. For years this Christian education board had developed and maintained job descriptions that coordinated the various educational ministries of the church. The job descriptions defined for ministry volunteers what was expected of them and what support they could expect in return from the church. Each person on the ministry team also knew who to report his progress to, who reported his progress to him, and what types of resources were available to fulfill the job, all the characteristics of a good job description.[16] Having these job descriptions was a positive development for the church, but something was missing.

Shortly after beginning my service on the board, I discovered that the morale of many of our volunteer workers was low. When questioned about their ministries, many of these volunteer workers and helpers felt like they were doing another job on top of their regular employment. This attitude seemed contrary to serving the Lord with gladness as the psalmist exhorts us to do (Ps. 100:2). I decided to try a change in nomenclature from job description to service description. At the top of each service description I included citations from Scripture which underscored that volunteer work is an act of service to Christ. That simple change in nomenclature did something wonderful for our ministries. Our board began focusing on persons rather than programs, and our volunteers expressed their appreciation for our efforts. The end result was an increase in the performance of our volunteers and an increase in the success of our recruitment and retention efforts. The original job description material was still in each service description, but the underlying attitude for having the descriptions had changed.

Revising the Job and Service Descriptions

Job and service descriptions are often created when a new position is added to support a ministry team. But more frequently, churches and Christian organizations will find themselves creating job and service descriptions for existing positions staffed by employees or volunteer personnel already on the job.

There really is no ideal time to create a job or service description, except to do so as soon as possible whenever it is evident a description is missing for an employee position or a volunteer service role. For example, in situations where a job or service position is brand new, a description can be created from scratch without the baggage of accumulated expectations. However, the lack of operational experience with the position may result in the description being largely theoretical, even if it is designed around previous experience in similar positions. In situations where a position has been in existence for some time but lacks a job or service description, the existence of operational experience with the position is more likely to result in a description that accurately reflects roles and responsibilities. However, developing a job or service description for a position "in play" carries with it the danger of creating a description that may be largely reactive to negative experiences with personnel in the position.

No matter when a job or service description is created in the life span of a position, it is essential that the description reflect accurately the primary duties and responsibilities associated with the position. The description should also include the flexibility to incorporate into it the specific talents and skills of the person filling the position.[17] By building flexibility into job or service descriptions, the needs of the organization can be accommodated through the listing of primary duties and responsibilities, and additional abilities and interests brought to the position by the employee or volunteer can also be appropriated.[18] The primary duties and responsibilities related to the position would not necessarily change across persons filling the position, but accommodating individual talents and skills would modify the position with each change in personnel.

When a vacancy occurs in a ministry position, the corresponding job or service description should be evaluated and revised.[19] Revisions made to job or service descriptions should include input from personnel at the same level as that of the position being updated, as well as from persons who work immediately above and below the position.[20] When possible, input from the person vacating the position should be sought and taken into consideration as appropriate.

After a position has been filled for approximately six months to a year, the job or service description should be revisited and modified to accommodate the additional gifts and contributions the employee or volunteer has brought to the position.[21] Thereafter, the description should be updated on an annual basis to ensure that the needs of the organization are being met and that the abilities of the employee or volunteer are being appropriated in such a way that the position remains challenging and rewarding.[22] The end result of this extra effort will be greater performance outcomes for the organization and greater job or service satisfaction for the employees or volunteers.[23]

Because job and service descriptions are not static documents and will change over time and personnel, they should not be made a part of the official documentation of the organization. Any change to the job title, duties and responsibilities, and/or qualifications for the position may require an amendment to the constitution or bylaws.[24] Job or service positions are best kept on file in the main office or personnel office of the organization where they can be easily accessed for distribution or modification.

Ingredients of a Job or Service Description

Although the content of a job or service description will vary according to the needs of the organization, there are core elements that should appear in any description. For example, a job or service description should include not only what the organization expects of the employee or volunteer, but also what those personnel can expect in the way of support from the organization.[25]

It is important that the wording of job or service expectations and subsequent supportive measures be stated as concretely as possible.

Concrete wording will help diminish misunderstandings and false assumptions about duties and responsibilities. Abstract or theoretical wording leaves duties and responsibilities too open to misinterpretation.

Figure 10.1 is an example of a service description that was prepared for the volunteer position of director of educational ministries in a local church. This service description contains the following core elements that should be part of any job or service description:

- official title of the position,
- purpose of the position,
- qualifications for the position,
- working or serving relationships,
- general duties (primary areas of service),
- expectations of and provisions for the position, and
- personalized areas of work or service.

Official Title of the Position

The title of a position is more important than one might generally think. A title of a job or service position communicates: (1) the level of the position in the organization; (2) the level of power and authority that can be exerted by the person in the position; and (3) the perceived competency of the person filling the position.

A position title can also have a significant impact on the morale of the employee or volunteer as well as the morale of others working or serving alongside him or her. Nothing is more demotivating or embarrassing to an employee or volunteer than to be identified with the wrong title in print or addressed with the wrong title in a public forum. "Terms such as 'director,' 'minister,' 'coordinator,' or 'facilitator' each communicate something different."[26] For example, a minister usually has more training than a director. If a pastor introduces the youth minister as the youth director, the person in that position may feel slighted, and rightfully so! A misused title may happen inadvertently, but it may also communicate a lack of respect for the employee or volunteer. A misused position title may also communicate that the job or service role is not as essential to the organization as the official title would indicate. Therefore, job and service position titles should not be treated lightly and should be used correctly in print as well as in verbal references to the employee or volunteer. Never underestimate the power of a title![27]

It is important to keep the title of positions descriptive and yet as short as possible. Chances are a shorter title will be remembered and used more accurately than a long, complicated one. At one point in my own ministry, my job title was seventeen words long. I almost needed a second business card just to list my position title! Though the title was descriptive of my role within the organization, rarely was the full title

Figure 10.1

Service Description—Director of Educational Ministries

*And whatever you do, do it heartily, as to the Lord and not to men, knowing that from the Lord you will receive the reward of the inheritance; for you serve the Lord Christ.
(Col. 3:23–24 NKJV)*

And whatever you do in word or deed, do all in the name of the Lord Jesus, giving thanks to God the Father through Him. (Col. 3:17 NKJV)

Service Title: Director of Educational Ministries (DEM)

Ministry Purpose: The Director of Educational Ministries is responsible for overseeing the administration, development, and evaluation of all educational ministries of the church.

Service Qualifications: The DEM should have proven teaching and leadership skills. Time management skills are essential as are good people skills.

Serving Relationships: The DEM serves under the direction of the Associate Pastor of Church Ministries. The DEM attends all Christian Education Committee meetings and serves as an ex-officio member of the committee. The Youth Coordinator reports to the DEM and is supervised by the DEM. The DEM serves as the Christian Education Board liaison to the Board of Deacons.

Primary Areas of Service: Service responsibilities will be in four general areas: administration; education; development; and ministry.

Administration: design and maintain the total educational ministry within the mission statement, goals, and budgetary guidelines of the church. This will involve recruiting qualified personnel; developing and adjusting Christian education programs to meet congregational needs and accomplish educational objectives; providing for requisite curriculum, resources and educational media; and monitoring and reporting on expenditures and progress to the appropriate serving relationships.

Education: train and equip persons for effective service for Christ. This will involve designing clearly stated educational objectives and goals compatible with the mission statement of the church; developing, communicating and modeling a biblical philosophy of teaching and learning in the church and home; training leadership; and evaluating and administrating curriculum selection and utilization of resources.

Development: plan and lead the expansion of the total educational program. This will involve initiating and maintaining outreach efforts in conjunction with other church ministries; measuring and assessing growth; planning short-term and long-range ministry goals.

Ministry: model and implement a shepherding, caring fellowship that supplements and complements the ministry of the pastoral staff. This will involve caring about and for the needs of personnel serving with you; exhorting, counseling, strengthening, and encouraging leadership; creating ways to build a caring fellowship; and guiding individuals in identifying and maximizing their spiritual gifts and God-given abilities in ways that enable them to serve the Lord effectively.

Continued on the next page

Continued from previous page

Service Expectations: The DEM is expected to recruit and delegate responsibility as necessary rather than be seen as doing the ministry of education by himself or herself. The DEM is to be recognized as a fellow servant of Jesus Christ and minister of the gospel, being held accountable to God for the spiritual condition of the congregation in the same way the pastoral staff is held accountable. Other service parameters include:

▪ The work load is expected to be approximately twelve hours per week, which includes time in preparation for and participation in Sunday morning, Sunday evening, and Wednesday evening ministries as necessary in fulfilling the duties of the position.

▪ The DEM is encouraged to participate in local opportunities for professional growth and allowed to attend one major conference per year budgeted by the church.

▪ The DEM will be provided a budget appropriate to cover expenses related to the Board-approved educational ministries of the church.

▪ **Personalized Areas of Service:** The DEM is encouraged to appropriate his or her God-given abilities and spiritual gifts in the fulfillment of this service position. Specific areas of service subject to change include (specifics would be bullet listed below):

▪
▪
▪
▪
▪

Date revised:

---

used accurately by my peers—sometimes even I couldn't remember the whole thing. While long titles are not uncommon in academia, the larger churches or Christian organizations are becoming, the longer job and service titles seem to be becoming to distinguish levels of job and service positions. However, with these longer titles comes the responsibility to use them accurately so employees and volunteers are not embarrassed or insulted.

Purpose of the Position

A statement of the purpose of a position is another core ingredient of a job or service description. The purpose section introduces the role and responsibility of the position and its function within the organization. Written as a short statement, the purpose section essentially identifies the broader objectives, tasks, and/or goals that the position is intended to encompass.[28] All of the other content in a job or service description flows from this purpose statement.

Qualifications for the Position

A list of the essential qualifications required and/or desired in the person filling a position is another core ingredient of a job or service description. Common qualifications that will be described include, but are not limited to, the amount and types of previous experience needed for the position or related positions and a list of the skills needed to perform duties and responsibilities.[29] Depending on the job or service role, additional qualifications may need to be identified, such as: (1) educational background; (2) position-related training and/or certification; (3) personal character qualities and interpersonal skills; and (4) indicators of the level of spiritual maturity.[30]

Qualifications for a position should be organized with the *requisite credentials* first, and then any other *desired credentials* listed after them. When qualifications are organized in this fashion, essential and/or non-negotiable qualifications do not become overlooked or overshadowed by other attractive qualities a person may bring to the job or service role. Arranging qualifications from requisite credentials to desired credentials assists recruiters in identifying appropriate personnel to fill positions and alerts applicants and volunteers to the true level of expertise needed to serve in the position.

Relationships

When working or serving relationships are identified in a job or service description, the employee or volunteer will understand "how [the] position fits into the organization structure; who the individual is responsible to, and who the individual is responsible for."[31] Relationships that need to be identified include: (1) the chain of command; (2) lines of authority; and (3) committee involvement. By identifying these relationships, employees and volunteers will know who the appropriate personnel are to contact and connect with for approvals, permissions, and appropriating resources.

The chain of command identifies who is in authority over the position and who the employee or volunteer will be supervising. The identification of lines of authority expands upon this chain of command by setting and/or clarifying decision-making boundaries associated with the position. Whatever the working or serving relationship in the context of the hierarchical structure of the organization, it is vital that "if a person is assigned responsibility for a certain action, he or she must also be allowed a corresponding degree of authority to accomplish it. If the two are not given in equal amounts, the employee is set up for failure."[32]

Board and committee responsibilities are additional working or serving relationships that need to be identified in a job or service description. An employee or volunteer will need to know the decision-making bodies he or she will need to attend and/or make reports. The role or level of participation expected in these decision-making bodies also needs to be indicated (e.g., observer, chair, voting member, ex officio member, etc.).

General Duties

Apart from the title of a position, a list of general and specific duties is probably the first element that comes to a person's mind when a job or service description is mentioned. Duties and responsibilities will vary from position to position, and even from person to person in the same position. Generally a job or service description should include two levels of duties: (1) *general* activities and responsibilities that anyone in the position is expected to do; and (2) *personalized* activities and responsibilities that are unique to the person currently in the position.

In the general duties section of a job description (primary areas of service in a service description), the nonnegotiable activities any person in the position is expected to perform are identified. These duties and responsibilities reflect the primary purpose of the position emphasized earlier in the description and are intended to work together with other positions for the efficient and effective operation of the church or Christian organization. As personnel filling the position change over time, or as duplicate positions are created at the same level (e.g., having more than one youth leader), these general duties may need to be updated, but usually no drastic changes are made to the general duties section unless the position itself changes.

Expectations of and Provisions for the Position

A job or service description should include some indication of essential attitudes or behaviors expected of the employee or volunteer and what he or she, in turn, may expect in the way of tangible support from the church or Christian organization.[33] Common expectations made by organizations include attitudes and behaviors such as: (1) being faithful in fulfilling the duties of the position; (2) agreeing to adhere to biblical and organizational standards of personal conduct and spiritual integrity; (3) maintaining confidentiality; (4) showing respect for consumers/members, peers, and superiors, etc. These expectations are not so much tasks as they are parameters within which general duties and responsibilities should be completed.

In tandem with the statement of expectations for the employee or volunteer, tangible forms of support provided by the organization to help the person in the job or service role should also be indicated. Common forms of tangible support frequently needed by an employee or volunteer include provisions, such as budgetary support, a positive and productive working environment, opportunities for continuing education or training, clear and open forms of communication, etc. These forms of support should be realistic within the resources available to the church or Christian organization, and every effort should be made to provide them. It is important to remember that the performance and retention of an employee or volunteer is often directly related to the provisions made in support of his or her position!

Personalized Areas of Work or Service

Personalized duties in a job description (personalized areas of service in a service description) are the negotiable activities *a specific person* in the position brings to the organization as a result of unique skills and/or interests. As a result, these activities will vary from person to person filling the position. Specific duties and responsibilities are enhanced or advanced as activities *related to the position* that the specific employee or volunteer brings to the position. These enhanced or advanced activities expand the value of the position to the organization while increasing the morale and job or service performance of the employee or volunteer. Every time a new person is brought into the position, the personalized duties section must be updated to reflect the unique skills and/or interests of the new hire or volunteer.

Conclusion

Job and service descriptions can be invaluable tools in coordinating the ministries of the church or the functions of a Christian organization. Through these descriptions, duties and responsibilities can be more easily managed across positions so that all activities work together without omissions, competition, or duplication of effort. The end result will be the overall advancement of the organization with less conflict, more cooperation, a greater sense of teamwork, and a higher level of satisfaction on the part of the employee or volunteer.

BY
DENNIS WILLIAMS

Chapter 11

Conducting Effective Meetings

SOMEONE ONCE MADE THE statement that "committees keep minutes and waste hours." Anyone who has ever served as a member of a committee at a church or other Christian organization will no doubt shout a heartfelt "amen" to that statement. We spend a great deal of time in meetings, so we must recognize our need to be efficient stewards in the use of other people's time.

Perhaps it would be good to first define what we mean by the term *meeting* so the reader can understand the direction this chapter will take on the subject. Broadly speaking, a meeting refers to the gathering of individuals together for a specific purpose. This includes boards and committees.

In this chapter I want to begin by first affirming the importance of the social nature of meetings. From there I will discuss the different types of meetings that most Christian organizations conduct over the normal course of their operations. Third, we will explore ways to facilitate an effective meeting and then identify some practical ways to make them successful experiences for all concerned. Finally, I want to present some guidelines and a practical checklist that you can use to evaluate the effectiveness of the meetings you lead and/or attend.

Meetings as Social Events

Sociologists would agree that most meetings can be summarized as social events since people are always involved. Since it must be recognized that not all social events are positive, it is important to get to know people and to foster the social dynamic of the group. A leader can do this by talking to the participants and learning about their hobbies, reading habits, sports interests, travels, friends, and family members. A wise leader does not ignore the realities of meetings being social events. Not everyone attends meetings to "get things done." Many people come to enjoy the process and the social interactions associated with gathering together with others.

To foster this kind of environment, you should plan an informal get-acquainted period so people will feel at ease. Perhaps during the first meeting of the group everyone should be given an opportunity to talk about themselves, their interests, and how they feel about an important topic under consideration. Another idea would be to adjourn the first meeting early so people can spend some social time together.

Another approach is to provide a discussion-starter activity that provides information on the group. Many different kinds of questions have been developed by those who study group dynamics, but nothing profound or overly esoteric is needed—just something to break the ice and get feeling comfortable being together. Examples of such nonthreatening questions might include:

- Where did you live between the ages of nine and twelve?
- Who was the center of human warmth in your home?
- When did God become more than a word to you?
- Who has made the most significant impact on your life and why?

Another helpful suggestion is to ask the group to complete a personal profile sheet with statements such as these:

- My favorite food is . . .
- My favorite childhood vacation was . . .
- When I get spare time I like to . . .
- My favorite type of movie is . . .
- After church I like to spend the afternoon . . .
- My dream car would be . . .

By sharing with one another we get to know more about those with whom we are serving. Taking the time to build community is an important precursor to team building and the development of a conducive climate for service.

Along with the obvious social dimension that such activities develop, they also nurture a degree of group cohesiveness. Cohesive means sticking together or being united. It is what holds the bonds of friendship together and unites us as a ministry team.

Here are some important ways to make this happen successfully:

1. Identify as a group. Use inclusive terms to describe the group such as *us, our,* or *we.* Avoid personal ownership terms such as *my, I,* or *mine.*

2. Build a group tradition. Find something unusual, exciting, or funny that the group can remember.

3. Emphasize teamwork. Don't worry about who gets credit for success as long as the group succeeds. This is not the place for superstars.

We hear a lot about team ministry today, and this is healthy. Be certain that it is part of the group process as well.

4. Help the group to recognize good work. Praise good work in terms of the importance of the contribution to the group. Obviously we must be honest in this assessment because our credibility is on the line. It is most helpful to state before the entire group special recognitions and awards given to the group. Also, when a project or ministry planned by the group is successful, it should be communicated to the entire group for praise and recognition.

5. Set clear, attainable group goals. A goal for a given meeting, for the coming week, for next month is more likely to increase morale. Good goals will set the course of the group for the future, and it keeps everyone on track.

6. Give group rewards. Reaching a clear goal is a group reward. Commendations such as "We could not have accomplished this without each of you" is always in order. We often limit commendations, but they are essential to building group morale and motivation.

7. Treat members like people, not machines. Do not ignore the human and social dimension. Members quickly discover whether the leader is interested only in accomplishing objectives or in the needs and concerns of the people. Yes, we have God-given goals to accomplish, but part of this is to minister to those whom God has brought together in ministry.

Three Types of Meetings

Meetings can be formal or informal, which is probably another way of saying that some are planned ahead of time and some are more impromptu. Obviously some meetings may be scheduled ahead, but that doesn't necessarily mean that they are well planned.

The first type of meeting is to announce or inform. People are brought together for an announcement of a decision that has been made. It is similar to a press conference where questions are not permitted from the group following the announcement. If there are questions, they are only to bring a better understanding of the decision and not to change the decision. There is no vote of approval, and the announcement stands.

An example of this meeting might sound like this: "I've brought you all together for this meeting to announce that effective immediately, all budgets are being frozen and no new staff will be hired until we see some improvement in our fund-raising efforts."

The second kind of meeting is to obtain the support of the group. Again, the decision has been made, but in this case there is an appeal for the group to accept the decision and give their support. Follow-up questions would be in order, and the climate is more open and positive than in the first kind of meeting. It is important to recognize, however, that this discussion is not intended to change the decision. It is for the specific purpose of gaining support for the decision.

An example of this type of meeting might sound like this: "We have called this meeting today to let you know that the search committee has made their decision and has extended an invitation to Mr. Jones to serve as our new president. We believe he will bring a new sense of direction to our organization, and we trust each of you will make his transition smooth. If you have any ideas or suggestions about how we can accomplish this, we would be happy to entertain your input at this time."

The third type of meeting focuses on problem solving. The decision has not yet been made, and the group is brought together to discuss the issues and to come to some kind of resolution of the problem. It does not mean that people have come to the meeting unprepared or unsure of how they intend to vote. It means that the decision has not yet been made and there will be ample opportunity for discussion prior to the final vote.

An example of this type of meeting might be this: "As you know, we have enjoyed a significant degree of growth at our church this year. However, with this growth has come some big challenges in terms of sharing facilities, resources, and program allocations. It is our desire today to brainstorm ideas on how we can accommodate this new growth and work together toward reasonable solutions. We may not finalize our decisions today, but it is our desire to have everyone's input and suggestions before a decision is made at a later time."

Knowing the three types of meetings will help individuals understand the purpose of the meeting they are attending and what is expected of them in the process. Unfortunately some people think they are in a problem-solving meeting, when they actually are in a meeting where the decision has already been made. In many occasions where this is the case, it can lead to frustration, resentment, and disagreement among members. Most people want to have a say in decisions. When the process or type of meeting is misunderstood due to poor communication, it can result in a negative reaction and sometimes in resignations.

Suggestions for Conducting Effective Meetings

Since so many people spend so many hours in meetings, it is important that every effort be made to make the best use of the meeting time. Some helpful insights and suggestions will be offered here with the hope that they will contribute toward effective use of your committee member's contribution.

The leader is the first key to conducting effective meetings. First, as the discussion facilitator, set a premium on the expression of ideas. Encourage "what if" kinds of suggestions. Encourage members of the group to think outside the box if you are looking for new ideas.

Let the members know that you want to hear their ideas, even if they may seem unorthodox and bizarre. If people recognize the leader's willingness to listen to their ideas, without judgment, it will free them up to think of new ideas that will help the group.

Another way to foster a creative climate is to spotlight the areas of challenge that the group is facing. One person said that "a problem well defined is half solved." The leader should carefully articulate the issue at hand so the group can process it. Give the group time. The leader should encourage the group and demonstrate a willingness to help individuals develop their ideas. This fosters a team approach.

Effectiveness is hindered when the leader "freezes" people out. This happens by refusing to listen to new ideas or nontraditional solutions. If we listen only to those whom we like or want to hear from, we have in effect kept other members outside the process. Without the entire team, we are not as effective as we could be.

When successful ideas come about, we should reward the contributors with words of encouragement and affirmation. It is also important to encourage the ideas that were not successful because without some affirmation of the suggestion, though it was not used, people will hesitate to make future suggestions. They will not be open to trying new ideas or solutions in the future.

With all of this we need to emphasize the benefit of what is accomplished. It is highly motivational to point out the advantages of an idea developed by the group. It is what we called a group reward earlier.

In addition, an effective group leader should spotlight the area of challenge. Pinpoint the problems and be specific. Do not merely say, "Things around here are a mess." Be more specific. What are the real issues, and how can we solve them? In some cases it will be necessary to personalize the problem in practical and immediate terms but avoid casting blame or conveying negative criticism. This may not be an easy thing to do, but a good leader must be willing to identify the issues and move ahead.

When dealing with issues, if no ideas come from the group, it will be necessary for the leader to "prime the pump" by suggesting a line of attack at the problem. Use this to get people started. It certainly is not the final solution. One of the hardest things to do is to get a group started. Once this takes place, the opportunity for creativity in people is enhanced. If the leader just sits by passively and lets the conversation flow, the meeting can be a waste of time and can become demotivational.

As the group continues to work on the issues, the leader must keep in touch. A method must be in place to check on progress on a regular basis. Remember, it takes time to succeed. Some ideas or solutions are action-oriented and others are thought-oriented. In creative problem solving we must use both from time to time.

Some of the best ideas for solutions to problems come from a group effort and not from a single individual. When ideas are proposed the leader should work to develop and refine them. Help the person giving the idea to make it fit the needs of the group. Preparation is a key, and this takes time. Quick-fix solutions seldom last very long.

Arrange for a tryout of the idea. If it will require a major change, then more time in preparation will be essential. If possible, try the solution on a smaller group to see how well it will work. Be certain to build a full evaluation into the process, and make certain that there is a final evaluation process as well.

Reward the one who gave the successful idea. Many times this will be the entire group. Though in Christian ministry we serve because of our commitment to the Lord, it does not hurt for leaders to share a word of affirmation for those who have been faithful in service and have found ways to make the work of ministry more effective.

Elements of a Good Meeting

The following elements of a good meeting may be easy to write down, but it will be more difficult to implement them on a regular basis. The elements work together. If some are missing, the meeting may miss the mark.

1. **State Your Purpose.** The first step is to have a clear understanding of the reason for the meeting. Is it a regular monthly meeting to check on the progress of a program? Is it a special meeting to make a major decision? Is it primarily for fellowship and inspiration? Is it a meeting because we always have one? People are busy, and they do not want to waste their time in meetings that have no purpose. The rule of thumb should be that if there is no clearly defined purpose for the meeting, then don't have it. Meetings just for the sake of meeting have limited value and can cause negative reactions and a lack of effort on the part of the group.

One way to underscore the purpose of the meeting is to set specific goals. This provides a way to measure how much was accomplished. It can be very motivational at the end of the meeting to review what was accomplished.

2. Remind Participants of the Value of Their Involvement. A key for a successful meeting is to have the right participants present. Sometimes in a special called meeting, the leader selects who will be part of the group. At other times it is a group that is already appointed. Either way, it is important that the key players be present and ready to do their work. Select participants on the basis of what they can contribute to the issues at hand. It is unfortunate that people with absolutely no background for the task are sometimes appointed to committees. This certainly limits their effectiveness.

3. Preparation Is Essential. Both the leader and those in the group must come to the meeting with their "homework" finished. It is difficult to make good decisions when key information is lacking. Though we do not like to "check up on people," it may be necessary to make a phone call or send an e-mail note to make certain that people are ready with their work completed. Without important information in place, the success of the meeting is in jeopardy.

4. Location, Location, Location. Don't underestimate the importance of meeting location. It should be held in a place that will minimize interruptions and distractions. It should be held at a place that is convenient for the largest number of people. Sometimes people like to have meetings in conjunction with meals. If held in a public location, little actual business can be conducted. Try to find a place that will facilitate a good meeting with limited distractions. Don't meet in educational classrooms where the desks and chairs are designed for children.

5. Provide Tools for Effective Communication. It is important to have adequate communication tools and resources available for those in attendance. People understand more if they can see the proposals. When questions come up, the information should be readily available. Obviously, if you are presenting a document, all members *must* be given a copy (preferably in advance). These are practical issues, but when they are missing, meeting time can be wasted.

6. Prepare an Agenda. Agendas function as planning documents, and a well-prepared agenda can facilitate a successful meeting. Agendas can be used in a number of ways. They can state the purpose and goals of the meeting. They can spell out the items that will be covered, the time frame in which they are to be covered, and the people who are responsible. It is wise to have the agenda posted so people can check off the items as the meeting progresses. When it is placed before everyone, it helps to keep the group on track.

How can agendas be a guide and stimulus to thoughtful group discussion? First, agendas should be realistic. How much time is allotted for the meeting and what can we reasonably expect to accomplish? It is important to assign time limits for the various actions on the agenda. If it is discovered that there is too much to cover in a given meeting, another meeting should be scheduled. Agendas should not be overcrowded. It is important to list the names of the people responsible for the various elements of the agenda. This, along with time estimates, will keep the meeting moving in the right direction.

Some items on the agenda will require thought on the part of the group, and time should be given for open discussion and interaction. Items of this nature may need to be postponed for a future decision if adequate time is not allotted. Following a major conference, a time of debriefing and evaluation is in order for the planning group. Without time limits for the evaluation, several hours could be spent. It is beneficial to allot a certain amount of time, say forty-five minutes to an hour, for the evaluation time. People will know that if they have something to contribute, they must do it in this time limit. Actually this keeps the evaluation time fresh and keeps the energy level high for the meeting. It also allows time for other business to be conducted.

The order of items on the agenda is also important. It is a good idea to begin with some of the easy items and then move on to the more complicated ones. Be certain that they are in a logical order of sequence. If you begin with the "heaviest" item first, you may not get around to conducting other important business.

It is a good idea to list suggestions on the agenda about how the group can deal with items. If you are seeking nominations for positions, it is a good idea to list some possibilities. People seem to work better from a few suggestions than from a blank page. These suggestions should not be complicated or merely be simple notations. Be aware that the leader is not trying to control the group with these suggestions but is trying to move the meeting along. It is expected that the members will contribute and build on what is suggested.

It is essential for people to see the agenda before the meeting. This will help them know what materials to bring and give the group an opportunity to think about the issues beforehand. It will also avoid possible misunderstanding about topics to discuss and will keep unwanted surprises from coming up. If the chair or leader is given agenda items that are not appropriate or should not be part of the discussion, they can be eliminated early on and save the group important time. The importance of an agenda cannot be underestimated. Without it or with one that is weak or vague, the success of the meeting is in doubt.

7. **Keep Control of the Meeting.** It is the leader's responsibility to keep the meeting moving in the right direction. Avoid distractions and impromptu comments and stories unless they relate to the issues at hand. Attending a meeting is a sacrifice of time for everyone. When time is wasted, it can diminish the desire of members to serve.

8. **Summarize the Accomplishments.** Finally, when the meeting is about to end, review with the group what has been accomplished. Identify the next steps and list the unresolved issues. Make this a time of appreciation for the investment of people's time and energy. Let them leave feeling that their contribution was worthwhile and important.

9. **Make and Review Assignments Before Leaving.** Often in a meeting, decisions will be made that require assignments. Be certain that you remind individuals who have been given assignments of their responsibility. Specify what actions will be taken in the future to handle the unresolved items after the meeting. The details of who is in charge, what resources will be allocated, when the assignment is due, and how the outcomes will be communicated should be clearly identified so there are no misunderstandings after the meeting.

Evaluating the Effectiveness of Your Meetings

It has been said that "anything worth doing is worth evaluating." This is certainly true when it comes to meetings. The purpose of evaluation is improvement, and this is exactly what we must do to continue to make our meetings effective.

How can we tell if the group is working well? Look for these signs:

- People are free to speak about what they think and feel.
- Decisions are being made by consensus.
- Ideas are welcomed and freely accepted.
- People are evaluated on the quality of their contributions.
- There is full participation among all members.
- Important topics are given adequate discussion time.
- There is an understanding of other's ideas, plans, and proposals.
- There is a focus on goals and tasks.
- People are respected and decisions and actions are God-centered.

How can you tell if the group is not working well? Obviously the opposite of the listing above will reveal serious needs. Here are some of the negative signs:

- Participation is dominated by a few individuals.
- People do not feel a part of the decision-making process.
- People with abilities do not contribute to the process.
- Items of minor importance seem to dominate much of the time.
- Even after decisions have been made, they seem to come back for further discussion.
- There is a fear of change.
- Communication to the group is limited, and only the leader or leaders know what is going on. The actions appear to be more self-centered than God-centered.

The following checklist is provided to help you evaluate the effectiveness of your meetings. Feel free to add your own items, depending on the context and purpose of your particular meeting.

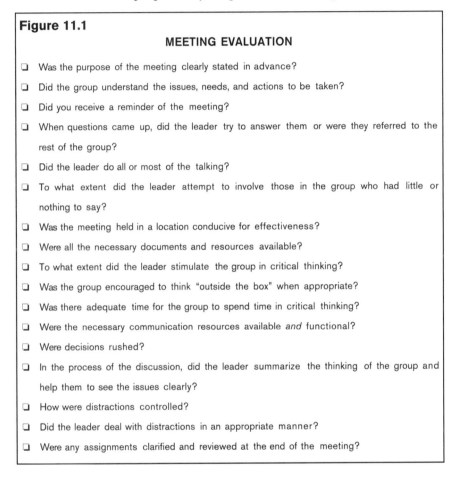

Figure 11.1

MEETING EVALUATION

❑ Was the purpose of the meeting clearly stated in advance?

❑ Did the group understand the issues, needs, and actions to be taken?

❑ Did you receive a reminder of the meeting?

❑ When questions came up, did the leader try to answer them or were they referred to the rest of the group?

❑ Did the leader do all or most of the talking?

❑ To what extent did the leader attempt to involve those in the group who had little or nothing to say?

❑ Was the meeting held in a location conducive for effectiveness?

❑ Were all the necessary documents and resources available?

❑ To what extent did the leader stimulate the group in critical thinking?

❑ Was the group encouraged to think "outside the box" when appropriate?

❑ Was there adequate time for the group to spend time in critical thinking?

❑ Were the necessary communication resources available *and* functional?

❑ Were decisions rushed?

❑ In the process of the discussion, did the leader summarize the thinking of the group and help them to see the issues clearly?

❑ How were distractions controlled?

❑ Did the leader deal with distractions in an appropriate manner?

❑ Were any assignments clarified and reviewed at the end of the meeting?

A final suggestion for evaluating the effectiveness of the meeting is to use an outside observer. Select someone who is not part of the group and ask him to observe the meeting. He should not participate in the meeting but should be seated in a location where he can see the group easily. The observer focuses on how people behave during the meeting. Special attention is given to what keeps the discussion moving in the right direction and what things interfere with the discussion. Keep track of who speaks and how many times. It may be helpful to develop a chart and mark an "x" for each person in the room and then draw a line from the speaker to the person spoken to. If the person responds to the first person, then draw another line back. If they speak to someone else, draw a line in that direction. This activity helps to discover who is doing most of the talking and also who did not speak at all or very little. It provides an indication of the balance and flow of communication. One of the elements of an effective meeting is that there is full participation on the part of the members. This is one way to track it.

The observer should try to look for feelings behind words spoken and see if the group responds to the feelings as well. Try to determine to what degree emotions and feelings are involved in the decisions being made. Watch the interest level during the meeting. If it is low or people seem bored, what could be suggested to "shift gears" and get people actively participating again? Do an assessment of the room itself. Are people comfortable? Can they see one another? Can they see the media easily? Is there good ventilation? Is the lighting adequate? Are there distracting noises? If the discussion lags, try to determine why. Have they been working on the topic too long and do they need a break? Is the topic of interest to the entire group, and is too much time being spent on the topic? Is the leader dominating the discussion and not allowing others to participate?

In the report, the observer should not pass judgment on the process but just report what was seen. Report the facts, not opinions. Let the group draw their own conclusions on how to improve the performance for the next group meeting.

Conclusion

It has been said with a great deal of truth that people working together can accomplish much more than a single person working alone. But the difficulty lies in the fact that many people are not used to working together in groups. Because of this, they do not see the benefit of teamwork. Leaders need to practice and teach this approach as they lead groups of people working together for ministry purposes.

Conducting effective meetings is not as difficult as quantum physics. Much can be accomplished with some forethought and prior planning. When this is done well, people will not resent having to attend a meeting and will begin to value the use of this time as an integral part of conducting ministry. The key to developing this attitude is being able and willing to apply the principle highlights in this chapter.

BY
JAMES ESTEP JR.

Chapter 12

Ministry Leaders as Change Agents

CHANGE IS A WORD THAT can evoke fear and apprehension or inspire and foster innovation. Just as people experience change throughout their lives, both beneficial and detrimental, organizations experience it as well. Changes within congregations and Christian organizations can occur for a variety of reasons. One of the most popular books of 1999 was *Who Moved My Cheese?* by Spencer Johnson. Through a simple parable the book highlights the dynamics of change through the reaction of four mice to the loss (change) of their prized cheese.[1]

Similarly, Mike Nappa's *Who Moved My Church?* provides a contemporary parable that addresses different relationships between the congregation and community. In it four parishioners seek their lost church building, and upon finding it implement their own version of ministry to the community.[2] What's the point? Congregations and Christian organizations have a choice. Either we facilitate change intentionally or we simply respond to the change that occurs and allow it to dictate the course of our ministry. Remember what we said earlier in this book: healthy growth requires change.

As Christian administrators entrusted with the ministry of reconciliation (2 Cor. 5), we must commit ourselves to intentional, proactive change within our institutions. Failure to embrace the positive potential of organizational change focuses our attention on the past and management of the present rather than helps us commit to engineering the organization's desired future. This chapter offers a brief insight into the nature of change and the means by which change can be introduced into a Christian organization. The management of organization and personal conflict is also addressed as part of the administration's pastoral responsibility to the congregation or organization.

The Nature of Change

Change is something we all talk about, but we rarely take time to either define or explain its nature. Without establishing a basic understanding of change, it becomes almost impossible to introduce change effectively into an organization. We will start with five basic assumptions about the nature of change: Change is natural, inevitable, necessary, a process, and value-based.

1. Change Is Natural

Put another way, change simply happens. Just as it is quite natural for us as individuals to be born, grow, live, and inevitably die, it is also the life cycle of organizations. To deny that change is natural is to deny reality itself. Who among us has *never* experienced change of some kind or another?

Figure 12.1 illustrates the change that naturally occurs within an institution's life cycle.[3] This model tracks the trajectory of change naturally present in the life cycle of an idea, ministry, program, or organization. Beginning at the lower left of the figure, organizations are shown to be born through active, intentional, progressive change. They focus on the future and engineer a ministry to achieve their desired dream. The organization continues to grow through purposeful planning and continued advancement, striving to reach its full potential. However, eventually the program, ministry, or organization will reach a plateau, a point at which the maximum effectiveness is achieved. Hence the objectives of the original dream are achieved and fulfilled. With the loss of forward momentum and movement, what happens next?

It is an institutional myth that organizations can simply maintain their current levels of effectiveness without any significant change occurring. In reality, one may have to change the program, ministry, or organization just to maintain present levels of achievement. The maintenance myth has led to ineffectiveness and the eventual death of many congregations and Christian organizations. The only way to maintain growth of the organization and the further expansion and accomplishment of its ministry is to reengineer the organization, to recast the vision that was discussed earlier in chapter 3. In essence, we are asking, "What does God want us to do next?" Failing to do this commits the organization to a change pattern driven by entropy and gradual decline rather than intentional progress driven by God's will.

The right side of the diagram illustrates what happens when reengineering does *not* occur. The ministry diminishes because the original dream, having already been achieved, no longer inspires or has the momentum for forward progress. Hence the organization *institutionalizes* and begins to exist and work for its own continued existence, not the achievement of ministry. Its focus becomes a glorified past, when the dream was still alive. Eventually the ministry or organization collapses due to lack of sufficient reason to exist or continue in an ineffective ministry. It simply dies. This is the end of the normal cycle of an organization's life, *if* the organization never recasts its vision.

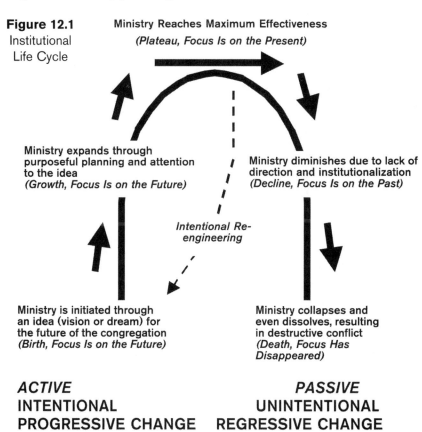

Figure 12.1 Institutional Life Cycle

Ministry Reaches Maximum Effectiveness
(Plateau, Focus Is on the Present)

Ministry expands through purposeful planning and attention to the idea
(Growth, Focus Is on the Future)

Ministry diminishes due to lack of direction and institutionalization
(Decline, Focus Is on the Past)

Intentional Re-engineering

Ministry is initiated through an idea (vision or dream) for the future of the congregation
(Birth, Focus Is on the Future)

Ministry collapses and even dissolves, resulting in destructive conflict
(Death, Focus Has Disappeared)

ACTIVE
INTENTIONAL
PROGRESSIVE CHANGE

PASSIVE
UNINTENTIONAL
REGRESSIVE CHANGE

Change is a natural aspect of life, for individuals or organizations, is a myth. To deny this can be life-threatening. While some change is intentional and beneficial, like the left side of the paradigm, and other times unintentional and degrading, it is nevertheless part of the natural life cycle of organizations.

2. Change Is Inevitable

Based on the previous paradigm institutional change it is not only natural but inevitable. Even *if* the active, intentional, progressive type of change is never fully realized by the organization, the passive, unintentional, regressive demise of an institution is inevitable. In the presence of genuine leadership, change is intentional; in the absence of leadership, change is a by-product of institutional entropy. As such, it is never a matter of avoiding change; it is a matter of which type of change we choose to experience. Change is inevitable.

3. Change Is Necessary

Just as change is natural and inevitable, it is also necessary. It is necessary for the advancement of the institution's mission and ministry, as well as to maintain its present level of ministry and, inevitably, its own survival. Failure to embrace the necessity of change creates a stagnant institutional environment that sees change as contrary to its mission. This is typical of administrations that rest on self-perception rather than institutional reality in decision making, strategic planning, and managing the organization, the images of the past rather and the reality of the present, over the future desired ministry objective. However, congregations and organizations that have proven themselves over time, having fruitfully endured changes in culture and demographics, are those that embrace the necessity of change.

For example, Sunday school has survived for more than two hundred years because it has intentionally reinvented itself numerous times throughout its history. In fact, most people are surprised to discover that the first Sunday school was a social outreach program that met in a restaurant with a paid instructor who taught more than the Bible (e.g., hygiene, literacy), and was not initially supported by the church. For most of us, our experience was almost the opposite of the original Sunday school established by Robert Raikes in 1780. It has indeed reinvented itself over the centuries, and had it not done so it might not be in existence today.[4] Change is necessary.

4. Change Is a Process

Change involves a process of generating a new idea, accepting it, implementing the idea, responding to conflict, and making what was once new part of the routine. In short, change is a process that involves the mind and heart of the individuals comprising the organization. In regard to the change process, congregations and organizations have five different types of individuals, each with his or her own function in the process of institutional change (see Figure 12.2a):

Initiators. These are the innovators, the change agents, the creative individuals who generate new ideas. This group is typically a minority of the congregation or organization.

Early Adopters. These are not the change agents themselves, but those who value the initiators and tend to agree with the new ideas, and hence they tend to adopt the idea early in the process. This group is typically larger than the initiators.

Middle Adopters. These make up the majority of the congregation or organization, typically comprising 55 to 65 percent of the people. They tend to follow the lead of the early adopters, and hence are cautious of new ideas until they see others adopting them as their own.

Late Adopters. These are the skeptics, who are not prone to adopting new ideas, and in fact will tend not to adopt them until they see a vast majority of the congregation or organization behind them. They typically are about the same in number as the early adopters, but they wait until the middle adopters have moved.

Stragglers. These are the opponents of change. This group tends to vehemently oppose change, and hence typically work against it or leave the congregation or organization when the change is adopted. They are typically in the minority of the congregation or organization, numbering about the same as the initiators.

Figure 12.2a: Balanced Organization Change Process

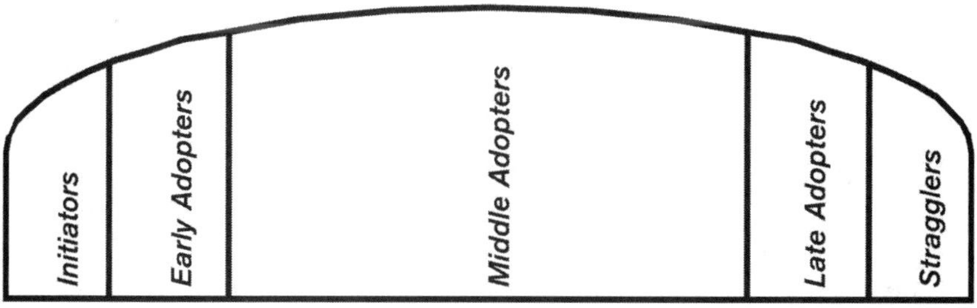

The process of adopting change is like watching a light turn green in a long line of traffic. The first car responds to the green light perhaps immediately (initiators). However, the second car (early adopters) must wait until the first car moves, and hence a slight delay occurs between the light turning green and the vehicles in the line moving. This process continues, with the third, fourth, and even fifth vehicle following in procession until all the traffic has moved and the light turns red. If all the traffic moved immediately, simultaneously, an accident would take place.

However, not all congregations and organizations are like the standard model for institutional change. For example, some are more amenable to change than others. Figure 12.2b illustrates this type of institution. In it, the initiator and early adopter groups comprise a larger part of the body than in the typical, balanced model. Hence, innovation and rapid adoption is typical for the institution.

In other instances, congregations and organizations are not as open to the idea of change (Figure 12.2c). In these institutions the late

Figure 12.2b: Innovative Organization Change Process

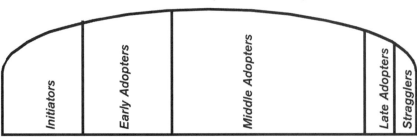

Figure 12.2c: Stagnant Organization Change Process

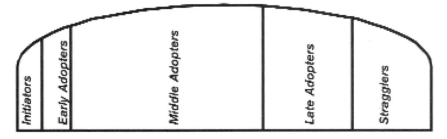

adopters and stragglers comprise a larger role, minimizing the voice of change by the initiators and early adopters. Such institutions would be traditional and somewhat stagnant, since innovation is improbable.

How do people _adopt_ the idea of change? Maxwell describes this change as a process of adoption, moving from ignorance to the acceptance of innovation. The chart below contains Maxwell's steps which individuals, congregations, and organizations move through from ignorance of an idea to fully accepting change and all its implications.[5]

Step 1: Ignorance. No unified direction or sense of priorities is felt among the followers.

Step 2: Information. General information is given to the people. Initially the ideas for change are not embraced.

Step 3: Infusion. The penetration of new ideas into the status quo may cause confrontations with apathy, prejudice, and tradition. The general tendency is to focus on problems.

Step 4: Individual Change. The early adopters begin to see the benefits of the proposed change and embrace them. Personal convictions replace complacency.

Step 5: Organizational Change. Two sides of the issue are being discussed. Less defensiveness and more openness concerning proposed changes can be observed. The momentum shifts from antichange to prochange.

Step 6: Awkward Application. Some failures and some successes are experienced as the change is implemented. The learning process is rapid.

Step 7: Integration. Awkwardness begins to decrease and the acceptance level increases. A growing sense of accomplishments and a secondary wave of results and successes occur.

Step 8: Innovation. Significant results create confidence and a willingness to take risks. The result is a willingness to change more rapidly and boldly.

Change should be viewed as a process, but upon what is the process based?

5. Change Is Value-Based

Change is never neutral! In Christian organizations, changes should be theologically motivated, and in some situations must be opposed on theological grounds. As we assess existing structures in the congregation or organization, we in turn dismantle them in order to better analyze their components and relationship to the existing education ministry, and in turn reassemble them into a newly formulated approach to ministry. However, in each of these stages, the congregation's theological values and concerns provide direction. In generating new ideas, analyzing them, advancing priorities within the institution, and facilitating ministry, *all* steps are based on theologically informed values. Since change is value-based, not all change can be considered either Christian or desired. It must be assessed through the lenses of Scripture and theology, but theology must not be confused with the status quo.

Types of Organizational Change

Change is not always the same. As previously mentioned, two broad categories of change are present in the life cycle of congregations and organizations. *Active change* is what was indicated on the left side of the life cycle chart. It indicates organizational change due to intentional planning and structuring, dream-driven, future-focused administration of the ministry. In this instance, administration is congregational or organizational leadership. On the other hand, *passive change* refers to the right side of the life cycle diagram. It indicates change due to purposefulness, irrelevancy, institutionalism, and past-focused (nostalgic) administration of the ministry. Seen in this light, administrators respond to institutional change rather than leading it. Rarely is passive change a conscious decision of administrators, but simply an accepted institutional entropy in the absence of genuine leadership capable of facilitating active change.

However, another dimension to the idea of change is the pace or degree of the change introduced into a congregation or organization. *Gradual change* refers to small or incremental changes, minor alterations within the congregation or organization's existing administrative framework—change decisions made within the matrix of the mission, vision, and core values of the congregation or organization. *Radical change* refers to large-scale changes, those that alter the very framework of the congregation—change decisions that reengineer the congregational and organizational matrix. It is within the combination of these four factors that the kinds of change can be identified and better understood. Figure 12.3 illustrates these four possible combinations of change.

Figure 12.3
Kinds of Institutional Change

	Gradual	*Radical*
Active—planned and intentional	*Tweaking*, gradual change; e.g., changing the times of Sunday school or forming a new Sunday school class.	*Transformation*, radical change and crisis management; e.g., Switching from a Sunday school format to a small groups/mid-week Bible study format.
Passive—reactionary and unintentional	*Evolution*, e.g., monitoring the continual slow decline of participation in Sunday school, deciding to reduce the number of classes.	*Crisis or Reactionary*; e.g., a church camp decides to sell property in order to meet the financial deficit of the general fund.

Tweaking and *Transformation* are active, planned, and intentional modes of change. They represent positive action to increase the potential of the congregation or organization's ministry. As such, they seek to bring the organization into a desired future. *Evolution* and *Crisis/Reactionary* are passive, reactionary, and unintentional modes of change. They represent action to maintain or minimize the decline of the congregation or organization's ministry. As such, they accept the inevitable future and seek to adapt to the changing ministry environment.

Healthy congregations understand and embrace change. Those bodies engaged in managing a congregation or organization in a climate of passive change do not seek to create a desired future, but they accept the inevitability of their declining future and simply change in response to it. This chapter focuses on the promotion and implementation of active, intentional change in congregations and Christian organizations. This is far more desirable.

Promoting and Implementing Organizational Change

The promotion and implementation of intentional change in a congregation or organization is a threefold process, forming a never-ending cycle of continual reengineering to incessantly advance its ministry potential. As such, innovation and creativity are desired characteristics of an institutional leader. The three phases are thawing, flowing, and freezing.

Figure 12.4
Process of
Implementing
Change

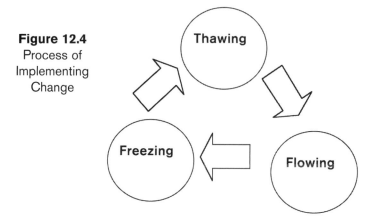

Phase 1: Thawing. This is a period when the idea is introduced, resistance is countered, and individuals are motivated to both adopt and participate in the change. This is only the initial stage. The proposed change can simply be snuffed out with little effort on the part of stragglers and advocates of the status quo. It is the period when the reason for change is given, and a call for commitment to the proposed change is made. During this phase, the status quo is undergoing review and discontentment is surfaced over the current circumstances so as to motivate the acceptance of change. The proposed change is being sold to the congregation. In short, it is a time of loosening our grip on the past . . . thawing, becoming fluid, able to move.

Phase 2: Flowing. This is a period of strategically moving from the past to the future in the present—moving from what *is* to what *is desired*. It is the implementation of the idea. During this period, managing the implementation process is critical. Jim Herrington, Mike Bonem, and James Furr identify four "disciplines" that aid a congregation during this period of organizational change.[6]

- *Discipline One.* Generating and Sustaining Creative Tension. Communication, decision making, initial conceptualization of the proposed change.

- *Discipline Two.* Harnessing the Power of Mental Models. Metaphor, assumptions, and paradigms for the congregation and ministry.
- *Discipline Three.* Enabling Team Learning. Those responsible for the change must become specialists on the subject, not as individuals, but as a group.
- *Discipline Four.* Practicing Systems Thinking. Congregations are complex organizations with interrelated systems all of which are impacted by proposed changes.

This phase is comprised of the tactics of change, the step-by-step process of implementation. This is generally accomplished by frequent and clear communication, structure and support for the change, and continual assessment of the process. During this stage, the proposed change is being formulated. In short, the ice having thawed is now flowing along a predetermined path toward a desired destination.

The freezing phase is a period of empowerment, when the new idea becomes the status quo. The change reaches its penultimate and final form. Freezing still involves the process of implementation, but it is the final step to making the proposal the new status quo. The implementation is completed and it becomes the standard practice. In short, the idea now freezes, becomes solid and recognizable within the congregation.

Figure 12.5 summarizes this three-phase process of implementing change. However, it is critical to remember that it is an ongoing process, since what is frozen from the last change initiative must be thawed in favor of a better one in the future.

Figure 12.5
Three-Phase Change Process

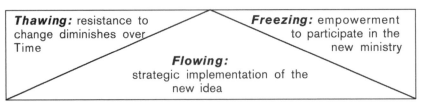

Organizational Change Strategies and Tactics

Successful institutional change involves moving strategically, forming a proper approach to the overall matter, and tactically taking specific actions to accomplish the strategy. Hence, change tactics are twofold: (1) tactics that advance the cause of the proposed change, and (2) tactics that minimize the opposition or resistance to the proposed change.

Figure 12.6 provides a strategic view of how to implement change within a congregation.[7]

Figure 12.6: Strategy for Change

Change Stage	Challenge/Issue	General Response (Strategy)	Action Steps (Tactics)
Thawing	Overcoming resistance to change	*Build a case for the necessity of change*	Identify and explain the dissatisfaction with current ministry or situation.
			Provide opportunities to participate in the change process.
			Recruit those who support the change initiative.
			Provide pastoral attention to those who continue to disagree.
			Provide time for the thawing process to occur.
Flowing	Managing the process of change	*Establish a detailed process for change*	Formulate a clear concept for the desired change initiative.
			Communicate the change initiative to the congregation through a variety of means.
			Develop a support system (organizationally, materially, and spiritually) for the transition period.
			Design a system of evaluation and assessment for feedback on the progress of change.
Freezing	Implementing the proposed change	*Accentuate the congregational dynamics for change*	Gain support from key leaders, individuals, and groups in the congregation.
			Use diverse voices in support for change, e.g., men and women, generational representation.
			Develop slogans, symbols and language in support of the change initiative.
			Provide stability by celebration and acknowledgement.

In light of these general strategies for implementing change, tactics for achieving change are critical for the successful execution of change.

Thawing Tactics

Effective change requires tactics that cause members of the congregation or organization to recognize the need for change and to embrace the willingness to move toward it by adopting a new idea or paradigm. This is typically the most difficult phase of implementing organizational change. Several recommended tactics to achieve this are as follows:

- Provide biblical and theological reasons for the change, but avoid the negative implication that failure to support the idea is unbiblical or unfaithful.
- Tie the proposed change to the mission and vision of the congregation or organization.
- Objectively illustrate the need for change, for example, catalog unmet needs, analyze a decline in attendance, and publish survey results.
- Seek out the opinion of key congregational members, organizational participants, and even key members of the community early in the process.
- Suggest that the proposed change is not a replacement, but an alternative to the status quo, and hence does not necessitate the omission of existing programs, policies, or procedures. However, because the proposed change is an improvement over the status quo, in time it would replace it by attrition.
- Avoid the appearance of railroading by giving individuals time for consideration, reflection, and discussion. In short, don't vote for the proposal the moment it is proposed.
- Several months prior to introducing the proposal, introduce the idea of change through a sermon, lesson, or staff address.
- Present the proposed change as an extension or revision of an old one, and hence as more of a modification or adaptation of the past and present.
- Use external examples of other congregations or organizations that have made similar changes. Point out institutions, but avoid the possible "me-to" appearance of these arguments.
- Do your homework on the subject; consult external authorities, for example, journals or experts for support, even a congregational or business consultant.
- Have the proposed change well thought through, including purpose and objectives, plan for implementation, resources dedicated to its completion, and a means of assessing its impact. This process will continue into the second phase.

Flowing Tactics

Once the case for the necessity of change is won and the decision is made to change, administration must engage in planning the step-by-step process of incorporating the decision into the congregation or organization, moving toward the desired change. The following methods are associated with the flow phase of the change process:

- Form an implementation team to manage the details of the implementation plan and respond to unexpected difficulties.

- Storyboard the steps necessary for moving from the current point A to desired point B. Heller and Hindle explain that in addition to identifying the steps required in the change process, two additional features of the story board should be to dovetail tasks. Align the steps to complement the overall task of change and quantify tasks. Give a predetermined deadline for each step or number of days for completion of a given step.[8]
- Make the proposed change manageable, divided into a specific set of singular action steps that are readily achievable individually but cumulatively move the congregation or organization toward the desired destination.
- Determine resources and a timetable for implementation; assign dates and dollars.
- Visit diverse congregations and organizations to glean from their experience and achievement.
- Develop a thorough institutional communication strategy. How will the institution be informed and kept informed on the progress of the proposed change? You could say it is a matter of locution, locution, locution.
- In addition to information sharing, commit to a process of gaining congregational input, town-meeting sessions, polls (not votes), and questionnaires.
- One-on-one selling of the idea. Spend private time with key individuals and voices in the congregation and organization.
- Maintain a checklist for completion and responsibility to ensure coordination of the implementation measures.

Freezing Tactics

How does the proposed change become the institution's status quo? This is the task of the third phase, freezing. It is the final phase in the implementation of change. Several administrative tactics facilitate the engraining of the new idea into the organizational culture.

- Communications about the change should focus on positive implications and benefits of its adoption and completion.
- Emphasize the *why* and *what* rather than the *how* of the proposed change. Explain and focus on the purpose and objectives, not the methods.
- Solidify the completion of change by formalizing it into organizational policies and procedures.
- Throughout the process, maintain a heightened level of communication, both in terms of frequency and overlapping means of communication.

- Organizational change is accomplished by the team, not just individuals. Hence, acknowledge the success of the team over individuals.
- Celebrate its completion! The celebration also serves as a point of finality to the proposed change.

Each phase of the change process requires a different type of tactic, each utilized to accomplish a necessary effect on individuals and the organization itself.

Recognizing Change Resisters

A fatal error in many organizational change endeavors is to underestimate the possible negative reactions to change. This is not just the matter of dealing with stragglers, but with all the implications of change. For some people, the process of accepting change is traumatic, even resembling the stages of death—inability to act, denial, anger, bargaining, depression, testing, and acceptance.[9] So it should come as no surprise to experienced administrators that conflict arises during these traumatic encounters.

Resistance may come from a variety of sources, but it all shares the common element of a fear response to the proposed change. It is a reaction to the loss of something held sacred or that will be altered beyond recognition. These barriers may originate with beliefs and values that are threatened, personal and interpersonal barriers, and organizational barriers, even failure to trust leadership. The following are possible sources of resistance of which administrators must be aware:[10]

Interpretation and Theology. Perhaps unique to congregations and Christian organizations is change resistance based on differences of interpretation or theology. Example: Opposing social outreach ministries to the poor and underprivileged based on a belief that the gospel requires only spiritual outreach. Solution: Formulating a sound theological perspective on the proposed change may aid in minimizing the resistance.

Worldviews and Values. Since change is never neutral but reflective of values and priorities, resistance to change can arise from individuals holding different values and priorities. Example: Those valuing status quo over innovation, or the general difference in perceiving financial debt as unacceptable vs. necessary. Solution: Communicating how the proposed change is aligned with the congregation or organization's mission, vision, and core values will help minimize this source of resistance.

Interpersonal Issues. Organizations change because the individuals in the organizations change. Resistance can occur due to the relationships within the institution. Example: Personal feelings, perceptions of nepotism. Solution: Being aware of this potential source of resistance and considering key individual's feelings and perceptions in the planning process can address this concern.

Procedural Matters. Change can be resisted on the basis that its determination and implementation violate an expected or agreed-upon procedure. Example: A Christian school announces the finalization of a decision to change admission requirements prior to the faculty having had their voice in the decision. Solution: Concerns for procedure can be addressed by not only predetermining the approval and implementation procedures, but communicating them to the congregation or organization prior to the implementation of the proposed changes.

Institutionalism. "We've never done it that way before!" This is resistance based on the value placed on the status quo and sacrosanct traditions that are taboo. Example: Opposing a change toward elective adult Sunday school classes because the congregation has always had age-graded adult classes. This is perhaps the most difficult form of resistance, since many of those advocating it are sincere and simply unfamiliar with what other congregations and organizations are doing. Solution: The best way to minimize this is to introduce change through inductive discussions and present it as an addition or alternative, but not a replacement.

Nearsighted Ministry. Resistance can result from a lack of perceived need, which creates a problem for the thawing phase of implementing change. Example: A church camp does not recognize the need for a special needs or disabilities week of camp and subsequently rejects the idea of scheduling such a week. Often this problem is due to their inability to see beyond their own needs or that of their relationships. Solution: Resistance can be countered by providing an accurate portrait of the need, utilizing the thawing tactics, providing even testimonies and illustrations to emphasize the need for change.

Distrust of Leaders. Christian leaders are called to "be above reproach" (1 Tim. 3:2 NIV), "blameless" (Titus 1:6 NIV), and "worthy of respect" (1 Tim. 3:8 NIV). When leaders have failed to provide leadership, or even have given the appearance of impropriety or trustworthiness, those listening to a proposed change may not feel compelled to rally in support. Example: Someone questions a new expansion to a facility when one of the decision makers is a building contractor. Solution: To resist this problem leadership should be held to a high standard, be available and accessible, maintain a visible presence, and admit when failure occurs and work toward correcting it.

Complexity of Change. Resistance can occur when change is misunderstood or simply so complicated that it is not readily comprehended. An effective response to this source of resistance is to provide a clear, accurate portrait of the change proposal. Example: Outlining a forty-step process for changing the curriculum at a Christian school rather than describing it in terms of five phases, each comprised of eight steps. Solution: Presentations should identify the rationale for change, the phases for its implementation, and emphasize future opportunities for clarification and updates.

Generational Innovators. Implicit in the process of implementing change is that what is an innovation today becomes the status quo tomorrow, only to be challenged by the next generation of leadership within the congregation or organization. Resistance can arise from an unlikely source, another innovator, who feels the need to preserve his or her creation. Example: A new camp manager recommends changes to the standard camp schedule to his board, on which sits the former camp manager who created the schedule template originally. Solution: One way of addressing this concern is to seek the advice of generational innovators early in the process and allow them to become part of the process. Also, demonstrate the affiliation of the proposed change to theirs rather than identifying the previous innovation as being wrong, lacking, or ineffective.

Personality Traits. Often change is resisted based on a sense of personal fear about the proposal. For example, some individuals are simply not inclined to risk, favoring the security of constancy rather than seeing the need for change. Others may be unwilling to suffer the pain or sacrifice that it may take to birth a new idea and see it grow to fruition. Complacency is likewise a common problem, seeing no one's need but their own. For those involved in the existing organizational structure, if change challenges it, they may perceive a threat to status within the institution, or fear the possibility of increased responsibility with a new position. Solution: A pastoral presence is the best response. These concerns and fears must be allayed by a sympathetic presence, providing spiritual counsel.

Assessing Fields of Force

How does an administrator know when sufficient support has been raised to undertake a change initiative? One can utilize a fields-of-force analysis. Figure 12.7 illustrates such an analysis. It depicts the support for and resistance to the idea of changing the curriculum in Sunday school to an application-focused curriculum from a content-focused curriculum. Those in favor of the change are the Christian education minister, most Sunday school teachers, the congregation's Christian education board, most parents, and denominational leaders. The relative strength of each of these supporters is represented by the arrows, ranging from +1 to +5.

Those opposing the change, favoring the status quo, are the youth minister, deacon chairman, some Sunday school teachers, the Sunday school superintendent, and some parents. As with the supporters, the relative strength of the resisters, those favoring status quo, are likewise assessed on a -1 to -5 scale. This analysis suggests that the forces in support of the change total 23 points, while those resisting change total 9 points.

Figure 12.7
Force Field
Analysis

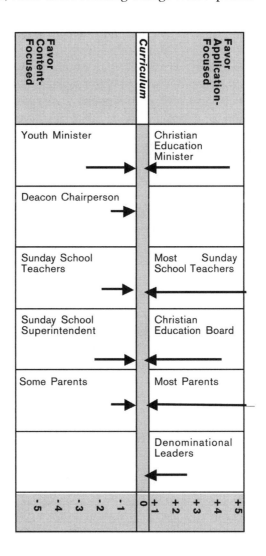

How do you know how to assess points? What makes someone a 2 and another a 5? Obviously the positive scale is for those in favor of change, and the negative scale are those opposing it. But how do you assign a numerical value? Several criteria may be used to assess the strength of these voices: (1) *Numbers.* Obviously a head count of individuals must be considered in assessing strength. (2) *Respected Individuals.* A respected individual may be assessed as being more influential than fifty individuals not recognized as leaders. (3) *Affected People.* Those directly impacted by the proposed change need to be included in the assessment and given more voice than those unaffected by it. (4) *Positioned People.* Weight must be given to those who hold leadership positions within the congregation or organization, or who are in a position of decision making about the change. While this process is not scientific, it is a means of objectifying the decision-making process innate to institution organizational change. It identifies areas where additional attention should be focused to facilitate the acceptance of change.

Preparing for Conflict

Change and conflict are two sides of the same coin. Resistance to change usually takes the form of some level of conflict. The competent administrator recognizes this fact and takes appropriate measures to manage the inevitable conflict that will arise on some level in resistance to the proposed change. Not all conflict is alike. It occurs at different levels of intensity. Speed Leas identifies five levels of "religious strife":[11]

Level 1: Predicaments. Individuals stay focused on the problem.

Level 2: Disagreement. Individuals stay focused on self-protection.

Level 3: Contest. Individuals openly engage in a win/lose scenario.

Level 4: Fight/Flight. Individuals break relationships with the opposition.

Level 5: Intractable. Individuals legitimize doing harm to the opposition.

Each level of conflict requires an appropriate response. Most congregational conflicts are manageable until they pass level 3. At this level common distortions begin to occur between the disagreeing parties:[12]

- Dichotomizing. Conflicting parties view the situation in absolute terms, e.g., right/wrong, black/white, with no gray.
- Universalizing. Conflicting parties speak in terms of "everyone," "all," "never."
- Magnification. Conflicting parties focus tightly on every issue, blowing minute incidents out of their natural proportion or giving grandiose interpretations.

- Fixation on Emotions. Conflicting parties emphasize the fear or hurt inflicted by opposition or demonstrate anger as a means of derailing the process.

The best response to level 3 is to increase clear and direct communication with the opposition, highlight areas of common ground between the disagreeing parties, and identify the values at the root of the issue.[13] After level 3 the necessity of a professional conflict manager, or an outside third party, may be required to facilitate conversation or to arbitrate a truce.

Approaches to Organizational Conflict

What strategy can we use to respond to conflict situations? In general, administrators must decide to respond with assertiveness, desiring to win, or in a spirit of cooperation, valuing relationships and discourse in working through the problem. When these two axes are combined, four possible approaches to conflict management emerge (Figure 12.8).

Figure 12.8 Strategies for Conflict Management	High	**Compete** (Win/Lose)	**Collaborate** (Win/Win)
	Assertive		
	Low	**Cower** (Lose/Lose)	**Compromise** (Lose/Win)
		Low Relationship High	

Compete and *collaborate* are highly assertive, with their distinction resting in the value of asserting organizational change. *Compete* sees a winner and a loser, whereas *collaborate* seeks to create a situation where all involved are winners. On the lower end of the assertive scale are those who *cower*, avoiding conflict and inevitably committing to a losing strategy; and a *compromise* approach wherein the necessary changes are thwarted to preserve the relationship. Of course, *compromise* and *collaborate* place high value on personal relations within the organization, while *compete* and *cower* do not. The most favored response is a collaborative, win/win strategy.

These approaches are further exemplified by Peacemaker Ministries of Billings, Montana, which has identified three general categories of behavior that address conflict within the church. Figure 12.9 identifies the behaviors and actions associated with these possible responses to conflict, noting that often conciliatory responses slip into escape or attack responses.[14]

Figure 12.9
Responses to Conflict

Escape Responses (Cower)	Attack Responses (Compete)	Conciliation Responses (Compromise, Collaborate)	
o Denial o Flight o Suicide	o Litigation o Assault o Murder	o Personal o One-on-One o Overlook an offense o Discussion o Negotiation	o Assisted o Third Party aid o Mediation o Arbitration o Church discipline

Conclusion

Change is inevitable in organizations. Whether Christian in mission or not, the world is always changing. Those organizations that operate in this world will undergo change as well. Whether it be positive or negative, change will occur. As Christian leaders we have the choice to stand by and respond to change or we can choose to manage its influence proactively in our lives. The healthier response is to be intentional about it. Unfortunately, change also brings conflict. Again, Christian leaders need to view conflict from a positive rather than a negative point of view. Conflict gives us an opportunity to facilitate dialogue and discussion. It brings us out of our comfort zone and creates a degree of disequilibrium in our lives. Not all of this turbulence is negative. In fact, most conflict has positive outcomes if managed properly and from a biblical perspective.

Regardless of the intensity of the conflict, administrators who are Christian must maintain a pastoral perspective and presence in the situation. In his book *Firestorm*, Ron Susek discusses six appropriate pastoral responses to conflict, each depending on the conflict situation:[15]

Step Out. Set a spiritual example, providing model behavior in the face of conflict.

Step In. Mediate the conflict, providing a common ground for conflicting sides.

Step Over. Rise above the conflict, providing a subject on which to focus that is greater than the subject of the conflict.

Step Up. Confront the conflict, providing a direct response to the source of conflict.

Step Back. Let the conflict burn itself out, providing space for a conflict to continue, but with a limited opportunity for expansion due to lack of consumables.

Step Down. Resign from the conflict, providing no support or engagement to a conflict that has no need for administrative involvement.

As Christian administrators, we have an obligation to both the individuals with whom we serve and the congregation or institution to provide a pastoral response to their circumstances, even those involving conflict. Change is difficult to embrace for some people, while others greet it with enthusiasm. In either case, a pastoral spirit must prevail in order to maintain the Christian nature of the organization.

BY
JAMES ESTEP JR.

Chapter 13

Decision Making and Communication within the Organization

WE MAKE DECISIONS EVERY DAY. As individuals we make mundane, routine decisions, such as what to wear or where to have lunch. Usually such routine, daily choices have little effect on the life of individuals. However, we also have to make decisions that are more significant, monumental—decisions that can be life-altering, such as choosing a college, career, or spouse. The process of decision making is simplified by being answerable to only oneself. Regardless of how complicated or monumental an *individual's* decision, it does not even compare to the complexity of managing the decision-making process of a group of individuals. Boards, committees, groups, teams, or task forces inevitably make decisions. While some of their decisions are routine and others are monumental, managing the process of decision making is critical.

Decision-Making Myths

Misconceptions about decision making are numerous. They confuse and confound the process of rendering a sound decision and hence jeopardize the purpose or task of the decision makers. The following are commonly held misconceptions about decision making:

Decisions are not all theologically based. For evangelicals, everything is theological. Regardless of how seemingly routine in nature or unrelated to theology, decisions reflect our values, which are theologically informed. Also, in every decision a search for biblical precedents should occur. For the Christian leader, all decisions are directly or indirectly theologically informed.

Decision making occurs only at the highest levels of the organization. In fact, decisions occur throughout the organization. Leaders, managers, or directors of specific programs and tasks make decisions. While perhaps the more strategic decisions are made by the organization's leadership, operational decisions are made throughout the organization.

Accurate and readily accessible information ensures a good decision. Accurate and accessible information is essential for a good decision, but it does _not_ insure good decisions. A faulty process, such as one that does not provide voice for every stakeholder in the decision, or biased interpretation of data, can render a poor decision in spite of superlative information.

Decisions are as easily made individually as corporately. As previously noted, the complexity of corporate decision making is exponentially more complex than individual decision making, even under the most ideal situations. An individual faces only his or her perspective and concerns when making a decision, but a group encounters the sum total of all the perspectives and concerns of the individuals within the group, as well as managing the collaborative interaction of such individuals.

Decisions are better made by small groups. While smaller groups have fewer relational bonds and fewer individual perceptions with which to contend, it does not mean the decision is better. A decision may be made more easily, but this is not necessarily better. Additionally, if the group is too small, it may not be representative of the entire organization and may still use a poor decision-making process. There is no correlation between the size of a group and the success of decisions made by them.

Decisions should be based on strictly objective reasons. Humans are not strictly objective beings; they have emotions, values, and commitments that may even border on the irrational. Decisions must be in response to more than simply objective concerns and criteria, and must be supported by more than cognitive means, with appeals to emotion and values. Similarly, problems or issues require a decision that may address the emotional as well as the intellectual needs and concerns of individuals. While objectivity is valued, it cannot be considered the only or best reason for a course of action.

Decisions are made by people taking action on their own. In fact, the opposite is true. Administrative decisions are a product of a corporate decision-making process, not simply individuals making decisions on their own. In fact, individuals acting on behalf of the group may be usurping the group's intentions.

In short, administrative decision making is a complicated matter not to be underestimated. A proper understanding of decisions and decision making safeguards the process and advances the potential for effective decisions.

Types of Decisions

Not all decisions are alike. For example, Hersey and Blanchard maintain that there are two essential issues within decision making for change: diagnosis, deciding what should be done, and implementation, deciding how to do it.[1] However, the characteristics of decisions even within these two broad categories may be distinct. Heller and Hindle identify eight different kinds of decisions:[2]

1. **Irreversible.** The decision, once made, cannot be unmade—such as when signing an agreement to sell or buy a company.

2. **Reversible.** The decision can be changed completely—either before, during, or after the agreed action begins.

3. **Experimental.** The decision is not final until the first results appear and prove themselves to be satisfactory.

4. **Trial-and-Error.** The decision is taken in knowledge that changes in plans will be forced by what actually happens in the course of action.

5. **Made in Stages.** After the initial step, further decisions follow as each stage of agreed action is completed.

6. **Cautious.** Decision allows for contingencies and problems that may crop up later. Decision makers hedge their bets.

7. **Conditional.** Decision altered if certain foreseen circumstances arise. An either/or decision, with options kept open.

8. **Delayed.** Put on hold until decision makers feel the time is right. Go-ahead given when required elements are in place.

While decisions are made at every level of the organization's administrative structure, decisions made at various levels differ in their significance and impact on the congregation. Figure 13.1 depicts the three basic administrative levels in any organization (leadership, management, and program director) and the three levels of decision making associated with each (long-range, strategic, and operational), with each level influencing the one below it. Leaders make the most influential decisions, those of long-range importance, such as the organization's mission, vision, or values. Managers, those supervising the directors of several programs, make strategic decisions, such as enrollment objectives and course offerings for a Sunday school over a three-year period or five-year expansion plans for the facilities of a Christian camp. The day-to-day decisions of operational importance are made by those leading programs within the organization, such as a Bible school superintendent deciding how much curriculum to order for the next Sunday school quarter. The degree of complexity and significance rises as a higher level of leadership engages in the process of decision making.

Figure 13.1

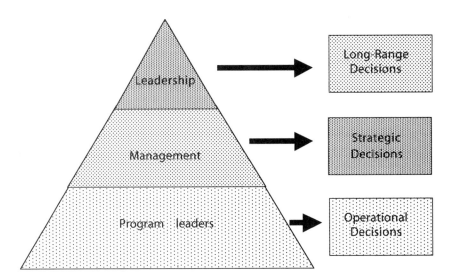

Decision Making by the Numbers

Formulas offer almost absolute certainty. For example, 2 + 2 = 4. Two hydrogen atoms plus an oxygen atom produces water (H_2O). However, decisions are *not* formulas. The process of making a decision does have some definable steps outlining the tasks in determining a direction (diagnosis) and implementation (action plans) within the organization. Figure 13.2 lists the basic steps in the decision-making process for both individuals and groups.

Continual Spiritual Preparation

This is both first and last in the steps of making an effective decision. Can a decision be *spiritual?* Absolutely! Decisions can be spiritual in several ways. Those participating in the decision-making process should prepare themselves spiritually by committing to prayer, fasting, devotion, and personal theological reflection during the period of decision making.

Wayne Jacobsen suggests several guidelines for corporate prayers in a team:[3]

- Prayer must be dynamic and flowing, sensitive to the uniqueness of each meeting.
- Members must be helped to understand that God is looking only for simple, sincere prayers.
- This is corporate prayer . . . jump right in with conversational praying.

Figure 13.2
DECISION-MAKING STEPS

Decision as Diagnosis
- Continual spiritual preparation.
- Clearly define the problem or issue.
- State the desired outcomes.
- Gather relevant information and materials.
- Collect alternative ideas.
- Explore and debate the best alternatives.
- Make the decision.
- Formulate policy/procedure.

Decision as Implementation
- Develop an implementation plan.
- Implement the idea.
- Assess the decision.
- Assess the whole process.

- Comments should not focus so much on conclusions for the business items ahead as on our attitudes and perspectives.
- Everyone must want God's will for the fellowship.
- No one person has a monopoly on God's wisdom.
- We must trust one another.
- Above all, don't be afraid to make mistakes.

Those participating in the decision-making process should approach the decision from a theologically informed perspective. Regardless of the nature of the decision, it should match several overarching theological criteria:

- Does the decision honor and glorify God?
- Is the decision consistent with God's revealed will in Scripture?
- Does the decision address the spiritual nature of humanity?
- Is its success based on a call to a maturing faithfulness?
- Does the decision affirm the nature of Christ's church and advance its mission?

These questions would serve as overarching criteria for the decision. They provide a theological context in which to make strategic, long-range, and operational decisions. Finally, decisions can be rooted in biblical precedent. The ability to examine a decision in light of a similar decision made by God's people in Scripture would provide a connection to the spiritual heritage of the faith community in the past.

Clearly Define the Problem or Issue

Decision makers require a target. The more clear the target, the more accurate the decision. Groups must explore, clarify, test, and summarize what exactly must be decided. It is possible, even probable, that every individual in the decision-making group will have at least a slightly different understanding of the problem or issue. Hence, without a clarifying step the group will experience confusion in the decision-making process. In this step, decision makers engage in either *linear thinking,* assuming that problems or matters are simple and require a singular response, and/or *systems thinking,* which assumes that problems or matters are complex and hence require a multifaceted response. Until the decision makers can agree on a commonly articulated, written definition of the matter requiring a decision, they cannot even engage in the appropriate type of thinking, let alone render an effective decision.

State the Desired Outcomes

What are the criteria for a successful decision? If the problem is solved, or the matter is fully addressed, what would be the *desired effect*? Typically, the criteria are a mirror reflection of the definition provided in the previous step. For example, if a Christian school is deciding how to award scholarships, and one issue is fairness in awarding scholarships to females or minorities, then a desired outcome would be that females and minorities will be equally eligible for scholarships. Once again, until the decision makers can write a set of desired outcomes, an effective decision cannot be rendered. As previously noted, some matters require systems thinking because they are so complex that no singular response will adequately address the matter. Likewise, the desired outcomes may not be singular, presenting a complex set of desired outcomes to address the situation.

Gather Relevant Information and Materials

Effective decisions require accurate, reliable, and current information. Decision makers must engage in fact finding, collecting materials and insights, even engage in surveying the congregation to generate needed information. While a decision has not yet been made, nor have alternatives been presented, it is important to gain an accurate portrait of the current situation and further define the subject at hand. Pertinent information may take many forms, depending on the matter being addressed:

Theological. Decision makers should engage Scripture and their own theological tradition to provide spiritual insight to the issue being discussed. In so doing, Christian administrators avoid the pitfalls of pragmatism and institutional expediency. As Karen Yust comments, "The primary purpose of every church committee is to discover God's will for church life."[4] In any organization that is Christian, the pastoral aspect of the decision must be maintained.

Statistical. In order to more accurately define or gauge the significance of problems or issues requiring decisions to be made, quantitative data may be necessary. For example, if a Christian education committee is deciding to create new Sunday school classes based on a sudden increase in church attendance, it would be prudent to know such statistical items as how large the increase in attendance has been, the number of current Sunday school classes, their enrollment and potential class sizes, and the number of available teachers in reserve.

Legal. In some instances legal advice may be required. Therefore, an attorney may become a consultant to the decision makers; for example, a camp's board of directors formulating a personnel manual, including hiring and termination policies, or designing a child-safety policy and procedure manual at a church. In both these instances, legal insight is necessary to insure that no state or federal statutes are violated or circumvented.

Historical. Part of planning and decision-making processes is understanding the organization's past as well as its present. It may become necessary to engage in historical fact finding to ascertain what factors or events contributed to the current situation being discussed. What caused the problem? What made the issue surface now? How has the organization dealt with this subject in the past?

Financial. Many decisions have budgetary implications. In fact, most decisions eventually have a budgetary impact. Information about the current situation's financial impact is critical, particularly if the decisions being made are due to financial problems. How much capital or credit do we have? Also, many of these budgetary decisions made by the organization ripple into the budgets of individuals, homes, and other constituent bodies. For example, a Christian college deciding to raise tuition should ask how such a tuition increase not only impacts their overall budget, but how it impacts the financial picture of parents and students, how it changes the potential for student grants or the greater dependence on student loans. Gaining an accurate financial picture before debating alternative ideas is essential.

Organizational. Assessing the current condition of the organization itself may also provide information necessary to make a decision. The health of the organization must be considered before making any decision. While some of this may take the form of statistical information, decisions must be made in light of the institution's mission, vision, and values. Hence decision makers should reflect on the issue through the institution's own lens as well.

It is critical to gather *all* the available information and make it readily available to *all* the decision makers, with no selective screening or restrictive access. In short, everyone involved in the decision-making process starts with the same portrait of the current situation.

Collect Alternative Ideas

Decision makers should engage in brainstorming. Without assessment or comment, every possible idea should be presented by decision makers. The purpose of brainstorming is that participants' ideas can be presented in rapid-fire succession in order to generate as many ideas as possible. Hence, groups must engage in the act of risking ideas, encouraging innovations, and recording *all* the results of the brainstorming sessions. Groups may place the responses into categories of similar alternatives in order to provide a preliminary level of analysis to the information processing. One critical note to remember is that this is *not* the actual decision-making stage. The decision itself may eventually be one of the ideas or a fusion of several ideas presented in the brainstorming session, *but* a decision is premature during this step.

Explore and Debate the Best Alternatives

Following the brainstorming exercises, the decision-making body must decide what ideas are most desirable. Which alternatives fulfill the desired outcomes? In order to address the matter properly, all the brainstorming alternatives must be assessed to determine which ones best fit the stated desired outcomes. This can be done by performing a SWOT analysis (strengths, weaknesses, opportunities, and threats). In this analysis, decision makers can assess how each of the brainstorming alternatives either targets (strength) or misses (weakness) the criteria. (See chapter 5 for additional information on conducting a SWOT analysis.) It may also be advantageous to return to the information gained in step 4 to assess which alternative is most favorable. The more accurate alternatives are then further assessed to determine the potential positive outcomes (opportunities) and potential risks (threats) to their implementation.

Figure 13.3 provides a graphic framework through which to make such assessments of ideas, gauging the certainty of a successful decision on two factors: (1) the precision and accuracy of desired outcome statements (Did decision makers know what needed to be addressed?) and (2) the degree of confidence in the methods recommended by the decision makers.

As this decision-making process ensues, favored alternatives rise to the surface, narrowing the field of options for consideration. A high level of precision and confidence yields certainty, whereas a low level of either yields uncertainty, with risk being between the two.

Make the Decision

By this step, the alternatives that have the most promise for addressing the subject of the decision are self-evident. Having already assessed the brainstorming alternatives, those that remain at the top of the list are obviously the ones from which to choose. One critical matter is to determine *when* the decision is finalized. This may require establishing deadlines for rendering a decision or an agreed-upon set of developments after which the decision must be rendered. Regardless of the

Figure 13.3

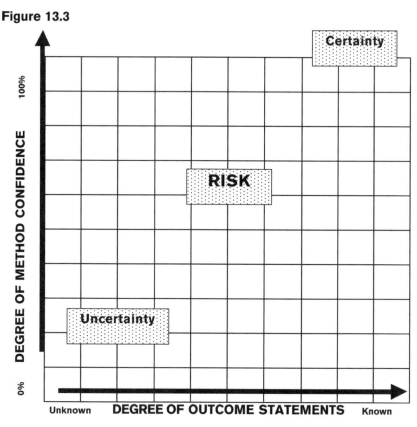

method used in decision making, the diagnosis stage of the decision-making process must be recognized as being completed before moving on to the implementation stage. This determination should be based on the aforementioned criteria and adhering to a predetermined process, *not* the acceptability or rejection of the final decision by some.

Is there ever an occasion to amend or overturn a decision? Only when it is evident that inaccurate data and information was used in the decision-making process, or when the situation being addressed has obviously changed to the degree that the previously determined definition and desired outcomes no longer fully or accurately address the subject. The decision-making process may have to be reentered at step 5 or 6, or be reengaged entirely at step 2.

In general, four possible decision modes are common to organizations, all of which are based on the relationship between the group and its leader.[5] Decision making is either done by an individual—the leader—or by the group itself through corporate decision making. When the leader is responsible for rendering the decision, it is accomplished either through *dictation,* which is an authoritarian approach to decision making, or *consultation,* in which the decision maker provides some opportunity for question and explanation of the decision. Decision making done by a leader is often simpler than that done by the group, simply because the necessity of maintaining group dynamics, reaching consensus or a suitable vote, and dealing with the implications of a potentially divided group are avoided. This does not make a leader-driven decision process *better,* only *simpler.*

The latter two decision-making modes rely on the group to render the decision, with a decreasing influence of the group's leader. *Facilitation* assumes that the group and leader must jointly reach a decision, and hence it is the leader's role to facilitate the process and aid the decision makers in making the decision. The second group-oriented decision-making mode is *delegation.* In this instance the group is self-managing, able to work through the decision-making process on their own. Leadership is provided by the decision-making group itself, and hence the appointed leader can delegate decision-making authority to a group of these highly capable individuals.

It is at this level of making decisions that the issue of *vote* or *consensus* arises. Voting simply renders a decision by majority opinion, leaving possibly 49 percent of the decision makers out of the loop, generating potential resentment and a divided public face about the decision. Consensus is always favored over a vote. In consensus, the decision makers reach a *general* acceptance and agreement about the direction that should be taken and commit to support the decision, even if as individuals they do not fully endorse every aspect of the decision. James Means identified six possible shortcomings of a group leader in decision making:[6]

1. Leaders press for goals not owned by members.
2. Leaders use manipulative methodologies.
3. Leaders fail to motivate people.
4. Leaders fail to assess group capacities.
5. Leaders fail to enlist essential people.
6. Leaders fail to grasp group dynamics.

Formulate a Policy/Procedure

If the decision addressed something other than a policy or procedure, it may be necessary to form a policy and procedure to solidify the decision. Policies are predetermined decisions, whereas procedures are predetermined actions. If the decision was a policy or procedure, it will be necessary to incorporate the newly formed policy into the existing institutional policies and procedures manual. This step formalizes and finalizes the decision making.

Develop an Implementation Plan

Now that the decision has been finalized, attention turns toward making it a reality. This starts the implementation phase of the decision-making process. The new challenge is one of formulating a step-by-step action plan for moving from the current situation or position to the newly determined position. The group must think through the process of change and develop a tactical plan for implementing the decision. The plan should consider elements such as these:

- *Who* needs to be informed of the decision? Who is impacted by the decision?
- *How* will the constituents or congregation be informed?
- What *resources* (human and other) are needed to implement the decision?
- What needs to be *produced* (materially and immaterially)?
- What general *phases* of action are required?
- What *specific* action steps must be taken?

In so doing, unforeseen obstacles for implementing the decision may be recognized and addressed. Many excellent decisions are thwarted by poor implementation because more attention was given to making the decision than to implementing it.

Implement the Idea

This step is easier said than done. As one implements the previously designed plan, some adjustments will have to be made. However, several general axioms for implementing a decision should be followed.[7]

- All those involved in making the decision must share the same vision and voice the same decision, thus presenting a unified decision.
- Mobilizing must begin at the top and must never stop; forward progress is essential for implementation in order to avoid stalling.
- Radical change is easier to make when the need is readily recognized by the organization.
- As will be discussed later in this chapter, increased formal communication and consistent conversation with the congregation are essential to implement a decision, with leadership providing updates on the progress of implementation.
- Since numbers give individuals a sense of security, acknowledging a high degree of acceptance from the congregation is one means of promoting further acceptance by holdouts.

Assess the Decision

How do we know if the decision was effective? How do we know if the criteria were addressed not only in theory but in practice? How do we know if the decision had its desired effect? It is negligent to assume that a decision was made so perfectly in theory as to never require the confirmation of its accuracy in practice. Depending on the nature of the decision, assessment can be accomplished through a variety of means: feedback from participants and organizational members or statistical analysis of participation in a new program. The criteria for a successful decision should simply be made measurable, with priority given to voices outside the decision-making body.

Assess the Whole Decision-Making Process

What can be learned about decision making from the experience of making this decision? To increase the probability of effective decision making in the future, learning from the process used in previous decisions is essential. Learning from both successes and errors, the decision-making group will be better prepared to make future decisions.

Biblical Portrait of Decision Making

While Scripture does not provide an outlined, systematic process of decision making, it does provide insight into decisions made by God's people. One such example is in the life of the early Christian community. Figure 13.4 depicts the previously mentioned steps to decision making (left column) as they relate to the decision rendered by the apostles and Christian community in first-century Jerusalem (right column).

The early Christian community obviously considered decision making a priority, worthy of their full attention. They demonstrated a commitment to mission and a willingness to review alternatives and select the most effective means of achieving their pastoral objectives, as well as a sensitivity of the congregation's perception and acceptance of the Christian community.

Institutional Communication

The classic Abbott and Costello routine "Who's on First?" is an example of a failure to recognize the two-way nature of communication. In this routine, Abbot continues to explain the placement of the various baseball players on the field, much to the confusion and consternation of Costello. However, the communication failure is not simply Costello's inability to comprehend Abbot's communications, but Abbot's failure to recognize the feedback provided by Costello indicating miscommunication. In short, communication is a process, not simply content or means of transmission.

Figure 13.4

Prescribed Process	Example from Acts 6:1-7
Continual spiritual preparation	The apostles were part of an active Christian community that was frequently noted for its spiritual commitment (Acts 2:42; 4:31; 5:41-42).
Clearly define the problem or issue	The early Christian community experienced continued growth in excess of the apostles' ability to minister to the body, particularly the Hellenistic widows (Acts 6:1). Hence, the problem was actually fourfold: (1) Widows were not being fed, (2) numerical growth was not being addressed, (3) limited workers in the church, the Twelve, and (4) possible ethnic/cultural issues, e.g., Palestinian vs. Hebraic widows.
State the desired outcomes	The apostles had obviously identified their desired outcomes: (1) See to the physical needs of the widows, (2) continued numerical growth, (3) better management of the situation, and (4) address the perceived ethnic/cultural concern (Acts 6:2, 4).
Gather relevant information and materials	The apostles obviously were aware of the situation at hand, as Luke explains the conditions that confronted the early Christian community. While Acts 6:1-2 does not explain *how* they became aware of it, their response to it demonstrates a thorough understanding of the situation.
Collect alternative ideas Explore and debate the best alternatives	The apostles could have considered a wide variety of options. For example, halt the growth of the community and hence maintain the current condition. The apostles themselves could have become frustrated and decided either to quit doing *social* ministry and focus solely on *pastoral* ministry (as if the two could truly be separated). The apostles could have decided to change their focus of ministry from outreach to "serving tables." Likewise, the apostles could have facilitated a Jewish/Gentile splinter of the congregation by deciding to minister to their own ethnic group (Jewish). The verbiage of Acts 6:2 indicates that alternatives were at least considered.
Make the decision	"Therefore" (Acts 6:3). The apostles reached an accord with one another regarding their desired direction for the Christian community. They rendered their decision in light of the church's mission, and what would advance the mission (continue in the ministry of the Word) and address the ministry needs of the congregation.

Continued on the next page

Continued from previous page

Develop an implementation plan	The apostles explained their decision to the Christian community and invited them to participate in the ministry. The decision was implemented by the congregation's selection of seven individuals to serve, according to predetermined criteria and approval/ commission of the apostles (Acts 6:2–3, 5–6). It should be noted that all seven chosen had *Greek* names, hence possibly addressing the cultural/ethnic concern.
Formulate Policy and Procedure	The selection of the seven to serve at the Hebraic widows' tables is precedent setting for the start of lay ministry within the church, subsequently giving rise to the appointing of deacons, elders, and other apostolic designates (1 Tim. 3:1–13; Titus 1:5–9).
Implement the idea	The apostles commissioned ("laid hands their on them") the seven men selected by the congregation and allowed them to perform their ministry (Acts 6:5–6).
Assess the decision	The effect of the decision was positive feedback (Acts 6:5a) and continued numerical growth (Acts 6:7). Presumably the desired outcomes were met (at least temporarily). The continued reference or presence of members of "the seven" seems to acknowledge the validity of the process and the ministry it produced (Acts 21:8).
Assess the whole process	The decision of Acts 6 mimics a similar process used later by the early church when addressing yet another issue of mission and direction (Acts 15:1–35).

Effective communication is usually an assumption of most organizations and administrators. It rarely receives attention or consideration until a complication occurs due to communication failure, leading to an investigation that asks such questions as "Who knew what?" "Who said what to whom?" "How did someone know this?" and "Who was supposed to know this?"

Communication is more than word selection, sentence structure, or forms of sharing information. Communication is not a one-way phenomenon but a two-way experience. Figure 13.5 illustrates the process of communication. It begins in the mind of the sender, with his or her ideas and perceptions. These ideas and perceptions become a message when they are encoded with words, symbols, and images, allowing the message to be shared. The transmission process is the actual sending of the message, using a variety of means such as speech, paralanguage, nonverbal, audiovisual, multimedia, or iconographic methods. The message is now received by the listener, who has his own ideas and perceptions, and the process of decoding begins, wherein comprehension and interpretation of the message is being understood by the listener. Feedback to the message is given from the listener's ideas and perceptions.

Figure 13.5: The Process of Communication

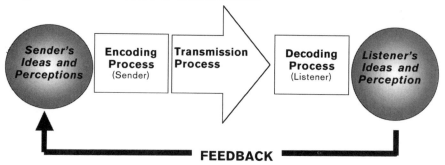

For this reason, in every single communication endeavor several possible versions of the message are present throughout the process of communication:[8]

- what the sender intended to say, or the idea;
- what the sender actually said, or the encoded message;
- what the sender actually thinks was said, or the sender's self-assessment;
- what the listener heard, or the received message;
- what the listener wanted to hear, or his ideas and perceptions;
- what the listener interpreted according to his perspective, or decoding;
- what the listener thought he heard, or his understanding of the message; and
- what the sender heard from the listener about what the sender said, or feedback.

Administrators are responsible for safeguarding the communication system of the organization. Communication problems are most commonly encountered in the divergence between the desired vs. the perceived message. This places a strain on the transmission phase of the communication process. Figure 13.6 illustrates how major decoding problems are often the result of limited or ineffective means of transmission, whereas decoding problems are minimized when the transmission means are intensified and more concrete ways of encoding the message are increased.[9]

Decoding problems are particularly evident in theological contexts, since terminology is laden with implied meanings. For example, the term *baptism* may convey immersion, pouring, or sprinkling or even be

Figure 13.6

Major Decoding Problem

Sender's Desired Message	*Transmission Means*	Listener's Received Message

Minor Decoding Problem

Sender's Desired Message	*Transmission Means*	Listener's Received Message

considered literal, in terms of water baptism, or metaphoric of immersion in the Spirit. This has often created confusion and miscommunication for congregations and for Christian camps and schools. Hence, the means of transmission must be multiplied and diversified in order to insure accurate communication, such as defining the term the first time it is used, or speaking in terms of its mode rather than using the term *baptism*, or providing a picture on a written document or handout.

Principles of Organizational Communication

Organizations are dependent on developing a culture of communication. They are places where influence, ideas, innovation, and initiatives develop. The style of communication that a particular ministry demonstrates reflects its values and priorities toward ministry. The following principles are helpful guidelines for ministry leaders to remember when seeking to communicate, both to their staff as well as their constituents.

1. Those who serve in leadership capacities should model and champion the cause of open communication throughout the organization.

2. Ministries need to be vigilant to guard against sending out poor communication, particularly anything that generates miscommunication or misunderstandings.

3. Christian organizations should insure harmony between the communication in word and deed. They should model integrity in what they say they do and what they actually do.

4. Ministry leaders should communicate regularly with the organization and broader community. A variety of formats for this is recommended (newsletters, memos, meetings, etc.). Face-to-face dialogue is always the preferred approach.

5. Organizations should appoint an individual or team to monitor communications, especially written communications, and develop a schedule and collection for communication. Larger organizations should designate someone as their public information officer and train her for her responsibilities.

6. Ministries must adopt a culture of communication, one in which it is a common experience for members, without degenerating into gossip.

Methods of Communication

Perhaps the two most common forms of verbal communications in organizations are *written* and *spoken*. Newsletters, Web sites, or e-mail are perhaps the most common forms of written communication, but other means of written communications are also common, ranging from manuals to public relations pieces. When writing a piece for publication or making a presentation, four general suggestions are as follows: (1) Explain the reason for the communication. Let the reader know your main point. (2) Use summary statements throughout the document or presentation in order to guide the reader's mind through your reasoning. (3) Select your verbiage carefully, using precise wording. (4) Finally, provide visual guideposts such as fonts and symbols to mark transitions in communication.[10] Most ministries limit themselves in their communication methods, but more can be done to creatively present the information that is necessary for effective operation.

Symbolic communication as demonstrated in one's use of body language can be a powerful means of communication. Be conscious of communication through gestures or body signals. For example, positive body gestures might include smiling, nodding the head in approval, raising the eyebrows to show attention, or moving one's hand to add emphasis. Negative activities might be chewing on a pen to show uncertainty, placing the hand to the face or neck to show concern, or placing the hand on the forehead or bridge of the nose to signal tension or conflict.[11] Being conscious of our own body language or that of others can aid in the communication. Likewise, intentionally using body language can aid in facilitating communication.

Visual communications often accompany other forms of communication in the organization. Such items as handouts, still photographs, maps, charts, and other supporting information materials can be used to augment presentations and other forms of spoken communications. While the use of such materials in conjunction with verbal communication does not insure the transmission of the message, it does increase the means of transmission and hence raises the probability of accurate and comprehended communication between individuals and within the institution.

Modern technology provides a variety of new methods of communication. This is perhaps the one area of communication that many organizations have not fully embraced. A cartoon in *Leadership* seems to readily acknowledge this, showing a church secretary using a

Guttenberg-style printing press in her office and asking, "Any word yet, Pastor, about my request for a photocopier?"[12] Such technological innovations as computer-generated projections in worship or group meetings and the use of Web sites and e-mail are becoming more common in congregations and Christian organizations. Helpful instructional applications such as Web-based research capabilities advance the educational agenda of congregations, church camps, schools, and higher education institutions. However, such technologies as video conferencing or meeting via nationwide walkie-talkie have yet to make their way into the communication plans of most Christian organizations.

Perhaps the most common form of face-to-face communication is a *meeting.* Chapter 11 has already provided insights into the form and functions of meetings. However, three basic questions should be used to assess the communicative dynamic of meetings:[13]

1. Does your staff have weekly or regularly scheduled staff meetings? Without such meetings, the staff lives in the tyranny of the urgent and must address matters as they arise. Regularly scheduled meetings allow items to be placed on agendas and hence provide an opportunity for concerted attention by participants.

2. Have the meeting participants shared their expectations of communication? Meetings are at their optimal performance in a climate of open communication where information is readily available. If participants' expectations of communication are not met, the meeting will be conducted in a climate of confusion and even suspicion.

3. How often does the team evaluate its communication effectiveness? Often communication becomes an assumption, without receiving any direct attention. It is always wise to conduct periodic evaluations of the communication shortfalls and successes in order to enhance it in future meetings. They are the setting wherein most organizational decisions are made and work is accomplished. The success of meetings relies on effective communication.

Conclusion

The process by which decisions are made and communicated within a Christian organization is an essential dynamic. Understanding the fundamental elements involved in decision making will contribute to leadership effectiveness. Once decisions have been made, however, they must be communicated throughout the organization. Great care must be taken to ensure that there is institutional integrity in the manner in which decisions are made as well as the methods used to communicate them.

PART 4

STAFFING

Ask any nonprofit ministry director what is the most difficult decision he or she has ever had to make and he or she will always respond with the same answer: staffing. No other decision will have as lasting an impact on the ministry as staff selection. Recruiting, selecting, and training the right people is critical for the long-term success of every ministry. That's because people are the organization's greatest asset. Staffing is at the heart of everything we do in ministry.

In generations past, God chose and gifted those whom he wanted. He made it clear to each prophet, king, shepherd, or pastor that they were his chosen vessels. Each was expected to employ his gift or talent for God's glory. In the New Testament, we find several detailed lists which explain the various gifts that are given to believers (Eph. 4:11–12; Rom. 12:6–8; 1 Cor. 12:7–10, 28–30). God's plan is for shared ministry service based upon the gifts that have been distributed. As each person uses his gifts, the church will experience healthy spiritual and numerical growth. The challenge for those of us who serve in ministry leadership positions is in knowing who is gifted for what positions of service and whether they are called into service. Kenneth Gangel put it well in his book *Building Leaders for Church Education*:

> There is in Christian ministry a dynamic tension that must be maintained between the concepts of *gift* and *call*. We know from the New Testament that the Holy Spirit sovereignly gives to every Christian a spiritual gift which He intends for that individual to use in the service of Christ through the church.

> But the other tension, the concept of the call, is rather like the rudder that steers a ship. The gift rather describes the what of ministry and the call then designates the where of ministry.

It is quite obvious that those who have the responsibility of supervision and administration of people in collective ministry must recognize both of these crucial ingredients as biblical components.

The concepts of *gifts* and *call,* if taken seriously, have profound implications for the way we recruit workers in the church or Christian organization, the way we supervise their activities, and the way we evaluate their performance.[1]

Every ministry leader understands the tension that exists between hiring the people who will provide forward-thinking insights as opposed to those who are easy to get along with. Trail-blazing visionary leaders are usually difficult to corral while compliant, easygoing staff may be challenging to keep motivated. Rarely do both character qualities exist in the same staff member. As one experienced organizational leader reflected:

Selecting new staff members for an organization usually involves a subtle contest between the needs of the organization for broad diversity and the needs of the hiring manager for conformity or compatibility (usually called the "right chemistry"). Complicating this situation is the experiential truth that any working group can handle only so much variety or dissimilarity among its members before it begins spending the bulk of its time dealing with members' differences—to the detriment of achieving common work goals.

Each opportunity to add a person to the staff of an organization is, therefore, an opportunity for its top manager(s) to assess the current mix of the work force as a whole, test the diversity level, and assert whatever leadership is necessary to achieve an appropriate balance and mix. The chief executive needs to decide on the best strategic mix for his or her organization and *require* that the recruitment and selection practices do, in fact, achieve that outcome and thereby optimize the organization's human capabilities.[2]

The managerial function of staffing gets at the heart of these and other vital issues. Simply defined, staffing is viewed as "filling, and keeping filled, positions in the organization structure."[3] Never has there been a definition that is easier to write than to practice! Since most ministries are already in operation, it starts with knowing the mission, vision, and strategic plan of the organization. Then an inventory needs to take place which identifies the available staff and where staff members are needed. In some cases staff members are already available but not necessarily in the right positions. At that point, some adjustments may need to take place to ensure that everyone is where they "fit" the best.

When further staff are required, a detailed analysis needs to be done to determine how many staff are needed and with what qualifications. This knowledge is essential to future staffing success. How to recruit the staff who are needed and the process by which these individuals are screened is the substance of chapter 14. Countless churches and non-profit ministries have been the target of lawsuits in recent years because they did not screen their staff properly. Courts are holding nonprofits liable for not being diligent in their screening of staff, both paid and volunteer. It is important that ministry directors understand what the law requires and how the information is gathered. Recruiting and screening volunteers is one of the most time-consuming jobs of a ministry director. Knowledge of how to do it effectively and efficiently will be advantageous to you.

Chapter 14 is also designed to help the ministry leader understand how to equip and train teachers for their task of educating the congregation. Most volunteer teachers come with little qualifications other than a willing heart. Therefore, it is incumbent on us to train them for their job. Without this training they will quickly lose heart and quit. This results in disgruntled church members and poor morale. Important details such as classroom management and instructional methodologies will be discussed.

Developing the paid staff member is far more difficult than working with volunteers for some ministry supervisors. This is due, in part, to the dynamic which exists between the paid ministry staff leader and his or her volunteer workers. When volunteers don't perform according to expectation, staff members can become frustrated and anxious. This can result in feelings of ill will among the ministry team. "One of the greatest fears among managers of volunteers is [the] tension between volunteer and paid staff. So prevalent is this fear that when asked to name the most difficult aspect of their job, twenty-nine out of thirty managers of volunteers in organizations that have paid staff responded that it is tension between that staff and volunteers."[4] This strain, if left unattended, can wreak tremendous havoc on the organization.

The purpose of chapter 15 is to identify the key elements of staff development. What motivates a staff member to serve may be different from a volunteer. Knowing this difference will be helpful when seeking to motivate them toward excellence in their service. Keeping the staff member engaged in the task and committed to quality performance is the focus of this chapter.

The final chapter in this unit addresses the subject of legal and ethical issues in ministry. Written by an attorney who once directed his own legal team in Denver, this author is now serving on staff at the Crystal Cathedral in southern California while completing his doctoral degree.

He brings to the writing team a wealth of knowledge and experience about these most critical areas of ministry practice. The chapter is replete with extensive documentation for the reader who desires further information about any of the topics discussed. One simple mistake in a ministry can result in significant damage to the future of the organization. As the saying goes, "ignorance of the law is no excuse." This is certainly true when the ministry leader stands before a judge and jury. This chapter is designed to provide the ministry leader with the essential facts needed to stay above the law and within the guidelines clearly given to us in the Scriptures.

BY
LARRY PURCELL

Chapter 14

Recruiting
and Screening Volunteers

MY FIRST EXPERIENCE OF being recruited to serve in a church was during a Wednesday evening annual business meeting. I had returned to my home in Kentucky from serving in the military a few months earlier. The small rural church that I had grown up in was having its annual business meeting to elect church officers and teachers. This service was usually not well attended. Not attending this particular service could be a dangerous practice because it meant you could be volunteered for a position without your knowing about it. The position I had been "volunteered for" was to teach five boys in a beginner class, first and second graders. Their mothers had attempted to teach this class during the previous year, but each had resigned very quickly. I could tell after attempting to decline this position by offering the parents and congregation numerous possible outcomes that the task was mine.

For the next year these five boys would begin a journey with Rick and me that would be life-altering as it was our job to shepherd these five boys through some challenging life issues. I approached this task with fear and trembling, feeling overwhelmed by the task. I thought my filling this position was for the benefit of these poor boys who had control of their parents. Little did I realize that I would be the benefactor of relationships that have lasted a lifetime. In a very clumsy manner, Rick and I began to build relationships with these boys both inside and outside the classroom. We were instilling into these five boys what had been taught to us in our earlier years. One of the most profound facts I learned from this early experience was when the mother of one of these boys would confront me with a truth. She cautioned me to be careful what I said and where I went because her son was watching every move I made. What a weighty truth! I learned that I actually had

244

influence over someone else. This would impact my spiritual growth and journey in a profound manner.

The purpose of recruiting volunteers should not be to find warm bodies and place them where no one else desires to go. Rather, recruiting volunteers must take on a *kingdom focus*. While Rick and I both grew as a result of this early experience, the manner in which it was handled did leave a lot to be desired.

This chapter will review how to recruit and screen volunteers for service in church ministries and Christian organizations. We will first explore the biblical and theological rationale for involving all believers in the work of ministry. The next section of this chapter will survey the problems with recruiting volunteers in today's church. The last part of this chapter will focus on ways some churches are screening volunteers.

A Biblical Mandate for Volunteer Ministry

You will hear much today about how the success of any business venture depends on its knowing its purpose. *Mission* and *vision* are terms frequently used in both secular and sacred areas to describe or define purpose. A business can spend a lot of its time and energy developing its mission and vision statements. The church has already been assigned its mission statement by our Lord (Matt. 28:18–20). These verses are referred to as the Great Commission, which is the mission of his church. This takes out all guesswork and saves a congregation many hours of research. It is from these verses that a church's leadership will pray and seek from the Lord his vision for them. The term *vision* refers to how a church expresses its specific fulfillment of the Great Commission. See chapter 3 for an expanded discussion of these critical terms and concepts.

Unfortunately, many Christians view the work of ministry as the sole responsibility of professionals. We are used to going to entertainment or out to eat and being served. This consumerism has moved into the pew! This is often expressed by hiring a minister or staff person to fill positions and meet specific needs. Is this a biblical model?

Ephesians 4:11–12 differs with this modern model of hirelings. The task of the Great Commission is a global assignment. This mission will seem overwhelming if only vocational ministers perform it. God has already thought of that and has provided churches with the solution in these verses. Ephesians 4:11 identifies several gifted persons whom God has loaned to the church. These persons must be seen as gifts from God on loan to a congregation for a specific purpose. Ephesians 4:12 presents the purpose of the *pastor and teacher* as equipping saints. Vocational ministers are often referred to as being "hired" by a congregation. Pastors and staff ministers are brought into a church to perform tasks for the congregation. This model of hiring the works of ministry betrays the biblical model presented in Ephesians 4:11–12.

Pastors and staff persons will usually bring to congregations a high level of skill and training. This will entice the vocational minister to feel he or she is the resident expert to perform ministry tasks, rather than the equipping of the congregation. This consumer mentality can lead a congregation into a mind-set of being served, rather than being a servant. Ephesians 4:11–12 teaches a church that equipped saints are to do the work of the ministry. This is what builds up the church, which is the body of Christ.

This biblical rationale of the mission of the church, the task of the vocational minister, and the role of the individual members offer a model for leadership multiplication. The casual observer can see that too many people are doing too little in today's church. The solution to this is to return to a biblical model of discipleship, volunteer ministry, and leadership multiplication.

First Peter 5:1–5 calls for volunteer leaders to *shepherd* those for whom they have responsibility. The use of the metaphor *shepherd* reframes the task of a leader into more than just a set of competencies or tasks. Rather, it causes both the leader and the follower to see the work of ministry as that of investing in the kingdom of God by investing in the life of others. Titus 2 offers a similar leadership multiplication model by the act of mentoring. The younger men are to be mentored by the older men, and the younger women are to be mentored by the older women.

Vocational leaders must take on the task of developing the members whom God has provided them for the fulfillment of the Great Commission. This is not to infer that vocational ministers do not do the work of ministry, but that they do not do it alone. It is the task of the vocational minister to invest in the persons whom God has provided for his work. Multiplying leadership is another expression often referred to as discipleship.

Problems of Recruitment

My early experience of directing a classroom that no mother wanted has been a guide for how *not* to recruit volunteers. Too often churches and other nonprofit ministries recruit volunteers to fill immediate needs rather than plan for the future. Such recruitment practice develops a culture of crisis. My awareness of the culture of immediate needs in my home church caused me to want to miss the annual business meeting, but I was too afraid of what job I might be assigned. This is only one example of why churches have difficulty finding enough volunteers to meet their ministry needs. Dennis E. Williams and Kenneth O. Gangel address a number of problems related to recruiting volunteers.[1] Some of these problems will be summarized in this section of the chapter.

Spiritual Problems

Any argument that relates to problems of having enough workers to do ministry must be viewed first as spiritual. In Matthew 9:36–38, we learn that as Jesus looked upon the people, he had compassion on them. As we view the work of ministry, we must see it as an act of spiritual compassion. This would lead to the motivation of praying to God, the Lord of the harvest, for workers. Do we present the work of ministry as a task to be accomplished or as an act of spiritual service? We are not to pray only to fill positions, but to seek to help equip people for spiritual growth and service.

Lack of Commitment

Many churches carry an inactive membership roll. This roll usually designates those who are unable to attend because they have moved away or are homebound. This roll could be even larger if most churches were honest. We have too many ministry observers and too few workers in the harvest. This is sometimes due to worker exhaustion. I have seen volunteers who were reluctant to get involved in ministry because they felt it was a lifetime assignment. Others may have been hurt in some past experience and are hesitant to get involved in the next series of changes at their church. In one recent study on this issue it was found that seven out of ten churches now expect their members to be involved in ministry as a requisite for membeship.[2] This culture of crisis is slowly being addressed as more churches intentionally plan and communicate their expectations for members getting involved in their ministries. One southern California church expressed this as one of their core values: "Every Member a Minister."

Lack of Leadership

Many churches are experiencing a vacuum in leadership because they have insufficient *closed group* opportunities for their members. Discipleship training or leadership development has given way to time pressures. A *closed group* is an experience that is essential to the discipleship and leadership development of the individual member. It is the time that present and future leaders participate in more in-depth spiritual training and equipping for service. This is a time for intentional spiritual growth and service development. The *open group* is often thought of as the time a Sunday school class or cell group meets for Bible study that is focused on evangelism and fellowship. It has less demand for service and is seen more as foundational for elementary Christian education.

Paul uses the metaphor of a farmer in 2 Timothy 2:6 to describe how young Timothy was to relate to faithful men. The farmer knows that to grow a good crop takes patience and effort. Leadership development must be seen as an act of discipleship. The type of discipleship that is carried on in too many churches does not lead people to service. Those who are attending may be soaking in all the fellowship and study, but these must be provided as channels to express their gift of ministry.

Administrative Problems

In a time when leadership appears as the key word, administration appears as the ignored word. Administration is not a nasty essential in churches, but it is essential. Leadership is doing the right things, while administration is doing things right.

I was recently looking through a file cabinet and found a folder filled with completed spiritual gifts inventories. I asked the church's secretary when these had been completed and how they had been utilized by the leadership. Her look of exhaustion and comments was evidence of someone's poor planning. During a moment of excitement, the church's leaders had administered the spiritual gifts inventories but had never used them in their planning. This resulted in a culture of reluctance in that church. When new leaders assumed their roles, the members knew it would be just a matter of time and the excitement would disappear. Fewer and fewer of the congregation would participate in training classes or complete surveys, believing it would not be used in planning.

A leader's vision without the proper planning and execution can lead a congregation to frustration. The vision can assist the membership in seeing a different and better future. However, without good planning the congregation is unable to see how this vision can be accomplished. Good planning will motivate the membership to serve because it will provide the essential steps to facilitate vision accomplishment.

The task of good leadership is to provide the vision and the vehicle to arrive at that destination. Organization is the vehicle that accomplishes this task. Organization includes the structures and staff necessary to fulfill God's desire in that specific context. The terms *systems thinking* and *systems alignment* are critical to the task of organizing a body of believers to accomplish God's vision for them. *Systems thinking* is the *big picture*. The big picture is when a leader can carefully review the entire structure of a church by looking at its budget, paid and volunteer staff, ministries, available space, and community context. *Systems alignment* is the practice of the leader moving these structures in a manner to enhance and support the task of a church fulfilling its vision. It is critical to present these two principles because too many leaders attempt to place new wine in old wineskins. As the community and the congregation change, the organization of the church must be adjusted to meet the needs of such changes.

Evaluation is also an aspect of organization. Williams and Gangel call this the weakest area of churches.[3] First-class evaluation requires good organization. The purpose of evaluation is not punishment but improvement. This requires a clear understanding of expectations before a task is undertaken. A clear job description can include assigned roles, expectations, and standards of excellence. This allows the volunteer to have a clear definition of the task and how it will be measured. Vague or ambiguous job descriptions and standards can lead the volunteer to a diminished view of the importance of the task or assignment. A volunteer worker wants to know that his or her work does make a difference. This can increase the volunteer workers' motivation and the desire to enlist others in the work.

There can be many additional comments as to why there are problems recruiting volunteers to accomplish God's work. We live in a fast-paced society. Many households have dual-career spouses. When you add to this the responsibility of parenting, time is a premium. For this reason, we must make every effort to encourage spiritual growth and leadership development requisite to church membership. Effective administration must also limit the number of jobs a leader is assigned. Church leaders must take heart and not give up, for the Lord of the harvest will accomplish his will. God has given to each of us the same amount of time. It is the task of a church's leadership to examine and identify ways to remove the obstacles that discourage its members from service.

Recruiting and Retaining Volunteers

How does your church identify and locate new recruits? The story of my first experience of being volunteered is not a good example of identifying and locating new recruits. My beginning experience did not discourage me from being involved in God's work, as it does some people. This church recruited workers the same way it had for the past fifty years. A very small church can often conduct its recruitment in a casual manner because it organizes itself as a family. Ministries and workers may be few in number, and thus the task is much easier to manage. Churches that organize themselves for growth must take a more deliberate approach. The following steps will be reviewed in order to serve as a primer for a church's leadership recruitment team.

Once the leadership team has developed a better understanding of where it is and where it is going, it is vital to list the ministries. The strategic plan may identify some existing ministries that are no longer effective or that may need some small changes. See chapter 5 for a detailed discussion of this issue. A review of the neighborhood may also identify gaps between the needs of the community and ministries presently being offered. This step may identify a new population that is not being reached. It is evident that skillful planning will always identify the need for new recruits.

Prepare a directory of the existing ministries of your church and list the names of those presently serving in leadership positions. This will assist in identifying the personnel needs of the church. This directory can be placed on bulletin boards or be included as an insert in the weekly worship service bulletin. This directory of ministries and recruitment needs can be used in new member training classes and to encourage further leadership preparation.

The next step is to identify the giftedness that God has brought to the congregation. Designing a plan to enlist as many members as possible to complete the spiritual gifts surveys is critical. This can be accomplished by completing the surveys in Sunday school classes, discipleship classes, or as part of the new member classes. The key to success is to ensure that the surveys get into the hands of as many people as possible. This task requires a strategy and will take some time to complete. For this reason, it is advisable to enlist a leadership team that will guide this process. This team will need to create a system that encourages those who have the spiritual gifts inventories to return them completed. The pastor can encourage the congregation's participation in this event through his sermons. A Sunday morning worship service can be developed that would promote the membership to complete the surveys. The completed surveys could be carried to the altar as an act of commitment and a time of prayer.

The leadership team would follow the completion of the spiritual gifts surveys with a letter to those who participated. The letter would be an encouragement and appreciation for their participation. It would also explain the next steps that would be used to encourage the participants to be involved in training and ministry. The team could utilize a small group or individual setting to review the spiritual gift survey with the participants. Ministry opportunities could be presented by using the directory of ministry positions. The participant needs to have time to explore his or her gifts, interests, past experiences, and previous training. The recruit can then be matched to a ministry position and introduced to a mentor.

Mentors can be those who have been serving in positions of ministry. Paul, in Titus 1:5–6, commanded Titus to appoint elders who were above reproach. We need to have leaders doing ministry who have demonstrated godly character. It is essential to develop a team ministry approach. This will enable each new ministry and recruit to grow and will reduce frustrations. Mentors will be able to assist the new recruit in developing the competency and motivation essential for success. Careful steps must be taken to provide a volunteer with sufficient information and relationship to reduce the rate of attrition. It will also be helpful for the leadership team to develop training for the mentors. This practice can be useful in developing leadership at every level of the church's organization.

In Exodus 18, Moses' father-in-law offered Moses sage advice for developing leaders at numerous levels. Tribes would identify specific persons to handle the minor issues, and the larger issues would be brought to Moses. This practice of developing several layers of leadership is best facilitated in a team environment. Training mentors to lead this process at each level of a church's ministry develops this new team ministry culture.

The practice of developing mentors can be generally seen as producing shepherds. The shepherd cares for the sheep and hears the sheep (John 10). Mentors, who shepherd their group or team, must see their task as developing faithful followers of Christ, not just accomplishing a task. We often focus on the completion of a task to the exclusion of the individual. This shepherding model better reflects the relationship between Christ and his disciples. In 1 Peter 5, the apostle Peter commanded leaders to shepherd the flock of God. Peter encouraged those leaders to exercise their position of authority or leadership by being the example. What a scene this produces in my mind of the Chief Shepherd taking lead with his sheep following. With such a scene in mind, it is easy for the shepherds to see that as they follow Christ the sheep will also follow.

A high-expectation church can only be achieved by developing a culture of high-expectation members. This can be encouraged by using the above steps to effect the necessary changes in the church's organization.

Motivating Volunteers

Dennis Williams offers the following nine suggestions to facilitate the motivation of volunteer church workers:[4]

1. Church leaders must be person-centered and not task-oriented.
2. Ministry leaders must earn respect by demonstrating godly character.

3. Every effort should be made to place persons where their wants and desires can be fulfilled.
4. Volunteers should be appointed for a definite period of time.
5. Sustained motivation requires that people know what is expected of them.
6. Praise, recognition, and appreciation should be given when merited.
7. Church leaders should emphasize teamwork rather than competition as a group incentive.
8. Sustained motivation occurs when workers have opportunity to participate in planning and decision making.
9. More attention should be given to effective supervision at all levels of church organization.

A believer's basic motivation to volunteer is to serve God. It is a way in which we can be fulfilled as disciples.

Screening Volunteers

Matt, the minister of education at a rapidly growing church, had been hurriedly enlisting and assigning workers in the education ministries of his church. Matt intended to increase the training as soon as he got caught up on having enough workers in each of the church's ministries. Matt received a call from a concerned parent of one of his youth. At first Matt wanted to discount the parent's concerns as an overprotective parent. The complaints became too many to ignore, so Matt began to investigate the accusations. When Matt checked into the background of the new worker, he found a history of similar complaints in previous church ministries. This concerned Matt about the worker, who was always so eager to volunteer.

This caused Matt to begin implementing a new and improved volunteer workers screening process. Matt had gotten caught up in the process of enlisting workers to meet needs. This story has been played out across thousands of churches and nonprofit ministries across North America. This scenario should raise questions in the minds of pastors and other ministry leaders. How should workers be enlisted and recruited? The first section of this chapter has sought to answer this question. The second question raised by Matt's dilemma relates to the reason for screening volunteers.

Jesus told his followers, "I am sending you out like sheep among wolves. Therefore be as shrewd as snakes and as innocent as doves" (Matt. 10:16 NIV). God can read the heart of a person, but we cannot. We are limited in knowing someone's heart by examining his or her life. A church has the responsibility of screening volunteers for a variety of reasons. One such reason is because we are to entrust the work of God to those who are faithful (2 Tim. 2:2). The work of Christ should clearly reflect the character of Christ. Just as he has been faithful and true to his character, so must all who do his work. For this reason, it is recommended that all workers, staff and volunteers, be screened. A number of steps will be offered to assist in screening staff and volunteers, and especially those who work with children and youth.

All church workers should provide references and agree, in writing, to have a background check before being interviewed. You will need written documentation of the contact with references and information obtained during the personal interview. Interview and document the person's Christian testimony, special interests, past teaching and volunteer experiences, and other related information. All information obtained during the interview and screening process is confidential and must be kept filed in a secure area.

A second reason to screen volunteer workers is the safety and responsibility to those whom they have been entrusted. The first thought parents have, when the media reports some impropriety at a park, school, or church ministry, is *this could have been my child.* Church leaders must be proactive in establishing a plan to increase the safety and security of every member, especially children and youth.

Another reason to screen volunteer workers is because of today's litigious culture. Lawsuits are such a phenomenon of our society as revealed by reading labels on prescription drugs and the length of disclaimers and disclosures on products. Notice all the waivers you must sign to enroll your child in a sporting event. What steps can a church take to ensure that its volunteers and employees do not hurt someone and render the church liable in the process? A word of caution: your church should always consult an attorney when reviewing safety policies to prevent it from being sued.

The National Child Protection Act of 1993 was established to encourage states to improve the quality of their criminal history and child abuse records. The act was passed in October of 1993 and amended in the Crime Control Act of 1994.[5] This act establishes safeguards for children and agencies caring for children. As a result of this act, states are mandating that organizations complete a nationwide criminal history background check on prospective employees and volunteers serving children, youth, the elderly, and individuals with disabilities. Churches are not exempt from completing a nationwide criminal history background check of its employees or volunteers. In fact, it is imperative that a church complete such background checks for a higher moral reason.

Populations that are most at risk of being damaged and in need of special attention are our children and youth. J. W. "Bill" Phillips has offered a number of suggestions to assist churches in providing for the safety and responsibility of its employees and those to whom they minister. Phillips encourages all churches to adopt written policies for children and youth ministries in church business session. He offers the following policies that your church can adopt:[6]

1. Require a criminal background check of all staff and volunteers who work with children and youth.

2. Develop a worker's application form that includes a place for the worker to sign, giving permission for a background check. No exceptions can be made.

3. Require that all childcare groups have a minimum of two workers present, no exceptions. One of the two must be an adult.

4. Require that a person be a member of the church for a minimum of six months before he or she can teach any class.

5. Provide regular orientation of all teachers and workers about the church's policies relating to childcare and sexual abuse issues. Teach them how to recognize a child who may have been abused. Local police and social service agencies can offer suggestions.

6. Schedule and conduct an annual review of childcare policies, worker's personnel files, and so forth. Make updates as needed, informing all workers in writing.

7. Require that if any person acts questionably or fails to follow the policies, that person will be suspended immediately from working with children until the situation is investigated and resolved.

8. Determine who will serve as the media spokesperson for the church if a problem arises. Allow only one person to speak to the media on behalf of the church. Warn all others to adhere rigorously to this plan.

A church's screening process will help its volunteers and leaders meet its moral, spiritual, and legal responsibilities. When a church seeks to implement this process, it must be done with caution. The staff and volunteer leaders must be included in development and implementation of the screening process. Including staff and volunteer leaders in the development of this new system will help them recognize that these steps are to protect the children, youth, themselves, and the church. It is recommended that an attorney be consulted to review a church's documents and screening processes. An attorney should always be consulted when a complaint has been made against a volunteer or staff member. The church's insurance provider can be consulted to make certain that there is adequate coverage to protect its volunteers and staff.

Conclusion

In this chapter we have looked at ways to recruit and screen volunteers for ministry. We have seen how the church's task is the fulfillment of the Great Commission from Matthew 28:18–20. The biblical model of leadership development is identified as Ephesians 4:11–12. Paid staff members cannot do this alone, but they must be at the task of developing their church's vision, identifying volunteers' giftedness, and empowering the membership to do works of ministry. The biblical model of developing volunteer leaders has been identified as a shepherding model. God's people glorify him and grow in grace and knowledge as they engage in the work of ministry. The problems identified in recruiting volunteers (spiritual problems, lack of commitment, lack of leadership, and administrative problems) have become a measurement of a church's culture. This culture can be replaced with a biblical model as church leaders train and enlist the membership in works of service.

The critical nature of screening ministry workers has been reviewed. In our litigious society, church leaders must develop policies and procedures that ensure the safety of those receiving and those performing ministry. Suggestions have been offered to assist you in implementing these steps. Professional agencies can be consulted to aid a church in developing safety and security processes. Always consult an attorney as you develop, review, and implement a screening process with staff and volunteers.

Review Questions

1. Does your church have processes in place for the training and recruitment of volunteers? When does your church search for volunteers—only when there is a need, or does it have an ongoing training program? If your church does not have a volunteer recruiting and training process, how would you lead it to do so?

2. Does your church have a list of its ministries available to the membership? How would you lead the development and use of such a tool?

3. Does your church have a new members class? How would you lead in developing such a class, and what would you teach? Does your church give the spiritual gifts inventory? How could such a tool be helpful to volunteer recruitment and placement?

4. Does your church screen paid staff and volunteers? How would you lead a church to develop and adopt a screening process? Who would lead this process? What would it look like?

Volunteer Application Form

Name

Address

City   Zip

Pager   Work phone

E-mail   Cell phone

1.   Marital status: (check all that apply)

    ❏ Single   ❏ Married   ❏ Divorced
    ❏ Divorced and remarried   ❏ Separated

2. Briefly state how you came to know Jesus Christ personally.

3. Have you been baptized as an adult? ❏ Yes ❏ No. If not, are you willing to be baptized? ❏ Yes ❏ No.

4. What attracted you to come to our church? _____

5. Why do you want to serve at our church? _____

6. Are you currently serving in an area of ministry at our church?
       ❏ Yes ❏ No. If yes, where are you currently serving? _____

7. Are you currently a member of a small group for accountability and spiritual growth? ❏ Yes ❏ No

8. What previous leadership experiences have you had? _____

9. Are there any broken or impure relationships in your life? ❏ Yes ❏ No
      If yes, please explain: _____

10. Are there any patterns of sin in your life that would reflect poorly on Jesus Christ or on this church?
❏ Yes ❏ No   If yes, please explain:

11. Have you ever been under church discipline? ❏ Yes ❏ No
    If yes, please explain: _____

    _____

    _____

12. What regular practices do you participate in to grow and develop your
    relationship with Jesus Christ? _____

    _____

    _____

13. Have you ever been arrested or charged with a felony?
    ❏ Yes ❏ No If yes, please explain:

    _____

    _____

    _____

14. Are you willing to submit to the authority of the church leadership team
    (pastoral staff/church board) ❏ Yes ❏ No

15. References: Please provide the names, addresses and phone numbers of three
    people we can contact on your behalf:

    1. Church staff member: _____

    2. Name _____
       Address _____
       Phone _____

    3. Name _____
       Address _____
       Phone _____

_____   _____
Signature   Date

STAFF USE ONLY

Interviewed by: _____   Date _____

Ministry Director Signature: _____   Date _____

Executive/Senior Pastor Signature: _____   Date _____

Leadership Position: _____

This person will report to: _____

Comments: _____

_____

_____

_____

BY
MICHELLE ANTHONY

Chapter 15

Developing Staff Members

OFTEN THE IDEA OF STAFF development in a church or Christian organization is characterized by the thought, *I wish I had staff to develop.* Most churches and nonprofit organizations have little or no resources to provide for the development of their staff. Even in organizations that have plentiful staff, the leader is often too busy running the organization to take the time to train and nurture their staff.

Frequently, these same organizations have failed to provide meaningful middle management. In some cases the structure has reduced the supervisor's role to basic oversight with little or no concern for the long-term vitality of the staff or the organization itself. Whether the challenge is in the scarcity of staff or the challenges associated with leading a large staff, a proper understanding of staff development is essential if the organization is to experience lasting success.

The Biblical Basis of Staff Development

Ministry teams are made up of people who are abundantly diverse. As we begin to explore this subject, we must not neglect the Creator of our diversity and unique needs as human beings. Scripture gives a great deal of insight and direction about the development of Christian leaders. It addresses such pertinent issues as understanding the vision of the ministry, selecting the team members, communicating the goals, understanding the unique contributions of each individual member, and partnering with them over the long haul to accomplish the mission. These factors are at the very heart of staff development. We will briefly review some of the more obvious passages of Scripture that relate to these important themes.

Old Testament Examples of Staff Development

One of the most obvious examples in the Old Testament is seen in Joshua as he and the Israelites prepared to enter the promised land.

258

Joshua understood the goal as God had given it to him. He was commanded to cross the Jordan River and enter the land that had been promised to him and his fathers. In addition, he was commanded to be strong and courageous, to obey the Lord's commandments, and to utterly destroy all the nations inhabiting Canaan (Josh. 1:1–9).

Joshua was given further instruction on the selection of his team as he commissioned the Reubenites, Gadites, and the half-tribe of Manasseh to cross over the Jordon River with their brothers so they could participate in the various battles which were necessary to take possession of the land. Joshua understood the weight of his call on their lives, as he reminded these warriors what they would be leaving behind: their wives, their children, their farms, and their livestock. He understood that the sacrifice was great and that some people might never return home (Josh. 1:10–18).

We find Joshua to be a zealous commander-in-chief and leader. He led the people through spiritual rituals and experiences into numerous battles. He administered justice and admonished the people when they needed it. In addition, he read aloud the Scriptures in the presence of the entire assembly, led an obedient life before them, and never let them forget that God was a holy and jealous God who demanded nothing less than complete obedience. Joshua died at the age of 110, leading and developing the twelve tribes of Israel just as he began, strong and courageous (Josh. 5:3; 7:22–26; 8:34–35; 24:19–25, 29).

Throughout the Old Testament we find several examples of leaders who selected their team members to serve alongside them in order to partner with them in accomplishing a goal. The ultimate source of these goals was God himself. He articulated them with clarity and detail to those who would share in their fulfillment. After Joshua we see David and his mighty men of valor conquering some of the strongest armies ever assembled. Nehemiah commissioned his diverse and talented team with the task of rebuilding the temple in Jerusalem. Many people throughout the Old Testament could be cited as excellent examples of leaders who developed their staff.

New Testament Examples of Staff Development

As we enter the New Testament, we become eyewitnesses to a staff selection process like no other in history. Jesus embarked on choosing his disciples and began to unfold the mission that would shape their lives for years to come. Little did any of them know that when they decided to follow Jesus, all of history would hinge on this selection process. Jesus is the master leader, and we can learn from his example. First of all, Jesus was intentional about who he chose for his team. Nowhere in Scripture do we see him posting an advertisement asking for applicants to join his staff team. On the contrary, Jesus was clear about whom he wanted, and he chose each with an individual invitation.

Second, although many others were invited to follow and have their lives transformed by Christ, it would be these twelve who would receive a special invitation to join his inner circle of disciples. They fulfilled his plan to evangelize the entire world with the message of God's love and redemption. He relentlessly taught these disciples about his unique method of reaching the world with the gospel message. He wanted to be sure that they had a clear understanding about why the Father had sent him. Not only did he understand the uniqueness of each disciple; it appears that he chose each one because of their unique contribution to the team as a whole. He even chose a disciple whom he knew would become a betrayer. Although sympathetic to their faults and weaknesses, Jesus never allowed his disciples to use them as excuses to grow stagnant in their personal faith. Jesus' example left an indelible mark on their lives. In addition, after he returned to heaven, the Holy Spirit was dispatched to abide with them in order to ensure their long-term effective service.

Throughout these biblical examples, and many more that could also be cited, we see five consistent principles for developing ministry staff. They may be summarized as follows:

1. Develop a clear sense of direction.
2. Select a compatible team.
3. Articulate the goals and objectives.
4. Understand the complexities of the team and their ministry context.
5. Commit yourself to both the organization's goals and individuals on the team.

These timeless principles of staff development provide us with valuable insights about how we should develop our ministry teams today as well. The tension is often found in conflicting desires between meeting the goals of the ministry organization and nurturing the staff of that organization. Often they are mutually compatible, but sometimes they are not.

Have a Clear Sense of Direction

Achieving direction is multifaceted. It starts when you know your ministry's reason for being. Obviously, no ministry enterprise can be all things to all people. For example, in the context of ministry we have churches, schools, relief agencies, mission boards, camps, etc. Each serves a beneficial purpose. When any one of them gets fuzzy vision about their unique niche in ministry or contribution to the kingdom, danger is not far off. For example, it is possible for a church to also serve the needs of those less fortunate within their community. However, if a church becomes too involved in this type of ministry, it runs the risk of losing its distinction as a church.

According to Kenneth Gangel, a church or Christian organization begins with the assumption of the three following premises for goal setting:

1. **The Organization Has Goals.** They may be unwritten, forgotten, or fuzzy, but the mere existence of the organization implies some sort of goal orientation.

2. **The Organization Has Some Structure to Facilitate Goal Realization.** This structure can vary from one person making everything happen to a large and complicated staff system to implement goals through multiple levels of management.

3. **The Organization Requires Effective Leadership If Goals Are to Be Reached.** Goals rarely, if ever, are just achieved out of the blue. There are specific procedures and accountability structures that need to be in place in order for goal achievement to take place.[1]

Since most organizations begin with some form of goal structure, many misunderstand this to be enough to guide the staff. Nothing could be further from the truth. In order for staff members to fulfill the goals of an organization, they must understand not only *what* they are, but also *where* they came from.

Most organizations begin from the inspiration of an individual or group of people. The top-level leaders of the organization must have a clear sense about *why* the organization was founded and *where* it is going. They need to be able to articulate the reason for its existence (both biblically and philosophically) and to have clearly defined targets for ministry activity. If this is not done, staff development is futile. This revelation is sometimes misunderstood, but it is an important foundation for staff development. A brief description of each of these elements is critical before we move into the details of staff development. Some are so important that they have entire chapters dedicated to them in this book, so I will refer to them only briefly as we move through the discussion.

Mission. When one talks about mission, he or she is referring to the foresight of something that "could be." The visionary leader sees down a path some time in the future past hindrances, obstacles, and problematic issues, to a "possibility." These people envision, for the rest of us, what this ministry will one day look like and begin to articulate their passion for what could be. They slowly begin to turn their dream into a reality as they put structure and shape to their dream. The language used to describe this process is called a mission statement. This statement should be biblically based and simple yet inspiring, since this is the wellspring from which all other issues in goal setting flow.

Vision. Vision differs from mission in that it gives specificity to the organization's dream. It usually tells us how we will arrive at the articulated mission and what the final outcome of our labors will look like one day. It is descriptive in language and should also inspire the hearer.

Core Values. Once the leader of an organization clearly communicates his mission and vision for the ministry, the task of setting core values should be implemented. These values are at the heart of the institution and describe the qualities that will be present in the staff members, the processes, and the programs of the organization. These values often determine budgets, staffing, and conflict management among other issues and should be agreed upon by the key stakeholders in the organization.

Setting Goals. Soon after the organization's mission, vision, and core values are determined, goals and objectives should begin to be formulated. It is tempting to rush to goal setting, because we have a natural tendency to want to get to the activity of the organization. This can be dangerously shortsighted without the proper formulation of the broader issues that the big picture provides. Goals are part of a greater strategic plan, as discussed in greater detail in chapter 4 of this book.

Goals should be strategic, measurable, and attainable. Unlike a to-do list, goals should be challenging enough to take the longevity of the specified period of time, usually one year, and yet realistic enough to attain in that time frame. For instance, "Start a memory verse program" would be something you would put on a task list, but this would not serve as an effective goal. Rather, a goal in this area might be worded something like this: "Review the age groupings in the children's departments over the next six months in order to develop an age-appropriate program for Scripture memorization that follows weekend curriculum for ages 6–10." The latter language gives strategy because it is linked to current curriculum, measurability because it gives a six-month review time followed by an implementation program, and is attainable because the group is a reasonable size (ages 6–10).

Assessment. Gangel suggests that "goal achievement moves forward step by step, and its progress must be monitored."[2] He suggests using the framework of evaluation, reinforcement, and reward. Evaluation must be done by the entire team and should be done regularly. This can also serve as a reinforcement time to remember the goals and to have accountability about their progress. Reinforcement can also come in the form of monthly one-on-one times with staff members and their supervisors to review the current progress of that month's steps toward completion. Reward is a time for members to celebrate either verbally or tangibly significant steps made toward the success of goal advancement. It should not be neglected.[3]

For a staff to make a significant contribution to the organization, they must be clear on the overall direction of that organization. This includes the ability to articulate the mission and vision, to demonstrate through their caring demeanor the core values, and to have a working knowledge of the goals and objectives of the ministry venture. It is the responsibility of the leaders of the organization to be able to articulate these to others. Once the leaders are able to do this, they are ready to begin to select the other members of the ministry team who will assist them in making the dream of the ministry a reality.

Staff Selection

In the best-selling book *Good to Great,* Jim Collins comments on the importance of selecting the right members for the organization's team. He uses the metaphor of "getting the right people on the bus" to describe the process of staff selection. Referring to the importance of this task for the leader, he declares, "First Who . . . Then What." Collins researched a set of elite companies which made the leap from good to great results and then sustained those results for more than fifteen years. This is what he found to be consistent in those companies regarding their staffing practices.

The good-to-great leaders understood three simple truths. First, if you begin with "who," rather than "what," you can more easily adapt to a changing world. If people join the bus primarily because of where it is going, what happens if you get ten miles down the road and you need to change direction? You've got a problem. But if people are on the bus because of who else is on the bus, then it's much easier to change directions . . . Second, if you have the right people on the bus, the problem of how to motivate and manage people largely goes away. The right people don't need to be tightly managed or fired up; they will be self-motivated by the inner drive to produce the best results and to be part of creating something great. Third, if you have the wrong people, it doesn't matter whether you discover the right direction; you still won't have a great company. Great vision without great people is irrelevant.[4]

One of the most critical choices a leader will ever make in the church or organization is who he selects as his staff. Often we are tempted to take the first person who has a beating heart and a willingness to work for the salary being offered. We think naively that things will be easier this way so that we move quickly to fill the gaps and then get back to the "more important" issues. But the wise ministry leader understands that staffing is one of the most important things he will ever do as an administrator.

When the organization has the wrong people on the bus, its leaders will spend a disproportionate amount of time dealing with issues of conflict management, motivation, correction of errors, and lack of competence. All of these erode the productivity level of the organization and hinder the leader from doing what only she can do. Collins warns that the main point of staff selection is not just assembling the right team, but to get the right people on the bus (and the wrong people off) *before* you figure out where to drive it.[5]

Not only is the aspect of hiring the right people one of utmost importance, but so is identifying those individuals who are currently occupying the wrong seat on the bus. Churches and other Christian ministries are notorious for not being willing to terminate an employee, so they reshuffle the deck and place the poor performer in a different job instead. This allows the administrator to avoid the difficult task of documenting poor performance, confronting the individual with the evidence, and then terminating him from his position.

For churches and Christian organizations, this can be a serious ethical and spiritual dilemma. The church is supposed to be a safe place that is full of love and grace. It is a family. However, the church today is also a vibrant organization with accountability for goals and objectives, budgets and boards. How does one reconcile the ideal of family (which you can never be kicked out of) with the reality of an organization (from which you can be removed at any time)? It is within this tension that pastors and administrators alike find themselves either giving the ineffective employee another seat on the bus (of which he may or may not be competent) or creating an unprofessional environment that lacks promotion, incentives, or conducive working conditions. Either of these avenues is not honest or beneficial for the overall integrity of the institution or the believer. In short, it is poor stewardship of God's resources.

Admittedly, there are times when just shifting someone's seat on the bus can make a positive contribution to the ministry's goals and objectives. Sometimes a person's fit isn't obvious until he has the opportunity to grow into the organization. This should always be a consideration before termination, but Collins urges that when you know you need to make a people change . . . act![6] We are urged in Ephesians 4:25 to speak the truth in love and to allow our words to bring grace to the moment (Eph. 4:29). Ultimately, God governs people choices in ministry, and he may be urging someone to move from one area of ministry to another. Sometimes he appoints us as spiritual leaders and supervisors to be the spokesperson of that message. We can never underestimate the primacy of prayer when choosing a staff to carry out the Great Commission of our Lord, considering the importance of the decisions that have been entrusted to us.

The right people have ownership of where they are going. In fact, they are a large part of figuring out the right path of how to get there. A leader of great people will set forth a basic goal or elevating idea and allow the staff to pool resources, gifts, and creativity on what exactly that looks like and how to get there. This model takes an effective but humble leader who is willing to allow her staff to share in the molding of the direction. This model, as opposed to a more stereotypical executive leader, has lasting greatness because the passion of ministry achievement is in the very DNA of every individual working on the project or goal. The more typical executive leader will appear successful and may even be able to create a dynamic feel during his leadership, but the many worker bees whom he has enlisted to do "his" goal will be left visionless when he leaves or retires.[7]

In ministry, we cannot afford for our influence to be great and full of returns only for the duration of our short contribution. We must be willing to choose the individuals who have enduring character qualities and giftedness to contribute wholeheartedly to the mission of the church if we are to change this generation for the sake of Christ. We must have eyes to see beyond the here and now to build lasting teams that, with or without our leadership, will understand the mission and will be dedicated to its success.

Understanding the Uniqueness of Team Ministry

This next section will deal with the individual staff member as a person. Often we are tempted to develop staff in order to better accomplish *our* goals. The challenge before any executive leader is to take a step back and see the development of the individual also from the perspective of an end and not just as a means to an end. People are highly valued in Scripture and by Jesus himself. The person was always more important than the program or what was even proper. Jesus valued people as the hallmark of his ministry. We do a disservice to our ministries, and ultimately to our Lord, when we neglect this care for our own staff members. When we do, we are guilty of using people rather than developing them, and therein lies a great secret about effective staff development. When you develop your team as individuals, you also build a foundation for effective team achievement. In essence, a healthy team is comprised of healthy individuals. When team members experience high levels of personal job satisfaction, it translates into team ministry satisfaction, as well.

Though it may appear simple on the surface, it is actually quite difficult to manage because it involves a multifaceted process of:

(1) developing an awareness of what motivates staff members, (2) understanding human nature, (3) dealing with unrealistic expectations, (4) assessing individual staff members' strengths and weaknesses, (5) managing change and conflict, and (6) helping shape attitudes and behaviors in the workplace.

While each of these issues is central to the achievement of an organization's goals, *how* we treat our staff will in many ways determine the lasting success of those goals. Many senior leaders focus on the accomplishment of ministry goals with eyes focused so far down the horizon that the staff members (who carry those goals) are often overlooked or abused along the way. A brief overview of each of these critical elements is essential to a skillful team builder.

Motivation

There are a number of motivational theories that we can glean from in order to better understand what inspires an individual to action. Perhaps the one with the most direct application to ministry was developed by Frederick Herzberg. His model is referred to as the two-factor or hygiene-motivator theory. In his theory, Herzberg identifies one set of factors in the work environment that produce job satisfaction and another set that produce job dissatisfaction. Those factors which lead to job dissatisfaction are called hygiene factors, while those factors which lead to job satisfaction are called motivators (see Figure 15.1).

Hygiene Factors. Hygiene factors are the primary cause of unhappiness in the work environment and relate to the context of the job, not the day-to-day content of the position. When these are not provided, the employee will become dissatisfied, but when appropriately given, they will not necessarily increase satisfaction. These factors include: salary, job security, working conditions, status, company policies, quality of technical supervision, and quality of interpersonal relationships.

Motivational Factors. Motivational factors are the primary causes for job satisfaction. They deal directly with the content of the job itself and relate to the real nature of the work that people perform. When an employer neglects to provide these factors, the staff member will experience no job satisfaction. However, if the employer does provide a sufficient quantity of these, they provide high job satisfaction and productivity. These factors include: achievement, recognition, responsibility, advancement, the work itself (challenging and an opportunity for self-expression), and possibility of growth (personal and professional).[8]

Implications for ministry staff development in light of Herzberg's hygiene factors rest primarily on the shoulders of the administration within the organization. After reviewing the list of factors needed for job satisfaction, you will see that all of these elements are within the power

Figure 15.1

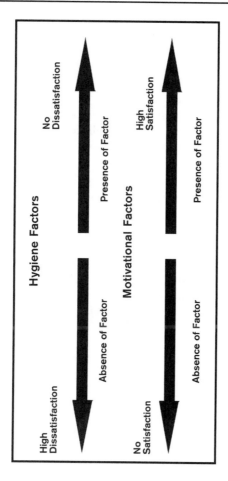

of those in supervisory roles. As Christians, we should provide the best working conditions of any comparable organization. To make our employees' jobs more rewarding, to grant them responsibility according to performance, and to praise their accomplishments does much to increase job satisfaction as well as to treat them with the love and self-worth we are called to as Christ's ambassadors.

Human Nature
in the Context of Building Community

Central to any working environment is an accurate biblical understanding of human nature. The Bible tells us that man was created in the image of God (Gen. 1:27), created for the purpose of glorifying God (1 Cor. 6:20), for his good pleasure (Phil. 2:13), and yet born with a sinful nature imputed from Adam's fall (Rom. 5:12–21). As sin entered the human race, we were destined for certain death and separation from

God. After having given our lives to Christ, we live in constant battle between our sin nature in which we were born and our new redemptive relationship. Our hearts are torn between wanting to do good and doing the very evil that we hate (Rom. 7:14–20).

As we contemplate this tragic situation in light of developing our staff in churches and Christian organizations, we must remember that we're dealing with fallen and sinful people who desperately long to be completely sanctified once and for all. We must provide authentic and grace-filled environments for this struggle. Developing an environment where staff members are free to acknowledge this spiritual battle in their lives allows them to share a sense of community with other believers. Unfortunately, far too many Christian leaders pretend they are above the battle and are no longer fighting the battle. This creates a false illusion of having attained spiritual maturity that is beyond the struggle between a fallen nature and a redeemed soul. Sharing personal struggles can have a profound impact on the growth of staff members both personally and professionally. This authentic lifestyle must be demonstrated before our staff if they are to respect us and see us as sincere Christian leaders.

Unrealistic Expectations

Another aspect in understanding the complexities of staff members is to understand the unrealistic expectations that can arise in our ministry settings. Often a new staff member enters into his or her new job with rose-colored glasses, similar to the honeymoon phase of a marriage. Their expectations of working conditions, ministry accomplishments, promotion opportunities, and meaningful interpersonal relationships are at their highest. However, once the reality hits that life in ministry can sometimes be hard and demanding, these expectations are shattered, leaving the individual with feelings of bitterness toward the supervisor or the institution as a whole.

Taking the time to walk through both the positive and negative aspects of the position before hiring the staff member can return dividends later. We are tempted to extol the many positive points of the organization and the position to potential workers because we want to hire that individual. We try to convince him that our staff is worthy of his efforts and allegiance. Less often do we find a supervisor who sits down with a potential staff member and says, "Hey look, this is a really great place to work, but I've got to be honest about a few things." How refreshing this would be in today's world! Perhaps this technique might keep new staff members from creating and feeding unrealistic expectations that could, in the long run, be hazardous to the unity of the entire staff.

This is particularly true for those who are in their first ministry assignment. Fresh out of college or seminary with a degree in ministry, many of these interns come into our ministries with an expectation that life will be filled with victory after victory. What they fail to realize is that victories generally come after prolonged battles. All ministries have their share of heartaches, politics, and pressures. Long hours are coupled with the occasional misunderstanding—and our young ministry interns find themselves searching through the classifieds on Monday morning looking for any other career option that seems less stressful and intensive.

Assessing Staff Members

Each staff member brings a plethora of strengths and inherent weaknesses to any team. Unlike the previous paragraphs that deal with the potential lack of honesty on the part of the employer, this area deals more with how staff members portray themselves during the interview process. Most Christian organizations spend ample time asking spiritually related questions during the interview process. Some even investigate the candidate's area of spiritual giftedness. Less often do these organizations dig deep into the strengths and weaknesses of an individual. God has designed each of us with diversity, and it serves the administration well to explore this diversity and consider their job placement accordingly.

For example, traditionally we have a job opening and we realize what it takes to do that job, so we go in search of "that" individual. On the other hand, we could find an individual who could bring great giftedness to the team but has a weakness in one area of the job description or position description. That same weakness might be an obvious strength of another staff member already on the team, but that person has been unable to exercise this strength because it was not in her original job description or position description. The wise leader takes frequent assessments of new and current staff members' strengths and weaknesses and changes areas of involvement and management accordingly, thus allowing for achievement, promotion, effectiveness, and ultimately, job satisfaction.

Managing Change and Conflict

Two guarantees of any ministry employment are change and conflict. We live in a hyperchange society in which trends and ideas rarely last a year, as opposed to twenty to thirty years ago, when you could count on something at least surviving the decade before changing. Compare this with our grandparents who went their entire adult lives with relatively little change in society's norms, spiritual rituals, and worship patterns. In light of this trend, what will the next generation face?

Although change can have positive features and make contributions to an organization, change can also create a destructive blow to the internal and external supports of that organization if it is not managed effectively. The number one focus during a season of change should be *communication*. Seldom do people respond after a time of radical change in their church or school with the statement, "Everything went OK, but I just felt so overcommunicated with." Our goal should be to overcommunicate to our congregations and stakeholders in such a way that their response is, "We get it. You can stop telling us this now."

We generally *think* we are overcommunicating because we are privy to the abundance of conversations, meetings, and information about a particular situation.[9] We grow weary of hearing about it, so we make the assumption that others feel the same way. This false assumption inevitably leads to conflict.

Successful staff development requires a "heads up" approach on the part of the leadership to anticipate how the change will impact the staff. When it is perceived that it will have a negative impact, efforts should be taken to communicate with the staff before the information becomes public. It should be obvious that their feelings as well as their jobs were taken into consideration and that the end result of the change will be much better for the kingdom in spite of the hardships involved. However, because the end does not justify the means, the staff should know that their feelings do matter and that everything possible will be done to mitigate any unnecessary damaging effects of the change.

When conflict among staff arises, as indeed it will, wise ministry leaders take the time to gather all the information necessary to implement an intervention strategy. This approach is discussed in more detail in chapters 13 and 18, so I won't take the time to expound on it here. Suffice it to say that staff development requires an intentional and proactive approach toward resolving interpersonal conflicts among staff. Never underestimate the value of positive morale. It may take months to build it but seconds to lose. Trust that is broken can be difficult to repair.

Shaping Attitudes and Behaviors

There are really two key components of shaping attitudes and behaviors of your staff in a Christian organization—and these are prayer and keeping short accounts. As believers, we have a tremendous privilege and responsibility to pray for those in our care. We sometimes categorize only the lay people in our churches, the children in our schools, or those we are ministering to as "sheep" that need our care, but as supervisors this designation also includes our staff members. The Bible is clear that we are to take seriously those who are under our care. We are to be constantly and consistently in prayer for those who are in the service of the Lord for their strength, for their boldness, their spiritual growth, and their resistance toward the evil one. Unlike any of our efforts, the Holy Spirit, through prayer, can do the impossible in the lives of our staff members.

Second, foster a culture of keeping short accounts among your staff. The organization that meets with a staff member once a year for an annual review should not be surprised to discover a variance between the mission of a particular department and that of the organization. When behaviors or attitudes become even slightly skewed, it is prudent to address the situation immediately. Often this can be done over coffee, or as a side note to a conversation. This can be done naturally during the periodic meetings discussed in the ministry by objectives chapter. Many times the issue can become corrected without any lasting damage to either the person or organization.

But left to fester and grow, these negative attitudes or behaviors can continue for months and even years before their exposure. At this time, it is nearly impossible (aside from God's intervention) to unravel the host of negative emotions and feelings of bitterness to the satisfaction of both the employer and employee. Unfortunately, many professional relationships are severed along the way. Clearly, there is a triad relationship between the Holy Spirit, the supervisor, and the staff member in which each person must be responsible to do his or her part.

Staying Committed

When we look at great biblical leaders we find Moses, Joshua, Isaiah, Jeremiah, Nehemiah, Jesus, Peter, and Paul (among others) who committed themselves to the long haul of ministry with those who were entrusted to their care. Each of them had ample opportunities to get frustrated and leave their ministry altogether. However, each of these men recognized the specific call of God on their lives. Only he could release them from their leadership positions.

As Christian leaders mobilizing diverse staffs in the twenty-first century, we have been commissioned to lead as long as God calls us to that particular ministry. However, the best staff development is always done in the context of lifelong learning. Interestingly, those who have had the deepest and most meaningful impact on our lives and ministries are not necessarily those who have "wowed" us with their talent or insights, but rather those who have stood beside us over the long haul of life's ups and downs. They have been there through the difficult times, encouraging and comforting, and they have been there on the sidelines cheering us on during our fifteen minutes of fame. They see us for who we are, accept the most radiating qualities of our Father in us, as well as the qualities that are far less than we hoped anyone would ever discover . . . and they love us anyway.

Those who desire to develop their staff need to keep this kind of perspective on their job. Being a life-impacting leader of staff requires a long-term perspective. Try to see each opportunity as one that can pay dividends not only today but years from now. Having this mind-set will require you to confront some issues that you might be tempted to let slide at the moment. However, when you realize that in the greater context of time the issue will not resolve itself and that they are much easier to deal with when they are small, it will motivate you to handle it sooner rather than later.

You'll also need to keep in mind that you have been entrusted with this individual's ministry development by the Lord. This young man or woman has been entrusted to your care by him for their preparation and training. They may only be under your watchful eye or care for a few years and then move on to other fields of opportunity. The training and staff development nurturing that you provide them may have a lifelong impact on their values, beliefs, and ministry practices. If you are faithful and do your job well, you may be fortunate enough to have them come back many years later and thank you for all you did to see that they were nurtured and loved during some challenging seasons of their career development. What greater reward could anyone want than that?

Conclusion

Staff development is complex and yet at the heart of any effective Christian organization. It starts with focusing on the big picture (knowing why your ministry is in existence and what it is destined to do). Beyond the big picture of purpose, you need to have a firm hand on selecting the right people for the right positions. When you discover that poor placements have been made, you will need to intervene and make the necessary changes. Until that occurs staff development will be undermined by factors which may be beyond your control. However, once this has taken place you are free to move on to the next important step, which is the ability to articulate your direction. This generates a degree of excitement and staff esprit de corps.

Contrary to popular belief, most staff do not join the ministry team purely for the good of the organization. As altruistic as it would be, it simply isn't realistic. Staff members are also looking for something they can take away from their partnership. It might be expanded training, a sense of making a contribution to God's kingdom, gaining a sense of personal well-being, gaining some specific job skills, or developing a mentoring relationship with someone in the organization. The wise and discerning leader takes the time to explore those reasons and seeks to negotiate how to make those expectations a reality in light of the organization's purposes. Facilitating a win-win arrangement can have a lot to do with a staff member's personal motivation for service. When a match is made between the two, successful and meaningful long-term working relationships will be the outcome.

When these mutual expectations are not met, disillusionment and disappointment are the inevitable outcomes. Conflict management techniques rise to the forefront of concern, and intervention strategies are implemented. Time and energy are drained from the enterprise, and ministry becomes tedious work.

Perhaps more than any one aspect of staff development that needs to be emphasized is the need for the ministry leader to shepherd his or her staff flock. Being a caring and nurturing person who lives an authentic life out in the open before his staff is foundational to healthy staff development. Taking the time to meet individual staff needs while at the same time directing ministry efforts toward organizational goals is a difficult challenge with sometimes conflicting aims. However, it is essential for the development of healthy staff who will experience life-long ministry satisfaction. The dividends will be worth the effort.

BY
MARK HENZE

Chapter 16

Legal and Ethical Considerations in Ministry

IN TODAY'S MINISTRY WORLD, the management and administration of Christian education requires at least a passing knowledge and understanding of the current legal climate. This climate is never static.[1] While it would be nice to believe that a Christian ministry may operate independent of legal considerations, this is neither realistic nor biblical. Many ministries tend to embrace the law when useful, but complain that the law should have no applicability whenever it is burdensome. This attitude, together with a cultural tendency to separate law and religion into nonoverlapping categories, often prevents a ministry from effectively utilizing the protections afforded while leading to great peril when other laws are ignored.

The idea that ministry is exempt from civil law is not biblical. Nor is the belief that ministry should operate independent of available legal protections. In Old Testament Israel, the civil law and religious law were synonymous.[2] The civil law constituted God's very revelation to humanity. By Jesus' day, much of the law had been misapplied and stripped of its original purpose. Although Jesus promoted respect and obedience to the law, he nevertheless showed little hesitancy to disobey laws that had lost their purpose.[3] Yet, he never suggested that he and his disciples were exempt from the burdens of appropriate civil law due to his religious mission.[4] Likewise, Paul never suggested that he was exempt from the law. In fact, he not only preached compliance and obedience, but he also didn't hesitate to call on the law to provide the protections that it might afford.[5]

Indirectly, this chapter considers ethical issues as well as legal issues. Despite recent attempts to separate law from ethics, it seems that both are integrally entwined. While there may be occasion to ethically oppose a specific provision of civil law, attempts by a ministry

274

to disregard or claim ignorance of the law will not suffice. Nor will Christian ethics support the actions of a ministry that blatantly manipulates or takes advantage of our God-given freedoms. It still remains a valid presumption that ethics dictates compliance with the law on the vast majority of occasions, while violation of the law tends to be associated with the unethical. The idea that one cannot legislate morality may recognize the law's inability to change one's heart, yet it fails to recognize that moral claims are often the chief source of legislation that limit and define acceptable activity.

Ministries cannot benefit from the law while at the same time claiming to be above or exempt from it. I vividly recall a time when I was approached by a church that was angry over another charitable organization's utilization of curriculum material that had been obtained from the church without its permission. Despite the church's desire to bring litigation, I found myself privy to information that this same church was being considered for legal action due to their refusal to obtain ASCAP and CCLI licenses. They had argued that "all music is God's music." On the other hand, a church cannot shirk its stewardship duties out of a belief that it should not fight an appropriate and righteous battle.

For example, one church was requested by a bankruptcy court trustee to return the full amount of an individual's prior annual tithe to the court. Despite the fact that the issue involved was the subject of both controversy and continuing legal argument, and the fact that a national Christian legal organization was willing to underwrite all the costs of litigation, the board determined that a church should avoid participating in legal disputes and paid the funds to the court while signing an agreement not to contest the matter. Less than one month later, Congress passed a new law resolving the issue in favor of churches. Yet, this ministry had waived its right to have the contributions returned.

Basic Legal Concepts

Legal and ethical considerations within Christian ministry fall under every aspect of the management and administrative process. This chapter is located under "staffing" only due to the proliferation of legal issues involving employees and the use of volunteers. In fact, legal and ethical issues also populate the process of planning, organizing, directing, and evaluating. In fact, the sheer number of such issues requires that this chapter be intentionally abbreviated. Any attempt to cover all the various treatments afforded by federal and state law or to treat the myriad of specific issues addressed in volumes of case law would be neither wise nor helpful. Instead, a worthwhile objective would be to stimulate an understanding of the categories and concepts into which these issues may be organized. With proper conceptual development, a ministry or institution would be better able to recognize and anticipate potential issues as they arise.

There are some preliminary concepts that need to be understood. First, we must realize that there are a variety of sources of law. There are foundational sources which, depending upon one's worldview, may be described as inalienable rights or as constitutional, foundational, God-given, or natural law. While the foundational sources in today's Christian world are not as pervasive as those handed down in Deuteronomy, they do serve as the underlying basis for all other sources. From these foundations, a body of law based upon historical acceptance and use has developed. This is typically referred to as the common law, or sometimes case law. Finally, specific decrees or rules are enacted to flesh out situational and administrative aspects of the common law. This is typically referred to as statutory law.

Second, certain areas of the law tend to apply to everyone, while others apply only to specifically defined segments of the population. For example, while the laws of contracts and liability apply to everyone, the specialized fields of maritime, banking, health care, creditor, school, or church law do not. However, one application may easily cross over between specialized fields as in the case of a church school or a religious psychology clinic. Similarly, any time that one of these fields hires employees, labor and tax laws will come into play.

Third, certain special bodies of law tend to incorporate a different mix of legal sources. For example, educational law often depends more on specific statutory directives while church law depends upon a larger complement of First Amendment and other constitutional or foundational issues. Figure 16.1 portrays four major legal quadrants: administrative law, organizational law, liability law and constitutional law.[6] Both organizational law and administrative law tend to apply more often within the public sector, while liability law and constitutional law often become issues within the private sector.

This figure shows, as an example, both the typical overlap and the different emphasis characterizing two specialized bodies of law—school law and church law. Clearly, there is a large area of law that overlaps and directly affects both bodies. However, it also becomes clear that school law tends to focus more on administrative and public concerns, while church law typically finds itself dealing with constitutional and more private concerns.

The four quadrants are divided as follows. *Constitutional law* deals with the very legal and ethical foundations upon which all other areas of the law are built. Today, these include the foundations of personal and economic freedom and the idea of inalienable rights, including the right to free speech, free press, free assembly and free exercise of

Figure 16.1

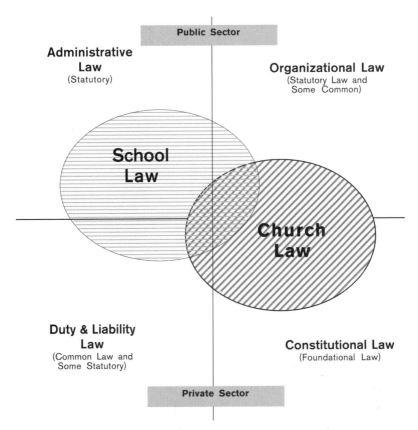

religion, the right to be free of government seizure or the institution of a government religion, the right to due process (including freedom from unwarranted discrimination), and some would argue, a right of privacy. Due to the characteristics of the free exercise and the establishment clauses of the Constitution, church law often finds itself embroiled in more constitutional issues than administrative or regulatory issues. In fact, within the body of church law, many areas concerning the application of statutory and common law necessarily encompass issues of constitutional law as well.

Under the rubric of *organizational law* we typically find issues concerning business organizations, corporations, nonprofit status, and taxation. These are typically statutory in nature, although some areas of common law may exist. One characteristic of statutory law is its mutability. Its authority depends solely upon the passage of legislation that can just as easily be modified or repealed by the simple stroke of a pen, signifying a change in the temperament of the majority. These laws have few gray areas and require strict compliance. For example, the failure to timely file a required 501(c)(3) application to obtain tax-deductible charitable status will result in the complete denial of the desired privilege.[7]

Within the category of *administrative law* we find special industry and profession-specific legislation, together with the bulk of labor and regulatory laws. These laws tend to be more specific and strict than the organizational laws. They depend largely on definitions and classifications, and they may also change swiftly if the time and culture warrant. Here we find issues such as professional licensure, securities laws, wage and hour regulations, environmental and occupational workplace laws, health codes, retirement benefit laws, building and zoning codes, equipment inspections, and many of our educational laws such as truancy, public finance, and curriculum laws. Here we find that school law is often replete with specialized regulations and requirements that must be adhered to before one can perform the defined function of a "school."[8] It is also here where church law often encounters the interaction of constitutional and regulatory law.

Liability law encompasses the area of fiduciary duties, trust, and tort law, together with criminal law. It is here that concepts of personal responsibility and liability for our intentional or negligent actions are given effect. Here there are two divisions of liability. Criminal law deals with the action and not its effect while seeking goals of societal tranquility, deterrence, punishment, retribution, behavior modification, and rehabilitation. On the other hand, civil aspects of liability law require only that a person who is injured or wronged be appropriately compensated for his loss. This category relies heavily on the common law, although some statutory definitions of "wrong" or liability exist.

It is in this area that we deal with child abuse, good Samaritan or volunteer statutes, negligence issues, and intentional torts such as assault, libel, and fraud. Constitutional concepts likewise establish rights which once infringed lead to liability. This allows compensation for intentional acts such as discrimination or the infringement of copyright and other property laws.

A Closer Look at Types of Law

It is now time to investigate further each of these quadrants.

Constitutional Law

Constitutional law is arguably the cornerstone of American society. To some, it represents the grand achievement of a communal and allegedly benevolent species. To others, it is a practical way to divide duties and majesteria . . . checks and balances, public vs. private, and religious vs. secular. Yet, to Christians, it is simply a reflection of God's universal truth and the dignity of his creation. According to the Declaration of Independence, "We hold these truths to be self-evident, that all men are created equal, that they are endowed by their Creator with certain unalienable rights, that among these are life, liberty and the pursuit of happiness."

The First Amendment of the United States Constitution, which was made applicable to the individual states through the incorporation doctrine of the Fourteenth Amendment,[9] provides two crucial areas of religious freedom. First, the Establishment Clause[10] provides that neither Congress nor state legislatures may pass any law that declares a state or national religion, compels any particular form of religious belief or worship, or endorses, aids, or promotes any set of religious beliefs or practices over another. Second, the Free Exercise Clause[11] provides that neither the states nor the federal government shall pass any law that impedes or prohibits any particular form of religious belief. Apparently, either the wording of these clauses was clear or there were few conflicts between the government and religious belief for the first century and a half after its adoption. There is little case law interpreting these clauses prior to the mid-1900s.

The establishment clause has never been held to require hostility between government and religion. However, it does require that government action avoid favoritism. Thus, government-sponsored religious activities, coercion of religious practices in schools and public forums, and providing aid or support based on or determined by religious factors are prohibited. According to Justice Hugo Black in the 1949 case of *Everson v. Board of Education*,[12] "In the words of Jefferson, the clause against the establishment of religion by law was erected to set up a 'wall of separation between church and state.'"

Since that time, the establishment clause has expanded to suggest that federal and state laws (1) must have a secular legislative purpose; (2) that the primary effect of the law must not advance, promote, or inhibit religious practice; and (3) that the statute must not foster excessive government entanglement in religious concerns.[13] Based on this analysis, corporate prayer[14] or Bible readings[15] in the public school have been prohibited; prohibiting the teaching of an accepted educational topic (evolution) for religious purposes has been outlawed;[16] and government aid to schools or other organizations may not be used for religious purposes.[17] On the other hand, the courts will generally not involve themselves in clergy hiring and termination[18] decisions or matters of ecclesiastical governance.

While the establishment clause typically involves cases filed by individuals against government agencies attempting to prohibit government action, the free exercise cases typically involve individuals seeking personal exemption from existing laws. In ruling on free exercise issues, the court must distinguish between a person's belief and his or her acting upon that belief. Clearly, the right to one's belief is unassailable, but is there a corresponding right to act upon that belief to the detriment of others?

To make this determination, the court in Sherbert[19] and Yoder[20] established another three-part test. First, did the person have a sincerely held religious belief that resulted in the issue in dispute?[21] Second, does the law unduly burden the free exercise of that person's religious belief? Finally, is the government's interest so compelling as to warrant the infringement of that person's free-exercise rights? A component of these last two parts includes an analysis of whether or not methods exist that would achieve the same governmental objective in a manner that would be less intrusive on the individual's religious rights.

Based upon this test, the court has permitted the existence of alternative parochial and Christian schools,[22] the right to witness door to door and in public forums,[23] religious access to other forums if they are routinely made available to nonreligious organizations, and discrimination on otherwise actionable grounds in the hiring of clergy.[24] However, the court has similarly rejected claims to polygamy, to protect religious practices that are illegal,[25] and actions that are detrimental to the health of another.[26]

In short, constitutional provisions, while providing the foundation for the entire American legal system, also provide for a variety of exceptions and protections against legal intrusion into good-faith religious beliefs. Where legitimate religious concerns exist (such as the right to conduct Bible studies in a home or to make contributions to selected ministries), we must be proactive in protecting our rights. However, where the matter has no real Christian significance (such as a constitutional right to discriminate in clergy hiring based on race), we are best to refrain from their use.

Organizational Law

Indirectly, organizational law revolves around the concepts of ownership and control (both external and internal), the liability of those in control, the structure of governmental entities (with some obvious constitutional ties), and taxation. A ministry may be structured as an individual effort or as the joint effort of many people. If only an individual is involved, the issues of control are uncomplicated. The individual is solely responsible (liable) to society and is in complete control of ministry decisions. However, joint efforts require more complex regulation of both internal and external control. The law of corporations and business associations (including partnerships and foundations) will apply equally to all private enterprises whether in the market or ministry.

In an effort to encourage organizations that focus on providing community services rather than monetary gain, a variety of special benefits are available to nonprofit organizations. However, the designation *nonprofit* means only that the organization has no stated goal to derive profits for its owners. It does not mean "charitable" or "tax-exempt." At the time of this writing, most of the airlines are "nonprofit," however this is not intentional, nor have they been organized as nonprofit corporations. In addition, the designation *charitable* is not the same as a *church*. A local homeowner's association is organized as a "nonprofit" corporation; however, it is neither religious nor charitable in nature.[27] On the other hand, World Vision is a nonprofit charitable organization, but it is not a church. The appropriate designation will have an effect upon the benefits that are bestowed, the rationale behind their bestowal, and the procedures to be followed in obtaining those benefits.

The benefits generally available to a nonprofit entity include (a) exemption from income taxes, property taxes and sales taxes; (b) allowing supporters to deduct their gifts and contributions; and (c) the provision of additional protections to officers and volunteers from contractual and tort liability. Note that tax-exempt status does not excuse the organization from filing tax returns or exempt it from paying income taxes on income that has nothing to do with its exempt purpose. Exemption or special treatment for income tax purposes is a matter of federal law while exemption from real estate and sales and use taxes is a matter of state law.[28] Many states will determine eligibility for state exemption by whether or not the organization has qualified under federal law.

Internal Revenue Code §501 confers and regulates tax-exempt status. Generally, subsection 501(c) (3) of the code determines whether or not contributions will be deductible. There are twenty-seven acceptable purposes or categories for tax-exempt organizations listed under §501(c) (3), the most common of which are (a) charitable; (b) religious; (c) scientific; and (d) educational purposes. In general, the requirements for an organization's approval depend upon (a) its organization, (b) its manner of operations, and (c) its objectives. The entity must have an organizational structure (normally as a nonprofit corporation or limited liability corporation) that clearly limits the activities of the organization to its intended purpose; prohibits the payment of monetary profits or benefits to its owners, organizers or members; and requires that any assets remaining upon dissolution or cessation of operations must be distributed to another qualified 501(c)(3) organization. The entity must be operated so that it clearly pursues its approved exempt purpose; avoids participation in political campaigns for public office; and spends only an insignificant amount of time and resources in attempting to influence legislation or political objectives.[29]

Tax-exempt status is neither a right, nor is it automatically conferred.[30] An application requiring strict deadlines and details must be filed with the IRS. The only exception belongs to recognized churches that, due to First Amendment issues, are automatically exempt and are not required to file with the IRS. Although the IRS code contains no specific definition of the term *church* and courts have relied on a number of definitions from other sources, the IRS eventually proposed a list of fourteen criteria to be considered in characterizing who is a church and who is not.[31]

1. a distinct legal existence,
2. a recognized creed and form of worship,
3. a definite and distinct ecclesiastical government,
4. a formal code of doctrine and discipline,
5. a distinct religious history,
6. a membership not associated with any other church or denomination,
7. an organization of ordained ministers,
8. ordained ministers selected after completing prescribed studies,
9. a literature of its own,
10. established places of worship,
11. regular congregations,
12. regular worship services,
13. Sunday schools for religious instruction of the young, and
14. schools for the preparation of ministers.

Although no single criterion is controlling and the applicability of all fourteen is not necessarily required, a number of courts have since adopted these or similar factors in defining a "church." Many believe that these factors form too narrow a definition and are thus flawed and subject to challenge.[32] Still, the lesson to be learned is that not all religious organizations will meet the definition of a church. Where a non-IRS statute refers to a church, it is important to review the definition used for that particular statute. As a result of the uncertain nature of the definition, many churches will file the IRS application to ensure that tax-exempt status is properly recognized.[33]

Most ministries will likewise wish to organize as a corporation or a limited liability corporation. Such status provides a great deal of liability protection. While an individual or partner will be personally liable for the contract and debt obligations of a solely owned or partnership ministry, the owners, members, and directors of a corporation will not be held indirectly liable for a corporation's activities. In addition, many of the statutory limitations of negligence liability are applicable only to nonprofit corporations.

Administrative Law

The fact that a nonprofit organization is tax exempt does not absolve it from labor and employment laws. In general, income taxes, Social Security, and other required taxes must still be withheld from employees. One notable exception is federal unemployment insurance.[34] The withholding of state unemployment taxes will vary state by state depending upon the applicable statute.[35] Additionally, licensed or ordained members of the clergy may exclude from their taxable income that amount of their compensation that has been designated as "housing allowance." The only limitations to the amount designated are that the amount (a) must be reasonable; (b) must be actually related to the costs of housing (including rent, mortgage payments, property taxes, insurance, repairs, improvements and yard care), furnishings and utilities; and (c) must have been declared by the employing church prior to making the applicable compensation payment.[36]

This is a very beneficial exemption and, if the clergy is making mortgage payments, can result in a form of double deduction (exempt from income and deductible on Schedule A for mortgage interest and property taxes). Recent litigation brought by the IRS sought to clarify some particularities of this exemption and resulted in a preliminary order from a federal appeals court indicating that it believed the entire exemption violates the First Amendment's establishment clause. However, in response, Congress stepped in and passed the Clergy Housing Allowance Clarification Act of 2002 which limits the amount of the exemption to "the fair rental value of the home, including furnishings and appurtenances such as a garage, plus the cost of utilities."[37]

Furthermore, confusing vestiges of a pastor's and church's exemption from Social Security still remain. While a qualified pastor may claim an exemption from participation upon grounds that his religious convictions are opposed to his or her receipt of benefits from a secular and public program, the application procedure is arduous with time-sensitive deadlines.[38] Should an exempt pastor later decide to participate, he will likely never have the opportunity to reclaim his exemption again. In addition, his church (as employer) may at the time of its incorporation elect to treat its qualified pastors as "self-employed" and become exempt from employee withholding and paying its employer's share of Social Security on behalf of the pastor. However, while this may benefit the church, it surely does not benefit the pastor, who will be required to pay the entire Social Security tax pursuant to the Self-Employed Contributions Act (SECA).

It is safe to assume that all other regulatory labor laws apply as well. However, many of these laws exempt organizations employing only a small number of people or with gross income below a certain level (the number varies from statute to statute).[39] Therefore, small organizations and churches may wish to consult the applicability requirements of each specific law. Worker's Compensation premiums are typically required;[40] wage and hour requirements apply in the same manner as in the "for profit" world;[41] immigration laws are in full force and effect; and the occupational safety and health laws apply although there remains some question whether churches and many charitable organizations may be characterized as being "engaged in business affecting commerce" as required by OSHA and other laws.

If the organization is a religious charity or a church, major differences begin to arise when we consider discrimination laws. For example, both Title VII of the Civil Rights Act and the Americans with Disabilities Act apply to all employers of fifteen or more, yet include specific statutory provisions exempting a variety of religious organizations and educational institutions that are owned or controlled by religious organizations.[42] These organizations may discriminate only concerning the hiring of those not belonging or adhering to the tenets of their particular religious affiliation. Despite popular belief, they are not immune from discrimination claims by nonpastors based upon race, nationality, disability, sex, or marital status unless such requirements can be established as an integral and reasonable requirement of their religious convictions.[43]

Other administrative areas include the statutory definition of a "minister" (for purposes of performing marriages and access to prisons, hospitals, and other nonpublic areas of ministry),[44] professional licensure for nonpastoral professions (such as the licensure of psychologists), securities laws, intellectual property and copyright law, charitable solicitation law, and bankruptcy law. With minor exceptions, these laws apply equally to both profit and nonprofit organizations. For example, the fact that a church does not charge admission to a worship service or class does not exempt its use of copyrighted materials in a manner otherwise violating copyright law.[45] In addition, while arguably the First Amendment should allow a church to raise support and contributions in whatever manner it deems appropriate, the fraud provisions of both state and federal securities laws have been held to apply.[46] Even the U.S. Bankruptcy Code contains a provision specifically applicable to churches and charitable institutions.

The Bankruptcy Code permits a trustee to recover any payments made by a debtor within a year prior to the debtor's bankruptcy filing if the payment was not in compensation for a reasonable value received in return.[47] Thus, the trustee is authorized to demand that a church or charitable institution return to the court all of the debtor's contributions over the past year. In addition, a person making payments to a bankruptcy court pursuant to an approved wage earner's (chapter 13) payment plan cannot make charitable contributions during the term of the plan.[48] However, after a number of challenges and attempts to change the law, Congress finally passed the Religious Freedom and Charitable Donation Protection Act of 1998. This law protects a debtor's previous charitable contributions that amount to less than 15 percent of his gross annual income, or amounts exceeding that percentage if the debtor has established a regular pattern of similar giving in the past. In addition, a Chapter 13 debtor is now permitted to continue these regular contributions during the course of his payment plan.

Liability Law

It's just a part of life that during the course of dealing with employees, volunteers, and the public, accidents and mistakes occur and people are harmed. In addition, contracts and monetary obligations are made by people on behalf of organizations where the organization may later be unable or may choose not to honor the commitment. Liability for contractual or monetary defaults tends to be less complicated than personal injuries. If the organization is structured as a corporation, the individual employees, directors, and officers will not be individually liable.[49] If the organization fails to pay its debts, the creditors may attach the assets owned by the corporation but may not collect from the individuals involved with the organization. On the other hand, if the organization is not incorporated, the debts of the organization become the individual liabilities of those in control.

Issues of personal injury are a bit more complicated. American common law provides that when someone is harmed, the person causing the harm has the responsibility to either correct the harm and/or compensate the injured party for their loss. Liability can arise from intentional and malicious acts, a failure to use due care, or even simple accidents. When they occur, the legal question revolves around who is responsible and to what degree. If the injured person (or a third party) is partly responsible, that partial responsibility must also be taken into account.

In general, both the organization and the acting employee are responsible for the results of the employee's actions, provided that the event took place within the scope of the employee's duties. This is based upon the common law principle of *respondeat superior*, meaning that the employer has final control over the actions of its subordinates and must respond for their actions. Therefore the liability of the employee is imputed to the organization. However, one must understand what acts are deemed to be within the "scope" of an employee's duties. Generally, this includes actions that were authorized or which could have been anticipated to arise from one's employment duties.[50] Yet, it normally does not include acts taken in direct and intentional violation of that authority. A distinction must be made between negligence (lack of due care) and intentional or criminal wrongs. The organization will not be responsible if the employee intentionally acts in contravention of his orders or authorized duties. As is the case with contracts, employees of nonprofit corporations who did not personally participate[51] in the action will also be insulated from personal liability.

A notion still remains among some churches and nonprofits that they benefit from a doctrine of "charitable immunity." This doctrine once prohibited a charitable organization from being sued or being held liable for its negligent acts. The rationale was to prevent random negligence from undermining the entire work of an otherwise beneficial charity. While this doctrine controlled court decisions as late as the 1940s, it has since been rejected in every jurisdiction. Remnants of the doctrine still arise on occasion when dealing with claims initiated by beneficiaries of charitable services.[52] Otherwise, unless liability is expressly limited by statute, churches and nonprofits face the same liability issues as any other entity.

Despite these limitations, today's legal climate suggests that no mistake, no matter how honest or minimal, should go uncompensated. As a result, the specter of being held personally liable for errors and negligence may cause individuals to avoid charitable and volunteer activities. On the other hand, organizations become concerned with the prospect of unavoidable liability resulting from the use of volunteers who are less trained, less committed, and less subject to control and oversight. Public concern for the viability of nonprofit organizations and volunteerism has prompted most states to enact statutes limiting the personal liability of volunteers who perform uncompensated services at the behest of charitable organizations.

In addition, Congress has passed a federal Volunteer Protection Act[53] which substantially limits liability. This act applies nationally[54] and covers most volunteers who aid nonprofit or governmental organizations. The statute does not apply if the individual's action is intentional or criminal, if the volunteer was not acting within the scope of his volunteer duties, if the volunteer was unlicensed and performing an act that required appropriate licensure, or if it involved the use of a vehicle where liability insurance is required by law. Additionally, the act covers only the volunteer. While the volunteer cannot be sued, the organization may still be responsible to others for the actions of that volunteer.

The volunteer immunity laws of most states and the federal Volunteer Protection Act also include the good-faith activities of uncompensated officers and directors of a nonprofit entity. Thus, while an officer or director is clearly immune from liability for the actions of others in the organization for which he or she had no complicity (by virtue of corporate limitations of liability), he is also immune from the decisions he makes as a board member unless his actions consist of obvious and gross negligence, are intentional or criminal in nature, or are outside of the scope of his authority and duties as a director. The scope and authority of a director is determined by both the specific authority granted to the director by the organization and by the standards of conduct set forth for directors of nonprofit corporations under the Revised Model Nonprofit Corporation Act that has been enacted by most states.[55]

Despite these protections, the organization remains at risk. In most instances, these risks may be managed through proper insurance coverage. This coverage may include a general liability policy covering the organization, motor vehicle coverage for those operating organization vehicles, D & O insurance (protecting directors and officers), and even umbrella coverage protecting the individual volunteer. However, even insurance coverage will not offer protection from willful and wanton misconduct, gross negligence, criminal activity, acts of self-dealing, or actions made in knowing disregard of applicable law.[56] Finally, a rash of insurance claims (even if frivolous in nature) may result in skyrocketing insurance premiums or even the unavailability of certain types of coverage. Other forms of risk management must complement the use of insurance.

Risk management techniques may range from providing quality training and supervision of volunteers and employees, to developing policy manuals clearly outlining one's scope of employment. Release forms requiring disclosure of medical information and waiving liability may be warranted for certain activities. Registration and check-in procedures for child care and Sunday school programs are helpful. The prohibition of counseling services by nonpastoral or nonlicensed providers is imperative. It would also seem advisable to regularly reevaluate programs and duties for possible legal consequences. Some of the hot areas of legal liability include the following:

1. **Negligent Hiring.** While an employer is generally not liable to third parties for the intentional or criminal misconduct of an employee, the employer may be held liable under the same circumstances for its own negligence. Often this involves a claim that the employer was

negligent in the selection and hiring of the wrongdoer. Did the organization use due care in hiring the employee or selecting the volunteer and placing him in certain areas of responsibility? Has the employee or volunteer been screened to discover and investigate prior misconduct or to discover attitudes that conflict with his duties and the safety of his clients and coworkers? If prior problems have been discovered, what actions have been taken by that person (and the organization) to ensure that they will not occur again? What prior training has the person received to ensure his competence and that he recognizes problems and misconduct when they occur?

In short, an employer has a duty to use reasonable care in investigating a prospect and evaluating his or her suitability for the position.[57] This duty is based upon standards of reasonableness, and the standard may increase when the employee or volunteer will be knowingly placed among clients or coworkers who are particularly vulnerable, as when working with children, seniors, or the disabled.

2. **Negligent Supervision.** Once a person has been hired, an organization has a duty to reasonably and properly supervise the actions of its employees. Many cases of negligent supervision involve incidents of child molestation or sexual misconduct. When it comes to children, several courts have held that the appropriate standard of care is that of the average responsible parent, yet the organization is not an insurer of the child's safety.[58] Thus decisions as to negligence often involve a balancing of the reasonableness, cost, and availability of preventative measures, together with a consideration of the measures commonly used in the community. Today, in many communities it is anticipated that attendance records will be kept, that children will not be released to strangers, that restrooms in children's facilities will be restricted, that counseling will not be crossgender unless conducted within the view of witnesses with open doors, and that multiple chaperones be utilized during off-site activities. While the failure to utilize these measures may be acceptable in a small rural community, it is likely that the same is unreasonable in a major urban area.

3. **Negligent Retention.** An organization may have acted responsibly in the hiring and supervision processes, but may be guilty of negligence if it unreasonably retains an employee after receiving information that the employee has developed a propensity, pattern, or disposition of placing others at risk of harm.[59] Negligent supervision and retention often go hand in hand. If it is possible to properly rehabilitate an employee and to supervise and insulate the employee from situations where harm may occur, it is generally not negligent to retain the employee. On the other hand, if such precautions are unavailable or unreasonable, it may make more sense to let the employee go. Finally,

the organization must balance issues concerning improper termination. If there is insufficient evidence of misconduct to warrant termination, it may be more prudent to establish proper prevention and supervisory measures.

4. **Malpractice.** Malpractice consists of a professional person's deviation from the reasonable standards of care expected of those within that profession. Claims for clergy malpractice have typically been appended to claims for intentional acts (such as criminal acts or sexual misconduct), or to claims for negligence in counseling. Most courts have rejected these claims,[60] partly due to problems in determining what specific duties are required from the profession of "minister"; partly due to the constitutional ramifications of establishing a standard of conduct applicable to all religious persuasions; and partly due to the fact that most of the claims of alleged malpractice consist of violations of criminal standards applicable to all, rather than standards specifically applicable to clergy.

However, there are clear professional standards applicable to the role of psychologist or mental health counselor. Virtually all states require the licensure of mental health counselors, yet counseling activities by clergy are typically exempted, or if not exempted by statute have been deemed exempt due to constitutional free-exercise issues. This exemption only applies to those meeting the definition of a minister or clergy and often applies only to spiritual counseling.

The clear overlap of spiritual and mental health counseling, together with the difficulty of determining what standard should be applied to spiritual counselors (secular precepts or biblical precepts), makes it difficult to determine whether clergy counseling efforts fall within the profession's standard of care. Because of these issues, many churches now require the referral of counseling or encourage clergy to obtain proper training and licensure as a psychologist while providing appropriate malpractice insurance. Strategically, many question whether mental health licensure opens the church up for additional liability while obligating its counselors to accept and practice within secular standards.

5. **Confidentiality of Communications and Clergy Privilege.** Confidentiality and privilege are two different concepts. Typically, there is no legal requirement that a minister's conversations with a parishioner remain confidential. In fact, unless a conversation occurs in private with no other parties present and with an expectation of confidentiality, the conversation is normally not regarded as confidential. In most cases, any duty of confidentiality is moral in nature, not legal. However, due to the fiduciary qualities of the relationship, confidentiality is often expected and required to maintain effectiveness and

trust. Arguably, these conversations by their very nature may imply a contract or expectation of confidentiality. Therefore, one of the first issues that should be clarified by a pastor during any consultation is the extent of any expectation of privacy. To avoid any confusion, it is imperative that the pastor's church or denomination have a written and established policy about the confidentiality of clergy communication.[61] The existence of such a policy will also be important when establishing any claims to clergy privilege.

Unlike the issues of confidentiality, the concept of privilege deals only with the ability to legally compel a minister to disclose confidential communications in a court of law. The rationale is that the privilege will protect a person's right to religious confession (penitence) and preserve the confidence and therapeutic value of such communications. At one time, all clergy conversations were privileged; however, today the existence of a privilege is governed by state law and communications are only privileged if they involve: (a) a legally recognized pastor or licensed counselor as a party[62] (b) to a private communication that was intended to be confidential,[63] (c) where the pastor or counselor was acting in his or her professional capacity as either a spiritual advisor or mental health counselor. The counselee need not be a regular client of the counselor or a member of the pastor's congregation.[64]

The clergy privilege may apply to marital counseling situations where another spouse is also present; however, this will vary state by state. State statutes also differ about who has the right to assert or to waive the privilege. The pastor may have no right to waive the privilege and may be compelled to testify against his or her own will if the penitent agrees to waive the privilege.[65] Such a waiver may be involuntarily made by a penitent who discloses the contents of privileged communications to others, thus destroying the expectation of confidentiality. The privilege may also be voluntarily waived by the penitent, provided that the court is convinced that the waiver is knowingly made and with an understanding of what will be disclosed and how it will be used against the penitent.

Despite any expectation of confidentiality or privilege, there are certain situations where a minister may have a legal duty to disclose. If possible, these potential duties should be revealed to the penitent prior to his or her decision to participate in the conversation. For example, neither an expectation of confidence or privilege serve to preclude a clergy from disclosing to law enforcement officials confidential communications about past crimes or future intent to commit a crime. However, a pastor's disclosure to proper authorities will serve merely as a "tip" and will not waive a future claim of privilege prohibiting testimony in court.

The authorities will likely need to find other evidence of the crime outside of the minister's tip.

A recently burgeoning area of the law concerns the reporting of child abuse. All states now have statutes designating persons in certain professions and situations as "mandatory reporters" of suspected child abuse. In many states, a minister (and in nearly all states a licensed teacher or counselor) are deemed mandatory reporters.[66] In exchange for the duty to report, a good-faith reporter is granted immunity from liability for the disclosure. On the other hand, the failure of a mandatory reporter to disclose either actual or reasonably suspected abuse constitutes a criminal act (typically a misdemeanor), and such a conviction may affect one's ability to maintain his or her professional license. In addition, many of the statutes permit the child or parent to bring a suit for damages against a person who unreasonably fails to report.

This requirement may raise a clear ethical dilemma for pastors. Do they maintain their confidence and continue to counsel an otherwise reluctant penitent? Do they report and breach their confidentiality? Or do they stop the person from confiding further if the issue appears to be unfolding? Many pastors and counselors have elected to disclose their duty and decision to report prior to the commencement of the confidential relationship. As a result, child abusers and victims may elect to avoid spiritual or mental health counseling that might be beneficial to both them and society. In either event, this is an area where nonprofit organizations and churches need to fully investigate their state's reporting requirements and develop a written and clearly articulated policy.

Conclusion

Legal issues are best dealt with before they become confrontations. This requires that they be investigated not only during the operational stages (staffing and directing), but also during the initial planning and organizing phases. Paradoxically, the law tends to provide its own evaluation through the plight of others. Case law and legislative proposals are often the result of the evaluation of others and are there to provide clear signals to those who are attentive.

Clearly, the legal issues faced by churches and nonprofit ministries are no more daunting than those faced by others. However, a scarcity of time and resources, together with a feeling that we deserve some absolution as we go about the Lord's business, has created trouble for some organizations in the past. On the other hand, knowledge of the law is neither a license to wield our religious freedoms for untenable positions nor a substitute for ethical action. Our witness to the world as individual Christians and Christian organizations should establish our realistic ability to balance the burdens and the benefits . . . all in an effort to bring about God's plan.

Special Online Sources:

www.ChurchLawToday.com. This Web site is managed by Christian Ministry Resources in Matthews, North Carolina, and Richard R. Hammar. This is a wonderful source that includes a resource center (bookstore), updated case law, articles of both practical and legal professional concern, copies of legislation, charts of state legislation concerning a variety of issues, and numerous newsletters. Their Resource Center may be reached at 1-800-222-1840. They are also the publishers of several print newsletters including the bimonthly *Church Law & Tax Reporter.* Additional materials and resources are available online for subscribers to their newsletters.

www.ChristianLaw.org. This Web site is managed by the Christian Law Association, an organization that publishes numerous books, articles, and pamphlets on church legal matters, offers legal advice and free legal defense when appropriate, and operates a daily radio program, "The Legal Alert." The Web site includes many articles, case updates, and legal abstracts of interest. They may be reached at 727-399-8300.

PART 5

DIRECTNG

If you've ever tried to lead or conduct an orchestra, you'll understand what it means to direct an organization. Harmony is achieved only if everyone involved is reading from the same page and has agreed to cooperate and share their talents until they get to the end of their assignments. Without this level of mutual cooperation and support, the task of the conductor is undermined. In fact, it is doubtful that success can be realized without it.

The managerial function of directing is much like the role of an orchestra's conductor. His or her job is to synchronize the efforts of the ministry team. The lead minister must understand how to delegate responsibilities wisely, to motivate the various members of the team toward staying on task, to coordinate the efforts of many in order to achieve the specified objective, to intervene when personal differences show themselves among the work force, and to facilitate change as the organization moves ahead in accomplishing its mission and vision. It's tireless work and frequently the point at which many Christian managers express a great deal of frustration because it's during this phase of the management process when conflict occurs most frequently. It's one thing to specify on a job or position description *who* should do *what*. It's quite another thing when all the individuals come together to perform those responsibilities with their various personalities and preferences.

Directing is concerned with managing people once they have arrived on scene. Up until this point, most of the work of management has been concerned with putting things in order conceptually and on paper. By now, mission and vision have been established. Goals and objectives have been committed to writing. Budgetary resources have been allocated, and tasks have been assigned to appropriate roles. Authority and corresponding responsibilities have been specified, and people have been recruited, oriented, and trained to perform those specific duties. Now is when the real challenge comes because the actual people have shown up to go to work.

Directing people comes with its own set of challenges compared to the other managerial functions we have discussed thus far. "In performing the directing function, the manager is faced with the challenge of providing leadership to the work group, building a climate in which individuals are motivated to perform their jobs effectively and efficiently, and communicating both operating expectations for performance as well as providing feedback on results. These individual elements of directing place a premium on the manager's ability to work with people."[1]

At some point every ministry supervisor will come face-to-face with the reality that people are hard to manage. However, the Scripture teaches that there is no method for accomplishing the Great Commission other than through volunteers (Eph. 2:11–16). God has chosen in his sovereign plan to use volunteers to accomplish his goals and objectives for humanity. As ministry leaders we are to train and equip volunteers for effective service. Chapter 18 is designed to provide the ministry leader with insights on how to develop ministry staff members. They are unique and distinct from volunteers, and it is incumbent on us to realize this important fact. Learning how to assess the needs of each staff member in your organization and to provide in-service training and development opportunities should be the goal of every Christian organization.

One of the more popular approaches to staff development has been the increase in the use of personal mentoring. This can be done through a variety of different methods, each discussed in detail in chapter 18. Mentoring has many positive effects on the ministry organization as well as the individual team member. When people are made to feel important and are respected as contributing members of the ministry organization, they feel a sense of goodwill toward the organization and are more successful in their levels of satisfaction. Learning how to format a mentoring program to accomplish this is part of the content of this chapter.

Chapter 19 deals with the important subject of transforming a group of individuals into a team. We all know that a team can accomplish a great deal more than a group of people working independently. However, to many Christian managers the secret to forming a team out of a group is illusive. Jesus demonstrated this for us while he lived upon the earth. He took a group of unskilled and relatively uneducated men and transformed them into a dynamic and gifted ministry team that would later turn the world upside down. This can be our experience as well by applying the insights gleaned from this chapter.

Christian managers have their own opinions about how to motivate and influence others. These different approaches are referred to in the literature as leadership styles. No one approach or strategy is appropriate in every circumstance. There may be times when a particular leadership strategy is more appropriate due to a particular internal or external threat or opportunity facing the ministry organizations. When an organization is facing a crisis, it may be appropriate for the director to take on a more authoritative and direct leadership style until the crisis is brought under control. After things have settled a more democratic and participatory approach may be appropriate, especially if the members of the ministry team are experienced and well trained. There are a variety of leadership strategies. Under what circumstances a particular approach is best is discussed in chapter 20.

The final chapter in this unit is focused on how to work with boards and committees. It is a law within our country that nonprofit organizations must have a governing board. These boards are comprised of men and women whose only qualification for service is a willing heart. Many Christian ministries suffer from the lack of proper board training. It is generally up to the ministry director to provide this training, but few were equipped for this during their seminary education. As a result, many ministry leaders find working with their board or supervisory committee to be a source of frustration and pain. What is needed in most cases is an understanding of proper roles and responsibilities. When one entity assumes the responsibilities of the other, conflict can result. A healthy understanding of the boundaries that should exist between boards and ministry executives can lead to productive and fruitful service for all involved. "Fences make for happy neighbors" is a saying that applies in this circumstance.

The process of directing men and women is fraught with many challenges and hazards. One poor choice or decision can spiral into many more. A poorly thought-out response or one ill-spoken word can cause significant harm to team morale. Small mistakes can lead to larger ones in an effort to cover up or compensate. If the Christian manager isn't careful, he or she will find the courtroom to be the end result of his or her actions. God desires for his people and his ministry to be led with effectiveness and efficiency and will provide the careful administrator with the necessary tools for service. The Holy Spirit is an excellent source for application in the directing function. He is willing to provide valuable counsel to those who seek it and can help settle even the most troublesome conflict. Blending a group of volunteers and staff members into a coherent and functioning team is not an accident and does not occur naturally. It is done as a result of wise decision making and disciplined direction of others. It is our hope that the chapters in this unit will provide the ministry leader with the necessary tools for accomplishing God's purpose in the various ministries where they will be applied.

BY
RICHARD LEYDA

Chapter 17

Developing Leaders

LEADERSHIP DEVELOPMENT FOR Christian ministry involves the growth and maturing of emerging leaders, under the direction of God's Spirit, in order that they might be prepared for effective servant leadership. The Christian leader has no more critical task than preparing future leaders to carry on the work of the ministry. This is essential both for any particular Christian organization's continued survival and effectiveness as well as for its mission of sending emerging leaders out to multiply God's work in the world. Christian and secular researchers often note the lack of qualified leadership in government, business, schools, religious organizations, and society in general, both here and around the world. This crisis in leadership might also be viewed as a *leadership development* crisis, due in large measure to the failure of leaders to fulfill their critical role of raising up others to replace them.[1]

The term *development* often refers to the long-term growth of future leaders in a wide range of dimensions. Leadership *training,* on the other hand, is sometimes a more focused term, used to indicate the teaching of skills to those in current leadership. In this usage, development includes training and a great deal more.[2] While we generally recognize this difference in usage here, sometimes the terms will be used interchangeably.

If you are relatively young or new to vocational Christian ministry, you may be struggling to see yourself as a leader, let alone a developer of leaders. It is the purpose of this chapter to help you see a vision of what God can do through you as you begin the process of training and equipping others for leadership roles in ministry. If you are a more seasoned ministry leader, this chapter might challenge your thinking and give you new frameworks to approach the vital task of preparing faithful leaders for ministry now and in the future.

Why Must We Train Others?

The Biblical Mandate and Pattern

The first and most obvious reason is that it is a biblical mandate for ministry leaders to equip others for service. Scripture reveals the importance of training future leaders for the work of God in the world. It appears bound up in the very nature of the Great Commission of Matthew 28:18–20 that the command to "make disciples" would involve developing leaders to do the work. Christ's practice was to prepare leaders for future ministry, and his three years of training the Twelve is a model of how it was to be done by those who would come after him.

Leadership is always charged with the responsibility of the reproduction of leaders and with their development. Paul's instruction to Timothy clarifies this: "And the things you have heard me say in the presence of many witnesses entrust to reliable men who will also be qualified to teach others" (2 Tim. 2:2 NIV). Leadership development is at the heart of the process by which the faith spreads and is passed on from generation to generation.

Servanthood, as Jesus makes clear in Mark 10:45, is the dominant biblical image of leadership. Greatness in God's kingdom is equated with serving others. Such servant leadership might best be exemplified in the preparation of others for leading; in this role success means helping others to succeed.[3] Sadly, some leaders do not engage in this task because they are threatened by the success of others; they instead may work to undermine the growth of others and to keep them down. This occurs with surprising frequency in churches and other Christian organizations and causes heartaches for young staff members.

A Vital and Strategic Function of Leadership

Developing other leaders is the essence of the leadership role. This second reason is clarified by Bill Hybels: "Leaders are at their very best when they are raising up leaders around them. When a leader develops not only his or her own leadership potential, but draws out the leadership potential of scores of other leaders as well, the kingdom impact from one life is multiplied exponentially. It produces far more fruit than any single leadership achievement could have. The impact of the leader's life will be felt for many generations to come."[4]

One of Robert Clinton's seven major leadership lessons states, "Effective leaders recognize leadership selection and development as a priority function."[5] In my role as director of a university vocational internship ministry program, my first recommendation to my students as they search for a place to serve is "find a site supervisor who sees the equipping and development of you as a major focus of her or his ministry." Such leaders have their antenna out for emerging leaders and want to have the widest and most long-term influence possible for the kingdom. This kind of ministry is time- and energy-intensive, but the potential payoff in the long run is phenomenal.

Because of the press of more immediate tasks and the consuming nature of developing others, a leader will likely not engage in this function unless he or she understands just how vital it is. Training others to do a task is highly inefficient in the short run. The leader in all likelihood can accomplish it faster with better quality. Over the long term, however, production is multiplied through the work of the trainee, and the leader is freed to focus on priorities only he or she can accomplish.

Only Leaders Can Reproduce Leaders

Based on informal research, John Maxwell contends that four out of five individuals who become leaders are prompted to do so by the influence of an established leader who mentored them. Generally speaking, "it takes a leader to raise up a leader."[6] Hybels likewise believes that leaders alone are uniquely positioned to multiply the impact of their role by impacting developing leaders. He contends that leaders learn best from other leaders.[7]

Insuring that an organization has continuity of qualified leadership may be the key role of any ministry's board of directors or governing body. One of the most important responsibilities a ministry leader will ever accept is his or her own succession planning. While not easy, corporate leadership recognizes the essential nature of this important task. Max De Pree declares, "Leaders are also responsible for future leadership. They need to identify, develop, and nurture future leaders."[8] Maxwell maintains that the leader creates a legacy only "when a person puts his organization into a position to do great things without him."[9]

Jesus spent the last three years of his earthly life in succession planning and development for the church phase of his mission program. The key to Jesus' greatness as a leader, according to management expert Ken Blanchard, was the lasting nature of what he created and of its leadership. "It's easy to get people to do what you want them to do when you are hovering over them. The key to your effectiveness is how well your followers carry on when you are not around."[10] A secure and wise leader has vision to plan for the long term.

A number of years ago, one of my students, an intern in a local church youth ministry, shared with me the philosophy of the youth pastor under whom he was serving. One of the pastor's goals was to prepare those working for him so well that if he were to leave his role at any time, the ministry could go on without skipping a beat. He eventually did leave, and the ministry continued to prosper under the student's oversight.

What a tremendous gift to this young man and a legacy to that ministry. Today my former student has developed into one of the finest youth pastors in the area. It is a testimony to the foresight of his ministry supervisor.

It's a Rewarding Task of Leadership

A leader must engage in the development and training of emerging leaders for the sake of his own soul because it is one of the most rewarding endeavors of Christian life and ministry, for both now and eternity. This may at first seem self-serving, yet Scripture promises rewards for those found faithful in service to Christ. Ask any seasoned ministry leader what is one of his greatest joys and rewards of ministry and he will tell you it is seeing people in whom he has invested his life becoming ministry leaders themselves. This replication of effort produces a joy that is hard to find anywhere else. In addition to the long-term payoffs of training others, the inherently rewarding relationships that are built with an enthusiastic and energetic young emerging leader can be exciting and revitalizing for the developer.

The Responsibility of Developing Ministry Leaders

This has some connection to a continuing debate in leadership theory about the question, "Are leaders born or are they made?" Many people see development as a combination both of innate and early life factors as well as later life education, work experiences, and mentoring. One authority contends, "Leaders, then, are a combination of the two schools of thought: they are both born and made. It is quite possible that many people are born with the prerequisites, yet of these, only a few go on to become leaders."[11]

From a Christian perspective one might ask the question in a slightly different form, "Is ministry service based solely on the particular gift that a person receives at conversion, or can an individual be trained in ministry leadership?" How one answers this question determines who is responsible for developing leaders. A balanced recognition probably is again the most realistic approach. Malphurs points out: "This means, in the right context, either a 'born leader' or a 'made leader' can accomplish much for God. And it would also appear that the above average or super leader is the person who is born a leader and develops those gifts to a great extent."[12] From a Christian perspective of leadership development, each of the following four considerations plays an important role in determining who is responsible for training others for leadership roles in ministry.

God Is the Developer of Leaders

In his sovereign working, God himself is actively involved in the process. He uniquely designs individuals with innate capabilities and talents, including those related to leadership, before they are born (Ps. 139:13–16). He moves their hearts to respond in faith and sends the empowering Holy Spirit to indwell them, granting such gifts of the Spirit as leadership and administration (Rom. 12:7; 1 Cor. 12:28). He works providentially as the Lord of circumstances, bringing events and circumstances into the life of the emerging leader and wasting nothing—including mistakes—in the enterprise of producing maturity and preparing the leader for the work he plans. Clinton notes that those who are sensitive to providential processes will realize who has designed their course of study: "It is God. Each of us has leadership courses that are individually tailored for us by the Academic Dean."[13]

The Emerging Leader Has a Responsibility to Look for Ways He Can Develop as a Ministry Leader

The individual's degree of responsiveness to God's working is a large factor in the developmental process. He or she may exercise veto power over growth initiatives. While some people debate whether common leadership traits can be identified, at least all would agree that willingness to take on a role of leadership is essential. A learning posture or a willingness to be taught and developed would seem an essential characteristic for those who would develop into godly leaders.[14]

Admirable qualities, development opportunities, and work experiences are pointless without the motivation to lead. Risk taking and the weight of responsibilities, along with the personal costs, may cause many people to decline the leadership role.[15] Receptivity on the part of the potential leader can result in a discovery of God's sovereign work and realization of God's gifting and preparation for service. Accepting these as a trust and cooperating as a faithful steward in one's own development is a vital part of the leader's maturing process. With growing maturity, the leader is increasingly responsible for self-motivation and a continued commitment to development. Leadership development in large measure is self-initiated development, and self-awareness is essential to success as a leader.[16]

The Leader-Developer Has a Unique Role

The role of the leader-mentor might be viewed as threefold:

1. pointing to God's sovereign work in events and human encounters in the life of the emerging leader;

2. helping the individual recognize God-given giftedness and capabilities; and
3. intentionally aiding in developing these endowments.

Mature leaders should help provide a divine perspective for the trainee. Their most important task is to live a life of dependence on God and to encourage this obedience and to model it actively before those they lead. Of the many qualities for spiritual leadership which Oswald Sanders lists in his classic work *Spiritual Leadership,* being spirit-filled and empowered is the one he views as indispensable.[17] The mature leader should help the emerging leader see from his or her own example what it means to walk by faith and not by sight. The transparency and honesty of the leader about his or her own weaknesses and failures and the challenges of ministry will give the trainee a realistic picture of service and permission to be less than perfect.

Finally, a leader cannot help another to grow beyond the level to which he or she has attained in any particular dimension of leadership capabilities; this is a foundational principle undergirding leadership mentoring. As Christ teaches, "A pupil is not above his teacher; but everyone, after he has been fully trained, will be like his teacher" (Luke 6:40 NASB). We reproduce what we are. A more detailed discussion of the function and activities of a ministry mentor is found in chapter 20.

The Church or Ministry Organization Has a Vital Role as Well

Often the power of the church or ministry organization to influence the growth of leaders is ignored or underutilized. The traditional approach to leader development has primarily been one of individual preparation and skill development; yet in recent years the socializing influence of the organization for developing vision and values has been increasingly utilized.[18] The family, church, and friends serve as formative and supportive environments for shaping a young person's beliefs, values, and understandings of leadership. Discovery and affirmation of giftedness takes place best in the context of community, where the emerging leader has the opportunity to serve and actually exercise giftedness.

The concept of peer mentoring and the mentoring group has gained more prominence over the last decade. Jesus formed the Twelve into what has been called an intentional learning community. Emerging leaders are discovering this process of learning together to supplement traditional training structures.[19]

A few years ago I had expressed some frustration to Howard Hendricks about the individualistic nature of the models of disciple making dominating the scene. Voicing similar concern, he commented on the impact he had seen on the spiritual development of individuals through the dynamic of the small-group community. Compared to the limited perspectives possible from one leader-mentor, the leader in training can receive multiple interactions with individuals who have a wide variety of insights and gifts. This environment provides fertile soil for the nurturing of future leaders. Leadership teams likewise have great potential for producing leaders.

Components of Leadership Development

Malphurs makes a distinction between the potential leader's God-given capacities and developed capacities.[20] The former are comprised of such divine endowments as spiritual and natural gifts, passion for ministry, and temperament.

Practically, assessing these might be approached from the framework of Rick Warren's SHAPE acronym.[21] One might come to understand life direction for ministry and leadership through tools and inventories that help to assess Spiritual giftedness, Heartfelt passion, Abilities, Personality, and Experiences in life. A variety of tools exist for helping individuals evaluate themselves in each of these areas. Malphurs and others include a number of these in their works.[22]

In addition to these God-given capabilities, there are also developed capabilities. These are leadership abilities that can be nurtured and cultivated over time. With God's help, the emerging leader can become a better leader as growth and improvement occurs. The leader-developer can have varying degrees of impact in these areas, depending on a wide variety of factors. While a number of overlaps between groupings exist, Malphurs organizes developed capabilities into the following four categories: character or soul work, head or knowledge work, skills or handiwork, and emotions or heart work. Development in each of these areas calls for a particular type of intentional focus.[23] Because of the importance of these components, a brief description of each is provided.

Character

A person's character, the sum of his distinct qualities, reflects the core of who that person is in his or her innermost being. Character is the foundation for Christian leadership and for the other three categories. The Scripture accords qualities of character a central place for determining selection of church leadership, as catalogued in passages such as 1 Timothy 3:1–7. The term *training* can be properly applied to most dimensions of leadership; yet, because of its deep-seated nature, one must "develop" character. When seeking to hire ministry leaders for a church or other form of ministry venture, great care must be given to the character of the applicant. Skills can be taught in orientation or in-service seminars, but character comes with the applicant and is imbedded deep in the core of the individual. Character is not learned in a short-term seminar because character traits such as faithfulness, integrity, and wisdom are harder to come by and take a lifetime to develop.

Knowledge

The leader must have attained and be able to use different understandings and types of information to be effective. We most often think of _intellectual_ or cognitive knowledge gained from a classroom or seminar. Indeed, much can be learned about leading from courses, training seminars, books on leadership, and especially from studying Scripture itself.

In addition to intellectual knowledge there is also _experiential_ knowledge. This is gained from actual experiences of leading ministry or general experiences in life. The combination of intellectual course work while being involved in a ministry internship or staff position serves as an excellent framework for gaining and retaining both kinds of knowledge.

Intuitive knowledge is a bit harder to define; the leader knows but cannot always articulate this source of knowledge. A leader may simply express that a certain decision was based on a "gut feeling" or a sense of what was the right thing to do. This intuition may spring from living over a long period in a leadership culture and may, at times, be based on sensitivity to the working of God's Spirit in the life of the leader.

Skills

Leadership behaviors—what the leader does—comprise this category. Trained skills are appropriate and useful applications of knowledge to ministry situations. One author puts skills into one of three groups: technical skills, human skills, and conceptual skills.[24]

Technical skills, the ability to work with things, are usually job specific and depend on what the leader will be called on to do; they are often task or "hands on" oriented. Preparing an organizational budget or planning and teaching a training session would fit in this grouping.

Human skills, or "people" skills, help the leader to work effectively with others toward the organization's goals. Trust building, motivating, conflict resolution, listening, and rewarding and recognizing contributions of others are among important skills the leader must develop.

Conceptual skills, the ability to work with ideas, involve applying abstract knowledge to the organization's needs. These often involve the "big picture" and include envisioning, strategizing, and problem solving.

While leaders at all levels need people skills, leaders at lower management levels usually need more training in the technical skills area. Those at higher levels will tend to need more development in the conceptual skills. Training processes mentioned later in this chapter are often appropriate for teaching skills, but since skills are about *doing* activities, the trainee must have the opportunity actually to practice them in simulated or real-work situations. Some skills are fairly simple and can be picked up early in a leader's career, while others are fairly complex and take a great deal of experience.

Emotions

Emotions are God-given and often neglected when addressing the topic of leadership development. A leader's mood and attitude have an important impact on those who follow, both negatively and positively. Improper emotional reactions can handicap a leader's effectiveness and give indicators about the necessity for deeper "heart work." The leader must understand his or her emotional life, including needs and drives; otherwise, the leader may be using the ministry to satisfy personal emotional needs—for control or approval, for example—in inappropriate ways. Proper emotional responses by the leader can be a great gift to followers, providing empathy and a sense of caring.

Leader-developers should pay particular attention to the emotional responses of emerging leaders with whom they work. They can then provide insights and teach them biblical ways of managing their emotions. In the area of the emotions, a teachable spirit and willingness to grow are essential for life change. The leader can provide assistance to a certain level but must be ready to refer the individual to professional counseling if necessary.

Each of these areas build upon and integrate with one another. To be effective, a comprehensive leadership training program should include elements of all four components.[25] Omitting any of these vital areas could lead to a dysfunctional leader who is missing or deficient in one or more of these essential elements. A healthy and well-balanced ministry leader should have training in each of these areas.

The Process of Leadership Development

The development of leaders is a complex process, whether viewed from the perspective of a biblical model or secular approach. The temptation is to present a few easy steps to development, but growing people to lead the church or other ministry organizations is not so simple. This is not to say that training sequences—as will be presented later—are not helpful in teaching some dimensions of leading. Although they help us in our understanding of the process involved, they should never be viewed as formulaic or automatic. Just because a person attends a "leadership development" seminar doesn't mean he or she will emerge as a Christian leader equipped for service to the kingdom.

A Lifetime Development Process

After an extensive study of the life of biblical, historical, and contemporary leaders, Robert Clinton summarizes his view of Christian leadership development like this: "God develops a leader over a lifetime. That development is a function of the use of events and people to impress leadership lessons upon a leader (processing), time, and leader response. Processing is central to the theory. All leaders can point to critical incidents in their lives where God taught them something very important."[26]

One who desires to train future leaders should take perspective and encouragement from this insightful description. First, as was mentioned earlier, God is superintending the process, which leaves little to chance. Second, God is concerned about transforming a person over a lifetime of preparation. We too frequently see only the short-term and not the big picture of a whole life. Even secular studies of leadership development recognize the limitations of a short-term approach. Many are currently advocating long-term strategies. Experiences that come early in life are helpful in developing leadership character and capabilities and may best serve as an awareness-building function for later learning.[27]

Third, it is a *process* involving lessons learned through many different events and people intersecting the growing leader's life. Periods of apparent progress and regress will be a natural part of it. Every circumstance, event, and encounter is useful to prepare leaders, if they will pay attention. In addition, God can and does use people, in particular a leader-developer, to impact that individual in strategic ways at critical times. Finally, as stated previously, the responsibility for growth, at least in some measure, depends on the responsiveness and receptivity of the emerging leader.

Clinton has suggested six stages of biblical leadership development, taking into account the processes nature of inner-life growth, ministry, and life maturing.[28] Although too detailed to describe here, this pattern would be a valuable framework to help developing leaders understand and cooperate with God's work in their lives.

Jesus' Pattern for Developing Leaders

Insight concerning the process that Jesus used in his leadership development plan is outlined in Mark 3:14: "He appointed twelve, that they might be with Him, and that He might send them out to preach, and to have authority to cast out the demons" (Mark 3:14–15 NASB). This three-step process outlined below parallels three points suggested by Hybels in his practical strategy for developing leaders. Three reasons were given by ministry leaders in response to the question, "How is it that you wound up becoming a leader?"[29]

1. **He Appointed.** Christ chose those who would be his key leaders—it was no accident. The first reason given for becoming a leader was, "Someone spotted my potential." A major emphasis for leaders is identifying potential and emerging leaders whom God is preparing. Those who train leaders must learn to recognize God-ordained qualities of character, gifts, and talents. They must also pray for willing potential leaders to emerge and for sensitivity to God's direction in understanding with whom to work. Churches and Christian ministries need to be proactive in their search for potential leaders, affirming their gifts and abilities and giving them further preparation in informal training as well as formal settings for biblical and theological training. The insightful leader should recognize that the most strategic individuals to focus energy and time on will be current leaders who need equipping and training for current responsibilities, as well as teachable future leaders who need long-term development.[30]

2. **That They Should Be with Him.** In Jesus' three years with his disciples, he provided them an immersion experience in leadership development. Everything he did, in word or deeds, had a teaching or training aspect to it. God desires to transform those who will lead the church into the image of Christ—to be like Christ and to lead as Christ would lead. This life-on-life context reveals powerful dynamics for life transformation and learning leadership. The second reason leaders gave about why they assumed a leadership role was, "Someone invested in me." The greatest opportunity to influence the beliefs and values of another person is in the context of a close personal relationship. The greater the time together, the greater the potential impact.

Paul speaks of this investment by the leader in the lives of others when he reminds his readers, "We were well-pleased to impart to you not only the gospel of God but also our own lives, because you had become very dear to us" (1 Thess. 2:8 NASB). Paul recognized the need for behavioral models in the development of disciples and leaders. In several epistles he encourages his readers to imitate him or live according to the pattern he gave. Zuck provides deeper insight in stating, "Paul's idea of imitation builds on his personal associations with his convert. The exhortations in the five epistles are addressed only to those churches he founded. Because they had witnessed his life, he could challenge them to remember him and follow him."[31]

3. **That He Might Send Them Out.** This is the eventual goal of leadership—to send out, to delegate, to scatter for the purpose of

accomplishing the work of ministry. Jesus first sent out the Twelve (Luke 9:1–2) and later the seventy (Luke 10:1) to gain experiential lessons that could be learned no other way. The final answer of Hybel's respondents for the reason they were leaders was, "Someone trusted me with responsibility." By this delegation the leader puts a stamp of approval on the emerging leader and shows confidence in the preparation. Logan and George see the primary purpose of delegation as developing people. They assert, "Proper delegation, one of the most powerful tools we have for discipleship, gets the job done and helps people grow in the process."[32]

On-the-job training experiences of many people in business and other fields seem to actually undermine their ability to function effectively on the job. We sometimes see young people in their first ministry role have such a negative experience that they become discouraged and leave vocational Christian service. We have discovered that one essential component of a successful internship experience is the opportunity for the intern to take on increasingly challenging projects and responsibilities, with an enhanced probability of success and a safety net in the form of a knowledgeable site supervisor or trainer. Through actual attempts to lead, the emerging leader experiences risk taking, failure, success, and the weight of responsibility. The person is stretched and learns valuable personal lessons concerning the self, others, and the practice of being in charge.[33] As Sanders states, "The departure of a strong and dominating leader makes room for others to emerge and develop. Often when the weight of responsibility falls suddenly upon his shoulders, a subordinate develops abilities and qualities he and others had not suspected he had. Joshua would never have developed into an outstanding leader had he remained one of Moses' lieutenants."[34]

In such experiences, young Christian leaders may be forced to draw on resources and capabilities never utilized and trust God in ways unknown before. The Bible is clear that trials and difficulties can produce the proven character and maturity essential for leadership in the church (James 1:2–4; Rom. 5:3–5).

When business leaders are asked where they gained their abilities to lead, the most common reply relates to their work experiences and the influence of their bosses. Far less evident is their reliance on formal education.[35] The newest paradigm in young employee and executive training for business has moved toward "action learning" whereby work assignments are tackled by a team of emerging leaders. Such an approach is based more on the real-life challenges facing an organization. This has become the dominant approach over the last decade, as opposed to the more traditional classroom-based model or an in-service training seminar.

This trend may have similarities to the current practice of some larger churches of producing pastoral leadership from training within the organization and not from formal theological schools. An action learning model taps into the motivations of adult learners, recognizing their desire to make current and valuable applications of their knowledge. Rather than separating theory from practice, immediate application of principles to real-life experience makes for enduring lessons.[36] If preparation for actual responsibility is the goal, developmental assignments may well be one of the best methods to use. Purely verbal transfer of information simply does not have the impact that engagement of the whole person in learning by doing or action learning does.[37]

Models of Leadership Development

Before any training sequence starts, individuals with the potential to lead must be identified and recruited, considering among other factors the qualities, experience, and willingness of the trainee as well as the needs of the organization. A leader must evaluate how well a potential leader matches with the needs of the team. Initial assessment of a potential leader's need for training and development in a wide variety of functions and tasks required by a particular position helps to determine areas for learning and goals for the training process.

Agreement on expectations and understanding between the trainer and the trainee about these goals is essential at the beginning of this process. Goals should be (1) appropriate to what emerging leaders need to be able to do, (2) attainable so that trainees do not become discouraged, (3) measurable in order for all to know when they have been achieved, (4) clearly stated to focus action, (5) challenging, so that trainees are stretched, and (6) written, to give a sense that the trainee is accountable.[38]

Such goals, especially when they emerge from a shared sense of vision and agreement between trainer and trainee, can serve as the basis for evaluation, a critical aspect of the training. Evaluation is integral to the whole process; it should consist of both ongoing feedback, serving as a means of encouragement and a measure of progress, and final evaluation to give a clear picture of the degree of achievement. Smith lists five criteria by which the trainer can periodically measure progress: (1) a good fit between the requirements of the job and the talents of the trainee, (2) willingness of the trainee to do the job with enthusiasm, (3) consistency of the trainee's efforts, (4) actual results and productivity, and (5) openness of the trainee to be evaluated.[39]

Logan and George outline an effective training process for church-related work, though it may be broadly applied across other training and development situations.[40] The leader begins a process of three

movements: *orient* trainees, *involve* them in ministry, and *equip* them for
it. While the typical schooling model places equipping before involvement, experiential learning theory says that people often learn best in the
context of doing and are more motivated and teachable when they discover the challenges for which they need to be equipped. In terms of
leader and trainee actions, the process progresses through a five-step
sequence.

Maxwell follows a similar process for training; his labels and description for each phase are included also.[41]

Step One: Model. *I do, you watch.* The leader has not only
verbally instructed the trainee, but now gives opportunity for
observation of a visual model of the whole process to be accomplished, performed completely and correctly from beginning to
end.

Step Two: Mentor. *I do, you help.* The leader continues the
work, but now limited participation gives the trainee a sense of
actually doing the task, accompanied by feedback and encouragement from the leader. The trainer continues to explain the
how of each step, but now includes the *why*.

Step Three: Monitor. *You do, I help.* Here, the trainee
takes over the reins of the task, and the leader assists and cor-
rects as needed. Consistency in proper execution of the task is
the aim here. Having the trainee explain the whole process can
be helpful and reinforce the learning.

Step Four: Motivate. *You do, I watch.* This stage indicates
completion of training, as the leader pulls out of the task but
still offers encouragement and support. The trainee's sense of
success can be a great motivator to refine the process and to
stimulate learning new tasks.

Step Five: Multiply. *You do, I do something else.* The completion of the cycle would entail the trainee eventually becoming the trainer of others on this same task and the leader
moving on to other tasks, especially development of other
leaders.

This final step is essential if the leader is to develop others and loose
them to be creative. Rush defines delegation as "the transferring of
authority, responsibility, and accountability from one person or group to
another."[42] Through it, emerging leaders are empowered and grow as
they are given permission to exercise power (authority), entrusted with
decision making (responsibility), and evaluated based on the degree to
which they have achieved established goals (accountability).

Situational Leadership Development. The processes noted above
show a number of similarities to a situational leadership approach that

has been used extensively in training and developing emerging leaders in Christian and secular organizations. I refer the reader to chapter 20, where a detailed discussion of this approach is provided.

Developing a Shared View of Leadership. Leadership is not a function of position, according to one view, but of certain skills and practices that can be learned by virtually anyone on a leadership team. A leader can promote an environment of "liberating the leader in everyone" by enabling people to act, as many individuals in an organization take on leadership responsibility and become to a great degree self-led. The capacity to operate in such a self-directed manner can be built in a number of ways.

Team members can be encouraged to take on ownership of the organization and its mission and can be given more freedom of choice about group direction. A growing sense of control over one's situation and self-determination inspires leadership confidence. Competence grows in emerging leaders in a climate where mistakes are simply a part of the learning, and communication and feedback flow freely. When each group member owns the mission and values of the organization, mutual responsibility for the organization's future is shared, and everyone takes initiative. The leader who wishes to engender such a climate might try some of the following behaviors.

1. *Stop making decisions.* Have those responsible for implementation make the decisions, but teach them how first.

2. *Stop talking at staff meetings.* Use them to listen and promote communication within the team.

3. *Set up coaching opportunities.* Put people in learning situations where the leader can support them and help them succeed in leadership roles.

4. *Share the big picture.* Help them see the overall plan and how their area of responsibility contributes to the whole.

5. *Let team members be the teachers.* The learning of more experienced, knowledgeable team members is enhanced as they teach, and newer team members learn as well.[43]

Conclusion

Developing other leaders may be the most crucial responsibly given to leaders in Christian ministry. They must be involved in this process for a number of reasons. It is commanded in Scripture, it is the most strategic task for multiplying ministry, only leaders can do it, and it provides tremendous rewards. A number of persons engage in and share responsibility for developing leaders: God, the developing leader, the leader-developer, and finally, the developing community. Ministry capabilities can be grouped as both God-given and developed. Developed capabilities of the emerging leader are divided among the categories of character, knowledge, skills, and emotions.

The process of God's development of leaders is lifelong, using events, circumstances, and people to teach and train. Christ's process of developing the disciples consisted of choosing them, investing his life in them, and sending them out into ministry responsibilities. While a number of training and development sequences have been presented, all generally begin with selection of potential leaders and utilize goal setting as the basis for continuing and final evaluation. Processes involve a progression of instruction, modeling, feedback, and active learning by the trainee, culminating with a complete delegation of tasks. The cycle of development is complete when the trainee becomes the trainer of others in these same responsibilities.

BY
JANE CARR

Chapter 18

Mentoring in Ministry

THE TERM *MENTOR* ORIGINATED in the *Odyssey,* an epic poem written by the Greek poet Homer. It was told that when the Greek warrior Odysseus went off to fight in the Trojan War, he left his young son Telemachus in the care of a trusted guardian named Mentor. The siege of Troy lasted ten years, and it took Odysseus several years to make his way home. Upon his return, he found that his son Telemachus had grown into a man under Mentor's wise tutelage.[1]

Based on this story, we now speak of a mentor as someone who fundamentally affects and influences the development of another through a significant relationship. Perhaps the best person to define mentoring is the one being mentored. Howard and William Hendricks describe it this way: "What matters is not so much whether you see yourself in that role, but whether someone else sees you in that role."[2] When others ascribe to us the title "mentor" we can be assured that knowingly or unknowingly, intentionally or unintentionally, we have had an impact on their life.

Stanley and Clinton describe the mentoring relationship as an exchange between two people. "Mentoring is a relational process in which a mentor, who knows or has experienced something, transfers that something (resources of wisdom, information, experience, confidence, insight, relationships, status, etc.) to a mentoree, at an appropriate time and manner, so that it facilitates development or empowerment."[3]

This type of mentoring relationship is evident in some of the great historical figures of our time. We readily recognize names such as Thomas Jefferson, Wolfgang Amadeus Mozart, Susan B. Anthony, and Martin Luther King Jr. because of their historic contributions that captured our attention. But what about men like George Wythe, who served as Thomas Jefferson's law professor and guided his reading and understanding of political philosophies. He was a man who reviewed drafts of the Declaration of Independence, and Jefferson often consulted with him on political matters even after departing law school.[4] Or what of Elizabeth Stanton, who forged a friendship with Susan B. Anthony that inspired Susan to be a public icon for women's rights to own property, pursue an education, and vote?[5] Or Joseph Haydn, an Austrian classical composer, whom Mozart greatly admired and emulated?[6] Or Benjamin E. Mays, who captivated the heart of Martin Luther King Jr. during chapel services at Morehouse College? King, enamored by the ministry of Mays, made it a point to regularly visit the office of Mays to explore his own thoughts and ideas about ministry and social activism.[7]

Hindrances to Mentoring

Though there are clearly many benefits to mentoring, it is not realistic to assume that the process is effortless. A good deal of effort is required on the part of both the mentor and protégé in order to make the arrangement work effectively. It is helpful for those contemplating establishing such a relationship to understand that there are a number of common hindrances. These include the following.

1. **Feeling Inadequate for the Job.** These people ask themselves the question, "What do I really have to offer?" One of the primary reasons we don't mentor is that we don't think we have anything to offer. Maybe we ourselves are just starting out, or we feel like we have so much still to learn. The fact of the matter is that a mentor is someone who is just a step ahead and who is still learning himself. As the saying goes, "Hindsight is always 20/20." Mentors simply share hindsight, the understanding that is brought to bear on something as a result of the passage of time.

2. **Never Having Been Personally Mentored.** People who are considering mentoring others may be hesitant if they have never been mentored themselves. They ask, "How can I mentor someone if I've never had a mentor myself?" The truth is that most of us have never had a formal mentor relationship ourselves. The word *mentor* sounds so ominous. How can we ourselves be something we have never seen or truly experienced? The fear of the unknown keeps us from doing so many things in life, including mentoring. Formal mentoring relationships are few and far between. However, all of us have had people in our lives who have impacted us in significant ways. Mentoring goes on around us all the time; we just don't often recognize it as that.

3. **Those Who Mistakenly Equate Supervision with Mentoring.** Individuals with this mind-set say to themselves, "I'm a supervisor; isn't that the same thing?" We often think that the terms *supervisor* and *mentor* are synonymous when in fact they are not. Many people think that because they assign tasks, monitor progress, and evaluate staff members

they are mentoring. Though some of the things we do in supervising are similar to the types of things mentors do, it doesn't mean that everyone who supervises also mentors. Chip Bell in *Managers as Mentors* states, "Not all mentors are supervisors, but all effective supervisors should be mentors."[8]

4. **Leaders Who Are Afraid to Risk Being Vulnerable.** Many leaders and managers find it difficult to be seen without pretense and ask, "What if I don't live up to their expectations?" Our fear of people finding out who we really are and realizing that we aren't what they expected us to be often hinders us from being mentors. Sometimes we have to simply get over ourselves. People don't want a picture-perfect, brush-stroked model; they want someone they can relate to in life and in ministry. They want people who struggle with real life issues just like them. They want people who from time to time blow it big and live to tell about it.

5. **A Misunderstanding between Mentoring and Discipling.** Some people ask, "How can I disciple this individual if I am not a spiritual leader myself?" These individuals confuse the mentoring process with discipleship. The two activities are qualitatively different. They have different purposes, goals, and methods. Making a disciple involves teaching the Scriptures, counseling, and living a life under close scrutiny by another individual who shadows your walk with Christ. Being a mentor involves training and equipping in matters that pertain primarily to another's vocational or professional development. Since both activities require a close interpersonal relationship, it is understandable why these two are often equated. However, they do have different ultimate outcomes.

Two Models of Mentoring

There are several ways that mentoring can be accomplished with numerous variations. For the purposes of this chapter and in the specific context of ministry mentoring, two models seem to provide the best choices. It may not be a matter of which one is best as much as which one is best, given the dynamics of the relationship and the purposes to be accomplished. The choices are the *peer mentoring* model and the *compass mentoring* model.

Peer Mentoring Model

Also referred to as the comentoring model, this approach to mentoring is based on establishing a peer relationship. Peer mentoring relationships are a unique model of mentoring. In peer mentoring relationships, both individuals are at about the same developmental level in terms of age (within five to six years of each other), situational pressures, spiritual maturity, and ministry experience. These shared realities often provide relational openness from the beginning and increased opportunity for mutual accountability. Peer mentoring differs from other models of mentoring in that it is relationship-focused rather than need-centered. J. Robert Clinton and Richard W. Clinton describe the Friendship Continuum[9] as identifiable stages by which proximity and continuity allow for movement through each stage from initial contact toward a comentoring relationship. The words in italics represent boundaries associated with moving from one stage on the continuum to another.

Stage 1	Stage 2	Stage 3	Stage 4	Stage 5
Contact	Acquaintance	Trusted Brother or Sister	Close Friend	Co-mentor
Acceptance	*Fun Time*	*Openness,*	*Confidentiality*	
Accountability				
	Together	*Trust*		

A biblical example of this type of model is the relationship that Jonathan and David shared. Both men were about the same age and were proven warriors and young leaders. They shared a heart to follow God and to do his will (1 Sam. 14:6; 17:45–47). They were committed to each other's best interests and to each other's future and family (1 Sam. 18:3; 20:12–17, 42). They looked out for each other, were transparent with each other, they strengthened and encouraged each other, and they were willing to take personal risks for each other (1 Sam. 20:3, 42; 23:16–17). First Samuel 18:1 describes the depth of Jonathan and David's relationship: "The soul of Jonathan was knit to the soul of David, and Jonathan loved him as himself" (NASB).

Not every friendship will become a peer comentoring relationship, but relationships that do will be characterized by unrestricted openness, trust, common commitments, and a sense of mutual responsibility for each other. Three relational ingredients are necessary for meaningful comentoring relationships. There should be fit, fun, and freedom.[10]

First, peers must be compatible with each other. There are people whom we connect with almost effortlessly. We are drawn to them in some way and have a desire to get to know them better. We are more alike than we are different. We share a natural fit. Second, peer mentoring relationships should be fun. If you enjoy being with your comentor, you will want to spend time together. Close relationships are fostered through time spent together and shared experiences. Informal times of simply enjoying a meal together, participating in a common interest such as shopping or golf, or just hanging out can provide opportunities necessary for building a relationship.

A final relational ingredient is freedom. This is the freedom to share openly and honestly with each other. Peer mentors must be willing to be transparent with each other, to hold in confidence things that are shared, and to encourage and spur each other on in mutual accountability. Perhaps this ingredient more than any other takes time to develop. Certainly there are levels of transparency that we experience in peer relationships, but the depth of transparency is an indicator of the effectiveness of a comentoring relationship.

Establishing a peer mentoring relationship is essential for leaders today. Studies indicate that few leaders finish well. Stanley and Clinton identified five pivotal points where leaders often go astray. These pivotal points include sexual relationships, power, pride, family, and finances.[11] Leaders can avoid these pitfalls if they are willing to seek out and submit themselves to comentoring relationships. In general, Christian leaders lack intimate friendships with peers. Upward and downward mentoring relationships help us develop in many ways, but often there are limits to these relationships. In a supervisory situation (upward mentoring), we may feel hesitant to share too deeply for fear of it reflecting poorly on our performance evaluation, or worse yet, we may fear losing our job. In a downward mentoring relationship, protégés usually lack the power or confrontational ability to speak strongly into our lives. Peer mentors typically are not constrained by either of these things. Stanley and Clinton surmise, "The higher a leader rises, the greater the pitfalls and the more important it becomes to develop accountable relationships with peers."[12]

So how do you get started in a comentoring relationship? A few steps to establishing a comentoring relationship include the following.

1. **Seek Them Out.** Ask God to bring people into your life, outside of your immediate ministry context, who can speak into your life. Look for opportunities to engage in conversations with people and explore chemistry.

2. **Share Your Desires.** As your relationship develops, invite them into your life, give them permission to ask questions and speak the truth in love to you. Let them know what you desire out of this relationship.

3. **Set Aside Time.** Make this relationship a priority in your schedule. Proximity and continuity are essential in developing strong comentoring relationships. The more your paths naturally cross, the easier it is to develop a deep and meaningful connection. However, scheduling regular and consistent time together is essential for busy leaders.

Compass Mentoring Model

As leaders, we must be intentional about surrounding ourselves with mentoring relationships. The easiest way to do this is to consider the directional points of a compass in light of three types of mentoring relationships. The first directional point of mentoring is upward (north) with mature followers of Christ who have life experiences that we ourselves do not yet possess. It is also essential that we have downward (south) mentoring relationships where we serve as the guide for someone else. Finally, we also need lateral (east/west) mentoring relationships with peers who can speak into our lives and hold us to the highest degree of moral and spiritual accountability. Each direction of mentoring contributes something unique that the others do not offer.

During the early stages of ministry the need for upward (north) mentoring is most evident. There are some things that you just can't learn from a textbook or a sterile classroom environment. A mentor who has gone before you and can give direction and perspective from a lifetime of real life experiences is invaluable when you are just starting out. Upward mentors also provide great inspiration and encouragement to crash through the quitting points of ministry by the example of their own perseverance and faithfulness. Even those who are well established in their ministries can benefit from upward mentoring when they maintain a lifelong learning attitude. There is always someone who is a step ahead of us no matter where we are in life. Just when you think you have seen it all or done it all, you are faced with some type of new reality. Leaders are continual learners who can benefit greatly from lifelong upward mentoring.

Despite our age, experience, or feelings of readiness, downward (south) mentoring is a significant part of ministry multiplication. If we have learned something, we must in turn teach it to someone else. It has been said, "There is no success without a successor."[13] There is always someone who is a step behind us. Even though we don't yet see ourselves as an expert, we probably know more than we think we know. Those who are just starting out in ministry have great opportunities to mentor college interns, youth workers, or lay volunteers. The first step usually begins by imparting to someone else something that we have learned or are in the process of learning. This often leads toward more formal mentoring relationships with those who have a deeper interest in ministry as their life's calling and toward whom we have a natural affinity.

Lateral (east/west) mentoring is among peers who are close in age and share commonalities such as hobbies, careers, lifestyle choices, and experiences. It is these very commonalities that allow peers to more readily understand and empathize with each other. A great source of mutual encouragement and accountability lies within these types of relationships.

In the compass mentoring model, multidirectional mentoring relationships ensure that leaders are benefiting from the strengths of a variety of models of mentoring. The compass model creates a circle of accountability and safeguards.

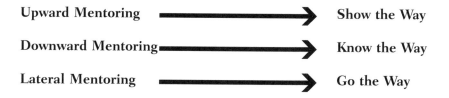

Upward Mentoring ⟶ **Show the Way**

Downward Mentoring ⟶ **Know the Way**

Lateral Mentoring ⟶ **Go the Way**

Upward mentoring allows those who have gone before to show you the way. Downward mentoring challenges you to know the way for others. Finally, lateral mentoring provides you with peers who can go the way with you through mutual encouragement, support, and accountability.

Formal and Informal Mentoring

We tend to think of mentoring only in terms of formal, highly structured programs. Though we have infrequent interactions or occasional experiences that shape our thinking and inspire us to want to be more, we fail to label these relationships as "mentoring" because they don't appear to be significant enough. What we must realize is that both formal and informal forms of mentoring do exist.[14]

	Short-Term	**Long-Term**
Formal	**1. Highly structured, short-term** The relationship is formally established for an introductory or short period, often to meet specific organization objectives. Includes orientation or assimilation into an organization or career field.	**2. Highly structured, long-term** Often used for succession planning, this relationship involves grooming someone to take over a departing person's job or function or to master a craft.
Informal	**3. Informal, short-term** This type of off-the-cuff mentoring ranges from one shot or spontaneous help to occasional or as-needed counseling. There may be no ongoing relationship. This type of intervention is often thought through.	**4. Informal, long-term** Peer mentoring often fits into this category. It includes being available as needed to discuss problems, to listen, or to share special knowledge.

The basic distinction between formal and informal mentoring typically revolves around the formation of the mentor-protégé relationship. Formal mentorships are structured and managed by the organization. Informal mentorships are typically spontaneous relationships that occur naturally and apart from any organizational sanction. At first glance we might view formal and informal mentoring as two opposing ends of a continuum. However, as Hendricks and Hendricks point out, "Formal relationships often involve informal activities, and informal mentoring relationships sometimes make use of more formal strategies for development."[15]

Formal programs for mentoring are becoming commonplace in business, government, and education. Although church and parachurch ministries have utilized the principles of mentoring for years, they have typically used other terminology to describe it. Among the laity, churches and parachurch organizations have promoted one-on-one discipleship programs and ministries such as Titus 2, where older women mentor younger women. Formal mentoring has also been evident in paid and unpaid internship programs in both church and parachurch organizations. Internships provide an opportunity for those who sense a call on their lives to vocational ministry to serve on a church or parachurch staff under the supervision of someone in pastoral ministry.

The most common form of mentoring is informal. Though rarely labeled "mentoring," it happens all around us every day of our lives. Here are two examples of informal mentoring:

> Two staff members get together for coffee. The newbie staff member asks the veteran staff member if she has ever been frustrated by not having enough volunteers. The veteran staff member shares her own frustration with a lack of volunteers, explains to the newbie what has worked and what hasn't worked in the past, and gives some insights she has about volunteerism in the church today. *That's informal mentoring!*

> A young man just starting out in ministry attends a pastor's conference where he meets an older man from another church. They strike up a conversation that leads to exchanging phone numbers and e-mail addresses. Every time the young man runs into a situation he is unsure about, he contacts his newfound friend to talk it through. Occasionally they get together for lunch just to share war stories. The young man is always encouraged by the example of the older man. *That's informal mentoring!*

Active, Occasional, and Passive Mentoring

Mentoring has also been categorized as active, occasional, or passive in nature. Active mentoring is often defined by words like *direct, guide, reinforce, motivate, encourage,* or *command.* It involves the intentional development of a plan that is dictated primarily by the needs of the organization or the personal preferences of the mentor. Occasional mentoring is less unidirectional and takes into consideration the desires of the protégé as well. It is characterized by words such as *counsel, instruct, support,* and *advise.* There is a higher level of mutual interaction and participation. Passive mentoring elicits words like *read, study, observe, admire, emulate.* The Mentoring Continuum[16] displays these basic differences.

The continuum carries with it the idea that mentoring has differing levels of involvement and corresponding degrees of intensity, based on the nature of the relationship. The various mentoring styles follow a progression of increasing intentionality and increasing intensity.

Passive mentoring encompasses both the contemporary and historical styles of mentoring. These are often the modern day "heros" and "heroines" of our lives. They may be people we admire because of who they are or something they have done. They may be people we have never met or even had a conversation with, and yet we have been impacted by observing their lives or reading something about them.

Occasional mentoring includes counseling, teaching, and sponsoring. These types of relationships are based on the changing needs of an individual. In a moment of crisis a counselor-mentor listens, gives perspective, and imparts hope. They are able to give alternative choices and present possible outcomes, leaving the final decision to the protégé. Teacher-mentors have experience and expertise in specific areas of ministry. These are the "go-to" people when you want to learn more about leadership, teaching, communication, or whatever. Teacher-mentors impart knowledge and link protégés to helpful resources that will broaden their understanding of the subject matter. A sponsor-mentor serves as an advocate for the protégé. He believes in the abilities of the protégé, builds confidence in him, and bridges relationships for him that enhance his ability to contribute to the organization.

Active mentoring involves the elements of discipling, spiritual guiding, and coaching. Discipler-mentors teach and model what it means to be a follower of Jesus Christ. They encourage protégés to develop a consistent spiritual growth plan that incorporates spiritual disciplines into daily living. Spiritual guide-mentors, on the other hand, help protégés discover God's movement in their lives. Stanley and Clinton state, "The primary contributions of a spiritual guide are accountability, decisions,

The Mentoring Continuum

More Deliberate ◄─────────────────────► *Less Deliberate*

Active Mentoring	Occasional Mentoring	Passive Mentoring
1. Discipler	4. Counselor	7. Contemporary Figure
2. Spiritual Guide	5. Teacher	8. Historical Figure
3. Coach	6. Sponsor	

Type of Mentor	Central Focus of Mentorship
1. Discipler	Understanding what it means to follow Christ
2. Spiritual Guide	Spiritual accountability and guidance in identifying the movement of God in one's life
3. Coach	Development of specific skills and motivation
4. Counselor	Providing timely advice; correct perspectives on viewing self, others, and ministry
5. Teacher	Imparting knowledge and instruction in a particular subject matter
6. Sponsor	An advocate who guides and protects a leader as they move upward in an organization
7. Contemporary Figure	A contemporary figure who serves as a living example to emulate
8. Historical Figure	A historical figure who is no longer living but portrays dynamic principles and values for life and ministry

and insights concerning questions, commitments, and direction affecting spirituality (inner-life motivations) and maturity (integrating truth with life)."[17]

The relationship with a spiritual guide is a highly reflective one. There are times in all of our lives when we must be willing to "review the whole narrative of our lives, seeking to make sense of it all" with the guidance of significant people in our lives.[18] Most people seek this type of relationship when they reach a plateau in their spiritual lives or feel stagnant in their ministry. A coach-mentor becomes necessary when protégés are faced with a new challenge or task for which they feel unprepared. Coaches train protégés in the strategies and skills they need to accomplish the task. They motivate the protégé to practice these skills. They observe them in action, evaluate them, and give feedback.

Characteristics of Effective Mentors

Over the years various authors have proposed characteristics of those who mentor well. Among these lists of characteristics are five common themes or indelible marks of a mentor. Those who mentor well are real, respectable, reliable, relational, and a role model.

1. **They Are Real.** Have you ever had a good friend pull you aside and whisper in your ear, "Hey, you have some mustard on your chin"? You think to yourself in utter embarrassment just how many meetings you sat through, how many people you passed in the hall, and how many conversations you had at the copy machine. Why didn't someone tell you sooner? The mark of a good mentor is that he is willing to be real with you. He is willing to point out the mustard on your chin or those areas in your life that everyone sees, but no one has the guts to tell you about. Mentors are also real about their own lives. They share with you the good, the bad, and the ugly. They allow you to see their struggles as well as their stresses. They don't have it all together nor do they pretend they do. There is no pretense about them. What you see is what you get. They are open, honest, and transparent about their ministries and their lives.

2. **They Have Earned Respect.** Another mark of good mentors is that they are widely respected by others. Two characteristics of church leaders mentioned in 1 Timothy 3:2 deal with respectability: "An overseer, then, must be above reproach . . . respectable" (NASB). This sense of respectability goes beyond the church to include the community. First Timothy 3:7 says, "And he must have a good reputation with those outside the church" (NASB). What do others say about this person, in Christian circles and beyond? Does he walk the talk? Is his character unquestionable?

3. **They Are Reliable.** A third mark of a mentor is reliability. Mentors who are reliable are people you can count on, people who are deeply committed to you, people who care more about your personal and professional development than what you think about them. Reliable mentors are people who embrace you like family. They realize that though your relationship will take different forms throughout a lifetime, like family it will always be a constant. The apostle Paul spoke of his young protégé Timothy as his "true child in the faith" (1 Tim. 1:2 NASB) and his "beloved son" (2 Tim. 1:2 NASB). So it is with those who mentor well.

4. **They Are Highly Relational.** Another mark of good mentors is that they are people magnets. When they walk in the room you know it because everyone wants to be around them. They may not be the loudest voice in the room, but they are certainly the most sought out. There

is a part of them that longs to be around people. They enjoy talking and listening to others. They make significant connections with people that go beyond the surface of, "Hi, how are you doing?" They ask questions more than they talk about themselves. They enjoy enlarging the lives of others. They serve as natural cheerleaders, and people gravitate toward them at parties and other social gatherings.

Similarly, mentors also maintain a vast network of relational resources. It is this vast network of relationships that lead people to say, "It isn't what you know, but who you know." Mentors who have well-established relationships outside the organization have the ability to connect protégés to an even broader learning community.

5. They Are Willing to Serve as Role Models. The final mark of mentors is their ability to show the way and lead by example. Is this person someone you look up to, someone who has something you need, someone who serves as a role model or example that you can follow? Paul declared to the Philippians, "Brethren, join in following my example, and observe those who walk according to the pattern you have in us" (Phil. 3:17 NASB). Several times throughout the epistles Paul echoes the sentiment, "Imitate me as I imitate Christ." In the same way mentors live a life that is contagious, a life that others want to imitate.

Mentors display competence in their field. They have the necessary skills, knowledge, and experience to make them experts. They have something that you need or desire to develop in your life, and they are willing to allow you to see them in action. They invite you to go with them, to watch them deal with a difficult situation or observe them teaching a large group. They say as Paul said, "The things you have learned and received and heard and seen in me, practice these things" (Phil. 4:9 NASB). They are teachers, not by trade, but by their very nature.

What Mentors Do

You may be reading the previous list and wondering, "Wow, do these kind of people really exist?" The answer is *yes!* They make valuable contributions in people's lives because they are willing to make the necessary investment that goes beyond simple friendship. They are intentional about the mentoring process and conscientiously strive toward the goal of replicating themselves in the lives of others. Because it is intentional, they accomplish their task by paying attention to a number of elements that are fundamental to the mentoring process. Some of these include the following.

Mentors Share Their Lives

Mentors spend regular time with their protégés just simply "doing life together." What this looks like changes depending on the protégé's season of life. A mentor must wear many different hats along the way. Some of those hats include being a source of information, sharing wisdom, giving feedback, acting as a sounding board, listening in time of need or personal crisis, nurturing curiosity, or teaching a specific skill. Whatever the need may be, the mentor and protégé journey along life's way together.

Mentors Are Willing to Ask the Tough Questions

In mentoring we often feel that the best way to help someone is to give answers, share insights, or simply make suggestions. Our tendency toward solving problems in a thirty-minute episode drives us to "tell" rather than "ask." It takes concerted effort to discipline yourself to ask probing questions rather than give ready-made answers. By asking questions mentors allow protégés the opportunity to explore their own thoughts and feelings on issues and gain the needed clarity to make decisions for themselves.

Larry Ambrose suggests that there are three distinct types of questions. They are investigative questions, discovery questions, and empowering questions. Each type of question fulfills a very different purpose. *Investigative* questions are fact-finding questions that seek information, background, and history. These are the kinds of questions that a good investigative news reporter would ask—the "who," "what," "when," "where," and "why" questions. Investigative questions provide mentors with basic information that will allow them to formulate more probing questions in the future.

Discovery questions prod protégés to explore the deeper meaning of experiences, to gain new insights about themselves, and to look at situations from various perspectives. *Empowering* questions challenge protégés to consider their desired outcomes, to chart a practical plan of action, and to establish a launching pad from which to move forward.

In a ministry situation investigative, discovery, and empowering questions might be differentiated in this way.[19]

Investigative Questions
- Tell me what you have accomplished so far.
- How long have you worked on this?
- Who else has been involved?
- Where do you think this project went off track?
- What were some of the reasons it got off track?

Discovery Questions
- What have you learned from this experience?

- What does it tell you about your approach?
- What's the best thing that could happen; what's the worst?
- What are your alternatives?
- How do you fit into this problem?

Empowering Questions
- What outcomes are you after?
- What do you have to do to make it happen?
- What's your first step?
- What resources do you have; what do you need?

Good questions begin with an exchange of information and lead toward creating insight. The ultimate goal in asking questions is not just to get people to talk, but to cultivate growth and awareness. The CEOs of some of the top Fortune 500 companies were asked what contributed most to their success as leaders. Many listed an effective mentor as one of the key contributing factors. To the question of what made these mentors so effective, the most common response among them was that they asked great questions.[20] Asking good questions doesn't come naturally. Leaders must be intentional and thoughtful about the questions they ask.

Mentors Provide Networking Resources

Mentors have a wide web of networking relationships and resources. For someone just starting out or stuck in a situation they can't see beyond, a mentor can provide valuable resources. Mentors are a walking encyclopedia of knowledge. Pick any subject matter, and they usually have an article or book you should read, a tape you should listen to, a Web site you should look at, or a person you just have to meet. With one phone call they have you connected to people whom you would have otherwise left voice mails for or spoken to through their administrative assistants.

Sure you can read, research, and make connections on your own, but it will take a lot longer and require more effort. It is very similar to the principle of "drafting" in cycling. Drafting allows you to gain an energy advantage by following in the slipstream of another cyclist. By allowing him to take the lead, his hard work and effort actually pull you along. In the same way protégés have an energy advantage when they position themselves behind a mentor who is willing to pull them along with his network of relationships and resources.

Pitfalls to Avoid in Mentoring Others

Mentoring is not easy, or more leaders would be doing it. If it were simple, far more ministry interns would be able to recognize their own ministry mentors. The fact is, however, that mentoring is not easy and rarely comes about without some significant effort and work on the part of both individuals. The following suggestions are offered with the hope that they will aid in the application of mentoring relationships among ministry leaders and protégés.

Avoid Giving Advice

Isn't that what mentoring is about? Well, not exactly. Advice giving only sets one person up as the hero or heroine who always saves the day and the other person as the helpless victim by the side of the road who desperately needs to be rescued. Most protégés don't really want advice, though they value your experience, ideas, knowledge of how things work, and special insights into problems. Avoid telling protégés what to do. Instead share your insights and leave the decision making up to them.

You will do this best when you practice letting the protégé do the talking. Listening without interrupting is a lost art in our society today. Just look at the conversations around you. People talk over one another, interrupt in midsentence, and complete the sentences of each other in a rush to begin their own thoughts and endless ramblings. Listening allows for protégés to reflect and work out their own thoughts and ideas.

In addition it is helpful to feed back the emotions that are expressed to you in order to demonstrate that you understand how what they are sharing has touched them. Provide your own insights only when asked or after first having asked for permission. You might say something like this: "Would you mind if I shared a few thoughts from my own experiences" or "could I share with you some things that have been helpful to me in the past?" Protégés are more likely to appreciate what you say when they have asked you to say it or at the very least have given you permission to say it.[21]

Taking Too Much Personal Control

Gordon F. Shea says, "Effective mentors stick with helping, not interfering. They share, they model, they teach; they do not take over someone else's problems unless there is a crisis that requires immediate action."[22] A mentor by nature is an influencer, and with influence comes power. Power in and of itself is not bad, but how we choose to use it can be. In order to avoid this pitfall, mentors must respect the independence of the individual being mentored and keep their own motivations in check. One of the best ways to do this is to be intent about your own spiritual pilgrimage. The apostle Paul said to the Corinthians, "Follow my example, as I follow the example of Christ" (1 Cor. 11:1 NIV). As mentors we aren't in the business of making miniature models of ourselves. When our primary focus is on following the example of Christ ourselves, our need to control or mold others into the image we have for them will begin to diminish.

Create an environment of support and encouragement where protégés can work toward mastering new thoughts, ideals, and skills. At times mentors fall into the trap of rescuing protégés because they don't want to see them repeat mistakes or be embarrassed or discouraged. Mentors must honestly reflect on their own motivations for interceding and be willing to allow protégés room to fail.

Having Unrealistic or Unfulfilled Expectations

Often we expect more than we get. This can go both ways in a mentoring relationship. When our expectations exceed reality, we become discouraged and disillusioned. The irony of it all is that we tend to be unaware of our expectations until they aren't met. Our expectations can include putting mentors on a pedestal of perfection. But what happens when we discover that our mentors are less than perfect? They miss a meeting time, they respond wrongly to a situation, or worse yet they commit moral failure and disqualify themselves from ministry. Hendricks and Hendricks write, "The beauty of mentoring is that you have someone to look up to. But the risk and the inevitable reality is that this person who you think so highly of will also let you down."[23]

The best way to deal with expectations is to clarify them from the beginning.

- What does a mentor do?
- What is it that you hope to gain from this relationship?
- What is it you hope to give?
- If you had a mentor, what are the most important things this person could help you with?
- How often will you meet and what will be the length of commitment?

These types of questions are good starting points. Second, it is helpful to remember that there is no earthly relationship that will completely fulfill us. Throughout the New Testament we see a recurrence of "one another" passages. We know that relating to each other is an essential part of the Christian life, but we must remember that the only relationship that will completely satisfy us is a personal relationship with Jesus Christ.

The Benefits of Mentoring

The benefits of mentoring are many and varied to both the individuals involved as well as to the organization as a whole. The following material will suffice to outline some of the benefits to the various entities involved.

Benefits to the Organization

Organizations that facilitate mentoring relationships benefit from increased productivity. As staff members assimilate to the organization and acquire the necessary skills and knowledge, their contribution to the organization naturally increases. "Mentor-protégé relationships can also give a boost to productivity through performance planning and increased teamwork."[24] By working alongside one another the protégé's motivation to do well increases, and this leads to better performance and greater productivity.

"Mentoring relationships increase the rate of organizational growth, reduce turnover, and maintain organizational stability."[25] Many organizations are finding mentoring a beneficial process to support the need for more effective staff development. By reducing the time spent orienting new employees and shortening the learning curve, new staff members are promoted more rapidly through the organization, and employee retention is increased. This type of intentional staff development also provides a systematic succession plan for key leaders in an organization. Too often organizations operate under the assumption that the perfect person will appear out of nowhere to fill vacant positions when they arise. An organization with an intentional mentoring process can provide a systematic way to move people into higher-level positions.

In addition, mentoring can increase organizational communication and understanding. Organizations are discovering that one of the best ways to disseminate the values of an organization, its institutional practices and priorities is through mentoring relationships. People learn best through relationships. In the context of a mentoring relationship, protégés see the values lived out and come to understand what is important to an organization.

Benefits to the Mentor

Mentors often get into mentoring relationships for what they can contribute to the development of others. They soon discover that mentoring is a two-way street that involves both giving and receiving. Reading, discussing, and exploring ideas and concepts together has a broadening affect on the mentor. In addition, many mentors find that they do things naturally, giving little thought to the "how" and "whys" behind what they do. By mentoring others, mentors are better able to understand the processes behind their actions and the values that drive them.

Other benefits include enhanced self-esteem, renewed passion for ministry, close personal relationships, a larger sphere of influence, and a lasting legacy. There is great honor in being asked to mentor someone else. The request alone suggests that you are someone who is respected and admired by others. We don't often look at ourselves the way others do. When we look in the mirror our focus tends to be drawn toward our faults and flaws. Mentoring can enhance our self-esteem and help us see ourselves from a balanced perspective.

Mentoring can also give mentors a renewed passion for ministry. A young, energetic, idealistic protégé can be a breath of fresh air. Battered down by the realities of ministry, a mentor's vision can get blurry and his ministry practices boring. Hendricks and Hendricks put it this way: "Just as you help interpret what the world has been to your protégé, he can help interpret what the world is becoming to you."[26] Protégés can spark new ideas, challenge old ways of thinking, and be a tremendous source of information in an ever-changing society.

Mentors also benefit from the close personal relationship that often transpires in a mentoring relationship. We were not created to live isolated lives as our individualistic society might suggest. In Genesis 2:18 the Lord told Adam that it was not good for him to be alone. There are great benefits in knowing someone personally and in turn being known by them. In 1 Corinthians 9:27 Paul says, "So that after I have preached to others, I myself will not be disqualified" (NIV). It is this fear of telling people one thing and then doing another that often drives mentors to stay the course. Mentoring breeds a relationship of natural accountability for those who mentor.

Finally, mentors benefit by having an increased sphere of influence. Most of us want more than fifteen minutes of fame. When mentors reproduce themselves in others, their influence extends far beyond their direct personal influence. No longer does the mentor's ministry end when he changes positions, relocates, or retires. A mentor's ministry actually outlives him. A lasting legacy is left for generations to come in and through the lives of those they have mentored.

Benefits to the Protégé

In a professional setting, those who are mentored have a tremendous advantage over those who are not. Starting out in a new ministry can be a lot like being thrown into the deep end of a swimming pool. You either "sink or swim." This trial-and-error process is one way to learn something new, but it isn't always the best way. Protégés progress more rapidly when their learning is built on the experience of others. Fear of failure is often significantly reduced, and protégés naturally take more risks. As this occurs protégés develop the confidence and competence they need.

Not only do protégés progress more rapidly, but they also experience greater overall job satisfaction. Several studies indicate that those who have been mentored experience increased opportunities for promotions, higher compensation, and greater job satisfaction than nonmentored individuals. This is the case regardless of gender or level in the organization.

Mentoring also enlarges a protégé's connection points both inside and outside an organization. This is especially vital for new employees. Connection points inside an organization help protégés learn the inner workings of the organization such as organizational culture, history, and the unwritten rules of the road. Mentoring also facilitates information networks outside the organization. These types of connections can provide outside perspectives, fresh new ideas, and be a source of career advancement when the time comes.

The Life Cycle of Mentoring

Though ideally mentoring relationships would span a lifetime, circumstances generally necessitate relational changes. Conflicts, job changes, relocations, new seasons of life, changing needs—these are just a few of the many factors that can affect a mentoring relationship.

Stanley and Clinton suggest that open-ended mentorships should be avoided. They recommend establishing "breaking up" points along the way. By setting up specific points (three months, six months, one year) for reevaluation of the relationship, it gives both the mentor and the protégé a polite way of bowing out if the mentoring relationship isn't quite what they expected. Conversely, if the relationship is going well it is easy to continue on and establish a new point of evaluation. In this way you have a built-in opportunity to evaluate the relationship on an ongoing basis rather than continue in a poor mentoring relationship that each person feels badly about ending.[27]

Hendricks and Hendricks point out three significant stages of the mentoring life cycle.[28] The first stage is the *definition stage*. During this initial period the relationship is defined, expectations are explored, and commitment is established. Zachary refers to the initial stage as a time of preparation and negotiation.[29] Both the mentor and the protégé must come to a shared agreement about such details as when to meet, how often, and deeper issues such as boundaries, confidentiality, and accountability. The second stage is referred to as the *development stage*. This stage is typically the lengthiest of stages and is marked by regular times of meeting, intense times of interaction, and visible signs of protégé growth and development. Zachary describes this time as a complex time. "Even when goals are clearly articulated, the process well defined, and the milestones identified, every relationship must find its own path."[30] The middle stage of a mentoring relationship is marked by days when the miles seem to fly by, large chunks of territory are covered, and amazing new lands are discovered.

At the *final stage* of the mentoring process there is recognition by one or both individuals in the mentoring relationship that the objectives for which the mentor and protégé first began meeting have been met. It may be that there were no specific objectives in the first place. In this instance the relationship may be simply in a lull. This brings the relationship to its final stage, the point of departure.

Though there is no magical timetable when it comes to the length of the mentoring life cycle, one thing is certain: almost all mentoring relationships have a point of departure. "Some experts estimate that the average mentoring relationship lasts between two and six years."[31] Even though the formal mentoring relationship may experience a point of departure, the relationship itself may continue on, taking the form of a friendship or occasional mentor. This is usually the case when the protégé has learned what he came to learn from the mentor and possibly even surpassed the mentor in some way.

Celebration and closure are essential ending elements in mentoring relationships. This is a time of mutual recognition of the meaningfulness of the relationship, an acknowledgement of contribution, and a celebration of life change. It may take the form of a simple card, letter, or one-on-one conversation. In more formal instances such as graduations, the completion of an internship, or job promotion, it may be appropriate to mark the ending with a ceremonial commissioning that indicates a rite of passage from one place to another.

Conclusion

Mentoring is a relational process that involves connection, communication, and commitment. In a day and age of instant messaging, online banking, and home grocery delivery, you can virtually live life without ever leaving home. Relationships are virtual, screen names are whatever you want them to be, and connections can be lost with the click of a button. Mentoring challenges our current way of thinking about relationships. It moves us away from our computer screens and back into the lives of people.

Mentoring relationships can have a profound, deep, and enduring impact. Though few of us feel like mentors, or ever aspire to be one, we usually are without realizing it. Any time we significantly impact the life of another person, there is a good chance that we have been a mentor. Mentoring is about influence. A mentor's influence far exceeds his personal reach. As a church we must embrace the need for mentoring if we hope to sustain the pace in a society that is set against the moral and spiritual truths we hold to. Mentoring relationships are a vital means of ensuring that current leaders finish well and that a future generation of leaders is poised to take their place.

BY
JAMES ESTEP JR.

Chapter 19

Transforming Groups into Teams

JESUS PROVIDES US WITH an example of the value of teams and team building. He met individuals at every level of unit development. He was familiar with the masses within cities, and he taught the crowds that followed him wherever he went. He likewise recruited a group of disciples who lived, traveled, and studied with him for three years, with the full intention of galvanizing the group into a team. He even encountered a cliquish faction within the team, James and John (Mark 10:35–45), and dismantled their desire for position and prominence among the disciples. Jesus formed a team out of an unlikely band of followers.

Jesus even demonstrated the role of leadership within the transition from a group to a team, from leading by directive to leading by collaboration. Mark's Gospel portrays this in Jesus' relationship to his disciples. In the early chapters Jesus does ministry and the disciples are more like spectators, watching him work (Mark 1:14–3:12). Later, the disciples begin to aid Jesus in his work, beginning to take active part in his ministry (Mark 3:13–6:6). Eventually, the disciples are able to do ministry themselves, but are still in need of Jesus' direct supervision and guidance (Mark 6:7–13, 30). Ultimately, the disciples are commissioned to carry out the ministry themselves, with Jesus still present among them, but no longer physically present (Mark 16:15–16, 20). Jesus had formed a *team*. Today, almost two millennia since the ministry of Jesus, his disciples still comprise teams to advance its ministry and mature its members. The intent of this chapter is to provide practical insights into the formation of ministry teams and guidance on how to turn a group of followers into a vibrant ministry team.

It isn't just those in ministry who are concerned with this topic. In corporate America there is a major emphasis on transitioning groups into teams. The book *Fish!* presents a contemporary parable for building community within the business world.[1] It relays the story of one leader's struggle to change an institution by changing the individuals and the dynamics governing their work relations. A highly effective and productive team is transformed from what began as a misdirected, unmotivated, and disorganized crowd occupying office space. Those who serve in positions of ministry leadership face similar challenges. Whether referred to as a group, committee, task force, or board, teams possess a *qualitative distinction*. Without this quality, regardless of the unit's label, it falls short of the ideal of *teamship*.[2]

Understanding Team Dynamics

What is the qualitative distinction between a group of individuals and a team? In a word: *synergy*. This is what Solomon spoke of in Ecclesiastes 4:9–12. Synergy enables a team to accomplish more than the work of one individual or the sum of individual contributions, becoming more than the sum of its parts. Synergy is accomplished through a variety of means such as a unified sense of and orientation toward objectives; the individual team member's character, giftedness, and self-perception; and the relational dynamic that participants share within the team. A team ultimately develops a collective identity as it serves the education ministry of the community of faith. In short, a team's diversity contributes to its strength. Bolman and Deal identify six characteristics distinguishing a unit as a team (reflecting the qualities of individual identity and giftedness, high relational dynamics, and goal-orientation), which are as follows:[3]

1. Teams shape purpose in response to a demand or an opportunity placed in their paths.
2. Teams translate common purpose into specific, measurable performance goals.
3. Teams are a manageable size.
4. Teams develop the right mix of expertise.
5. Teams develop a common commitment to working relationships.
6. Members of . . . teams hold themselves collectively accountable.

There are a number of advantages to forming teams in the context of ministry. They assist the accomplishment of the ministry's objectives in a number of important ways. These include the following:

1. Teams help individuals gain confidence in their personal giftedness and ministry potential.

2. Teams aid in developing meaningful and faithful relations within the congregation.
3. Teams integrate new members into the community of faith and education ministry.
4. Teams heighten the potential for successful achievement of desired ministry objectives.
5. Teams increase the base of support for addressing change and conflict within the ministry.
6. Teams provide for the nurture and spiritual formation of potential congregational leaders.

However, teams are not capable of addressing every circumstance or ministry endeavor in a congregation. While ministry teams present an advantage to ministry leaders, an overdependence or overemphasis on teams can sometimes be a detriment to both individuals and the congregation. Kenneth Gangel notes that teams are not always advantageous and are not always required. He asserts that "teams are not a cure-all for organizational problems," "an end unto themselves," "a substitute for involvement with the entire institution," or "a substitute for personal interaction."[4] Hence, ministry leaders should never limit a response to congregational matters to teams or teamwork.

Relational Complexity

It is easy to underestimate the complexities of teams. While teams may bring effective individuals into a positive, collaborative, relational dynamic, they can also complicate relationships too. Even in an ideal situation, the number of relationships within a team increases dramatically. The following formula illustrates the number of potential relational bonds that can be associated within a unit:

(Number of Unit Members) X (Number of Unit Members − 1) ÷ 2 = Total Unit Relationship-bonds

For example, perhaps a Christian education ministry unit has eight members. While eight may sound relatively small and manageable, when one takes into account the *twenty-eight* relationships upon which the work of the team rests (8 x 7 ÷ 2 = 28), one realizes the complexity of forming and maintaining teamship (see Figure 19.1).

However, not all units function within the context of such ideal relational bonds, and hence are not teams. Rather, the unit's goal orientation may be thwarted by poor relational dynamics, or individual giftedness may not complement other participants or the objective, and hence the unit never quite achieves the quality of a team.

Figure 19.1
Team Interaction

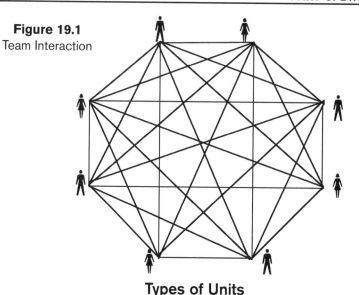

Types of Units

The dynamics of any unit determines its status as a team, or some other set of individuals. Figure 19.2 describes a number of possible unit dynamics.

Using this matrix, it is obvious that all units are not created alike. Most lack the qualitative elements necessary to achieve a sufficient level of team identity, relationship, and goal orientation that is required in teams. Some units lack these elements, falling short of the ideal, while in other units the relational dynamic overrides the task orientation, thwarting the purpose of the team. Typically the units in congregations are either groups or teams, or possibly cliques. The challenge comes in taking a group and transforming it into a team. The process is difficult but well worth the effort.

Transforming a Group into a Team

The main difference between a group of individuals and a team is goal orientation. While this is not the sole contributing factor, it is a key qualitative dimension of teams. It also tends to influence most heavily the traits of individual identity and relational dynamics. Olan Hendrix once identified two kinds of units (groups):[5]

1. Centric Group: Personal concerns are greater than group concerns.

2. Radic Group: Group concerns are greater than personal concerns.

By definition, a *team* must be a radic group. Figure 19.3 illustrates the goal orientation of the five units mentioned previously. Masses and crowds do not possess any discernible agreed-upon goal, although by

Figure 19.2: Unit Dynamics

Masses	A unit of individuals not viewed as assembled together and all acting independently from one another (e.g., people walking on a busy sidewalk) • Individual as an individual, no unit identity. • Relationship is inconsequential. • Objectives are individually determined.
Crowd	A unit of individuals assembled for possibly a common reason, *but* all acting independently from one another (e.g., attending a sporting event) • Individual as an individual, casual unit identity. • Relationship is low. • Objectives are individually determined, but share some commonality with those around them.
Group	A unit of people assembled for an apparent purpose, but *not* necessarily oriented to a joint task (e.g., disengaged office coworkers assigned a task) • Individual as an individual in a prescribed unit. • Relationship is moderate, communication less than ideal. • Objective is communal, but individualistic in character, no joint consensus.
Team	A unit of people that is assembled and identified by a common task, and has assumed responsibility for achieving it (e.g., a winning athletic team) • Individual as willing participant within a unit. • Relationships are high, ideal. • Objective is central and paramount.
Clique	A unit of people that is assembled and identified by the relationships within the group, to the exclusion of others and no task relations (e.g., a Sunday school class that has no desire for new members) • Unit as the individual, individuality lost. • Relationships are exclusive. • Objective is relationship.

coincidence some may have the same goal independently. Groups have attained some degree of goal orientation, but not perfectly aligned nor jointly held by the members. Teams have a unified sense of goal orientation and alignment with its achievement. To the extreme, cliques have virtually abandoned the goal of the unit, or replaced it, in favor of an exclusive relationship.

There are a number of ways to distinguish the differences between units and teams. A variety of these are displayed in Figure 19.4.[6]

Every team member approaches his responsibilities and tasks with innate preconceptions. Individuals carry the baggage of their own personal desires, skills, biases, personalities, as well as their representative capacity for their own ministry or interest group with a natural instinct to protect turf. However, for a team to be successful its participants must rise above their individualistic concerns, focusing toward the

Figure 19.3
Goal Orientation in Units

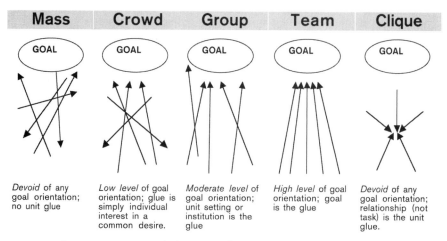

Mass	Crowd	Group	Team	Clique

Devoid of any goal orientation; no unit glue

Low level of goal orientation; glue is simply individual interest in a common desire.

Moderate level of goal orientation; unit setting or institution is the glue

High level of goal orientation; goal is the glue

Devoid of any goal orientation; relationship (not task) is the unit glue.

potential greater accomplishment of the team for the ministry of the church.

Regardless of whether one is part of a group or a team, it is still comprised of individuals. Hence, attention must be given to the individual's needs within the unit so that the actual participation within the team is pastoral. Myron Rush noted four basic personal needs that can be readily addressed by serving on a team:[7]

1. the need to use my skills, gifts, and creativity to assist the team's efforts;
2. the need to be accepted by the other team members;
3. the need for my personal goals to be compatible with the team's goals; and
4. the need to be allowed to represent others not on the team.

All this presupposes a collaborative environment. Hersey and Blanchard comment that "cooperative goals promote people's working together to ensure each other's success. . . . Research demonstrates that individuals and groups perform better where there are cooperative goals."[8] Within a team, little room is left for competition, only collaboration. Competition is acceptable, but collaboration is favored. While a team may be formed to be in a competitive relationship with another team or organization, the dynamic within the team is collaborative. Maddux comments about the four obvious benefits of collaborative teams as follows:[9]

1. Collaboration builds an awareness of interdependence.
2. When people work together to achieve common goals, they stimulate each other to higher levels of accomplishment.

Figure 19.4: Groups vs. Teams

Group Dynamics		Team Dynamics
Members think they are grouped together for administrative purposes.	← →	Members recognize their interdependence and understand both personal and team goals are accomplished by mutual support.
Members tend to focus on themselves. They approach their job simply as hired hands.	← →	Members feel a sense of ownership and unite to accomplish the team's goals.
Members are told what to do rather than being asked what the best approach would be.	← →	Members contribute to the organization's success by applying their unique talent and knowledge to the team objectives.
Members distrust the motives of colleagues. Expressions of opinion are considered divisive.	← →	Members work in a climate of trust and are encouraged to be openly expressive.
Members are so cautious about what they say, e.g., game playing and communication traps.	← →	Members practice open and honest communication. They make an effort to understand one another's point of view.
Members may receive good training, but are limited in applying it.	← →	Members are encouraged to develop skills and apply what they learn on the job.
Members find themselves in conflict situations which they do not know how to resolve.	← →	Members recognize conflict as a normal aspect of human interaction. They work to resolve conflict.
Members may or may not participate in decisions affecting the team.	← →	Members participate in decisions affecting the team.

3. Collaboration builds and reinforces recognition and mutual support within a team.
4. Collaboration leads to commitment to support and accomplish organizational goals.

Collaboration is necessary in a team because it fosters the sense of individual significance within the team, maintains the high relational dynamic present between participants, and focuses attention on an accepted objective.

Not All Teams Are Made Alike

Teams are *not* homogeneous. Diversity is not limited in terms of composition, but in terms of team types. Teams are not all alike. Business administrative books often itemize the various forms of teams, for example, executive, crossfunctional, formal support, project, task forces.[10] Confusion on the nature of the team on which one serves or what role it plays within the congregation can create goal confusion, relational dysfunction, and personal frustration. However, teams basically fall into four categories of team types. Figure 19.5 provides a filter to discern what types of teams exist in the typical congregation.[11]

Figure 19.5: Types of Teams

<table>
<tr><td colspan="2"></td><th colspan="2">DURATION</th></tr>
<tr><td colspan="2"></td><th>Temporary</th><th>Permanent</th></tr>
<tr><td rowspan="2">FUNCTION</td><td>Advisory</td><td>Research/Report Teams

e.g., brainstorming teams for new programs, building committees, feasiability study for a new Christian school</td><td>Church councils, committees, standing ministries

e.g., evaluation or assessment teams that monitor programs and make recommendations</td></tr>
<tr><td>Administrative</td><td>Short-term projects
Staff Search committees

e.g., VBS committee</td><td>Boards
Standing committees

e.g., a recruitment team responsible for staffing educational programs</td></tr>
</table>

For this reason it is clear that all teams are not created equally. While they may share the same fundamental characteristics, their function and duration make them different.

Leadership and Teams

Every team has a leader and needs a leader. It is never enough to simply place highly motivated, self-directed individuals into a collaborative environment. Leadership is always needed. Team leaders assume the responsibility for facilitating the teamwork within the unit and in essence creating, maintaining, and advancing the team's orientation and progress toward the goal, while guarding the team from dysfunctional elements. Robert Owens comments that "the sense of unity and pride that is so often observed in seemingly effective groups [i.e. teams] (and often called *morale*) is closely linked to the leadership present."[12]

Characteristics of a Team Leader

First, the leader must possess *spiritual maturity*. This is necessary to maintain the team's focus on ministry, its objective, and the theological worldview through which it must view its mission in light of the congregation. Christian leaders should also be concerned with maintaining a spiritual focus within the team. Karen Yust comments that "the primary purpose of every church committee is to discover God's will for church life."[13] She recommends that teams commit to acts of worship (such as a liturgy or ritual prior to the start of every meeting), prayer, Bible reading, personal reflection, and commitment to seek justice (reminding the members that their work is on behalf of others) as a means of maintaining spiritual focus on the team's purpose and task.[14]

Second, leaders must possess the ability to *think*. Leaders must think critically and creatively in order to provide adequate leadership to a team. Likewise, they must be able to think beyond their own agenda or personal interests. One's ability to reason, assess, and provide innovative responses to new situations is essential for a team's success.

Third, leaders must *value the team process*. Dictators do not form teams. A leader must genuinely accept and appreciate the contribution of each team member and the dynamics that govern the relationship within the team. Without an appreciation for this, members and discourse are perceived as encumbrances to the leader's will and decisions, which were typically made without input from the team. In short, a team leader must value the team, its role in decision making, problem solving, and achieving the task assigned to it.

Fourth, leaders must practice what Steven Covey describes as *Quadrant 2 Living*.[15] According to Covey, we live in a matrix of urgent/not urgent vs. important/not important tasks (Figure 19.6).[16] Quadrant 2 refers to those tasks that are important, but not urgent. Such tasks might be preparation, clarifying values, planning, building relationships, empowerment, or personal development. Successful leaders tend to spend 65 to 80 percent of their time in Quadrant 2, as compared to 15 percent by individuals characterized by a lack of performance, typically favoring Quadrant 3 (urgent and unimportant matters, e.g., interruptions, some meetings, mail, e-mail, and reports, also popular activities).[17] A team leader must stay focused on Quadrant 2 items, while guarding against the incursion of Quadrant 3 items, and hence keep the team at a high level of performance.

Leadership's Role in Groups and Teams

Leaders exhibit influence on team members, and yet must strike a delicate balance between their influence as individuals in the team and

Figure 19.6

	Urgent	Not Urgent
Important	**Quadrant 1** • Crises • Pressing problems • Deadline-driven projects, meetings, and preparations	**Quadrant 2** • Preparation • Prevention • Values clarification • Planning • Relationship building • True re-creation • Empowerment
Unimportant	**Quadrant 3** • Interruptions, some phone calls • Some mail, some reports • Some meetings • Many proximate, pressing matters • Many popular activities	**Quadrant 4** • Trivia, busywork • Junk mail • Some phone calls • Time wasters • "Escape activities"

the desire for participation and interaction of the team members. Gangel identifies ten roles the leader may play on a team: administrator, organizer, decision maker, group facilitator, chair, conflict manager, motivator, reproducer, and mentor.[18] Figure 19.7 denotes the shift from a group under a leader's direction toward a self-governing team, noting the changing role of leader from providing all the direction to assuming a collegial role on the team.

Figure 19.7: Relationship of Leadership Style to Team Influence

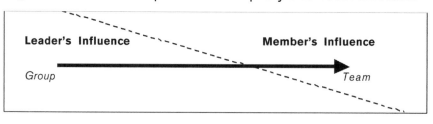

the

These leadership styles may be illustrated by the leader's relation to the team members, as demonstrated in Figure 19.8. The leader transitions from giving direction as a commander of the group to coaching the group or team. The leader then transitions from coaching them to being part of the team or group (still maintaining a noticeable presence in the deliberation and decision-making process), finally achieving a level of teamship wherein the leader can simply serve on the team as a colleague.

Figure 19.8

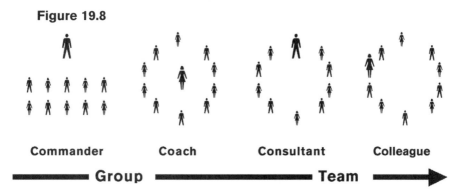

| Commander | Coach | Consultant | Colleague |

━━━━ Group ━━━━━━━━ Team ━━▶

Team Development Axioms

Setting up a team involves building consensus on goals, analyzing the team's potential, motivating its members, and then supporting the team by placing congregational resources at its disposal.[19] Several models of team building exist; however, they have a degree of similarity in principle. The following are core axioms for team building in a congregation:

1. Ultimate responsibility for team formation and development rests on the leader. While this is particularly true in the early stages of forming the team, regardless of the team's stage of development, the leader is needed as a commander, coach, consultant, or colleague.

2. Teams are established and maintained through a sense and statement of mutuallyaccepted purpose. Purpose can be thrust upon a group from a higher authority, but a group transitions into a team when the purpose is internalized and shared by all its participants and no longer has to rely on higher authority for impetus.

3. Teams develop best in an ethos of anticipated achievement; in an attitude of joint leadership via delegation, openness, encouraging innovation, and creativity. Team development can be impeded by a leader who does not transition appropriately, seeking to provide more direction than the team needs.

4. Teams develop when the process and ground rules of discussion and decision making are understood and accepted by team members. As with any unit of individuals, clear-cut processes and procedures for decision making, as well as an objective means or deadline for determining when the decision is final, must be accepted by all participants *prior* to the beginning of their work.

5. Teams develop when expectations are clearly articulated, defining and identifying each member's role. Five basic expectations of a team member might be participation, confidentiality, affirmation, preparation for meetings, and ability to work toward the shared objective.

6. Teams develop when achievements are celebrated. Teams must do more than work together. Perhaps the last celebration is the one for their decommissioning of service.

People Make the Team

Goal orientation and group dynamics are qualities dependent on the character of the individuals comprising the team. Hence the selection of members is a critical issue in determining the potential success or failure of a team. The following are critical questions that must be asked during the selection process:

1. What kind of individual is needed for the team? The answer to this assumes that the leader and/or team has a clear understanding of the team's purpose and agenda.

2. What are the spiritual requirements for the team? This will determine the necessary level of spirituality present in the team, as well as any particular spiritual giftedness and calling possessed by the individual.

3. Who within (or outside) our congregation possesses these traits? Teams cannot become dependent on one individual, and hence multiple individuals with the same general strengths may be considered for the same role on the same team.

4. How well do potential team members match the criteria? The team's strength is in its relational dynamics shared by its members. Are strength and weakness assessments viable? Just as puzzle pieces interlock to complete the picture, so the strengths and weaknesses of team members complete the necessary character of the unit.

5. Can they be accepted by the existing team, including the leader? Since relationships are implicit in the team dynamic, consideration must be given to the impact of introducing new members into an existing team dynamic as well as a new team.

6. On what basis does the team extend a call to serve? This not only refers to the nature of the team, for example, advisory or decision making, but to the expectations placed on the individual team member's role; that is, is it a permanent posting, temporary, or called simply for occasional consultation.

Assessing Teamwork Functions

While teams have a defined objective, their work is not always limited to the achievement of that singular aim. Teamwork occurs in more than one context. In fact, according to Ketchum and Trist, teams work in three frames of reference: Teams in action, meeting, and evaluation (Figure 19.9).[20] The first frame illustrates the team in *action*, when it is actually working toward achieving the team's objective. The second frame represents when the team is *meeting* to discuss the work and making decisions regarding its next actions. The final frame is an *evaluation* phase, when the team assesses its actions and decisions, stepping outside the two previous frames to gain a more comprehensive and objective perspective.

Figure 19.9

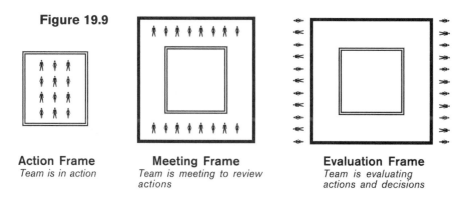

| Action Frame | Meeting Frame | Evaluation Frame |
| *Team is in action* | *Team is meeting to review actions* | *Team is evaluating actions and decisions* |

Team Member Roles

Members neither fulfill a singular role within the team, nor are roles themselves singular. Each individual on a team functions under the guidance of four different roles that must be in harmony, or it can create confusion and frustration for the individual and team. Most theorists of group dynamics have identified at least four components within *each* role, as follows:[21]

1. **Expected Role.** The team's expectations of the individual team member's role.
2. **Projected Role.** The communicated or expressed expectations by the team to individual team members.
3. **Perceived Role.** The individual team member's interpretation of the projected role.
4. **Functional Role.** The individual team member's actual actions or function within the team.

Failure to acknowledge the presence of these four role components, or to insure that the four are compatible and coincide, leads to an inadequate and incomplete perception of roles and their function within the team, and ultimately to dysfunction. Heller and Hindle offer a diagram illustrating the performance of teams (Figure 19.10).[22]

Figure 19.10
Team, Task,
and Individual

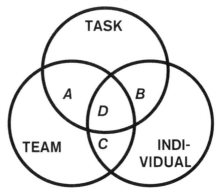

According to Heller and Hindle, section A denotes when "team works to[ward a] common end to complete tasks," since it denotes the overlap of team and task issues. B is "challenging tasks maintain individual interest," identifying the individuals' commitment to the objective. C is when the "needs of individual are addressed by the team," as individuals participate within the team relational dynamic. Finally, D illustrates when "each individual contributes to [the] team effort to complete the task at hand," denoting the core nature of a team. Hence, teamwork can be fulfilling to the individual participant, as well as rewarding for the congregation.

Productive and Disruptive Behaviors
An individual team member's behavior can contribute or detract from the team's relational dynamics or goal orientation. Figure 19.11 endeavors to identify some specific examples of these types of behaviors.[23]

Group Think . . . A Dysfunctional Team
A chief, yet unfortunately common, predicament to overcome in regard to teamwork is the potential enmeshment of a group's thinking or decision making process, that is, *groupthink*. Whereas most forms of disruption or dysfunction are readily evident, groupthink is so subtle that team members are often convinced that the team is functioning within expected perimeters, only to increasingly become ineffective and unproductive. What are the symptoms of groupthink and how is it recognizable? Here are several identifying marks:
*   Team adopts an uncritical attitude toward ideas and proposals, regarding themselves to be virtually infallible.

Figure 19.11: Productive and Disruptive Behaviors

Productive Behaviors	Disruptive Behaviors
• Stimulates relevant and clear communication	• Withdrawn, physically or mentally, from the team process
• Develops a fair and open process for decision making	• Places individual needs and ideas above that of the team
• Facilitates alternative ideas and brainstorming	• Volatile behaviors, e.g., displays anger, attacking personally, sarcasm
• Engages in intentional theological reflection	• Inconsistent convictions and positions
• Willingness to accept responsibility for assignments and tasks	• Distractive behavior, e.g., shaking head, doodling, audible noises
• Willingness to participate in the team process	• Major in the minors, unable to grasp big picture and resorting to hairsplitting issues
• Promotes and guards the relational bonds within the team	
• Establishes a safe environment	• Usurps the team process by making decisions individually or violating confidentiality
• Able to evaluate and assess ideas, not other individuals or the team	
• Advocates tolerance of alternative ideas and manages the potential for conflict within the team	• Advocates personal agenda rather than team's agenda
• Adheres to the agenda, maintaining progress toward the objective	• Tends to speak in "I" terms, or uses an unidentified "we"
• Tends to speak in "we" terms, rather than singular identity	• Dominates the relational dynamic and agenda
• Sets realistic timeline for accomplishments	• Anecdotal or selective interpretation of information
• Fair and considerate of team members' commitments and capabilities	• Uses "we-they" language, presenting an adversarial or divisive picture

- Team fails to heed cautions or concerns of the greater body in favor of their own ideas; failing to see their own weakness, seeing it only in others.
- Team addresses differences of opinion or disagreements with the majority of the team by pressuring individual team members into silence or capitulation; that is, forced consensus, manipulated or coerced.
- Team practices eisegesis (inserting a desired meaning into Scripture) rather than exegesis (ascertaining the intended

meaning of Scripture) with scriptural or theological validation of ideas and actions.

- Team regards itself as a consensus and unanimous opinion body, when in fact it has simply squelched opposition.
- Team disregards relevant information that opposes their position or view; for example, failing to address biblical or theological contradictions to their proposal.

How is groupthink prevented or reversed? The answer lies in safeguarding the team process and dynamic. Four safeguards can typically arrest the onset of groupthink. First, prevent its onset by preserving the productive behaviors and minimizing the disruptive behaviors previously mentioned. Second, preserve the integrity of each member's voice on the team, for example, listening attentively to individuals, summarizing their input after they are finished speaking, providing ample opportunity for sharing of ideas, and not allowing interruptions or emotional engagements. This can also be accomplished by providing an opportunity for individual written responses to agenda items *prior* to the unit processing the information, so that everyone's voice is heard. Third, while maintaining confidentiality, publicly voice favor on the team's progress. This keeps the team in touch with the reality of the congregation or constituency it serves.

Finally, provide for the critical examination of decisions and position. "The adverse effects of groupthink can be avoided if the leader is aware of the potential problem and takes steps to increase critical evaluation of alternatives under consideration."[24] This can be accomplished by the leader asking and promoting the critical examination of every proposal, as well as having an outside reader to serve as an *ex officio* sounding board for the team.

Conclusion

Teams have always been critical for the success of any institution. The failure to develop teams causes a diffusion of identity, lack of corporate goal orientation, and ineffective relational dynamics within the organization. Christian administrators must exemplify the leadership style that facilitates the formation of teams, and hence advance the mission and health of the organization.

BY
JAMES ESTEP JR.

Chapter 20

Leadership Strategies

HOW DOES ONE LEAD? It is not difficult to find resources posing definitions, theoretical frameworks, processes and procedures for leadership. Entering any bookstore, Christian or otherwise, one can typically locate one shelf or more filled with such items. In effect, leadership has become a buzzword for the twentieth and twenty-first centuries, but without a consistent definition. However, the nuts and bolts of leadership, or at least practical approaches to implementing leadership, are often lacking.

The emphasis of this chapter will be to address how one leads in a congregation or Christian organization through five venues: (1) identifying principles of Christian leadership, (2) highlighting the differences between leadership and management, (3) a brief look at leadership styles within an institutional context, (4) describing six strategies for implementing and maintaining leadership, and (5) presenting a model for leadership formation in a congregation or Christian organization. In so doing, this chapter will provide an overview of the nature, process, and formation of Christian leadership.

Christian Leadership Principles

What distinguishes Christian leadership from secular approaches has been the topic of discussion within the church for many years. It begins by asking the fundamental question, "What makes Christian leadership Christian?" It is our contention that a well-grounded biblical understanding of leadership will set itself apart from other more secular approaches in a number of important ways. These distinctives include an emphasis on four components: character, competency, context, and calling. Each adds an element which sets it apart from its corporate cousin. Figure 20.1 endeavors to demonstrate the relationship between these elements in relationship to understanding the nature of Christian leadership.

349

Components of Christian Leadership

The base component of any Christian approach to leadership is *character*. This is perhaps most evident in Scripture in the qualifications for congregational leaders, specifically elders and deacons set forth in the New Testament. As one reads Acts 6:3; 1 Timothy 3:1–7; 3:8–13; Titus 1:5–9; and 1 Peter 5:1–4, it becomes obvious that these are a series of life traits, designed to ensure that Christian leaders are "blameless" or "above reproach" (Titus 1:7; 1 Tim. 3:2). However, character is not enough. Being recognized as a "good person" does not insure he or she will be or become a good leader. However, character is foundational, essential, and nonnegotiable. Hence Paul places these life qualities as the bedrock for our understanding of Christian leadership.

The second component is *competency*. Leadership is not passive or uninvolved, nor is it done in isolation from others. Individuals must possess character and competency, the ability to perform ministry, and an area of recognized expertise or talent. You must be able to learn from a leader, and how can you learn from someone who is incompetent? What kind of a leader would a person make if he is incapable of basic leadership activities and abilities? This component emphasizes the *functionality* of leadership. Once again, Paul's list of qualifications in the Pastoral Epistles mentions one competency, their ability to teach (1 Tim. 3:2; Titus 1:9). One foundational competency of Christian leaders is the ability to communicate. Also, appointing an individual to a leadership role without requiring him to actually be able to work is adopting a practice of promoting the incompetent. Who wants to follow someone from whom he or she can learn nothing? In short, leaders must possess character and the competency to do ministry within the congregation or Christian organization.

As the third component, *context* places the individual with a position and frame of reference from which to be given a voice and a stage from which to communicate it. Character and competency can be thwarted without having the appropriate position or context in which to exercise leadership. It implies access to resources and the authority to guide and direct those serving with them. Context can likewise be a limiting factor, muffling or muting the voice of an individual, and hence detracting from the fulfillment of his leadership potential. Once again, Paul demonstrates the necessity of position when engaging his missions work in Asia Minor. Acts 14:23 notes that he "appointed elders for them in every church, with prayer and fasting, they committed them to the Lord in whom they believed" (RSV), illustrating the importance of having a recognized position from which to lead.

Figure 20.1

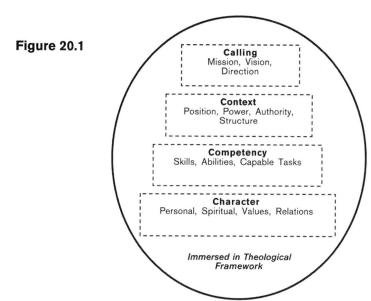

Similarly, the titles given leaders in the early church (deacon, bishop, elder, shepherd) not only depict their function (competency), but their placement in a position of responsibility and oversight for ministry (context). Context alone will never provide genuine leadership; it rests upon the character and competency of the individual in the position. Figure 20.2 illustrates the positional component of leadership in a congregational context.

Figure 20.2: Positional Leadership

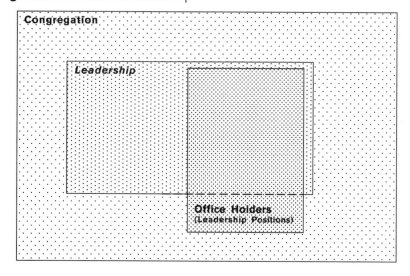

This figure illustrates four foundational facts about leadership in a congregation, some of which are so obvious that they are often overlooked: (1) Leadership comes from within the congregation. Even new pastors must become a part of the congregation, perceived as coming from within the congregation, before having a position from which to lead. (2) Leadership is not limited to office holders. Congregations have formal positional leaders (office holders) and also informal leaders (those recognized as congregational leaders without title or office). (3) Office holders are not necessarily leaders. Unfortunately, some individuals in office are not recognized as leaders, and therefore have a limited ability to actually lead the congregation. (4) The best leadership is one that is both recognized and holds office. In this case, those who are acknowledged as leaders within the congregation also hold the necessary position from which to provide leadership. For the context component of leadership to have its full influence and potential, the individual recognized as a leader must also be in a position of leadership, or the context diminishes the potential of the individual to actually lead.

The final component is *calling*. When Paul describes the qualification for an elder to Timothy, the first statement is one who desires the office (1 Tim. 3:1). This is not only a sense of divine appointment or recruitment to a context, but a commitment to the purposes of the ministry. Called people possess a consistent sense of purpose, an unrelenting passion to achieve something bigger than themselves. Leaders must be out in front, going somewhere, and have a following. In short, you aren't leading if you're not going somewhere! Leadership, in a word, is change: "To lead is to struggle. . . . Leadership always involves change, moving people from one point to another, from the old way of doing things to the new, from the security in the past to the insecurity in the future. Within us there is a built-in resistance to change which seems to threaten our stability and challenge our power. Even if our current situation is unhappy, we still dig in our feet."[1]

The divine calling of a leader identifies who he is in accordance with God's will. Calling is a culminating component, based on one's character, competency, and context. "Effective leaders help establish a vision, set standards for performance, and create focus and direction for collective efforts."[2] Defined this way, one's calling is a matter of direction and vision, as well as creating the climate and capability to fulfill God's purposes for the ministry organization.

Setting Christian Leaders Apart

What sets Christian leaders apart from their corporate cousins? Without belaboring the point of chapter 2, it is when the four components we discussed (character, competency, context, and calling) are theologically informed that the Christian nature of leadership is affirmed. For example, one of the most famous lines in movie history is from the 1987 blockbuster "Wall Street." In one scene the CEO of a major corporation, played by Michael Douglas, explains to stockholders, "Greed is good." This statement articulates the underlying values that corporate America has come to accept for doing business, but is this a characteristic that Christian leaders should emulate? Obviously not!

Other characteristics that are idealized by corporate cultures and idealized in popular media include such concepts as aggression, political manipulation, hedonism, and pragmatic values where the end justifies the means. Indeed, none of these are acceptable to the Christian leader. Swimming in this ocean of common practices is the Christian leader who is searching for a better way to conduct his or her affairs. From where do we derive our portrait of a desired character for leadership? God has expressed his desired character in Scripture, exemplified them in Christ, and supported them through the power provided in his Holy Spirit's presence. In short, the four components of leadership must be immersed in a theological framework to provide a model of leadership consistent with the theological organizations, congregations, or institutions in which leaders serve.

Several concluding observations about this model of leadership should be stated. First, the components are integrated and depend on one another, but this is not to say that some elements do not have a higher priority than others. Ideally, the pyramid shape would occur, with a proportionally tapered appearance of components. In this way, character and competency are never minimized by the context or call. Leaders who have a calling but lack character or context are dangerous commodities for any Christian organization.

Second, in light of the first observation, leadership formation should be sequential in nature. A young Christian who desires to become an effective leader should place a great deal of emphasis on personal character development before aspiring to fill an office or grasp a calling from God. Character development and basic competencies should precede context and calling. Moses spent eighty years developing character and being trained before he received his context and call. Likewise, David served as a seasoned shepherd for years before experiencing the context or calling of his life's work. Numerous additional examples could be provided to illustrate this point. God never circumvents the character development of a leader in order to rush the call of someone into office.

A final observation is that within the corporate body of Christ, the number of individuals in a congregation who have all four components will be relatively small. Quite a number may posses godly character, but fewer will have the necessary competency. An even smaller amount will achieve a particular context or position office, and far fewer of those will have been directly called by God to serve in a vocational sense. Hence, only a limited number will really serve in a leadership capacity in the congregation or organization compared to the overall number within the institution.

Moses as Leader

While the Scriptures are plentiful with examples of recognizable leaders among God's people, one of the most recognizable is Moses. Exodus 3–4 contains one vignette of his life, the burning-bush encounter. In it we see concern for the four previously mentioned components of leadership (character, competency, context, and calling), particularly in Moses' concerns and/or excuses for questioning the call of God. Figure 20.3 analyzes the account from these four lenses.

Figure 20.3: Moses as Leader

Category	Moses as Leader
Character	• 3:1–7: Moses demonstrates an acknowledgement of God and shows humility and respect before him by averting his face.
Competency	• 3:8–10: Moses received forty years of training in the household of Pharaoh and received an additional forty years of training in the wilderness. • 3:12, 4:1–9, 17, 21–23: God promises to provide miraculous signs through Moses' ministry to support his perceived incompetency. • 4:14–17: God provides Aaron as an assistant for Moses' mission.
Context	• 3:10: Moses is put into a position of leadership over God's people. • 3:18: Moses is promised a leadership role with the elders of Israel, and eventually the people recognize the mediating role of Moses between them and God.
Calling	• 3:10, 12: God commissions Moses to confront Pharaoh to release the Israelites. • 3:13: Moses understands that God is the one sending him on the mission.

Moses was a man of remarkable leadership based on his character, competency, unique historical context, and the distinct calling of God on his life. The same matrix could be used to formulate and analyze the leadership of Nehemiah, David, and a number of prominent New Testament leaders.

Leadership vs. Management

Administration as a concept encompasses both leadership and management. It is the capstone idea resting upon the corollaries of leadership and management. That is not to say, however, that leadership and management are synonymous terms. In fact, it's because so many contemporary authors have failed to differentiate between these terms in their writings that we have so much gross misunderstanding about them. Perhaps the leading spokesman for separating the terms has been Joseph Rost in his book *Leadership for the 21st Century.* In this text he lays out an overwhelming argument for keeping the terms distinct and then defines each as follows: "The definition of leadership is this: Leadership is an influence relationship among leaders and followers who intend real changes that reflect their mutual purposes."[3]

He then goes on to define management as "an authority relationship between at least one manager and one subordinate who coordinate their activities to produce and sell particular goods and/or services."[4]

Perhaps it would be helpful to illustrate these two terms in chart form.[5]

LEADERSHIP	MANAGEMENT
Influence relationship	Authority relationship
Leaders and followers	Managers and subordinates
Intended real change	Produce and sell goods and/or services
Intended changes reflect mutual purposes	Goods/services result from coordinated activities

Kouzes and Posner set about to draw a distinction between the terms by stating, "If there is a clear distinction between the process of managing and the process of leading, it is the distinction between getting others to do and getting others to want to do. Managers, we believe, get others to do, but leaders get other people to want to do. Leaders do this by first of all being credible. That is the foundation of all leadership. They establish credibility by their actions—by challenging, inspiring, enabling, modeling, and encouraging."[6]

Bennis and Nannis articulated it most simply: "Managers do things right, and leaders do the right thing."[7] Management tends to focus on operational items, working within the existing confines of the organization's mission, vision, structure, policies, and procedures. Management is bound by the institutional limits. Leadership tends to focus on the strategic items, reframing or changing the organization's mission, vision, structure, policies, and procedures. Leadership reshapes the institutional limitations. In short, managers function within the proverbial institutional box; leaders think outside the box. To confuse one with the other can be perilous to a congregation or Christian organization.

Administrators who are 100 percent *leadership* would have their heads in the clouds and trip over stones. On the other hand, administrators who are 100 percent *managerial* would be bean counters, never able to see the big picture. A balance must be maintained.

Administration requires both leadership and management, but in the absence of leadership, administration is diminished to the role of shop keeping, bean counting, and institutional maintenance.

Administration cannot separate leadership and management, but they are indeed different. Another attempt to draw a difference between the two concepts as displayed in action is set out by Stephen Covey. He provides a simple distinction between the two with profound implication for those involved in the application of theory within the context of Christian ministry. Figure 20.4 illustrates his leadership/people vs. management/things paradigm.[8]

Figure 20.4

Leadership (People) Paradigm	Management (Things) Paradigm
Effectiveness	Efficiency
Spontaneity	Structure
Discernment	Measurement
Causes	Effects
Release/Empowerment	Control
Programmer	Program
Transformation	Transaction
Investment	Expense
Customer Service	Administrative Efficiency
Principles	Techniques
Synergy	Compromise
Abundance	Scarcity

When one confuses the distinction between management and leadership in administration, adequate administration is never provided to the congregation or Christian organization. Institutions require managers and leaders within their administration. Failing to acknowledge this leads the institution to succumb to the inevitability of failure in its mission. Christian ministries need both dreamers and bean counters.

Leadership Styles

Strategies are linked to our style of leadership. Style of leadership refers to how leaders perceive their relationship to the organization and those working with them. Borrowing from the biblical metaphor of *sheep herding*, which is dominant in both the Old and New Testaments, two elemental styles of leadership are present in congregations and Christian organizations: shepherding and ranching. Figure 20.5 identifies the difference between the two.[9]

Figure 20.5: Shepherds and Ranchers

Shepherds tend to ...	Ranchers tend to ...
• try to personally meet everyone's needs	• strive to care for the flocks as a whole, not for lone sheep
• think the ministry will self-destruct without them	• operate by objectives and welcome all ideas for accomplishing goals
• exhibit drivenness	• handle change and conflict with maturity
• feel grateful to be needed	• encourage involvement by the laity
• have trouble delegating	
• do their planning on the run	• match jobs with appropriately gifted people
• live in the hectic present and overlook future trends	• delegate effectively and supervise with a light touch
• miss the big picture of "bodylife" because they are so focused on separate relationships.	• function as part of a team
	• rejoice when others succeed without them.

The success of a shepherd or rancher style of leadership is contingent on the maturity level of the followers. Several questions need to be addressed: Are they ready to assume responsibility for a task? Are they able to work in a team structure? Do they possess talents developed enough to be used with limited supervision? Two theories that provide further insight into the shepherd vs. rancher approaches to leadership are Paul Hersey and Kenneth Blanchard's theory of situational leadership, and the Four-Frame Model of institutional leadership.

Hersey and Blanchard's Situational Leadership Theory

Hersey and Blanchard's *Management of Organizational Behaviors* is now considered a classic of administrative literature. The theory rests on the basic principle that effective leadership resides in four styles (Telling, Selling, Participating, and Delegating) as they are used in relation to the readiness level of the follower. The *level of readiness* refers to the follower's ability (capability of doing a task, e.g., knowledge, experience, or skills) and/or his willingness (psychological readiness, e.g., confidence, commitment, or motivation).[10] From this, two possible axes of leadership response can be given: task-oriented or relationship-oriented responses to the follower's readiness.

Task-oriented responses are *one-way communications,* with the leader engaged in goal setting, organizing, establishing time lines and agendas, directing, and controlling followers. Relationship-oriented responses are *two-way communications,* with the leader providing support to followers, facilitating interaction (team building), active listening, and providing feedback to followers (evaluation and assessment).[11] Figure 20.6 captures the four possible approaches to leadership described by Hersey and Blanchard.

Figure 20.6

Follower Readiness Level	Appropriate Leadership Style	Description
1	Telling	• High task, low relationship orientation • One-way communication, primarily from leader to followers • Leaders should provide detailed instructions and supervise followers closely.
2	Selling	• High-moderate task, moderate-high relationship orientation • Two-way communication, primarily from leader to follower, but with heightened follower involvement • Leaders should explain decisions and provide opportunity for clarification.
3	Participating	• High-moderate relationship, moderate to low task orientation • Two-way communication, primarily discussion among followers with leader • Leader should share ideas and facilitate discussion and team decision making.
4	Delegating	• Low relationship, low task orientation • One-way communication, primarily from leader • Leader relinquishes control, giving responsibility for decision making and implementation to qualified followers.

Facilitative Leadership

How do Hersey and Blanchard inform the shepherd-rancher approaches to leadership? An approach to leadership that endeavors to move from shepherding to ranching is commonly labeled *facilitating leadership,* since the approach calls for the leader to facilitate leadership in others as a means of achieving the ministry potential and goals. Figure 20.7 identifies the difference between the two:

If one were to interpret this illustration through the lens of Hersey and Blanchard, the Telling and Selling approaches would readily align with the left side of the illustration, shepherding, emphasizing the leader's control and direct activity of the administration. Similarly, the right side of the illustration would reflect the Participating and Delegating styles of leadership, emphasizing group or team control and directing of the administration. The general difference between these

Figure 20.7

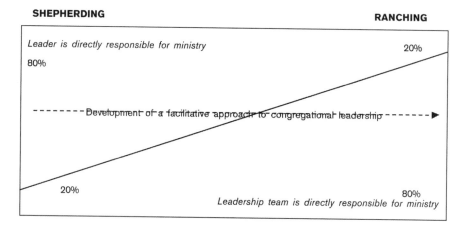

SHEPHERDING   RANCHING

approaches to leadership is that shepherds use their own authority to get things done, whereas ranchers empower others to get things done—by leading the group or being on the leadership team. One may have to begin as a shepherd, tending to the flock, but as the people and institution mature, shifting toward a rancher model is preferred and necessary. Being aware of this process allows the director of a Christian ministry with an understanding of the dynamic nature of leadership development and also of the situational issues that may impact one's leadership style.

Four-Frame Model of Leadership

But how does a shepherd or rancher actually understand their flock and grazing lands? In more literal terms, what is the corporate ethos in which leadership must function? The four-frame model of leadership provides insight into how leadership must engage the corporate ethos of congregations and Christian organizations. An appropriate leadership style is not only based on the appropriate response to the readiness level of the follower (Hersey and Blanchard), but on the self-determined identity of the institution in which one serves. Figure 20.8 outlines the four basic frameworks through which to ascertain the corporate ethos: structure, human resource, political, and symbolic.

While Christians may immediately respond favorably to the symbolic frame, with its obvious spiritual dimension and implications, it would be naïve not to identify the other three frames that are also at work within many of our congregations and Christian organizations. In short, every institution has a taste of these four cultures, but one will gain ascendancy within the institution (or perhaps two competing frames will vie for dominance). If a shepherd or rancher enters a

Figure 20.8: Four-Frame Leadership Model

	Structure	Human Resource	Political	Symbolic
Organizational Metaphor	Factory or Machine	Family	Jungle	Carnival, Temple, Theater
Central Concepts	Rules, roles, goals, policies, technology, environment	Needs, skills, relationships	Power, conflict, competition, organizational politics	Culture, meaning, metaphor, ritual, ceremony, stories, heroes
Image of Leadership	Social Architect	Empowerment	Advocacy	Inspiration
Leadership Challenge	Attune structure to task, technology, environment	Align organizational and human needs	Develop agenda and power base	Create faith, beauty, meaning

congregation or Christian organization, he must first determine the prevailing corporate ethos. Some refer to this process as exegeting the organizational culture. For example, as a shepherd in a political ethos, how do I provide leadership? As a rancher in a symbolic institution, how does this influence how I provide leadership? Hence, the prevailing corporate ethos will also shape the execution of one's leadership within a given context.

Myths of Facilitating Leadership

Several myths associated with facilitation as an approach to leadership within congregations and Christian organizations often detract from its successful use. Myths tend to restrict the implementation of a rancher approach to leadership by casting a disparaging assessment on its potential. Following is a list of these myths and their antithesis:[13]

- *Myth*: Facilitation is a loose approach to management that invites disorder and chaos!
- *Actual*: Facilitation creates a team-oriented approach to management that creates cohesion and direction.

- *Myth*: A facilitative leader simply agrees to everything the team wants.
- *Actual*: Facilitative leaders provide direction, but value the team members' insights and perspectives

- *Myth*: Facilitative leaders give up their own power and control.
- *Actual*: Facilitative leaders share their own power and control.

- *Myth*: It won't work in this culture.
- *Actual*: Facilitative approaches work very well when groups grow toward team status.

- *Myth*: Facilitation takes too much time. We won't get anything done.
- *Actual*: Facilitation may take time, but the *synergy* it produces makes the team more productive than the sum of the individual members' work.

- *Myth*: Facilitation encourages anarchy.
- *Actual*: Facilitation encourages ownership of the mission and values of the institution.

- *Myth*: The democracy of facilitation will water down the quality of decisions.
- *Actual*: Democratic process, or consensus more so, makes decision less unilateral and more of a product of those responsible for its success.

- *Myth*: Once we start a facilitative approach, we will have to do everything this way.
- *Actual*: Everything cannot be run by facilitation, only when the follower's readiness level is high enough to allow for a rancher style of leadership.

Facilitative leadership, where one moves from a shepherd characterized by solitary leadership toward a rancher marked by shared leadership, is far more desirable for leaders in congregations and Christian organizations.

Axioms for Leadership

How can leaders initiate, implement, or sustain a progressive culture of change and advancement in a congregation or Christian organization? While the specific may be different for each institution and individual leader, several broad responses can be made to this concern.[14] Failure to engage in the practices mentioned below cause a transition from institutional leadership toward institutional management and the erosion of progress toward fulfilling and expanding the mission of the congregation or Christian organization.

Axiom #1: *Leaders of successful congregations always engage in theological reflection on their ministry and that of their congregation or* *organization.* Leaders who fail to continually practice theological reflection diminish the Christian aspect of their administration. Theological foundations for educational ministry cannot simply be left behind for what may be considered more advanced or more contemporary models of educational administration. Everything we do in a congregation or Christian organization must be immersed in the theological framework of our Christian tradition. Hence we must constantly engage our theological convictions and heritage as *faithful* administrators. Every administrator must be at the least an amateur theologian.

Axiom #2: *Leaders of successful ministries never stop personal (and professional) development.* Closed systems always tend toward entropy. Batteries are always drained of power. Administrators who fail to engage in an intentional and regular plan for personal and professional development become entropic and drained, continually relying on a limited and ever-diminishing set of personal and professional resources. However, those who engage in personal and professional development, including genuine re-creation, serve in an open system, and are connected to the AC outlet. They will have a continual refilling of resources, insights, and personal networks. It creates a personal synergy. Committing to a plan for professional development reflects a humility of acknowledging the need for growth, that you are not finished, and do not have all the answers.

In short, the moment you stop growing, you start dying; the moment you start dying, your administration has an ever-diminishing shelf life. Your personal and professional development is an *investment,* not an expense, for the future well-being of your ministry and yourself.

Axiom #3: *Leaders of successful ministries think big.* As previously discussed, leaders think outside the box. They are not restricted by the dimensions of the institutional limitations, but they challenge the *status quo.* Leaders begin to become managers when their thoughts become restricted by the current institutional status. Successful congregations are those that endeavor to do the impossible and reap the benefit even when they miss their intended mark. The questions for every leader are "What's next?" and "What's new?" Leaders of congregations and Christian organizations can never stop thinking about the future of the institution, aiming ever higher and progressively capitalizing on the opportunities placed before it.

Axiom #4: *Leaders of successful ministries lead from the front.* One may manage from the rear, but leaders must be out in front. One cannot lead from behind. You can drive cattle, but you cannot drive sheep; they must be led. Leadership cannot be provided by remote, or at a distance. Christian leaders are actively engaged in the work of the ministry, and we must set the example and raise the level of expectation for those following us. Leaders must never be perceived as asking their followers to do something they are unwilling to do. The principle of MBWA, Management By Walking Around, applies to leadership as well. One cannot lead by residing in his office and engaging the congregational or organizational reality from a distance. Only when an administrator is perceived as being in touch and always moving forward at the head of the institution can he provide genuine leadership.

Axiom #5: *Leaders of successful ministries invest in the development of others.* The acknowledgement that God's call is too great to accomplish alone, and that others may be equally or more qualified to fulfill part of God's ministry in the congregation or Christian organization, requires that leaders provide attention to the personal and professional development of others. This is a hallmark of facilitative leadership. Christian administrators realize that people are more than resources and that they cannot be treated like inanimate supplies for the institution's machinery. For example, to run a pen out of ink or a copier out of paper, only to open another box of supplies and get a new pen or ream of paper, can *never* be equated with burning out an individual in God's service, simply seeking someone else as a replacement once they are used up. This would be an immoral and non-Christian practice.

Leaders who are Christian must provide pastoral and professional oversight to those serving with them. They should commit to the development of others. The lone ranger syndrome of the shepherd approach may lead to premature burnout, but the ranger approach requires a commitment to continual, rejuvenated service to the congregation or Christian organization.

Axiom #6: *Leaders of successful ministries value accountability.* Engaging in a routine practice of evaluation and assessment is critical for Christian leadership. It is a tragic flaw to assume theory will translate perfectly into practice. Leaders must hold themselves accountable for their performance and hold others likewise accountable. Leaders cannot assume that previous performance is equivalent to current performance. In short, accountability for one's efficiency and effectiveness must always receive concise, targeted feedback with an accompanying plan for developmental initiatives when necessary. Under performers not only hinder their own work, but potentially influence the entire congregation or Christian organization by setting a poor example, lowering levels of expectation, and causing others to neglect their responsibilities. In short, a lack of accountability will lead to institutional crisis and failure.

Axiom #7: *Leaders of successful ministries give attention to the core values and mission.* Regardless of how far a congregation or Christian organization advances, it cannot lose sight of its mission and values.

These are the *basics* for the institution. One must learn the alphabet, how to phonically sound out words, how to read, how to spell, and eventually how to construct sentences, paragraphs, and write papers. Regardless of how far one ascends up the academic ladder, one cannot forget the alphabet and continue to maintain his present level of success. Often in the midst of the hurried administrative agenda and ever-expanding list of responsibilities, it is easy to forget the basic rudiments of their institutional identity, direction, and reason for existence. Institutional vision casting, values clarification, and identity building are ongoing, lifelong processes, not one-time events.

Conclusion

Leadership is a paradoxical concept. It is almost always readily recognized when we encounter it, but on the other hand it eludes precise definition and classification. It is self-evident, but is difficult to capture fully in a theory and paradigm. As Christian administrators in congregations and Christian organizations, we are called to be leaders. We will bring to it our own character, including our personality, competencies, and deficiencies. We will be given a context, a position and title, from which to provide leadership. It will require us to exegete the institution, its corporate ethos, and the individual readiness level of those serving alongside us. Ultimately, we place our trust not in ourselves, not the institution, but as Luke wrote, "And when they had appointed elders for them in every church, having prayed with fasting, they commended them to the Lord *in whom they had believed*" (Acts 14:23 NASB, emphasis added).

BY
MICHAEL ANTHONY

Chapter 21

Working with Boards and Committees

SOMEONE ONCE SAID the greatest challenge in ministry is working with people. "You can't work with them and you can't work without them." It is true that working with people adds a considerable challenge to the process of getting things done. However, it is clearly the teaching of Scripture, and it makes sense because we maximize our effectiveness when we train and equip others for the task of doing ministry. God tells us in Ephesians 4:11–16 that one of the major reasons for providing all believers with a spiritual gift is for the express purpose of employing them in the business of getting them involved in ministry—whether it be through evangelism, teaching, acts of mercy and compassion, or administration. The gifts are given so that others may share in the responsibility of doing the work of the ministry.

In order for that work to be done with some degree of coordinated effort, boards and committees have been created. These entities have been the focus of frustration and disdain by many people over the years. We will discuss the benefits and drawbacks of working with these groups later in the chapter. For now, suffice it to say that working with teams such as boards and committees is both biblical and expedient. What we want to discuss with you in this chapter is how to effectively manage the process and share some tips on how to make this a beneficial experience for you as the ministry leader and for those who serve on the boards or committees with you.

The Biblical Basis of Boards and Committees

The Old Testament provides us with our earliest glimpse of ministry teams. The elders of Israel formed a body which provided godly wisdom and advice to the congregation. Moses recognized that he was not sufficient to attend to all the needs of the assembly, so he appointed mature men to listen to the disputes of the people and to govern them as they deemed appropriate (Exod. 18:13–27). These elders became the nation's leaders and continued to serve the people with a variety of responsibilities such as settling legal disputes and representing the people before God during important religious festivals.

In the New Testament, the best evidence for working through groups is demonstrated by Jesus himself as he selected a group of twelve men with whom he delegated responsibilities and prepared for ministry service. This "committee of twelve" would serve as a microcosm of community for conducting ministry ventures. Beyond this grouping he also selecting a subcommittee of three disciples who became the inner circle of his ministry.

After the ascension of Christ, these men appointed to the task others who were viewed as spiritually mature and attuned to the leading of the Holy Spirit in their lives. One of the first such ministry committees came in the early days of the church. The non-Jewish believers felt like second-class citizens when they discovered their widows were not receiving an equal share of food at the daily distribution. The twelve apostles gathered together to consider this claim and came to a greater realization that they should set priorities to their own ministry to avoid being brought into settling such secondary disputes. They commanded the body to appoint seven men who were well regarded as spiritually mature believers to oversee the daily distribution of food. This body became know as the first deacon board or committee in the church (Acts 6:1–7). This trend continued with the development of elder boards or committees in the churches that Paul established during his frequent missionary journeys. It would be safe to say that committees and boards have played a vital role in the life of the church ever since.

The biblical evidence of working with boards and committees has provided the church and religious nonprofit organizations with a paradigm for effective administration and stewardship of ministry resources. Whether functioning as a board of trustees in a Christian school, a board of directors for a mission or relief agency, or a financial auditing committee at a homeless shelter, these groups of caring people play a vital role in keeping the ministry on track toward the successful accomplishment of its institutional mission. Across North America religious nonprofit organizations are required to establish a board of directors (consisting of at least three members) who oversee the affairs of the organization.

In a church this body may be called by any of several names (trustees, elders, deacons, etc.), but regardless of the name it generally assumes the same function. It provides a link between the interests of the government (i.e., fiduciary and legal) and the members who have established it. In a church, the senior pastor may be an official member of the board or committee, but in many cases he is not. In most cases he serves as an ex-officio member depending on how the bylaws are written. The essential members of the corporate board (which is what the government calls a church board) will be a president, vice president, and a secretary-treasurer. More will be discussed regarding the structural composition of church boards later in the chapter.

Roles and Responsibilities of the Governing Board

This chapter is being written for a broad focus of appeal which will take us beyond the confines of the local church. For this reason, examples will be given of boards and committees which involve nonprofit organizations as well. In many cases, the principles that are applicable for the church board also apply to a religious nonprofit organization such as a Christian school, camp, or other form of parachurch institution. In order to appeal to the widest audience, examples will be given for both church application and other nonprofit organizations—likewise regarding the title for the leader of the board or committee. Some refer to this individual as a *chairman* while others prefer the name *chairperson*. In an age of inclusive language, the nongender specific term of *chair* is also used. Readers will need to take some liberty in making application of this term to their specific context.

What comprises the roles and responsibilities of the governing board depends on the nature of the organization. What elders do as they lead their church may be somewhat different from members of a school's trustee board. Likewise, a camp board may have somewhat different responsibilities from those who serve on a mission board. However, this is not to say that they do not all share some degree of common duties. There is a good deal of overlap in what they do and how they serve. These include the following:[1]

1. Drawing on the history and traditions of the organization's stated reason for being, the board interprets and sustains the mission of the organization, ensuring that each department and component of the organization is consistent with the stated mission.

2. The board represents the interests and concerns of the members whose resources allow the organization to pursue its mission.

3. The board selects the chief executive or professional director and then provides guidance, support, and accountability to this individual.

4. The board translates faith, traditions, beliefs, mission, and the institution's core values into policies and rules that guide the executive director and his or her senior staff in their activities.

5. The board works with the executive director to develop long-range plans, goals, and objectives for the organization and then monitors progress toward the completion of those goals.

6. The board is responsible for ensuring that the organization has the financial resources necessary to fulfill its mission and goals.

7. The board is responsible for ensuring that all of its decisions and actions meet the requirements of ethics and laws, including both civil and religious law where applicable.

8. The board ensures that the organization uses all of its resources, including financial and personnel, as efficiently and effectively as possible.

Board, Committee, Task Force, or Advisory Group: What's in a Name?

What one organization calls a board, another may refer to as a committee. What appears on one organization's chart as a task force may appear on another organization's chart as an advisory group. Much like trying to define the difference between a goal and an objective, it may come down more to the person making the distinction rather than any definitive source. The difference between a board and committee is a matter of authority. Boards have more authority than committees, and generally the latter are subordinate to the former. Virtually every board is divided into various subcommittees. These working groups of men and women form the basis of getting things done between board meetings. For example, in a church context, the elder board may be further divided into subcommittees with an elder as the chairman of each committee. Such committees may include finance, facilities, personnel, missions, etc. An example of this type of structure is illustrated in Figure 21.1.

Figure 21.1

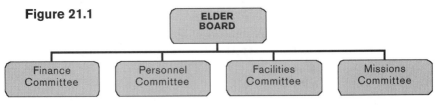

The work of the elder board is carried on during the month by the various committees, and then each committee chair (elder) reports back at the next elder meeting what is happening in his area of responsibility. The committees do not have any authority in and of themselves but serve to implement the policies of the board. They can make recommendations to the board which may include actions to be taken, policies to be formulated, or procedures to be modified, but the committees themselves report directly to the board. This allows a board to make use of the individual expertise of its members. A board member who is a building contractor by profession would be a logical person to chair the facilities committee. A chartered public accountant would chair the finance committee, etc.

A board can provide a level of engagement with an aspect of the board's larger responsibilities or with a specific issue that is difficult to maintain with the full board. The finance committee is a good example of this. The full board does not relinquish its responsibilities for the planning or oversight of an organization's financial well-being by creating a finance committee. Rather, by creating the committee, the board is calling on a few highly engaged and knowledgeable board members to monitor financial issues in greater detail and in greater depth on the board's behalf. The committee enables financial monitoring to occur between board meetings and makes it possible for complex aspects of financial performance to be properly understood and presented to the board in a cogent manner.[2]

At the beginning of each year the board gives a charge to each committee about the work that needs to be accomplished. Since the board is the only entity within the organization that has the "big picture," it falls to them to make the committee assignments. Each committee chair (also a member of the board) takes this charge from the board to the committee and directs the workload and timetable of the committee toward the accomplishment of its task. In this way the committee does not develop its own agenda and spend countless hours investing in completing a task, only to find out that the board neither wants nor appreciates the fruit of its labor. If this occurs, it is generally due to poor committee leadership and will result in hard feelings and tension between the board and the committee.

The work of a committee may be ongoing and continual. If the board has an assignment that is specific in nature and has a limited time frame attached (e.g., a building project, a conflict to be resolved, etc.), it may choose to create a task force. This group of individuals is assigned the responsibility of overseeing the particular assignment, and it is dissolved as soon as the task has been accomplished. Therefore, a task force is far more limited in nature, scope, and time than a committee. However, the task force is still accountable to the board and generally has a board member as its chairman.

One of the quickest ways to kill an organization's forward momentum is to increase the number of committees and then delegate visionary tasks to them. Committees are not by nature vision-building entities. Most committees are designed around the concept of control and maintenance and are by nature slow to respond to change. It has been recommended by a number of authoritative sources that all committees should be terminated at the end of each year and be made to justify their reason for continuing existence.

Some committees are obvious and need to have a continuous shelf life (e.g., finance, facilities, personnel, etc.). But others may have outlived their usability or perhaps have added members that have become counterproductive to the original intent of the committee. In such cases, they are terminated at the end of the year and not reconstituted. This allows the board to have a face-saving means of controlling the natural proliferation of committees.

Orienting New Members

Whether it is a board, committee, task force, or any other group of interested individuals, it is critical to the success of the group that all new members be oriented and "brought up to speed" about their responsibilities and duties. In many cases, the only qualifications volunteer members will have are their desire to serve. Beyond that, they will need to be trained and prepared for their role. "Part of the problem lies in the word *orientation* which smacks of learning where the lavatory, the coffee pot, and the desk supplies are located. Adequate preparation to shoulder the burden of strategic leadership requires something a bit more substantial. What is called for is job training, though the term may be offensive to new members who are accomplished in their occupations or in other board service."[3]

Probably the best person to conduct the orientation of new members is the chairman. This individual has most likely served on the board or committee for an extended length of time and is well acquainted with the procedural processes involved. He or she will no doubt have a complete history of the organization and will have a clear understanding of its mission, core values, strategic goals, and operational plans. Each of these elements of orientation are theologically informed, and hence orientation seeks to assure that participants are rooted in the theological perspective of the institution. This reiterates their conceptualization of the organization as Christian.

The orientation process should encompass three purposes. First, it should provide the member with a theological basis for the organization and for how the organization will operate. Second, it should provide the members with sufficient background information to give them some degree of historical context for decision making. Finally, the new member should be made aware of the process and procedural issues involved as a board member. Some discussion needs to take place about the tension between a board's role to set policy and the staff's role of implementing that policy.

The second purpose of the orientation is to provide a forum for the new member to ask questions. No one likes to ask questions in the context of a group if he feels he might be perceived as asking "dumb questions." Yet, most questions that a board member asks are not dumb at all. They reflect insight and wisdom. Generally, a question will be asked by a new member, and other members in the group who have been on the board for some length of time may respond by saying, "That's a good question. I've often wondered about that too." But they never had the courage to ask it themselves.

The orientation seminar should also include the organization's director. Together, the board chair and the executive provide the new members with an overview of the mission of the organization, its core values, annual goals and objectives, major policies and procedures where applicable to the new member's area of responsibility, and a review of the budget. The new member should have the freedom to ask questions such as the following:

- How long has it been since the board examined the organization's mission statement?
- Who was involved in deciding the core values?
- Has a long-range strategic planning document been developed for the organization? If not, why not?
- What are the organization's expectations of me about fundraising?
- How long has it been since the executive's job performance was evaluated, and how often is this conducted by the board?
- From a financial point of view, how is the organization currently situated, and do you foresee any significant changes in the near future?
- Is any litigation pending and has there been any recently? If so, are you at liberty to discuss it with me now?

During this session the new members should be given copies of the organization's policy manual so they have an opportunity to review it prior to attending any meetings. They should be walked through the organizational chart and provided with a brief overview of the executive's span of control. Regarding the method of new member orientation, some organizations use a buddy system, pairing a new board member with an experienced one. "This can be very helpful, as it compels the experienced board member to be as knowledgeable as possible in order to accurately teach the new one."[4]

Orientation and preparation of the new board member is important, but the process of training does not stop with this initial meeting. Ongoing board training should also take place on an annual basis. Viewed as professional board development, an organization that conducts such in-service training is serious about the quality of performance and gains the respect and admiration of its members, the staff of the organization, and the constituents who have put their trust in the organization's leadership.

Conducting Meetings with a Purpose

Boards and committees are generally comprised of people who are leaders in the organization's constituency. They desire to serve because they are committed to the mission of the organization and want to see it grow and flourish. Few people choose to serve on a board or committee just to see the organization plateau in growth and become insolvent. Meetings should serve a purpose and stay on course. An agenda should be developed and distributed at least one week before the meeting. Any supporting documents and reports should accompany the agenda as well. This allows each of the members to review them and conduct their own research before the meeting.

Once the agenda has been distributed and the meeting has begun, further items of business should be restricted from being added unless everyone agrees in advance. This prevents any last-minute surprises and develops trust among the members of the group. When last-minute discussion items are added and people have not been allowed to process their opinions in advance, they lose trust with the leadership of the group and quickly grow disenfranchised with the process.

Meetings should occur only when there is a reasonable purpose and the agenda has been clearly formulated in advance. If neither occurs, then the chairman should not hesitate to cancel the meeting or postpone it until a more appropriate time. Conducting a meeting simply because it is on the calendar is a surefire way to take the passion out of people's desire to serve. "Listless, ineffective committees can infect and detract from an entire board's performance. How long will a board member believe that his or her participation on the board is of value if meetings don't matter and committee assignments are an empty gesture?"[5] If the board or committee assignments are meaningful and the meeting follows the agenda, it ensures a more meaningful experience for everyone.

In addition to the previous guidelines, it is also essential that the leader of the board or committee follow some prescribed patterns of protocol. The most popular means of this is *Robert's Rule of Order.* Although most organizations choose to use this reference as their guide, many have been highly successful in creating their own set of guidelines to follow. The essence of either approach is to think through in advance the procedures that will be followed in order to set reasonable boundaries on discussion, encourage civility between members, and have an agreed-upon method for procuring votes. These rules should assist the organization in moving forward toward the successful accomplishment of its goals. They should not be viewed as technical or legal loopholes for the purpose of thwarting an unassuming member of the group.

Board and committee meetings that are most effective are characterized by mutual respect and honest discussion. If board members are intimidated or restricted from asking the tough questions, then the purposes of the board are undermined. Each member plays a vital part and should be respected for his or her contribution. Each individual should be encouraged to participate in the discussion, ask pertinent questions, and share ideas or opinions freely. Each member should feel the freedom to vote his or her conscience even if these views are not supported by the majority. If there is disagreement it should be done in such a manner as not to be offensive or disagreeable. Board members should learn to separate the issues being discussed from the personalities discussing them. Each must learn to "agree to disagree" while still holding an attitude of humility, mutual respect, and cooperation.[6]

Not enough can be said about the importance of keeping the meeting on track in terms of time frame for discussion. The board chair needs to take a firm hand to balance between the need for each member to have sufficient time to discuss the proposal at hand and yet prevent any one person from monopolizing the discussion. When sufficient discussion has transpired, the chair needs to cut off discussion and proceed toward a vote. Keep to the posted time frame stipulated in the agenda. If the chair does not maintain control of the meeting in this regard, members will become frustrated and lose commitment. They will find reasons not to attend future meetings, and interest in participation will wane.

One final thought should be addressed about the physical surroundings of the meeting itself. Numerous studies have shown that the physical surroundings of a meeting contribute or detract from the meaningfulness and effectiveness of the meeting, yet many nonprofit organizations choose to ignore such well-known findings. School boards that meet in a classroom while sitting in chairs designed for children violate this principle. The following list should provide the organization's chair and executive with reasonable guidelines to ensure that the physical surroundings of the meeting contribute to its effectiveness.[7]

1. A quiet, light, temperature-controlled room with adequate working space and comfortable chairs is an essential component of a

productive meeting. Many organizations feel compelled to conduct board and committee meetings on their premises, regardless of whether the organization's location is accessible and centrally located and whether suitable space is available. It is not necessary to use an organization's facility for meetings if participants can be more comfortable elsewhere.

2. Start on time, and end on time. If meetings consistently begin ten to fifteen minutes late, people will start arriving ten to fifteen minutes late, resulting in meetings dragging on past their scheduled end or important agenda items being left unfinished.

3. Adhere to a timed agenda, but maintain flexibility. All participants should share the responsibility for moving the business along. Peer pressure can be a deterrent to disruptive or distracting behavior from group members.

Establishing Boundaries:
Policy Formation and Implementation

One of the most important distinctions that can occur between members of the board and the staff of the organization is between policy formation and policy implementation. It is the purpose and privilege of the board to establish policy. These policies guide the organization toward the successful accomplishment of its goals and objectives for the year. Where many organizations get into trouble is when the line is crossed from policy formation to policy implementation. It is the responsibility of the organization's staff to implement the policy that has been created by the board. The staff do not create policy. It is their job to implement it. This may seem like a simple distinction, but it is probably the single largest cause of tension and conflict between the board and its organization.

An example of violating this simple principle is seen when a board member arrives at the church to drop off his child for a youth retreat. The board member doesn't recognize the counselors and informs the youth pastor that he will have to get different counselors because the ones he is planning on using are not members of the church. It is the opinion of this board member that only church members should be authorized to counsel the youth, since their theological beliefs as members have been examined and affirmed. This throws last-minute panic into the plans of the youth pastor. Since this is a board member, he must now consider canceling the trip because it is too late to recruit counselors who are also church members.

The youth pastor quickly calls the senior pastor for advice. Upon further examination, it is discovered that there is no official church policy requiring counselors to be church members. It is only the opinion of this board member that they should be. What is the youth pastor to do? How will this effect the relationship between the youth pastor and the board member if he continues with his retreat? Who has the authority to make the final decision in this case? Does the senior pastor intervene and tell the board member that he has no authority over the matter? You can imagine the conflicts that will be addressed at the next church board meeting! Numerous conflicts of this nature get played out on a regular basis all across North America each week.

This unfortunate situation can be avoided with a proper understanding of the boundaries that should exist between board members and staff members when it comes to church policies. The board member only serves as a board member when he comes to the board meeting. He is not functioning as a board member when he drops off his child at the youth event. In this capacity, he is a parent and does not have any authority over the youth pastor. If the board member sees something that concerns him, his job is to contact the board chair and discuss his concerns directly with him. If further action is required, the board chairman then calls the senior pastor and brings the matter to his attention. It is the senior pastor's responsibility to ensure that all of the church's policies are being implemented.

If there is no policy that counselors must also be church members, then that is the end of discussion unless the board member requests the matter to be put on the next board meeting's agenda. At that time, a proposal may be brought to the board about the formulation of such a policy. The time to discuss the matter is at the board meeting, not the church parking lot minutes before departure.

This violation of boundaries occurs frequently at Christian schools where board members (who are also parents) come into the classroom of their child and presume to instruct the teacher how they will perform their duties. School board members who abuse their role should be admonished, and if such actions continue, they should be removed from their position. Once again: boards establish policy and staff implement it. If the staff are not implementing the policy correctly, then the board holds the highest member of the staff (senior pastor, school principal, president, etc.) accountable. This individual must give an account and ensure that every policy that has been approved by the board is being implemented. If the policies are being ignored, then the senior staff member should be admonished, and if the problem is not corrected, subsequently removed from office.

Board and Director Relations

This is a natural place to discuss the relationship that exists between a board and its director. In the context of the local church, the senior pastor serves as the director of the organization. In a school context it is the principal. At a camp or other nonprofit organization it is the president or executive director. In the literature this individual is referred to as the chief executive officer (CEO). Though many have provided arguments why a senior pastor is not a CEO but rather serves as a shepherd, servant, etc., for purposes of our discussion, I will use the term CEO in order to be more inclusive about the leader "at the top." The CEO has the difficult job of maintaining a tenuous balance between board members, staff members, and members of the organization (e.g., congregation, campers, alumni, etc.). It is a task which comes with plenty of risk and peril.

The key to maintaining a healthy relationship between the board and the director is communication. Much like a marriage, the relationships that function well over time are the ones that are committed to open dialogue. The slogan "No surprise up or down" is a fitting reminder that the board does not like to be surprised by the actions of the director and likewise the director should not be surprised by what appears on the agenda of the board meeting. Catching people by surprise leads to distrust, disloyalty, and an undermining of commitment. The board chair and the director should maintain constant communication with each other as appropriate. This can be accomplished through a weekly phone call, an occasional e-mail, or perhaps a quick meeting during the week. It is in each other's best interest to foster a healthy dialogue on all matters pertinent to the organization.

When the director is made aware of a situation that could cause a concern for the board, he or she should call the board chair immediately and inform him or her of the various details. It is best if the chair hears the matter first from the director rather than from angry constituents. In the same way, if a board member has a legitimate concern about the actions of the director or a member of his or her staff, it is the responsibility of the board chair to bring the matter to the director's attention prior to any discussion at the board meeting.

The Board's Role in Long-Range Planning

Every organization needs to take a serious look at the future and prepare its resources to meet that future with intentional planning. Failure to do so threatens the existence of the organization as a whole. With that in mind, one of the first questions to be addressed is who actually does the planning. The answer to that question may depend on the nature of the resources at hand. For some churches a persuasive senior pastor provides the vision, and the board provides assistance to bring those dreams to pass. In other nonprofit organizations the board may prefer to bring in an outside consultant who guides them through the process of long-range planning. A third approach is for a subcommittee of the board to prepare an initial long-range plan that is presented to the board for consideration and discussion. Either way, it is essential for the board to be an integral part of the process. In the long run, it is the responsibility of the governing board to make the final decisions about the future of the ministry.

There are two essential steps for conducting this long-range strategic planning. The first step is to assess the various social, cultural, demographic, and environmental trends and their possible impact on the organization. It may seem like trying to gaze into a crystal ball to predict the future. But given the right set of data and information that is available to most organizations with a little research, it is a process that is essential.[8]

The second step is to take a serious look at the organization itself and reassess its mission, vision, and core values. Having done that, the board needs to be sure that its methods of accomplishing that mission are still viable. This is done on a periodic basis to ensure that the organization is staying true to its initial reason for creation. If changes are needed to the mission, then it is done intentionally after a good deal of forethought and planning rather than as a result of slow drift and organizational complacency. At the end of this step a document is prepared by the staff to specify progress on existing programs. This could include the following:[9]

- Statement of purpose: what the basic intent of the program is.
- Current status: what is now being done.
- Planned course of action: what changes are to be undertaken, and when.
- Targets: what points of measurable achievement, at what stated times, are set.
- Administration: who is going to do what and at what added cost.

This document provides the board with the information it needs to assess current performance and make decisions about the funding of current programs or making necessary adjustments. It will also provide them with the information it needs to make decisions about the initiation of new programs as well.

The end of the long-range planning process should involve the creation of a comprehensive document which specifies the various programs that are integral to the operation of the ministry with specific targets dates and measures. It should also identify people who are responsible (and accountable) for the successful implementation of the various programs. From the board's perspective, only the director is held accountable for the final outcome. However, by specifying other people (by name or department), the final document is a more accurate representation of the team-oriented nature of ministry.

Many organizations have found it beneficial to attend a long-range planning retreat in order to accomplish the goals of the planning process. The long-range planning process cannot be accomplished in one evening after work in the church conference room. Long hours of discussion and review of documents are essential to the integrity of the process. This should not be rushed. Many churches and religious nonprofits prefer to get away from the distractions of the immediate surroundings and rent a conference room at a local hotel or retreat center and conduct the meeting over the course of the weekend. In such circumstances, the format of the weekend would include the following elements:

Friday Evening. Spend some time in prayer asking God for guidance and direction. Enjoy a meal together and then begin reviewing any documents containing updates of local social, cultural, demographic, and environmental trends. In essence, you are asking, "What is happening in our area and how can we get ahead of the curve and prepare to meet these upcoming changes?"

Saturday Morning. Review the mission, vision, and core values of the organization and make any necessary adjustments. In addition, review what was accomplished during the past period of performance. You are asking, "Who are we and is this who we want to continue to be in the years ahead?" "How did we do last year regarding the accomplishment of our previous goals and objectives?"

Saturday Afternoon. Begin with the report from the director or board subcommittee about proposals for future direction. During this time the board is discussing the merits of various options and possibilities. Obviously resources are limited and decisions must be made about what can be done and what will have to be postponed or left for others to accomplish. During this session the board is answering the questions: "What challenges do we want to accept and what programs do we want to discontinue, change, or begin?"

Saturday Evening. The board meets to discuss the specifics about the new ministry ventures. This will include discussions about who will be responsible, what budgetary resources will need to be allocated, and what goals and objectives will be expected of this program. In this final session, questions are be asked such as "Who is going to take on this new responsibility?" "How much will this cost, and how will the funds be appropriated?" "What will be the measures of success for this new venture?"

Once this planning retreat is over, the secretary prepares a final document which specifies the details that were agreed upon. This document is circulated to those in attendance to be sure that it accurately represents the discussion and decisions that were made. The final draft of this record becomes the long-range planning document which is reviewed and updated each year at the annual planning retreat.

Some board members may be hesitant to become involved in the long-range planning process because it has been viewed as tedious, time-consuming, and sometimes contentious in nature.[10] It is true that planning does take time, but so does correcting the failures that take place due to lack of planning. Expectations regarding board member involvement in the long-range planning process should be communicated in the board member recruitment and orientation process. It should come as no surprise that each board member is expected to participate in the long-range planning retreat each year. Involvement by every member is essential for group ownership in the decision making.

The Role of the Board in Evaluation

Since you may end up serving as a member of a church board or committee, it may be appropriate here to include a section on one of the most important and difficult duties of a board member. This involves conducting either programmatic or personnel evaluations. There are several understandable reasons for this. First, nonprofit ministries generally have multiple performance criteria. Criteria for measuring success in the children's area will not be the same for measuring success in the missions area. Each will have their own performance criteria. Second, there is a lack of comparability between churches and other nonprofit organizations. What a megachurch does across town cannot be a viable standard of comparison for all other churches in the community.

Third, since the mission of churches and nonprofits is service, financial measures of performance are not always the best criteria for determining effectives. Fourth, there is an indirect relationship between cost and benefits provided. For example, just because a church has one youth leader with fifty young people in attendance does not automatically mean hiring another youth leader will produce an additional fifty young people. Finally, evaluation activities should not take so much time and energy that they take away from the day-to-day responsibilities of conducting the ministry itself. This limitation of staff resources is reasonable to assume and expect.[11]

One of the more challenging parts of being a board member at a church or nonprofit organization comes when it is time to evaluate the performance of the director. Evaluating the programs of the ministry is the responsibility of the director. However, the responsibility of evaluating the director falls to the board. It is one of the most important duties in their job description. This evaluation should be fair, comprehensive, and conducted at regular intervals.

It generally works best if there is a smaller committee appointed for the initial task of conducting incremental reviews. Many churches and nonprofits conduct a review on a quarterly basis as opposed to waiting until the end of the year. This committee, sometimes referred to as an executive committee or director's evaluation committee, meets periodically with the director to review the progress which has been made since their last meeting. Using the ministry by objectives method (see chapter 8), this committee receives a report from the director which identifies progress (or the lack thereof) on the goals and objectives which have been agreed upon prior to the beginning of the year. These markers are reviewed, and a discussion takes place with the director about his overall sense of how things are going. Several areas need to be covered in this meeting:

Personal. Time should be spent asking the director about health issues (physical, emotional, spiritual, relational, etc.). This is a time for the board to express their genuine concern for the well-being of the director beyond the work-related issues. If things come up that are a concern to the committee, they should seek to provide whatever resources are needed to help the director maintain peak performance. Some sample questions that should be asked would include:

- How are you feeling these days?
- Are you getting the time off that you need to maintain personal health and happiness?
- Are you able to enjoy time away with your family?
- Are you experiencing anything that is producing an undue amount of stress in your life?
- Are you giving an appropriate amount of time to your spiritual disciplines?

The spirit of these questions should be focused toward helping, providing support, expressing genuine care, and establishing a safe environment for sharing. Honest evaluation and openness will not exist outside an environment of safety and trust.

Relational. This is a time to reflect on their working relationships. Leading a ministry is not easy. There are times when making a decision will put the director at odds with those who otherwise honor and respect them. Some decisions can isolate a leader and cause emotional pain and heartache. This is particularly true when the director has been involved in managing conflict, conducting staff performance reviews, attending crises in the church (e.g., funerals, unplanned hospital visits, weddings, etc.), leading high profile programs (e.g., building campaigns, special conferences, long-range planning retreats, etc.) and during the development of the annual budget. Some time should be spent assessing the relational health of the director because it is critical to the successful foundation of all other areas within a team-focused ministry.

Performance. This third aspect involves walking through the agreed-upon goals and objectives and assessing progress. Where there is cause for celebration, the director should be affirmed and congratulated. Where progress has been less than expected, the director should be asked what additional resources are needed to provided assistance. A wise director will come to this meeting with a list of options and contingency plans already in mind. It will be the board committee's job to provide them where possible.

This is also a time to review the list of goals and objectives to see whether or not the projections have come to pass. Remember that these goals and objectives were developed with a degree of anticipated conjecture, so this is a good time to see whether or not those trends did indeed occur (e.g., "last year we thought the military base was going to be shutting down but instead they redeployed more people to the base"). Where goals and objectives need to be modified due to unforeseen circumstances, they should be revised and presented to the entire board for approval at the next meeting. Caution should be used, however, not to lower the bar of expected performance just because the director has not been able to provide proper supervision of the organization's resources.

At the end of the day it is the duty and responsibility of the board to ensure that the director is doing the job he or she was hired to do. If the director's performance is inadequate or consistently below expectations, this committee should bring the entire board into the loop and discuss what steps are necessary for a change. This may involve a sabbatical period for the director, a forced leave of absence, termination, or retirement. These are difficult and emotionally volatile decisions to make but necessary for the long-term success of the ministry.

Conclusion

There are few ways an individual can impact an organization as much as by participating on the board. As an elder, deacon, or in some other capacity, board members play a critical role in the long-term effectiveness of the organization's mission. If the board is to do an effective job, members must identify and stay focused on strategic priorities, use board and committee meetings intentionally, structure the board to accomplish consequential matters of interest, and acquire information that will inform for long-range planning. These are the critical tasks of a board which will ensure vitality and meaningful service.[12] "In sum, board members are limited part-timers with limited time and imperfect knowledge of the organization."[13] Though limited in a number of respects, they represent the future of the enterprise. Scripture clearly teaches that a vital link should exist between those who serve on the board of an organization and those who serve as its staff leaders. A partnership between the two is not only an ideal; it is an imperative.

PART 6

EVALUATING

Providing constructive feedback on an individual's performance is like trying to dance in a minefield. Everything can be going fine and suddenly without warning, the land mine goes off—causing a great deal of collateral damage. Performance reviews and evaluations can leave the Christian administrator feeling shell-shocked and hesitant to walk into that field again. However, our responsibility and duty is to travel down that path time and time again. Our job and the success of our ministry depends on it. That being the case, we need to travel wisely and try to find out where the land mines are located before we end up stepping on them. This unit addresses such issues. Providing honest feedback and assessment of performance is difficult to do, but it must occur at regular intervals.

In this unit there are two chapters which highlight the focus of our reviews: personnel and programs. Each has their own share of difficulties in terms of evaluation. In both cases, people and programs can be attached to strongly held emotional beliefs about how something should be done. When it isn't done according to these expectations, trouble can brew just over the horizon.

"Performance reviews stir anxiety in all of us, managers and employees alike. Partly to blame is the infrequency of such discussions. Like the child who fears going to the doctor once a year for a shot, we make the waiting game worse than the event."[1] It doesn't have to be so painful to go through or lead a personnel performance review as long as you have done your homework and collected the information you need. However, if you choose to neglect doing the hard work ahead of time, you may pay the price during or after the review. That hard price can include a loss of employee or volunteer morale, a decline in respect that others have for your leadership, their resentment or eventual resignation, or perhaps even being named in a workplace lawsuit. The latter alternative is fast becoming a growing trend even in Christian organizations. If only the manager had done due diligence and collected the necessary documentation before the personnel review had been conducted.

Such stress and anxiety have led many Christian managers to concede that they are not worth the work involved, but such reasoning is shortsighted—for both the ministry and the people involved. There are a number of reasons why conducting performance evaluations are valuable.[2] The first reason they are helpful is they provide us with an incentive to plan and set goals. It is nearly impossible to evaluate performance without some idea about where you expect to be a quarter or a year from now. Without goals and objectives you have no basis for future evaluation.

A second value in performance reviews relates to worker motivation. Knowing that a performance review is coming up generally motivates workers to meet certain expectations, at least in the short term. The meeting that occurs should provide impetus for high-achieving workers to continue their excellent performance for many months to come. As a rule, people prefer to receive good news rather than bad news, so conducting reviews can help motivate people to perform better for longer periods of time compared to not having any at all.

Third, conducting periodic reviews allows the manager and employee to get better acquainted. During these times of discussion new discoveries can be made about what employees like about their jobs and what they don't. Realizing that it is not always feasible to write a job description only for an employee's preferred activities, it does allow the manager to perhaps revise a job description toward the employees' successes rather than toward their failures.

The final reason why personnel evaluations are so beneficial is because the meeting allows the manager to ask if there are any sources of discontent such as an unclear job description, vague expectations, working conditions not conducive to high achievement, resources that need to be better allocated, or training that needs to be provided.

Performance reviews are critical for success for all entities involved. The employees should walk away from such a meeting with a sense that they know beyond any doubt how they are doing in their jobs. The manager has had a valuable encounter with an employee or volunteer and has taken the time to understand the working conditions and expectations of their subordinate. The ministry benefits from such an encounter through improved job performance and productivity. Chapter 22 expands on many of these issues and will provide the Christian manager with many valuable insights into the process of conducting performance reviews.

The final chapter in the book relates to the topic of programmatic reviews. Countless churches and nonprofit ministries across North America waste valuable resources each year conducting programs that meet few needs yet require excessive amounts of time, energy, and money. The reasons why it is so difficult to stop conducting certain programs in our ministry is because we have failed to take the time to establish measurable criteria to determine whether or not a program has been or continues to be successful. In the context of ministry, success is measured differently than in a corporate world.

For example, at what point do you decide that conducting the annual servicemen's appreciation Sunday is no longer beneficial if the local military base closed years ago and there are no longer any active duty personnel attending your church? When do you allow a program which was started years ago to meet a legitimate need to die because that need no longer exists? Can you discontinue the midweek service (which few people attend) in order to develop a small group program instead? For many people, canceling the midweek service is tantamount to leaving the faith. Tradition can be a difficult hurdle to overcome and often results in confrontation.

Many ministry leaders live the hope that the problem person or situation will simply go away. "However, most problems that require confrontation do not go away. They are infections: if we ignore them, they get worse. Soon that nagging pain in one toe becomes blood poisoning."[3]

What we need are specific, meaningful, and biblical measures for program evaluation. "It has long been understood in organizations that when you want to improve something, you first must measure it . . . measure is an integral part of continuous improvement."[4] These standards must be based on agreed-upon measures even though they may be hard to create. It is difficult to suggest that a program be discontinued if no criteria was set in advance to measure its success. Many churches are faced with such decisions every year.

At what point do we discontinue holding a Vacation Bible School if most of the congregation goes on vacation leaving few workers available? Should the effort and energy be put into the AWANA program that operates during the school year instead? Should the church van be sold and the youth be asked to rent a van each time they need one, or should we continue to fund the high maintenance bills that occur each year? Is the youth choir really meeting a need in the congregation, or is it simply the pet project of the retired music teacher in the church? Who gets to make these decisions and under what conditions? Walking into such emotionally laden discussions has brought about the demise of many a ministry leader.

The final chapter provides some helpful insights about how such criteria should be formulated. It is the hope of the author that the ministry leader will have the necessary tools to establish meaningful criteria for program evaluations. It is through such evaluations that we perform our God-given responsibilities of exercising proper stewardship over the resources he has provided for us. We can't do everything, so decisions have to be made about what is reasonable, needed, and doable in our particular ministries. Not every church can have a full menu of ministry programs. Navigating those tough decisions allows the ministry leader to move ahead through difficult days of increasing needs coupled with decreasing resources.

Evaluating nonprofit organizations such as churches, camps, mission agencies, and schools requires a different approach because of the extensive use of volunteer workers. The incentives are different, and factors which influence motivation are different. "Continuing struggles with, for example, recruiting volunteers, arresting high rates of volunteer burnout and turnover, relieving staff antagonisms, reaching mutually agreeable placements, and so forth, point to flaws in program design that must be addressed. By diagnosing such difficulties, a process of evaluation can enhance progress toward achievement of program objectives."[5] Getting at the heart of program evaluation is critical to future success. This chapter will provide you with helpful guidance to that end.

BY
JAMES ESTEP JR.

Chapter 22

Conducting Performance Reviews

SURPRISINGLY, MOST PASTORS ARE not terminated over issues related to doctrinal disputes or theological arguments. The mismanagement of resources constitutes one of the largest reasons why pastors elect to leave their ministry positions or are forced out. Most ministry leaders receive a great deal of training in preaching and counseling but receive little, if any, training in what will likely become a significant portion of their day or week. Being able to manage a staff member with a degree of professionalism and managerial ethics is not for the faint of heart. Measuring a person's performance and then meeting with that individual to review his performance is enough to make even the boldest of leaders shutter. Yet, in spite of this dilemma far too few ministry leaders spend the time necessary to do it right. As a result, they discover the hard way that the contents of this chapter may be among the most important of their entire ministry career.

Assessment, and specifically the appraisal of personnel, is perhaps the most neglected administrative aspect of any educational institution, particularly congregations. "Results [of assessment] typically disappear into the recesses of people's minds or the far reaches of administrator's file cabinets."[1] Conducting personnel reviews are often more complicated in Christian organizations. Unlike the business world, church-related organizations are often dependent on volunteer workers, making appraisals of service a more sensitive issue. Similarly, even paid employees at church-affiliated institutions often view their positions as a ministry, willing to assume increased responsibilities with limited financial compensation. Add to this the concerns for Christian relationships and valuing the individual, and the notion of assessing a brother or sister in Christ becomes even more complicated than many businesses experience. Michael Woodruff notes that failing to assess the performance of volunteers is "the high price of being too nice," identifying four benefits to performance assessment:[2]

- *Team members* are better off because they receive the coaching they deserve.
- *You* are better off because your stress level drops two hundred points.
- Your other *staff* members are better off because they see that what they do matters.
- The *church* is better off because the job is getting done and team morale is higher.

As Christian administrators we should consider personnel reviews as a matter of pastoral care. We are furthering the education and development of volunteers and employees, not criticizing or passing judgment. To accomplish this, administrators, employees, and volunteers within the organization have to be committed to the quality improvement of one another. It should become part of the institutional culture, not done simply in response to complaint or when need arises. Hence, individuals should have a voice in establishing criteria, procedures, assessment means, and possibly even the administrative response to assessment.

Perhaps one preliminary consideration about personnel reviews in congregations and Christian organizations is the distinction between employees and volunteer staff. While some distinction may be necessary, such as the expectations placed on individuals and the means of responding to appraisal information (e.g., financial or career incentives for employees vs. more altruistic motives for service for volunteers), the basic sequence of the appraisal cycle remains applicable. The distinction between paid and volunteer staff will be made when the subject matter necessitates it in this chapter.

The Biblical Basis of Personnel Appraisal

Is assessment a Christian ideal?[3] Too many Christians in administrative or staff roles have the notion that personnel reviews are contradictory to the injunction of Jesus, "Do not judge, or you too will be judged" (Matt. 7:1 NIV). However, Jesus was voicing his concern over the *unfair* and *unilateral* critical attitude of the Pharisees toward their followers and countrymen. "For in the same way you judge others, you will be judged, and with the measure you use, it will be measured to you" (Matt. 7:2 NIV). In another instance, he even commended the disciples for reaching a correct judgment in deciding a character issue between two individuals in a parable (Luke 7:43). Hence, it is the type of judgment given by the Pharisees that Jesus questioned, not the notion of assessing one's performance.

We also have the admonition of the apostle Paul to judge even the character of those in the church: "What business is it of mine to judge those outside the church? Are you not to judge those inside?" (1 Cor. 5:12 NIV). Similarly, assessment is implicit in the establishment of criteria for Christian leaders (1 Tim. 3:1–13; Titus 1:5–9; 1 Pet. 5:1–4). Some individuals will meet the selection criteria while others will not, hence requiring some form of review process to determine qualified candidates. Christian administrators must know how to judge without becoming judgmental and how to provide appraisal as critique, not criticism. In short, Christian administrators should *not* feel spiritual apprehension about reviewing their personnel.

How do we insure that performance review is Christian in character? Four criteria can guide us about the Christian nature of any form of organizational assessment: (1) Does it bring glory to God? (2) Does it edify the body, corporately? (3) Is it compatible with distinctively expressed Christian beliefs, biblically and theologically? (4) Does it encourage and aid in the personal development of the individual? In each instance, assessment can be Christian in its composition, function, and product. Four theological themes influence our approach to performance appraisal.

Assessment Is Part of God's Creation

Genesis 1 has repeated assessment statements in its depiction of God's creation: "It was good" (Gen. 1:10, 12, 18, 21, 25), and ultimately, "it was very good" (Gen. 1:31 NIV). Humanity was given the charge to care for the creation, which is the basis for Christian stewardship. Christian communities must be good stewards of God's provision. The review of personnel's performance enables us to assess those who have been entrusted as stewards over God's provision. It allows us to better comprehend, manage, direct, and even change and address problematic areas. Personnel review is part of the stewardship principle.

Assessment Is Part of God's Community of Faith

In the church at Corinth, Paul encouraged the believers to discern their giftedness as a means of assessing the unity and diversity within the members of the body of Christ (1 Cor. 12–13). Assessing must distinguish between unity and diversity, since both have value. Paul differentiated between gifts, workings, and service, all of which collectively form Christian ministry. Paul's concern in 1 Corinthians 12:1–11 was for the influence of each gifted individual's function and place within the ministry of the congregation. The mere presence of the gift within the congregation does not ensure that its presence is beneficial to the body of Christ; this calls for assessment of the function and fruit of the gift.

Paul's body metaphor for the congregation indicates that it is comprised of weaker and stronger members, and that weaker members should receive special attention. "But God has combined the members of the body and has given greater honor to the parts that lacked it . . . if one part suffers, every part suffers with it; if one part is honored, every part rejoices with it" (1 Cor. 12:24, 26 NIV). It is noted by some biblical scholars that 1 Corinthians 12 "deals with competencies, performances, attitudes, goals, and synergies from a beautiful theological metaphor" of the body.[4] First Corinthians also reminds us that assessment cannot quantify everything! For example, Paul provided detailed descriptions of the components of love in 1 Corinthians 13, but even with the list provided in verses 4–8, assessing the components would not equal the quality of love being described.

Assessment Is Part of God's Commission to His Community

The agricultural parables of Jesus in Matthew 13 provide images of assessing the fruitfulness of the Christian's work. The parables involve the concepts of fruit production and fruit inspection and provides measurable results in terms of yield. In 2 Corinthians 10, Paul encouraged us to continue to serve until "we take captive every thought to make it obedient to Christ" (v. 5 NIV). "Paul is providing a community assessment instrument in these verses that evaluates the content, competence, and character of who teaches and what is taught."[5] As such, assessment should be part of the community of faith's pastoral ministry.

Assessment Is for Edification of the Individual

As Paul wrote, his authority and assessment of the Corinthian congregation was an opportunity "for edification and not for destruction" (2 Cor. 13:10c NKJV). While not writing about theology, Bolman and Deal comment that "evaluation results help people relabel old practices, escape the normal routine, and build new beliefs."[6] Personnel reviews should take on a pastoral impact when they confront practices that are less than ideal, cause us to rethink and reflect on our service to Christ, and expand our theological understanding and commitment to his ministry. "To grow spiritually, feedback from others is essential. We often back away from this process because we are frightened of what we might hear. Our anxiety is an indication once again that we have centered ourselves on something or someone less than God. It is a sign that we have set ourselves up to filter out the positive and emphasize the negative— to hear praise as a whisper and negative comments as thunder."[7]

Prerequisites to Performance Appraisals

"Remember the central purpose of evaluation—improvement."[8] While we all may have experienced what we considered to be an unfair, confrontational, or judgmental performance appraisal, when one maintains the self-improvement and developmental purpose of personnel reviews, they are seen as necessary, beneficial, and collaborative. In order to appropriately design a process of performance appraisals for Christian organizations, it would be beneficial for the ministry leader to understand the basic cycle of personnel reviews. Figure 22.1 illustrates this basic review cycle which has four stages: (1) establishing a basis for appraisal, criteria, (2) conducting the appraisal, or evaluation methods, (3) reviewing the appraisal data, interpretation and analysis of the evaluation data, and (4) responding to appraisals, or rendering a decision on how to act in response to the personnel appraisals. By following this simple process we "offer acute and honest evaluation" as part of turning the vision of the organization's ministry into reality.[9]

Figure 22.1: Performance Review Cycle

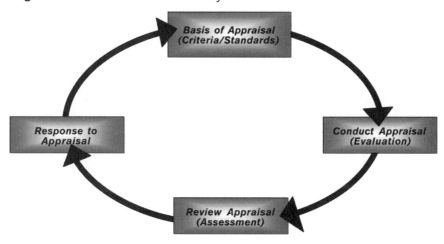

This cycle forms the basic pattern for conducting performance reviews. However, the actual process of creating and conducting an assessment of personnel is more complicated. Figure 22.2 depicts the process of personnel review that will be described in this chapter.[10] It denotes that the basis of appraisal must be correlated to the individual's job description. After this, the evaluation stage begins when the individual's actual performance is measured, generating evaluation data. Assessment follows when the evaluation data is compared with the expectations of the position as described in the criteria. A judgment of the evaluation data is made, and from this assessment a course of action is determined. Personnel maintaining a satisfactory rating, meeting the criteria, are commended; while those performing unsatisfactorily, not meeting the criteria, receive corrective action.

Figure 22.2: Process of Personnel Evaluation

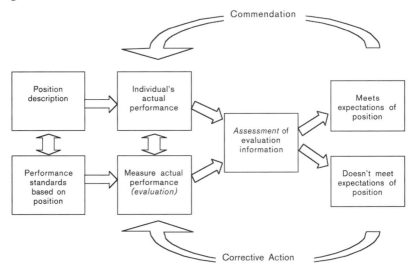

Rationale for Conducting Performance Reviews

What is the rationale for conducting performance reviews if they are so difficult to do with fairness and objectivity? The first step in performance reviews is to establish a set of performance standards and criteria for effective service. As previously noted, these criteria must relate directly to the stated position description of the individual. If not, assessment is virtually impossible or completely unreasonable, since an individual is assessed on criteria unrelated to his stated position. Several critical questions must be answered about establishing a set of base-line performance standards.

- *Who establishes criteria?* Do organizational leaders? Immediate supervisors? Appointed committee? Assessment or human resource/personnel officer? Colleagues and peers? Or in some instances, does an outside authority establish them, e.g., denominational, educational association, legal, or governmental agencies?

- *How are criteria established?* Dictated from institutional leadership or outside authority? Consensus among personnel? Voted in committee?

- *How are criteria stated?* Are they stated as outcomes? Measurable or subjective assessment? Do they seek to assess performance or motive?
- *How are criteria communicated?* Are the criteria part of training and orienting new personnel, or are they assumed by the institution? Are they frequently communicated or only mentioned when a situation presents itself? What is the standard means by which personnel, paid and volunteer, know what is expected?

For performance reviews to be effective, criteria do not have to be exhaustive, since this can exhaust both the assessor and those being assessed, particularly volunteers. Assessment criteria should be at about four to six well-stated expectations. They might be general statements, with several measurable criteria associated with each one. For example,

General Statement: Volunteers will be prepared to serve in junior worship.

Criteria 1: Volunteers will have materials prepared by Friday.

Criteria 2: Volunteers will arrive at least fifteen minutes prior to the service.

Criteria 3: Volunteers will spend time in prayer each week for the students in the junior worship.

Criteria 4: Volunteers will attend an adult worship service once a week.

But what kind of statements? What are we trying to assess? While *performance* is an obvious answer, Christian administrators must be concerned with more than an employee's or volunteer's performance. In the parable of the talents (Matt. 25:14–30), the "wicked, lazy servant" (v. 26 NIV) was not only assessed on his lack of proficiency, but on his deficient attitude and character. What are some general areas of personnel review in Christian organizations? The following list is by no means exhaustive, but it may provide a starting point upon which to generate criteria specific to a given organization.

1. **Theological.** Does the individual maintain beliefs and convictions consistent with the institution? For Christian institutions, particularly those engaged in teaching, this criteria is essential. If theological integrity is not present, we are simply doing social work in the Lord's name. This may not be a separate criteria statement, but would be present in other criteria statements.

2. **Cognitive Capacities.** Does the individual demonstrate the necessary thinking skills to maintain or advance his performance? Decision making, problem solving, and simply common sense are often critical issues in determining the performance of employees and volunteers.

3. **Life Characteristics and Traits.** In your institution, does character count? What life characteristics do you expect to be demonstrated

by your employees and volunteers? It is important that these be identified to some extent in order to avoid confusion regarding their personal presence and influence within the institution.

4. **Relational Abilities.** One's work performance is often not a matter of solitary service. Employees' and volunteers' performance in groups, their ability to maintain interpersonal relations, is an important assessment dimension. This may also be a crucial indicator of supervisory abilities.

5. **Performance.** As previously noted, performance is still critical. Assessing an employee's or volunteer's abilities and proficiency is necessary. To do so, specific and measurable criteria must be drawn from the position description and should be produced in such a way that it avoids confusion and makes the review as objective as possible.

Following the establishment of the standards and criteria, the institution must determine how to actually evaluate the individual's performance. In other words, what evaluation methods can or should be used?

Conducting Performance Reviews

Evaluation and assessment are two sides of the same coin, but they are *different* sides. Evaluation refers to the gathering of relevant information and insight upon which assessment can be rendered. Assessment is the actual process of decision making, rendering an appraisal of the evaluation materials. Hence, in this stage of the performance review cycle, *evaluation* is the key term; *assessment* comes in the next phase.

In designing a program of performance review for volunteers and employees, it is critical to decide whose voice needs to be heard. Who is doing the appraising? By developing a multifaceted approach to conducting a performance review, we provide a more accurate and clear depiction of the individual's actual performance, and hence guard against bias or one-sidedness in assessment. The possible voices of personnel evaluation are self, peer, subordinate, and leader (Figure 22.3).

Self-evaluation. How does the individual assess his own performance? Self-evaluations are helpful in that many times individuals are keenly aware of their shortcomings and successes. In these instances, the one responsible for assessing the individual need only agree and design an appropriate intervention. However, self-evaluations in most cases are regarded as an administrative mandate and often are not taken seriously and are considered busywork. Using self-evaluations successfully "includes involving the employee from the very beginning."[11] Hence, self-evaluation is viewed as a means of tracking one's own

Figure 22.3: Evaluation Voices

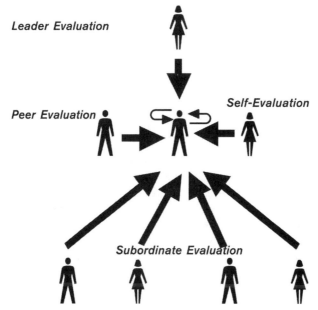

self-determined pattern of growth. Self-evaluation can provide an essential voice in the conducting of performance reviews.

Peer Evaluation. How do my peers assess my service? Peer review is a common form of evaluation, particularly in professional settings. Faculty in Christian schools and higher education institutions often engage in peer review as a means of evaluation, and to gain insight into teaching methods, course organization, and classroom management. Similarly, if assessment is to be a communal activity, it assumes the involvement of the whole community, not simply one's self and his or her institutional superiors. Peers provide a valuable voice in evaluation because they are *peers*. Who better to evaluate an individual than another individual who shares a similar commitment and conviction within the institution?

Subordinate Evaluation. How am I perceived by those over whom I have charge? Your ability to provide direction for a program or ministry is directly linked to the perception of those serving under your guidance. This voice is particularly valuable in evaluating those in directing or leadership roles within the congregation or Christian organization. Listening to this voice allows us to see beyond the individual's capabilities and skills and to gain insight into his or her ability to relate to others and provide direction to a program or ministry. As administrators, we need to listen to those whom we lead and supervise in order to evaluate our relational, organizational, and administrative skills.

Leader Evaluation. Perhaps the most commonly used and recognized voice of evaluation is that of the leader. How does my "boss" or supervisor perceive my work? Leaders need to evaluate those who serve with them as subordinates, not in a spirit of dictation, but of pastoral responsibility for those over whom they have been placed. The voice of leadership, as the organizational tier responsible for advancing the mission and vision of the institution and engaging in the process of strategic decision making and planning, is essential in the review of personnel in order to assure the success of the organization.

Often the voices involved in evaluation are in harmony, all agreeing on the relative strengths and weaknesses of an individual's performance. As administrators, we have assurance when all the voices are in agreement that we have a clear and accurate picture of the individual's capabilities. However, on occasion the voices will diverge rather than converge, creating a disjointed picture of performance. In such instances further evaluation and investigation might be necessary, even discussion with the individual, in order to clarify the portrait. Also, such assessments can also provide insight in regard to the individual's placement within the organizational structure.

For example, if an individual's self and subordinate evaluation provide a positive picture, but the peer evaluation does not, a leader may be wise to explore the individual's ability to relate to peers, or seek to discover the source of the negative assessment. This may preclude the individual from being promoted over his or her current peers. Hence, a comprehensive personnel review process would include a variety of perspectives, each evaluating the staff member's service.

Principles of Performance Reviews

How do you actually *do* performance reviews? What kinds of methods are valuable? One generally acknowledged principle of performance appraisals is *brevity*. A common error of performance reviews is overload, attempting to evaluate everything about an employee's and volunteer's service to the organization. When one goes to the doctor for an annual physical, the physician may perform some standard test (e.g., asking some general health questions, checking blood pressure, drawing blood analysis, taking a chest x-ray). The doctor does not order advanced diagnostic measures *unless* the standard tests indicate a possible problem that reveals the necessity of additional tests. Initial performance evaluation methods should endeavor to provide a basic insight to the performance of personnel, which can be further pursued if necessary.

Another general principle is the *frequency* of evaluations. Some recommend frequent evaluations, such as monthly or quarterly, while others recommend annual evaluations. The point is to establish routine, regularly scheduled periods of evaluation. Relying on *unprompted* or *spontaneous* evaluations can give the appearance that they are not important to the organization and even situation- or problem-driven. Whatever evaluation methods one may elect to use, they must be used on a regularly scheduled basis.

A final general principle for consideration is distinguishing between *quantitative* and *qualitative* data in evaluation. What type of data is needed for assessment? Evaluation methods are designed to generate different kinds of data. The two basic categories of evaluation methods are those that yield quantitative data and those that produce qualitative data. *Quantitative data* is statistical, i.e., quantities. An example of quantitative data might be a survey showing that 4.6/5.0 adult congregation members prefer elective Sunday school classes. Analysis of quantitative data relies on statistical analysis, such as, determining the mean, median, frequency, and standard deviation. In short, quantitative data is numerical data, and it requires statistical analysis. *Qualitative data* is more substantial. It deals with statements and opinions, which are not necessarily analyzed statistically, although it may be numerical. An example of qualitative data would be the verbal results of asking campers to list the top three problems with camp food. In this case, the data generated is not numerical, but verbal.

Often a thorough evaluation process will rely on both qualitative and quantitative evaluation methods. The qualitative methods generate the list of possible responses while the quantitative methods can be used to determine the strength of the responses. For example, the qualitative methods will raise most or all of the possible problems with camp food, and then a quantitative inventory can generate the quantitative data to determine if a single comment about the food is generally held by the campers. A camper may say that the food is cold when served, but when all the campers are surveyed only 1.2/5.0 agree or strongly agree with the statement, indicating a minority opinion, while 4.7/5.0 agree or strongly agree that the serving sizes are too small.

Personnel Review Methods

One basic means of evaluation is *anecdotal* comments. While virtually every institution uses this as a means of assessment, it is often not documented, and hence no official response should be based on what may have been just a passing comment. This is consistent with the scriptural admonition, "Do not entertain an accusation against an elder unless it is brought by two or three witnesses" (1 Tim. 5:19 NIV). Similarly, administrators should not accept anonymous feedback, since it leads to misunderstandings and does not lead to thorough assessment, only evaluation.[12] In some Christian organizations, e-mails can serve as documented anecdotal comments on an individual's performance. Anecdotal comments can be made from any of the four voices previously mentioned, as can any other evaluation method.

Interviews can be conducted with individuals or small groups, often called focus groups. Interviews should use a simple protocol of open-ended questions to facilitate open communication and generate unbiased feedback. For example, "What are Linda's best qualities as a teacher?" Or, "What areas would you change about Linda's teaching?" While the questions provide some direction for the responses, they do not state a conclusion about the individual in question. Protocols, the list of questions used in the interview, should consist of five or six questions, thereby keeping the interviews brief and focused on the subject. Interview data, as with observation data, can then be clustered or counted, requiring qualitative analysis.

Clustering creates categories of response. For example, the comments made about Linda's strengths have three common themes: She is knowledgeable, passionate, and caring. Counting would simply list the responses, counting the number of same responses, and/or noting the top three responses. For example, the three most frequent comments made about Linda's teaching were she is sometimes unprepared, absent too often, and tends to get sidetracked with questions. As previously mentioned, the protocol allows the responses to be focused and avoids changing the questions during the interview process.

Observations are similar to interviews, except the person conducting the evaluation directly observes the individual. Administrators may use a protocol to note actions or behaviors with which they are specifically concerned. Notes, both positive and negative, can be made about the individual's performance. The notes constitute qualitative data about the staff member's performance and can be used in evaluating his or her abilities.

Inventories can generate quantitative or qualitative data. Inventories, also known as surveys, designed to generate qualitative data are similar to interviews, consisting of open-ended questions to generate focused comments. Unlike interviews, written data rather than oral responses are generated; nor does it allow for clarifying questions to be asked. However, surveys do allow for anonymity. A simple yet effective inventory might consist of statements of the criteria. Have those completing the inventory indicate how well the staff member performs in relation to it (Figure 22.4).

For example, one criteria for a camp worker might relate to his or her ability to form healthy relationships with campers. On the inventory this would be listed in the left hand column and respondents would be asked to rate the worker's performance on a scale from "unsatisfactory"

Figure 22.4: Sample Simple Inventory Form

	① *Unsatisfactory* Rarely meets expectations	② *Fair* Meets most expectations	③ *Average* Meets all expectations	④ *Superior* Exceeds some expectations	⑤ *Excellent* Exceeds most expectations
Criteria 1					
Criteria 2					
Criteria 3					
Criteria 4					
Criteria 5					

to "excellent." It may be necessary to provide a brief description of the meaning of the 1-5 scale, such as unsatisfactory, fair, good, superior, and exceptional, and even define how these ratings are to be determined. Once again, this provides quantitative data about the camp worker's performance.

A similar form of inventory designed to generate quantitative data usually relies on Likert scales. They typically rely on a list of statements (not questions) with which respondents are asked to note their degree of agreement or disagreement, usually a scale of 1-5. One should also offer space for additional comments or explanations of responses. Figure 22.5 contains a sample Likert instrument. The performance criteria comprise the statements of evaluation, and respondents are asked to rate an individual's performance on a five-point scale.

Figure 22.5: Sample Likert Assessment Form

	① *Strongly disagree*	② *Disagree*	③ *Average*	④ *Agree*	⑤ *Strongly agree*
Criteria 1					
Criteria 2					
Criteria 3					
Criteria 4					
Criteria 5					

From this instrument, quantitative data can be generated about the degree to which an individual reflects the position criteria. For example, one criteria may be "Teachers should arrive prepared to teach." On the Likert inventory the criteria statement reads, "The teacher arrives prepared to teach," to which 4.6/5.0 agree or strongly agree, indicating a strong response. Likert inventories may also use the criteria as the basis for a set of questions on each one of them, and hence the instrument would still be focused on the position criteria, but this will be more extensive than an equal number of statements. As with all inventories, a place for comments and explanation for respondents should be provided in order to allow for some qualitative insight into their responses.

Frequent Evaluation Problems

Several problems frequently occur when using evaluation methods, particularly with inventories designed to generate quantitative data. The following is a list of the most commonly experienced problems:

Clarity of the Form. Does the evaluation instrument read clearly to the respondent? Questions or statements on an evaluation instrument should be *singular*, focusing on one issue, not multiple ones. All surveys should likewise offer an explanation about how responses should be made, e.g., darken the number on the Likert inventory, or write in the space provided.

Irregularity. Regular feedback, both written and oral, is crucial to paid and unpaid staff.[13] As previously mentioned, one problem is performing *situational* or *impromptu* evaluations. Not placing evaluations on a routine schedule indicates the relative unimportance of the act and does not allow for consistent and habitual review of performance.

"Halo Effect." This refers to Likert-type inventories, where the same rating is given on all the statements.[14] For example, students who evaluate a school teacher with the same rating typically do so because they are anxious to leave the class.

"Central Tendency." This is similar to the halo effect, but all the ratings are in the average column, e.g., all 3's.[15] This provides a null rating on the staff member's performance.

Clemency. This is similar to the previously mentioned two ratings, but all the ratings are in the high range, e.g., 4-5. While it is reasonable to believe that some personnel may average a superior or excellent rating, all the items on a Likert inventory will not necessarily be rated a 4-5.

Institutional Rigidity. It is critical that the evaluation instrument accurately reflects the stated position description. But not frequently reviewing the position description, criteria for assessment, evaluation instruments, or potential new means of fulfilling the position expectations can lead to ineffectiveness.

Using multiple means of assessment, particularly one that generates qualitative data and another to generate quantitative data, aids in the formation of a successful program of assessment.

Appraisal in Performance Reviews

Assessment and evaluation are different. As previously noted, assessment refers to the administrative assessment of evaluation data and determination of the appropriate administrative response to an employee's or volunteer's performance. Effective assessment of evaluation data rests on several principles. First, identify the source of the evaluation data, especially negative responses. This does not mean that anonymity must be abandoned, but rather to remember which "voice" is represented in the evaluation data. "When it comes to evaluating a congregation's response to a staff member, the reviews will almost always be mixed. As supervisors, we must decide which critiques hit the mark and which ones miss. This is hard to do when we focus primarily on what people say rather than who said it."[16]

Second, administrators should separate fact from opinion when assessing evaluation data. Administrators are responsible for rendering their opinions on the employee's or volunteer's performance, not on the opinions of those who provide evaluation data. Our assessment must rest on facts, not the opinions of others, lest assessment degenerate into popularity contests. Assessment must also be based on undisputable facts, not the interpretation of these facts.

Third, allow emotions to denote areas of concern, but do not regard it as data or react emotionally in response to it. Just as administrators cannot provide an emotionally-charged response, assessment cannot be based on strong emotions. For example, if during an interview a respondent begins to cry, this might draw our attention to the seriousness of the input, but it cannot be considered as part of the evaluation data, nor cause us to react emotionally.

Fourth, treat the person being assessed as you would want to be treated—with respect. "So in everything, do to others what you would have them do to you, for this sums up the Law and the Prophets" (Matt. 7:12 NIV). When approaching assessment from such a perspective, it maintains the developmental purpose of assessment, never allowing it to become disparaging.

Fifth, when evaluation data indicates unacceptable levels of performance, determine the reason for failure, not simply the degree of failure. Was it due to a personal trait? Is it a matter of lack of training or education, and hence can be readily corrected? Could it be an administrative issue? It is never enough to simply inform an individual of a low rating. Genuine and valuable assessment seeks to understand and explain a rating.

Finally, before assessing a volunteer or employee, assess your own possible involvement in the individual's performance, particularly in regard to shortcomings in performance. The following are some reflection questions that may be helpful in assessing administration's possible contribution to poor staff performance:[17]

- Did I communicate my expectations clearly? Does the volunteer know what is expected?
- Did I communicate the time demands or schedule accurately to the volunteer?
- Does the volunteer know when the performance objectives were to be met?
- Have I resourced this individual to succeed? Is it a lack of authority, position, equipment, funds, or assets to fulfill expectations?
- Did I provide enough training to adequately prepare the individual for the task? Is it a matter of training, or is the lack of performance related more to something else that is not related to training?
- Is the volunteer restricted by the organizational structure, policies, or organizational politics? Could the volunteer have achieved the expectations otherwise?
- Did I consider the personal or family life of the individual? Is the lack of performance due to a personal matter that should have been foreseen?

Once the assessment phase is completed and an administrator has rendered a decision about the individual's performance, the act of actually responding to the appraisal occurs. How do you actually communicate the assessment to the individual?

Personnel Review Decisions

Performance reviews involve reaching an administrative decision about the individual's level of performance. Administrators have four general possible responses to assessment decisions: reward, relocate, retrain, or release.

The first option is one of *reward*, wherein the evaluations represent an acceptable or above-average performance. While this is perhaps the easiest response for administrators, it is often neglected. In many cases, acceptable performance is expected and viewed as requiring no administrative response. In this instance, evaluation and assessment become nothing more than a search for poor performance rather than a staff developmental endeavor. Reward may be characterized as extrinsic and intrinsic. Promotions, financial stipends or raises, a larger office for employees, or a visible demonstration of appreciation, such as a plaque, for either employees or volunteers would be examples of extrinsic rewards. Intrinsic rewards are those that involve the personal satisfaction and contentment over a job well done, and are often the reward given by individuals to themselves.

Extrinsic and intrinsic rewards are both psychologically and spiritually uplifting. Remembering to openly reward and acknowledge exceptional service within an institution establishes an atmosphere of encouragement and support for service.[18] However, what about performance which does not meet expectations? Three additional responses must be considered in these instances.

Relocation of individuals usually is the result of recognized competencies, but they seem to be serving in the wrong position. The natural response would be to relocate them within the institution. Relocation does not mean promotion, since they may not be suited for a position with more responsibility. In such instances a promotion could lead to more poor performance by the individual. In addition, it could send a confusing message about performance expectations to those who serve within the institution.

Retrain is the most common administrative response to poor evaluation results. Administrators may have to commit to a more long-term, invested strategy to aid in the development of the individual's abilities and skills. "The spirit of consultive evaluation is coaching, not correcting."[19] It may involve providing a mentor for instruction, modeling, training, and equipping in order to raise performance to an acceptable level. The purpose of this intervention is to improve individual performance levels to retain the person in his position. It is best utilized when employees or volunteers are perceived as being valuable in the position they are in, but being in need of refinement and tuning in regard to their capabilities. If the individual's performance reaches acceptable levels, resolution of the matter has occurred through a constructive approach to personnel review.

Perhaps the option that is least favored by administrators is *release*. The release response may be temporary, such as a leave of absence, conditional, such as pending on accomplishing specified performance targets,[20] or termination, meaning a permanent release from the organization. Paul Borthwick provides some insight into determining when release is a necessary option. The following questions are valuable framing tools for making such a decision:[21]

- Has the congregation or organization outgrown the person?
- Has the person outgrown the congregation or organization?
- Is the person's ineffectiveness, poor leadership, or example actually blocking the progress of the organization's ministry?
- How much harm to the organization or other staff members is really being done?
- What if the position goes vacant for a while? Would that be better than the current state of affairs?

- What standard or criteria am I using to measure performance effectiveness?
- Who believes the person needs to be released?
- What will be the basis for dismissal? Relational, theological, performance, inability?
- Should he or she be given another opportunity for improvement?

In considering these questions, one can reach a decision to release with some assurance that all due consideration has been given to the matter. However, once one of the four assessment decisions has been rendered, how is the individual informed of his appraisal results? More importantly, how does one inform an employee or volunteer of poor performance?

Responding to Performance Reviews

"Follow-up is what really makes the process work."[22] Personnel review is incomplete if the evaluation information and its interpretation are simply filed and forgotten. The assessment must be shared between the administrator and the employee or volunteer to provide an agenda for continued or corrected performance. "Because Christian institutions are by nature nurturing organizations, there is a tendency to overlook discrepancies in job performance with the accompanying resolve that such individuals need a ministering supervisor or support group."[23] How does one actually respond to assessment decisions?

Conducting Performance Review Meetings

As Christian administrators, we should be committed to "creating a process that's positive, not poisonous."[24] How does an administrator actually share appraisal results with an individual? Several general principles that can aid in this matter are as follows:[25]

1. Be specific about evaluation results while maintaining confidentiality. Give them a clear picture of the basis of your appraisal decision. Share the *facts* with the individual.

2. Individualize your discussion with the individual, to an extent. While it is necessary to approach the appraisal meeting with a common core of content and intent, administrators can personalize the meeting as well. This may include addressing personal concerns and issues specifically related to the individual.

3. Document your conversation. This is not only to preserve the integrity of the decision and to insure that the individual understands the appraisal results, but it also demonstrates to the individual that his or her own response to the review is important and worthy of being recorded. It is also absolutely necessary in the event of subsequent legal action, e.g., the accusation of discrimination or wrongful dismissal.

4. Disarm tensions in the meeting. Tensions may be administrative (e.g., relations between a leader and subordinate), personal (e.g., when appraisal involves a friend or family member), or even pastoral (e.g., desire to assist while having to critique). Administrators should anticipate what tensions may be present and seek appropriate means to address them.

5. Keep criticisms confidential. Treating the individual with respect involves sharing only positives with others, while keeping areas of concern with confidence. Publicly complement individuals for their contributions to preserve their integrity and the integrity of the review process.

6. Offer encouragement in every instance of appraisal. Regardless of the resulting decision, the individual needs affirmation. Rarely is an employee or volunteer totally without merit. In fact, citing multiple positive traits for every one negative observation is a sound practice.

7. Respond immediately; don't procrastinate. Sitting on appraisal decisions does a disservice to the institution, the staff member, and yourself. Once the decision is made, whether it is positive or negative, set a meeting to discuss the results in a timely fashion.

8. Be prepared to handle emotional reactions. Regardless of how the staff member accepts or rejects the appraisal decision, the reaction to appraisal decisions must be addressed immediately and without a reversal of decision.

9. Discipline staff members when necessary. Sometimes an individual's performance is far below the level of expectation, demonstrates willful negligence, or is simply wrong (or even illegal). In such cases, the resolution or release option may require focused discipline—release of some form or serious performance targets.

10. Demonstrate a willingness to negotiate and compromise with an employee or volunteer. Reviews are typically not the setting for hard-line, unilateral discourse. A pastoral spirit is usually most advantageous, with the possible exception of discipline situations. Employees and volunteers should recognize administration's openness to listen to their opinion on their review. On occasion, it may be necessary to amend an administrative response in light of a staff member's response to it.

Meeting Arrangements

The entire process described in this chapter thus far becomes the subject of an arranged meeting. In this meeting the evaluation, assessment, and appraisal decision are communicated to the staff member. It is the culminating event of the review process. Managing the progress of the meeting is essential in making personnel performance reviews meaningful. Before conducting the meeting, several preparatory steps should be taken for the appraisal interview.[26]

- Review the individual's file or evaluation documentation, even up to two weeks prior to allow time for reflection.
- Insure that the meeting may be held in privacy.
- Schedule sufficient time for the meeting.
- Guard against interruptions. Silence the phone and intercom.
- Provide a nonthreatening, comfortable setting that is conducive to a conversation.
- Explain the purpose of the meeting to the staff member.

When the time comes to actually conduct the meeting, three basic components should comprise the agenda. First, begin with complements and positive reflections on a staff member's contribution to the organization. Identify the staff member's strengths of service and value to the organization. Second, focus on major areas of concern, just one or two items, avoiding specific instances or minor matters in order not to overwhelm the individual. Finally, reach an agreement on the appropriate developmental plan for the individual in order to improve service. Even in situations of reward, committing to developmental measures insures a continued exceptional level of performance.

Sharing Negative Appraisal Results

A negative or low rating of evaluation does not automatically lead to the release or termination of staff members. In fact, termination is the final option in a long line of interventions that may be used in response to poor performance. The following is a possible long-term response procedure for the under performing staff member:

- Evaluation and assessment indicates under performance of staff member based on the position description and criteria.
- Explain and outline the position description and criteria (again), highlighting areas of concern, offer assistance if needed.
- Evaluation and assessment, with focus on the highlighted areas of concern.
- Explain previous evaluation and provide performance targets if the problems persist.
- Evaluation and assessment, with focus on the performance targets.
- Meet and discuss staff member's progress or retreat on the performance targets; provide a probation period for a final attempt to accomplish performance targets.
- Evaluation and assessment, with continued focus on the performance targets.
- Determine a final administrative decision: release, relocation or resolution.

This long-term procedure reflects the pastoral concern for the staff member that underlies all staff relations within a Christian organization. Throughout the procedures three factors must be remembered. First, written documentation of every stage is critical. This may include formal memos to the staff member, minutes or records of meetings with the staff member, and a letter detailing and explaining the final administrative decision. It should also include notes detailing oral communications with the individual, such as an impromptu conversation or encounter, as well as any written communications received from the staff member. In fact, it may be necessary to have the individual sign or initial these documents as they are presented in order to acknowledge that he or she has read them.

Second, if resolution occurs at any time during the previously described process—that is, if the staff member was able to meet performance expectations—then the process ceases at that point. While administrators may want to continue monitoring specific performance concerns in the future, the process should only be continued if the concerns resurface. Third, the staff member may choose to resign or request relocation at almost any step of the procedure. This could be granted or denied based on the administrator's assessment of the individual and the situation.

Sharing negative assessment results with a staff member is often a difficult task for administrators. Staff members may be inclined to accept the appraisal of an administrator, but they recoil from the conversation. Similarly, staff members can refuse to accept the appraisal, responding with either denial or anger. This is where the appraisal conversation with staff members may become pastoral by necessity. Leroy Lawson refers to this as leaving the light on so that those who fly away in anger can return, and know they can return.[27] How does one map out a conversation about negative performance appraisal? Figure 22.6 contains a chart outlining the possible flow of conversation about negative personnel review. It is by no means a thorough discussion, but it does provide an outline for dealing with the three possible responses to negative performance appraisal reports.[28] However, there are advantages to providing a manuscript for such a meeting. It overcomes difficulties of face-to-face meetings, and it allows the performance assessment to be changed because of sensibilities or a meeting's consensus.[29]

Permanent Release: Termination

We have already mentioned the necessity of a procedure of continuing intervention and assessment and the possible options in the event of continuing unacceptable levels of performance. Termination is never the immediate response to performance concerns. These serve as the

Figure 22.6: Negative Performance Review Flow of Conversation

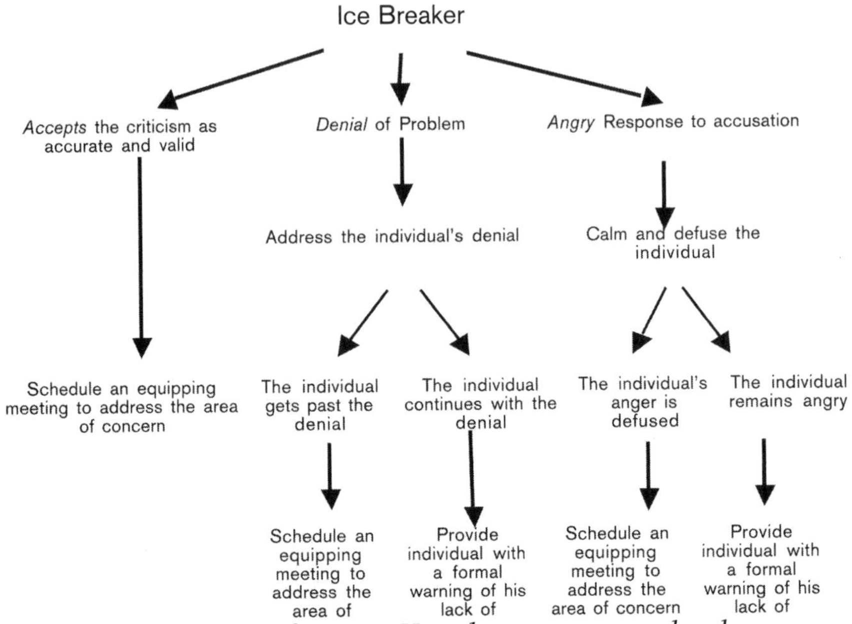

Ice Breaker

Accepts the criticism as accurate and valid   *Denial* of Problem   *Angry* Response to accusation

Address the individual's denial   Calm and defuse the individual

Schedule an equipping meeting to address the area of concern   The individual gets past the denial   The individual continues with the denial   The individual's anger is defused   The individual remains angry

Schedule an equipping meeting to address the area of   Provide individual with a formal warning of his lack of   Schedule an equipping meeting to address the area of concern   Provide individual with a formal warning of his lack of

basis for a termination decision. *How do you permanently release some-one?* Several general guidelines apply:

Personally. Termination should be done face-to-face. Even if the termination notice is in writing, it should be delivered by the administrator. The staff member should read it in the presence of the administrator.

Pastorally. Termination should be done gently, without judgment. The matter is settled, so there is nothing to gain by making critical or additional commentary.

Quickly. Close the staff member's responsibilities quickly. His or her lingering presence and continued underperformance can only further hinder the institution and create confusion in the organization.

Consistently. Terminations must be done on an equal basis to avoid any appearance of impropriety or personal agendas.

Discreetly. The decision to terminate is a confidential matter made by the administrator about the staff member, and it should never be intended for public viewing nor does it require public explanation.

Anticipate Possible Retaliation. One reason for the previous guidelines is to minimize the potential for staff members' destructive reactions to termination. One may need to consider possible negative reactions by the staff member and take precautions—backing up computer hard-drive files that may be erased in a moment of anger and frustration and possible legal action.

Conclusion

"Never be lacking in zeal, but keep your spiritual fervor, serving the Lord" (Rom. 12:11 NIV). Healthy organizations engage regularly in the appraisal of staff members' performance. The achievement of the organization's mission and ministry is dependent on the performance of its staff members. When performance appraisal is done in an atmosphere of pastoral concern and personal growth, it affirms the worth of the individual, commitment to community, and respectful relationship between Christians. "Each one should test his own actions. Then he can take pride in himself, without comparing himself to somebody else, for each one should carry his own load" (Gal. 6:4–5 NIV).

Appendix A

Suggested Resource: Adele Margrave and Robert Gorden, *The Complete Idiot's Guide to Performance Appraisals* (Indianapolis, Ind.: Alpha Books, 2001).[30]

Do's and Don'ts of Giving Performance Reviews	Do's and Don'ts of Receiving Performance Reviews
• Do your homework (be prepared). • Do schedule enough time so you don't have to rush. • Do meet in a confidential, safe place. • Do break the ice with small talk. • Do start with the positives. • Do remember your intention is to motivate. • Do make eye contact. • Do encourage participation. • Do listen–actively. • Do be honest, encouraging, and genuine. • Do use behavioral examples. • Do be open to new information. • Do agree upon goals for the future. • Don't be late for the performance appraisal meeting. • Don't take phone calls during the performance appraisal meeting. • Don't be disorganized or distracted. • Don't do all the talking or answer your own questions. • Don't interrupt. • Don't be too timid to speak the truth. • Don't overly focus on the negatives.	• Do your homework (be prepared–review your past performance). • Do be on time for your appointment. • Do be sincere, honest, and professional. • Do use behavioral examples to describe specifics. • Do participate–engage in the conversation. • Do make eye contact. • Do listen–actively. • Do take the time you need to formulate what you need to say. • Do participate in identifying goals for the future. • Do speak in a well-modulated tone of voice. • Do add your own comments in writing if you have the need. • Don't come in with a chip on your shoulder. • Don't stare–and don't focus on the ground or out a window. • Don't be negative or aggressive. • Don't let your emotions get the best of you. • Don't refuse to speak. • Don't be passive-aggressive. • Don't use sarcasm.

BY
MARK SIMPSON

Chapter 23

Evaluating the Effectiveness of Programs

Drawing Inaccurate Conclusions

FAITH FELLOWSHIP'S FIRST ANNUAL family night had been carefully planned over a period of nine months to kick off the new family focused ministries of the church. The educational ministries team had been given a budget sufficient to purchase food and resources so the event would be successful. Numerous methods of advertising were also utilized to invite the growing number of young families in the church to come and join in the food, fun, and fellowship.

Late in the afternoon the day family night was to be held, rainy weather turned into icy weather as a cold front moved through the area. Side roads became very slippery, and major streets were littered with traffic accidents. As a result, family night attendance was much lower than expected—families chose to stay safely at home rather than risk driving on the slippery road ways.

A few months later, the church's finance committee began developing the next church budget. The finance committee proposed to the educational ministries team that the funds for the next family night be reduced by 70 percent. The argument was made that the large amount of money spent for family night was not economical when low attendance was taken into consideration. Although the data the committee used to make this evaluation were accurate (i.e., attendance records and billing records), the conclusion reached *misinterpreted* that data because one vital piece of information was overlooked—the impact of the weather on the event.

At the same time the finance committee was making its program evaluations for budget purposes, the board of deacons was also making

411

its program evaluations for purposes of ministry effectiveness. When the attendance figures for family night were reviewed, the deacons reached the consensus that the low attendance was an indication of a lack of congregational interest in family focused ministries. The board informed the educational ministries team that family ministries were not proving to be effective in the church, and that other types of ministries more popular with the congregation needed to be developed. Although the information the board used to make this evaluation was accurate (i.e., attendance records), the conclusions reached were based on *unverified assumptions* about the meaning of the information.

Fortunately the financial committee, board of deacons, and the educational ministries team met together to discuss the future of family night. After looking more carefully at the data, the financial committee agreed to reinstate the full budgeted amount, the board of deacons agreed to survey the congregation for their perceptions on the effectiveness of family focused ministries in the church, and the educational ministries team breathed a sign of relief. Twelve months later the fastest-growing ministries of the church were found to be those that were family focused.

Evaluating the effectiveness of ministry programs is not an easy task. Data collection can be time-consuming, and the data collected can be misused or misunderstood if it is not interpreted correctly. However, the value of evaluation far outweighs the effort involved and the potential risks. Ministry evaluation can save substantially more time and effort than the time and effort consumed by the evaluation process itself. It also can prevent the waste of precious resources. The key to making evaluations effective is to collect data correctly and interpret the findings objectively.

Understanding the Need for Ministry Evaluation

"Evaluation is the process of getting answers to the question, 'How are we doing?'"[1] Every time we make comments about ministry, every time we express our feelings about how much we like or dislike ministry policies, procedures, programs, personnel, etc., we are making an evaluation.

Both formal and informal evaluation processes shape the way we do ministry. *Formal processes* of evaluation provide a church or Christian organization with objective data on "how we are doing." Objective measurements obtained from surveys and organizational records help ministry leaders make an accurate assessment of the health of a ministry, which in turn affects future ministry activities.[2] *Informal processes* such as casual observation and conversation also can yield objective measurements of the status of a ministry. However, if evaluation consists solely of informal processes, the danger is that more subjective and questionable data resulting from gossip, criticism, and unsubstantiated opinion will be included in the findings, which in turn can lead to a distorted assessment of the health of a ministry.

Therefore, to insure that evaluation shapes ministry in appropriate and accurate ways, the evaluative process must always seek to gather data as objectively as possible and interpret the data collected as accurately as possible. Informal process like casual observations and conversations can be included, but the data collected should be evaluated with great care.

Perspectives on Evaluating Ministry

"Some would argue that we should not evaluate the church or its people because it is a spiritual, not a secular, undertaking. Only God should appraise a spiritual ministry such as a church."[3] While it is true that only God can measure the spiritual state of the soul, it is also true that "by their fruits [which requires us to make an evaluative observation] you will know them" (Matt. 7:20 NKJV).

But even the church that does not invite evaluation engages in it. Whether we realize it or not, evaluation takes place every Sunday.

People are very discriminating. On the way home from church, a husband naturally asks his wife, "What did you think about the sermon?" Or, "Do you like the new Sunday school class?" Some go so far as to have roast pastor or roast church for Sunday lunch. Seeker church pastors are quick to remind us that when lost people visit our services, they do so with a critical eye. If ministry evaluation takes place on an informal level, why not move it to a formal level so that we can benefit from it rather than be a victim of it?[4]

Unfortunately, much of what passes for the assessment of ministry is more often criticism than evaluation. When criticism is accompanied by a critical spirit, it usually is made in the form of destructive comments that seek to harm persons and ministries rather than help them. Destructive criticism may contain a kernel of truth in its assessment of ministry, but the negative nature and intentions of the criticism usually cloud that truth from being taken seriously. Constructive criticism, on the other hand, does have its place in ministry. Constructive criticism, when offered as objective observations and the intention to help persons and ministries, can help correct errors and misunderstandings about ministry activities.

I have heard ministry leaders say that they never listen to criticism. To be fair, this statement usually means they will not nurture and perpetuate destructive criticism and a critical spirit by adding their voice to it. To participate in the perpetuation of a critical spirit is indeed inappropriate. However, to dismiss all criticism as being rooted in a critical spirit can cause us to have serious blind spots in our ministries. We *can* hear the comments of others without affirming them or adding to them, even the criticisms of those who intend to use them to do harm.

Sometimes the mere act of listening to the evaluations of our congregations or ministry constituents diminishes criticism without any further action on our part; some people just want to know and feel that their viewpoints and concerns are being heard. Yes, there are always those individuals who are never pleased with anything at any time and who thrive on letting everyone know it. But Christian leaders are not infallible; only God is. Many times we work so closely with our ministries that we fail to see problem areas evident to those for and with whom we labor.

Perhaps we would do well to follow in ministry the advice we are given about crossing railroad tracks: Stop! Look! Listen! Rather than dismissing all criticism as destructive and flowing from a critical spirit, we need to *stop* and hear the concerns of others, *look* for and consider carefully the validity of the concerns and reliability of the evaluations, and *listen* for the kernel of truth in what is being said. If we evaluate carefully constructive *and* destructive criticism, we could avoid being hit by an express train full of ministry problems just over the horizon.

Obviously not every criticism or evaluation can be accommodated. Faithfulness and obedience to God's Word must always take precedence over our desires and wishes and preferences. For example, many of the apostle Paul's letters to the early church contain teachings to correct believer attitudes and behavior patterns that were incompatible with God's standards for ministry. In those churches, incompatible preferences and practices had to be changed immediately. But sometimes an evaluation or criticism cannot be accommodated because the proposed changes would prove to be incompatible with the mission and goals of our ministry.

For example, I teach a doctoral-level course on educational research design. My mission is to prepare my doctoral students for the writing of their dissertations. Most of my students will tell you my research design course is one of the hardest seminars they have had to take. As a result, some of them will offer suggestions to make the coursework easier in the future. I try to incorporate these student evaluations that are compatible with the mission of the course into the next offering of the course. But if I followed all of the feedback I receive from my students, I would end up eliminating all assignments, which would make the course easier today, but dissertation research much more difficult tomorrow. In other words, if I accommodated all of their evaluations,

I would fail in my mission to prepare doctoral students for the writing of their dissertations.

It must be understood that resistance to evaluation is normal; no one likes to be evaluated. Fear of failure, fear of punishment, and fear of change compel us to resist evaluation. Even so, it is only through evaluation that we are able to move forward in our personal growth in Christ and our corporate growth as a church or Christian organization. Consider these valuable outcomes that evaluation can bring to ministry:

1. Evaluation accomplishes ministry alignment. Ministry efforts are aligned with the mission and values of the church or Christian organization.
2. Evaluation prioritizes ministry accomplishment. Ministry that is evaluated is given attention rather than being overlooked or neglected.
3. Evaluation encourages ministry assessment. Paid and volunteer performance is reviewed for purposes of enhancing ministry efforts.
4. Evaluation coaxes ministry affirmation. Morale is increased as personnel are given encouragement and shown appreciation for their efforts.
5. Evaluation emboldens ministry correction. Ministry strengths and weaknesses become evident, encouraging modifications where necessary.
6. Evaluation elicits ministry improvement. Changes to ministry are made based on objective feedback.[5]

Indicators for Measuring Performance

Once the decision is made to evaluate ministry to increase its effectiveness, the logical question becomes, "What do we measure?" The specific indicators of ministry effectiveness will vary from ministry to ministry because they are dependent on the mission and objectives or goals of the organization. However, there are four performance indicators that are common to almost every church or Christian organization, and each of the four needs to be evaluated:

1. Personnel. The performance of both employees and volunteers.[6]
2. Programs. The effectiveness of activities in light of the mission of the organization.[7]
3. Protocols. The efficiency and effectiveness of polices and procedures.[8]
4. Products. The outcomes of ministry in persons or as goods.[9]

In a local church, these four performance indicators would be measured in terms of ministry teachers, leaders, and workers; church ministries and resources; organizational structures; and spiritual maturity and learning outcomes respectively.[10] In a Christian organization, these four performance indicators would be measured in terms of leadership, management, and employee performance; services and resources; organizational structures; and sales or growth. It should be noted that the four performance indicators are interconnected to varying degrees. For example, the performance of personnel and the effectiveness of programs can be influenced greatly by organizational protocols.

Another way to look at performance indicators is to identify them in terms of their function within the organization, that is, as ministry outcomes or ministry processes.[11] "In general, outcome measures of performance refer to organizationally valued accomplishments of individuals or groups. . . . Process factors refer to measures of compliance with organizational procedures, rules or guidelines considered essential for the accomplishment of organizational goals."[12] Personnel and products are examples of outcomes factors; programs and protocols are examples of process factors.

Measuring Effectiveness

No matter how performance indicators are categorized, each one of them will require one or more types of data to be collected. Many churches and Christian organizations will be surprised to discover that some of the data that can be used to explore performance indicators has already been collected.

> For example, the congregation is constantly generating the geo-demographic trends of the congregation, the average attendance as compared to last year's attendance, financial patterns, growth patterns, staff and membership morale, average length of tenure of its professional workers, the number of social ministries it is carrying out, and the percentage of first-time visitors who visit a second time.[13]

This data can be used to evaluate performance indicators such as those related to program effectiveness (attendance and growth patterns), personnel performance (length of tenure in a position compared to attendance and growth patterns), and so on. Additional measures will also be necessary, but significant information can be gleaned from existing data collected "by the mere fact that [the organization] is operating. This information is generally cast off and lost, because the organization pays no attention to it."[14]

Measuring ministry effectiveness sometimes requires the collection of data over a significant period of time, usually one year or longer. These longitudinal studies involve gathering data multiple times from the same sources with the same instruments. The data gathered is then examined to determine the patterns and trends of changes in ministry effectiveness.

For example, if a church wishes to evaluate the effectiveness of new Sunday school curriculum in nurturing disciples, an accurate assessment cannot be made based on gathering data on just one Sunday. In order to get a more accurate assessment of the effectiveness of the curriculum, a church would need to measure knowledge, attitudes, and/or skills shortly after the new curriculum is implemented, and then again at the end of each quarter. At the end of a year, the data from each quarter would then be compared to determine what impact the curriculum was having on nurturing disciples. Longitudinal studies have the advantage of giving a more accurate picture of ministry effectiveness because the data represents changes over time, not just changes at one moment in time.

The effectiveness of some ministries, however, may need to be measured immediately. Churches and Christian organizations have numerous ministries that occur only once each year. In order to assess the effectiveness of these ministries, data must be gathered from one or more sources during the ministry activity or immediately afterward. This data can then be analyzed to determine the impact of the ministry on knowledge, attitudes, and/or skills as a result of the one-time event. Unlike the longitudinal Sunday school curriculum study, the data gathered only reflects a "snapshot in time." This immediate feedback can be extremely beneficial for purposes of future ministry planning and determining the immediate effectiveness of a ministry in changing knowledge, attitudes, and skills. However, in order to determine the long-term effectiveness of one-time ministries, a longitudinal study would be needed to determine the nature of those changes over time.

Protocols for Conducting Evaluations

In order to evaluate the effectiveness of a ministry, the protocols by which an evaluation will be conducted need to be determined before the evaluation begins. The following five parameters are common to most evaluation systems:

1. Content of feedback. What factors will be measured and what standards of performance will be used for purposes of comparison.
2. Temporal characteristics of feedback. How frequently will evaluations be conducted and how quickly will the findings be reported?
3. Mechanisms for gathering feedback. What types of tools will be used to collect data (e.g., interviews, surveys, tests and measurements, self-reports, etc.)?

4. Source of feedback. Who and what will be evaluated, and who will conduct the evaluation?
5. Recipients of feedback. Who will receive the findings (e.g., will the findings be made public or kept private; will they be made available only to the individual(s) evaluated or shared corporately).[15]

In recent years, accrediting agencies have begun requiring colleges and universities to develop a feedback system that evaluates every aspect of the educational institution. An integral part of this feedback system must be evidence of a clear link between the mission and goals of the institution, and the objectives and outcomes of each academic program or institutional service.[16] In helping two academic institutions prepare for their ten-year accreditation review, I developed an *Indicators of Success* feedback system to help track the evaluation process for every aspect of institutional effectiveness. This feedback system is easily adapted for deployment in a church or Christian organization. Figure 23.1 contains some (not all) of the indicators of success I have begun developing for my own online ministry resource center. The five parameters common to most feedback systems are represented in these indicators, as well as the intentional links between the mission, goals, objectives, and outcomes of the organization.

The initial investment of time in developing indicators of success will appear to be time-consuming at first glance. However, many organizations will have a significant amount of the information used in developing the indicators already on hand. For example, some organizations have a mission statement and corresponding ministry goals in published form. In those ministries, creating the indicators becomes a matter of transferring published information into the appropriate areas on the assessment table. Churches and Christian organizations that have not yet articulated their mission and goals may find that they do exist implicitly in the descriptions of their ministries. Ministry publications, bulletins, reports, slogans, service practices, etc. are often the operational description of an organization's mission and goals. Similarly, if ministry objectives and outcomes are not specifically articulated for each area of an organization, they may already be implicit in public relations materials, operations manuals, promotional items, and user testimonials, etc.

Once the information that defines the mission, goals, objectives, and outcomes of the organization are placed in the indicators of success table, the next task is to identify how each objective and outcome will be assessed. The assessment protocols that need to be identified include:

1. *Method.* What tools will be used to collect data, e.g., forms, surveys, reports, records, tests, etc.

Figure 23.1: Indicators of Success Terminology

Service Area and Time Frame
Identify the ministry or service the indicators assess, and the calendar or budget period for which the findings apply

Mission/Vison
Quote the mission and vision statements of the organization word for word

Goals
State the ministry goals of the service area

Objectives
List the measurable objectives that will be deployed to achieve the stated goals

Outcomes
For each objective, identify the measurable standards that will indicate the achievement of the objective; the standards should indicate who will be affected and how they will be affected

Assessments
For each assessment to be conducted on an outcome, identify the method, schedule, and evaluators that will be involved
Method: Indicate the tools that will be deployed to measure outcomes (forms, surveys, reports, records, tests, etc.)
Schedule: Indicate where and how often the assessment methods will be deployed
Evaluators: Indicate the persons who will be responsible for collecting, compiling, and interpreting the data

Findings
Record a summary of the results obtained from the assessments once the data is compiled

Impact
Describe specific and appropriate actions taken to shape or reshape ministry objectives and outcomes as a result of the findings

EDCOT® INDICATORS OF SUCCESS

Education with Digital Courseware and Online Technologies

Service Area	WEB SITE SERVICES
Time Frame	First Quarter 2004

Mission To provide educational ministry leaders with information on resources for electronic (digital) based classroom applications, such as PowerPoint and other forms of multimedia, and information on online courseware technologies, such as Web pages and discussion groups

Goals To provide resources on the instructional design of online classrooms
To provide form-processing services for online surveys deployed for ministry research
To provide training in the principles and practices of teaching online and designing online courseware
To host online discussion groups and Web sites that form ministry networks
To e-publish selected resources such as out-of-print books and research monographs
To edit and e-publish the *Digital Learning Journal*

Objectives	Outcomes	Assessments	Findings	IMPACT
Develop and maintain a Web site (www.edcot.com) that enables the mission and goals of the organization	Provide a user friendly online presence that is kept attractive and current in offering mission-related resources	**Method:** Solicit user feedback on Web design; Web site usage statistics **Schedule:** Monthly **Evaluator/s:** Web Master	Web site was launched this quarter; solicited feedback was very positive on Web design; Web site usage statistics indicate minimal site usage with 234 hits	Complete pages under development; continue to monitor site usage statistics; submit URL to Web search engines for increased visibility; consider options for promoting Web site
Serve as system operator of the *Web Crossing* discussion group software	Provide a user friendly platform for synchronous and asynchronous lines of communication that enable the networking of ministry leaders within and across hosted organizations	**Method:** Software billing statement containing discussion access statistics **Schedule:** Monthly **Evaluator/s:** System operator; Operations Officer	Software was launched this quarter; asynchronous linear discussions created for iComm, KidZatHeart, Ministers2Military, and Psalm One Ministries; 135 site hits; 57 messages posted; 12 registered users	Continue to monitor use of discussion groups; add threaded asynchronous discussion and synchronous chat room discussion options; evaluate open registration for participants rather than through the system operator
Edit and publish the online *Digital Learning Journal*	Expand the knowledge of the field on online learning in general, and expand the understanding of issues related to the theory and practice of online instruction in Christian educational ministries specifically	**Method:** e-publication of the journal and Web site usage statistics **Schedule:** Publish 3 times annually **Evaluators:** Journal editor; Web master	Journal is not yet available online; targeted release date of first issue: late summer 2004; site design and ISSN application in progress	Complete design of the journal Web site; secure associate editors and advisory panel; solicit journal articles

EDCOT® INDICATORS OF SUCCESS
Education with Digital Courseware and Online Technologies

Web Site Services Report: First Quarter 2004
The following report summarizes the outcomes of findings and impact developments made to the objectives and outcomes of EDCOT® Web site services. These modifications are based on the findings and impact of the assessments made of the *Indicators of Success* for the period of time specified.

Objective: Development of EDCOT Web Site
The EDCOT Web site was launched this quarter. Solicited feedback was very positive on the Web design. Web site usage statistics indicate only 234 hits of visitors to the site; this low access is to be expected given that the site is still under development. Additional pages for each service section are expected to be completed in the second quarter. Search engine submission of the home page URL is recommended. Advertise the Web site through e-mails to friends and colleagues in the hosted organizations. Promote the site at the 2004 NAPCE Conference using a promotional gift

Objective: Management of Web Crossing Online Discussions
The Web Crossing software was launched this quarter with asynchronous linear discussions created for iComm, KidZatHeart, Ministers2Military, and Psalm One Ministries. Site traffic consisted of 135 site hits with 57 messages posted. Threaded asynchronous discussions and synchronous chat room discussions are expected to be added in the second quarter. The system operator registered 12 participants needing access to restricted discussions and added them to the appropriate access lists. Consider making registration open to any visitor to the site, and moving access list management to the appropriate discussion hosts.

Objective: e-publication of the *Digital Learning Journal*
The first issue of the journal is planned for release in late summer 2004. The site design is to be completed by late spring 2004 in order to file the application for an ISSN for the journal. At the present time only one associate editor has been chosen; additional associate editors and an advisory panel need to be secured by late spring. Journal articles for the first issue also need to be solicited from the editor and associate editors, and submission guidelines need to be developed for future issues

End Report

2. *Schedule.* Where and how often the assessment(s) methods will be deployed.
3. *Evaluator(s).* Who will be responsible for collecting, compiling, and interpreting the data (there may be a different person for each).

Two columns in the indicators of success table remain blank until the evaluative data is compiled and interpreted. The *Findings* column is reserved for a brief, objective summary of the results obtained from the various assessments. The *Impact* column is reserved for a statement of specific and appropriate actions taken to shape new or reshape existing ministry objectives and outcomes as a result of the data under *Findings.*

Once the indicators of success table is completed, a *summary report* should be created that describes the status of each objective and outcome as a result of the assessments conducted. This report is essentially an abstract of the *Findings* and *Impact* data.

Tools for Conducting Evaluations

As noted previously, churches and Christian organizations already deploy several data-gathering tools that can help measure the effectiveness of ministry. These tools include the data gathered for budget reports, attendance charts, giving trends, sales reports, etc. Any data that is gathered on a consistent basis can be an invaluable source of information on the effectiveness of ministry. Other tools, such as job and service descriptions and program planning forms, also contain information that can be used to determine what indicators of success need to be measured by other means.[17] In addition to these existing data-gathering tools, ministry effectiveness can be measured directly by means of surveys or forms. When developed and implemented correctly, surveys and forms can yield extremely accurate perceptions about the effectiveness of ministry.

Paper Surveys and Online Forms

Paper surveys and online forms are data-gathering tools that measure ministry effectiveness in structured ways. Although the content of paper surveys and online forms can be identical, each of these tools has distinct advantages and disadvantages in gathering data.

Paper surveys can be given to anybody, and they can be distributed at any time before, during, or after a ministry activity. A copy of the survey will need to be made available for each person in the ministry activity, and in some cases, a pen or pencil will also need to be provided. Once the paper survey is completed, the data must be compiled into a database or spreadsheet—often by hand—and the responses for each question tabulated.

A disadvantage of paper surveys is that questions can be skipped, or multiple responses marked where only one is appropriate. When this occurs, the survey may be unusable if critical information is missing, or if the data cannot be categorized because of multiple responses. Also, the expense for paper surveys can be high once the cost of paper, photocopying, pens or pencils, and data compilation are taken into consideration.

Online forms require the person completing the form to have access to a computer and the Internet. Online forms almost always have to be completed at home or the office well after the ministry activity has ended (though the increasing popularity of Wi-Fi wireless connections and portable computers may change that in the not-too-distant future). *An online form should only be used in situations where most of the people participating in the ministry activity have easy access to the World Wide Web.* The Web address for the online form is the only thing that needs to be distributed to participants invited to complete the form. When the online form is submitted, the data can be automatically added to a database rather than having to be entered by hand. Once a predetermined amount of time has passed, the online form is removed from online access and the database records are tabulated.

An advantage of online forms is that responding to a question can be required, and the number of responses to a question can be limited. These form-processing rules insure that critical information is provided, and multiple responses are avoided as appropriate. The expense for online forms can be cheaper than paper surveys because no paper, photocopying, or writing instruments are involved. However, the costs can be higher if Internet service provider fees, Web-hosting fees, online form design fees, and database management costs are not already provided by the organization.

Both paper surveys and online forms are only as good in measuring effectiveness as the questions they contain. Although survey and form design is beyond the scope of this chapter, the following design principles should be taken into consideration when creating a survey or form:

1. Questions and statements "should be written in simple and clear language, should contain a single idea, and should be unambiguous."[18]

2. Demographic questions such as gender, age range, frequency of attendance, distance traveled to the activity, etc. should be included as appropriate to the ministry activity. This information will help you categorize your findings and look for patterns in responses. Please note that indicating age range will be less threatening to some participants than giving their exact age—age ranges also make data easier to process mentally (18–24; 25–29 as opposed to 18, 19, 20, 21, and so on).

3. You should not ask questions that might invade the personal privacy of the participant, nor should you ask questions that have no bearing on the area of ministry being surveyed. For example: asking participants their level of income is unlikely to be relevant to a survey on measuring the effectiveness of Sunday school curriculum.

4. Consider using a five-point Likert response scale for attitudinal items.[19] When a Likert scale is used, the item is presented as a declarative sentence, followed by response options that indicate varying degrees of agreement with or endorsement of the statement.[20] A separate sixth response point, "Does Not Apply," should be added only when necessary. For example:

The guest speaker enhanced my understanding of how to live for Christ.

A=Strongly Agree; B=Moderately Agree; C=Agree/Disagree; D=Moderately Disagree; E=Strongly Disagree

My overall *satisfaction* with the conference as a whole.
5=Very High; 4=High; 3=Appropriate-Average; 2=Low; 1=Very Low

The help desk staff was helpful in directing visitors to classrooms and answering questions about church programs.
5=Yes; 4; 3; 2; 1=No; 6=Does Not Apply

Please note that Likert response scales should start with the positive end of the continuum rather than the negative, i.e., Strongly Agree through Strongly Disagree, not vice versa. If numerical scales will potentially bias results, use letters (A, B, C, D, E) or abbreviations that represent the possible responses (SA, A, N, D, SD) rather than numbers (5, 4, 3, 2, 1).

When converting letters or abbreviations into numerical values, it is less confusing to give the negative end of the scale the low numerical value—low numbers for positive responses are psychologically unappealing. Also, you should never use zero as the lowest value for the end of a numerical scale on a continuum, or for a "Does Not Apply" response. There is always the possibility the participant's answer is not an absolute, and the zero value will not compute statistically, especially if you just need to count the number of times "Does Not Apply" was the response.[21]

5. Surveys and forms should be designed in such a way that they are easy to read, easy to fill in responses, and make data easy to compile.

Keep, Drop, and Add Surveys

Keep, drop, and add surveys are one of the fastest ways to gather data about ministry effectiveness. The data gathered are less structured than that of paper surveys and online forms because the three lines of inquiry involve open-ended feedback rather than true-false, multiple choice, or scaled responses. The keep, drop, and add survey can also be deployed in tandem with a paper survey or online form. Quite frequently the data collected with the keep, drop, and add method will clarify or expand upon the data collected through more structured instrumentation. Keep, drop, and add surveys can be given to anybody and distributed at any time before, during, or after a ministry activity.

The survey is conducted by giving each person a blank sheet of paper or a blank note card; in some cases, a pen or pencil must also be provided. Participants are asked to divide the paper or note card into three sections, and label one section "keep," one section "drop," and one section "add." Participants then write their feedback on the ministry activity under the appropriate sections. Once the survey is completed, the data must be compiled into a database or spreadsheet by hand, and the responses for each section tabulated.

A disadvantage with keep, drop, and add surveys is that critical information that could help interpret responses is not collected. For example, it could be helpful to know if repeating patterns of "keep" responses are coming from men or women, or from a specific age range. Also, the flexibility of open-ended responses makes the compiling of data more difficult. To sort the data, repeating patterns of keywords or response themes must be identified from the surveys themselves rather than determining them beforehand. Throughout the data compilation process there is also the challenge of deciphering the handwriting of the participants in the survey.

A significant advantage of keep, drop, and add surveys over paper surveys and online forms is that participants can be debriefed about their responses even before the written responses are compiled. This oral feedback often highlights the more critical perceptions that were recorded on paper or note cards, providing ministry leaders with the opportunity to probe responses as necessary in order to clarify participant feedback. Participants in a keep, drop, and add survey are also free to comment on any aspect of a ministry activity, rather than just the areas identified by the questions and statements on a paper survey or online form. The open-ended responses of a keep, drop, and add survey often yield insights into ministry effectiveness that may be missed when a more structured tool is used.

Drawing Accurate Conclusions

Once assessment data is gathered, no matter the method, the findings must be evaluated carefully in order to avoid drawing erroneous conclusions. The process of evaluating data "should include these elements: (1) careful examination of the information to determine its validity; (2) determination of the reasons for past success and failure; and (3) the feeding of information back into the process for future ministry planning.[22] Using the indicators of success protocols as an example, the Findings data would be studied carefully, the new data compared to the findings of previous evaluations, and then appropriate recommendations would be framed that shape or reshape ministry objectives and outcomes. These recommendations would be formed as impact statements.

The temptation in interpreting assessment data will be to draw conclusions apart from the data presented. Sometimes when the data indicates we are not being effective in ministry, we may become defensive and discount or ignore objective findings. If that happens, subjective opinions tend to become "the data" that justifies maintaining or dismantling the status quo. "Failure to use the results of evaluation is a disservice to the people with whom you work and, if done intentionally, dishonest."[23]

We must always remember that "the most important result of evaluation is what happens in and to the persons involved. . . . The church belongs in the people-mending and people-maturing business; therefore, evaluation should contribute to that process."[24] If we are willing to look objectively at our ministries and are willing to make appropriate modifications suggested by the data we gather, we will increase our effectiveness in building up the body of Christ, and in so doing make a valuable contribution toward fulfilling the Great Commission.

Notes

Part 1: Integration

1. John Dewey, from the introduction of *Theology of Administration: A Biblical Basis for Organizing the Congregation* by Harris W. Lee (Minn: Minneapolis: Augsburg Publishing House, 1981), 4.

2. The following list in a paraphrased form comes from Harris W. Lee, *Theology of Administration: A Biblical Basis for Organizing the Congregation* (Minneapolis: Augsburg Publishing House, 1981), 6–7.

3. Ibid., 7.

4. Gerhard Kittel and Gerhard Friedrich, eds., *Theological Dictionary of the New Testament*, s.v. *"Kubern EQ kubernesis"* (Grand Rapids: Wm. B. Eerdmans Publishing Co.), 1036.

Chapter 1

1. I would like to acknowledge the contributions made by several of my Ph.D. students who assisted me in gathering the biblical references for this chapter. They are Joyce Brooks, Mark Henze, Seung Lee, and Myeong-Shin Nam.

Chapter 2

1. Cf. Patrick J. Montana and Bruce H. Charnov, *Management* (Hauppauge, New York: Barron's Educational Series, 2000), 11–35.

2. Cf. Lyman Lundeen, "Theology and the Management Mystique," *The Lutheran Quarterly* 25 (1973): 339–50.

3. James N. Poling and Donald E. Miller, *Foundations for a Practical Theology of Ministry* (Nashville: Abingdon Press, 1985), 94.

4. William A. Johnson, "Process Management: Bad Theology in the Service of the Church," *The Christian Century* (1976): 625.

5. Myron Rush, *Management: A Biblical Approach* (Wheaton, Ill.: Victor Books, 1983), 11.

6. Loren Broadus, "What in the World Does Theology Have to Do with Leadership," *Lexington Theological Quarterly* 2 (1976): 75.

7. Poling and Miller, 108.

8. Kenneth O. Gangel, *Competent to Lead* (Chicago: Moody Press, 1977), 18.

9. Cf. Ray S. Anderson, "A Theology of Ministry," in *Theological Foundations for Ministry,* ed. Ray S. Anderson (Grand Rapids: Eerdmans Publishing Company, 1979), 9.

10. Cf. James Riley Estep Jr., "Biblical-Theological Foundations of Christian Education," in *Foundations for Christian Education,* Eleanor A. Daniel and John W. Wade, eds. (Joplin, Mo.: College Press, 1999), 13–33.

11. Lawrence O. Richards, *A Theology of Church Leadership* (Grand Rapids: Zondervan Publishing House, 1980), 199.

12. Cf. Lewis Sperry Chafer, *He That Is Spiritual* (Grand Rapids: Zondervan Publishing House, 1967), 17–21.

13. Ronald T. Habermas, "Practical dimensions of the *imago dei,*" *Christian Education Journal* 13 (1993): 90–91.

14. Cf. Lawrence O. Richards and Gib Martin, *A Theology of Personal Ministry* (Grand Rapids: Zondervan Publishing House, 1987), 130–132 for complete discussion of gifts in administration.

15. Kenneth Gangel, *Competent to Lead* (Chicago: Moody Press, 1974), 21. Gangel used the Septuagint rather than the Hebrew Old Testament as a means of completing his word study of κυβήρνητης.

16. Fritz Rienecker and Cleon Rogers, *Linguistic Key to the Greek New Testament* (Grand Rapids: Regency/Zondervan Publishing House, 1980), 430.

17. Ibid., 395.

18. Warren S. Benson, "Jesus Christ and Paul as Christian Education Specialists," in *Directing Christian Education,* Michael S. Lawson and Robert J. Choun Jr. (Chicago: Moody Press, 1992), 33.

19. Cf. earlier edition of this figure in James Riley Estep Jr., "Can a Christian be a Dean? Toward a Theology of Academic Administration in Christian Higher Education," *Christian Education Journal* 6NS (2002): 35–54.

20. Gareth Morgan, *Images of Organization,* 2nd ed. (London: Sage Publishers, 1997), 347.

Part 2: Planning

1. M. Peterson, "Analyzing alternative approaches to planning," in P. Jedamus M. Peterson, & Associates (eds.), *Improving Academic Management* (San Francisco: Jossey-Bass, 1980), 113–163.

2. A. MacKinney, "Planning in Academic Institutions," in *Professional Psychology: Research and Practice,* Vol. 15, No. 5 (1984): 637–44.

3. H. Koontz and H. Weihrich, *Essentials of Management* (San Francisco: McGraw-Hill Publishing, 1990), 49.

4. Ibid., 49.

5. This is modified from "The Planning Pyramid" depicted in the *Essentials of Management* text on p. 47.

6. MacKinney, 640.

Chapter 3

1. George Barna, *Without a Vision the People Perish* (Glendale, Calif.: Barna Research Group, 1991), 145.

2. William G. Caldwell, "Mission," in *Evangelical Dictionary of Christian Education*, ed. Michael D. Anthony (Grand Rapids: Baker Academics, 2001), 475.

3. Barna, 38.

4. Barna, 38–39.

5. Barna, 40–41.

6. Rick Warren, *The Purpose-Driven Church* (Grand Rapids: Zondervan, 1995), 81.

7. George Barna, *Turning Vision into Action: Defining and Putting into Practice the Unique Vision God Has for Your Ministry* (Ventura, Calif.: Regal, 1996), 145.

8. Barna, *Without a Vision*, 28.

9. Joel Hunter, "Clearing," *Leadership Journal* (Spring 1999): 120–124.

10. Josh McDowell, Dave Hannah, and Rick Warren, "Influential Things Come in Small Packages," *Christianity Today*, October 2003, 52–53.

11. Ibid., 52–53.

12. Bill Hybels, *Courageous Leadership* (Grand Rapids: Zondervan, 2002), 29.

13. Hybels, *Courageous Leadership*, 29–30.

14. John 1:14, Eugene H. Peterson, *The Message: A Paraphrase of the New Testament with Psalms and Proverbs* (Colorado Springs, Colo.: NavPress), 2000.

15. Vision Statement. Neighborhood Christian Fellowship. Covina, California, 1996.

16. Terry Wardle, "Keys to Communicating Vision," *Ministry Advantage* 4 (1993), 2.

17. C. E. Larson and M. J. LaFasto, *Teamwork: What Must Go Right/What Can Go Wrong* (Newbury Park, Calif., 1989), 24–26.

18. Ibid., 27.

19. W. Bennis and B. Nanus, *Leaders: The Strategies for Taking Charge* (New York: Harper and Row, 1985), 28. Quoted in Larson and LaFasto, *Teamwork*, 27–28.

20. Kevin Lawson, *How to Thrive in Associate Staff Ministry* (Bethesda, Md.: Alban Institute, 2000), 55.

21. Ibid., 59.

22. Ibid., 66.

23. Barna, *Turning Vision into Action*, 154–160.

24. Hybels, *Courageous Leadership*, 32.

25. Ibid., 32–37.

Chapter 4

1. Edward R. Dayton and Ted W. Engstrom, *Strategy for Living* (Ventura, Calif.: Revel Books, 1976), 41.

2. Robert Kreitner, *Management,* 8th ed. (Chicago: Houghton and Mifflin, 2001), 6.

3. Lee G. Bolman and Terrence E. Deal, *Reframing Organizations* (San Francisco: Jossey-Bass, 1997), 165.

4. Kreitner, 174.

5. Bolman and Deal, 268.

6. Adapted from Kenneth Gangel, *Feeding and Leading* (Wheaton, Ill.: Victor Books, 1989), 93.

7. Based on Andrew Seidel, *Charting a Bold Course: Training Leaders for 21st Century Ministry* (Chicago: Moody Press, 2003), 229–230.

8. Bolman and Deal, 53.

9. Louis Carroll, *Alice in Wonderland* (http://www.textlibrary. com/download/alice-wo.txt).

10. Dayton and Engstrom, 50. Their text uses the term *goals* whereas this one has substituted the term *objectives.*

11. Quote taken from President John F. Kennedy's address to a specially called joint session of Congress on May 25, 1961. The session was called to address the Cold War tensions with Russia, the failure of the Bay of Pigs invasion of Cuba, and the state of national security. Full text of the message is available from The John F Kennedy Library and Museum at http://www.cs.umb.edu/jfklibrary/index.htm.

12. Michael Kay, "Achieving that Everest Feeling," *Management Review* 88 (April 1999): 13.

13. Paul Hersey, Kenneth Blanchard, Dewey Johnson, *Managing of Organizational Behavior: Leading Human Resources* (Upper Saddle River, N.J.: Prentice Hall, 2001), 31.

14. Edwin Locke and Gary Latham, *Goal-Setting: A Motivational Technique That Works!* (Upper Saddle River, N.J.: Prentice Hall, 1984), 120–193.

15. Ivan Scheier, *When Everyone Is a Volunteer* (Philadelphia: Energize, 1992), 9–16.

16. Kreitner, 175.

17. Gene Greeson, *Goal Setting: Turning Your Mountains into Molehills* (St. Louis: Potential Unlimited, 1994), 79.

Chapter 5

1. Peter Blackerby, "History of Strategic Planning," *Armed Forces Comptroller* 39 (1): 23–24.

2. A. Lumpkin, "Strategic Planning in Health, Physical Education, Recreation, and Dance," *The Journal of Physical Education, Recreation and Dance,* 68 (5), 38–41.

3. Ibid., 38–39.

4. Aubrey Malphurs, *Advanced Strategic Planning: A New Model for Church and Ministry Leaders* (Grand Rapids: Baker Book House, 1999), 61.

5. Ibid., 104.

6. Ibid., 139, 140.

7. Ibid., 79.

8. Christine D. Keen, "Tips for Effective Strategic Planning," *Human Resources Magazine* 39 (8): 84.

9. Roger Kaufman and Jerry Herman, "Strategic Planning for a Better Society," *Educational Leadership* (April 1991): 7.

10. Keen, 84.

11. Keith Orndoff, "Developing Strategic Competencies: A Starting Point," *The Information Management Journal* (July/Aug. 2002): 60.

12. Paul Hersey and Ken Blanchard, *Management of Organizations: Utilizing Human Resources* (New Jersey: Prentice Hall Publishers, 1969), 382, 383.

13. Gene Mims, "Using Kingdom Principles in Church Planning," *Church Administration*, 38 (8): 10.

14. John Bryson, *Strategic Planning for Public and Non-Profit Organizations* (San Francisco: Jossey Bass Publishers, 1995), 188.

15. Henry Klopp, *The Ministry Playbook: Strategic Planning for Effective Churches* (Grand Rapids: Baker Book House, 2002), 31–34.

16. Ibid., 28, 29.

17. Kaufman and Herman, 8.

Chapter 6

1. Fritz Rienecker and Cleon Rogers, *Linguistic Key to the Greek New Testament* (Grand Rapids: Zondervan Publishing House, 1980), 430.

2. Larry J. Michael, *Spurgeon on Leadership: Key Insights for Christian Leaders from the Prince of Preachers* (Grand Rapids: Kregel, 2003), 101.

3. Ibid.

4. Aubrey Malphurs, *Advanced Strategic Planning: A New Model for Church and Ministry Leaders* (Grand Rapids: Baker Books, 1999), 194.

5. Kenneth O. Gangel, *Team Leadership in Christian Ministry*, revised (Chicago: Moody Press, 1997), 170.

6. Bobb Biehl, *Stop Setting Goals If You Would Rather Solve Problems* (Nashville: Moorings, 1995), 189.

7. Bruce Powers, ed., *Church Administration Handbook*, rev. ed., ed. Bruce P. Powers (Nashville: Broadman & Holman, 1997).

8. Bruce Powers, *Christian Education Handbook*, Rev. ed. (Nashville: Broadman & Holman, 1996).

9. James Riley Estep Jr. "Policy/Procedure Formation Template" (CE240/CE601 course handout, Lincoln Christian College and Seminary, 2003).

10. Powers, *Church Administration Handbook* (1997), 174.

Chapter 7

1. Robert N. Gray, *Managing the Church: Business Administration* (Enid, Okla.: NCC Publication, 1979), 75.

2. James Estep, "Basic Budgeting Design," Handout in CE601 Educational Leadership and Administration (Lincoln Christian Seminary, Lincoln, Illinois), Fall 2003.

3. Margaret J. Barr, *Academic Administrator's Guide to Budgets and Financial Management* (San Francisco: John Wiley & Sons, 2002), 37–42.

4. Ibid., 37.

5. Ibid., 39.

6. Ibid., 40.

7. Ibid., 41.

8. Gray, 75.

Chapter 8

1. P. F. Drucker, *The Practice of Management* (New York: Harper & Row Publishers, 1954), 135–136.

2. G. S. Odiorne, *Management by Objectives: A System of Managerial Leadership* (Belmont: Pitman Publishing Company, 1965), 55–56.

3. F. Luthans, and Jerry Selentin, "MBO in Hospitals: A Step Toward Accountability" *Personnel Administrator* 21, no. 7 (October 1976): 42–45.

4. F. V. Malek, "Managing for Results in the Federal Government," *Business Horizons* 17, no. 2 (April 1974): 23–28.

5. Education has been a major focus for the integration of MBO. One of the leading educational institutions which has pioneered this integration is the Management Institute of the University of Wisconsin. I recommend you obtain one of the first references to this adaptation by Norman C. Allhiser, chairman of the department of business and management. See his chapter entitled "MBO in the Management Institute" which is found in Dale McConkey's book cited below. Another excellent source is Steven Knezevich, *Management by Objectives and Results* (Arlington: American Association of School Administrators, 1973).

6. Michael J. Anthony, "Management by Objectives for Camp Administration," *Journal of Christian Camping* 17, no. 1 (Jan.-Feb. 1985): 12–13.

7. D. McConke., See chapter 5 "MBO in Church Organizations" in *MBO for Nonprofit Organizations* (New York: The American Management Association, 1975). See also Daniel L. Mead and Darrell J. Allen, *Ministry by Objectives* (The Evangelical Training Association, 1978).

8. Sister Rosemary Miller, "Living by Objectives," *Management by Objectives Journal* 1, no. 2 (October 1971).

9. Odiorne, op cit.

10. G. I. Morrisey, *Management by Objectives and Results* (Reading: Addison-Wesley Publishing, 1970).

11. John W. Humble, *Management by Objectives in Action* (New York: McGraw Hill, 1970).

12. Arthur D. Beck and Ellis D. Hillmar, *Practical Approach to Organizational Development* (Reading: Addisoon-Wesley Publishers, 1972).

13. McConkey, 172.

14. George Odiorne, *MBO II: A System of Managerial Leadership for the 80's* (Belmont: Fearon Pitman Publishers, 1979), 74.

15. Jim Collins, *Good to Great* (New York: HarperCollins Publishers, 2001), 13.

16. Knezevich, op cit., 37.

17. Anthony Raia, *Managing by Objectives* (Glenview: Scott, Foresman and Company, 1974), 149.

18. This list has been significantly modified from material found in Richard Babcock and Peter F. Sorensen, "An MBO Checklist: Are the Conditions Right for Implementation?" *Management Review* 68 (June 1979): 59–62.

19. Harold Koontz and Heinz Weihrich, *Essentials of Management,* 5th ed. (New York: McGraw Hill Publishing Company, 1986), 71.

Part 3: Organizing

1. Harold Koontz and Heinz Weihrich, *The Essentials of Management* (San Francisco: McGraw Hill Publishers, 1990), 134.

2. Arthur J. Lynch, "Modification to the Management Processes: A Proposal for Combination and Addition in Elements of Management," *Training and Development Journal* (July 1967): 51.

Chapter 9

1. Some of the content of this chapter was adapted from Michael Anthony, "Organizational Structures in the Church," chapter 8 in *The Effective Church Board* (Grand Rapids: Baker Books, 1993).

2. "Session Manual," Faith Presbyterian Church, Indianapolis, Indiana, p. 3.

3. James A. F. Stoner, *Management* (Englewood, N.J.: Prentice-Hall, Inc.), 225.

4. Bruce W. Jones, *Ministerial Leadership in a Managerial World* (Wheaton, Ill.: Tyndale Press, 1988), 120.

5. Session Manual, 8

6. Jones, 123.

7. Wayman D. Miller, *The Role of Elders in the New Testament Church* (Tulsa: Plaza, 1980), 79.

8. Ken Gangel, *Leadership for Church Education* (Chicago: Moody Press, 1970), 56–57.

Chapter 10

1. Harold J. Westing, *Church Staff Handbook: How to Build an Effective Ministry Team,* revised and updated (Grand Rapids: Kregel Publications, 1997), 93.

2. Kenneth O. Gangel, *Team Leadership in Christian Ministry,* revised (Chicago: Moody Press, 1997), 239.

3. Chris W. Tornquist, "Reading Between the Lines: The Problem of Unwritten Expectations," *Christian Education Journal,* Vol. 10, No. 2 (1990): 17.

4. Michael J. Anthony, *The Effective Church Board: A Handbook for Mentoring and Training Servant Leaders* (Grand Rapids: Baker Books, 1993), 78.

5. Westing, 94.

6. Ibid., 95.

7. Anthony, 78.

8. Westing, 95.

9. Gangel, *Team Ministry,* 329.

10. Judy J. Stamey, "Equipping the Saints to Serve," in *Church Administration Handbook,* rev. ed., ed. Bruce P. Powers (Nashville: Broadman & Holman, 1997), 239.

11. Michael A. Bechtle, "The Roles and Responsibilities of Christian Education Personnel," in *Foundations of Ministry: An Introduction to Christian Education for a New Generation,* ed. Michael J. Anthony (Wheaton, Ill.: Victor Books, 1992), 239–240.

12. Ibid., 240.

13. Westing, 98.

14. Ibid., 97.

15. Ibid., 93.

16. William G. Caldwell, "Administering Personnel," in *Church Administration Handbook,* rev. ed., Bruce P. Powers (Nashville: Broadman & Holman, 1997), 73.

17. Anthony, 80.

18. Caldwell, 73.

19. Ibid.

20. Robert K. Greenleaf, *On Becoming a Servant Leader,* ed. Don M. Frick and Larry C. Spears (San Francisco: Jossey-Bass, 1996), 182.

21. Westing, 93.

22. Gangel, 329.

23. Westing, 93.

24. Ibid., 97.

25. Gangel, 329–330.

26. Anthony, 80.

27. Ibid., 78.

28. Westing, 96.

29. Bechtle, 239.

30. Anthony, 80.

31. Bechtle, 239.

32. Anthony, 79.

33. Gangel, 329–330.

Chapter 12

1. Spencer Johnson, *Who Moved My Cheese?* (New York: G. P. Putnam Sons, 1999).

2. Mike Nappa, *Who Moved My Church?* (Tulsa, Okla.: River Oak Publishing, 2001).

3. Cf. Robert D. Dale, *To Dream Again* (Nashville: Broadman Publishing, 1981).

4. Cf. Nadya Labi, "The New Funday School," *Time* (December 16, 2002): 60–62.

5. John Maxwell, *Developing the Leader Within You* (Nashville: Thomas Nelson, 1992), 65.

6. Jim Herrington, Mike Bonem, and James H. Furr, *Leading Congregational Change* (San Francisco: Jossey-Bass, 2000), 100–157.

7. Adapted and based on David A Nadler *et al.*, *Discontinuous Change* (San Francisco: Jossey-Bass Publishers, 1995), 64.

8. Robert Heller and Tim Hindle, *Essential Manager's Manual* (New York: D. K. Publishing, 1998), 715.

9. Cf. Heller and Hindle, 730.

10. Cf. Phillip V. Lewis, *Transformational Leadership* (Nashville: Broadman & Holman, 1996), 130–131; Aubrey Malphurs, *Values-Driven Leadership* (Grand Rapids: Baker Book House, 1996), 130; Kenneth K. Kilinski and Jerry C. Wofferd, *Organization and Leadership in the Local Church* (Grand Rapids: Zondervan Publishing, 1973), 112–114.

11. Speed Leas, "The Varieties of Religious Strife," *Mastering Conflict and Controversy* (Portland, Ore.: Multnomah Press), 83–94.

12. Ibid., 88–90.

13. Ibid., 90–92.

14. "The Peacemaker: Responding to Conflict Biblically," promotional pamphlet (Billings, Mont.: Peacemaker Ministries, 1996).

15. Ron Susek, *Firestorm: Preventing and Overcoming Church Conflict* (Grand Rapids: Baker Book House, 1999), 136.

Chapter 13

1. Paul Hersey and Kenneth Blanchard, *Management of Organizational Behavior*, 6th ed. (Englewood Cliffs, N.J.: Prentice-Hall, 1993), 364.

2. Robert Heller and Tim Hindle, *Essential Manager's Manual* (New York: D. K. Publishing, 1998), 165.

3. Wayne Jacobsen, "A Board's Guide to Praying Together," *Leadership*, 6 (1985): 31.

4. Karen Marie Yust, *Attentive to God* (St. Louis: Chalice Press, 2001), 7.

5. Hersey and Blanchard, 456–458.

6. James E. Means, *Leadership in Christian Ministry* (Grand Rapids: Baker Book House, 1989), 159–164.

7. Cf. James Champy, *Reengeneering Management* (New York: Harper Business, 1995), 75–95.

8. Cf. Bill Creech, *The Five Pillars of TQM* (New York: Truman Talley Books, 1994), 321; Kenneth Gangel, *Team Leadership* (Chicago: Moody Press, 1994), 410–412.

9. Adapted from Richard M. Hodgetts, *Modern Human Relations at Work* (Chicago: Dryden Press, 1980), 359.

10. Trista Yarbrough, "Put It in Writing!" *Church Administration* 31 (1989): 24–25.

11. Robert Heller and Tim Hindle, *Essential Manager's Manual* (New York: D. K. Publishing, 1998), 25.

12. *Leadership* 6 (1985): 46.

13. Based on Judy J. Stamey, "Does Your Staff Know What's Going On?" _Church Administration_ 39 (1997): 8–9.

Staffing

1. Kenneth O. Gangel, _Building Leaders for Church Education_ (Chicago: Moody Press, 1981), 227–228.
2. Robert D. Herman, _The Jossey-Bass Handbook of Nonprofit Leadership and Management_ (San Francisco: Jossey-Bass Publishers, 1994), 536.
3. H. Koontz, and H. Weihrich. _Essential of Management_ (San Francisco: McGraw-Hill Publishing, 1990), 218.
4. Robert D. Herman, 515.

Chapter 14

1. Dennis E. Williams and Kenneth O. Gangel, _Volunteers for Today's Church: How to Recruit and Retain Volunteers_ (Grand Rapids: Baker Books, 1993), 27–45.
2. Thom S. Rainer, _High Expectation: The Remarkable Secret for Keeping People in Your Church_ (Nashville, TN: Broadman and Holman, 1999), 59.
3. Williams and Gangel, 38.
4. Dennis E. Williams, "Recruiting, Training, and Motivating Volunteers," in _Introducing Christian Education: Foundations for the Twenty-first Century_, ed. Michael J. Anthony (Grand Rapids: Baker Books, 2001), 175.
5. National Child Protection Act of 1993, http://www.casanet.org/library/juvenile-justice/ncpa93.htm
6. J. W. "Bill" Phillips, _Sexual Abuse: Protecting Your Education Ministries_ (2 of 3), LifeWay Christian Resources, http://www.lifeway. com/lwc/lwc_cda_article.

Chapter 15

1. Kenneth O. Gangel, _Team Leadership in Christian Ministry_ (Chicago: Moody Press), 276.
2. Ibid., 281.
3. Ibid., 281.
4. Jim Collins, _Good to Great_ (New York: HarperCollins, 2001), 42.
5. Ibid., 44.
6. Ibid., 56.
7. Ibid., 46–48.
8. Warren R. Plunkett and Raymond F. Attner, _Introduction to Management_ (Boston: PWS-Kent Publishing Co.), 348–350.
9. Paul Hershey and Kenneth H. Blanchard, _Management of Organizational Behavior_, 3rd ed. (Englewood Cliffs, N.J.: Prentice-Hill,), 288–289.

Chapter 16

1. The law is constantly in flux. As a result any written treatment of legal issues requires an appropriate disclaimer. This chapter is intended to provide a general and conceptual overview of the law affecting churches and ministry. It should not be relied upon as a substitute for legal consultation and advice. At

the end of this book is a bibliography providing a variety of additional sources of information on specific areas, including several Web site and reporting services that can keep the reader abreast of current changes.

2. In Exodus 21:1, the Lord said to Moses, "These are the laws you are to set before them." Then "When Moses went and told the people all the LORD's words and laws, they responded with one voice, 'Everything the LORD has said we will do.'" (Exod. 24:3 NIV).

3. Jesus picked grain and healed on the Sabbath (Luke 6:10–11), drove merchants out of the temple area (Luke 19:45–46), failed to follow all of the cleanliness laws by failing to wash his hands before eating (Matt. 15:1–9), and associate with both sinners and the unclean (Matt. 9:10–11). Although not civilly disobedient, Jesus did stand in the way of the execution of prescribed punishment meted out to the adulterous woman (John 8:1–8).

4. Note that Jesus paid and taught his disciples to honor the temple tax (Matt. 17:24–27), attended each of the required Jerusalem feasts, and even suggested paying appropriate taxes to Caesar (Matt. 22:15–22).

5. For example, Paul used and called upon his special privilege as a citizen of Rome to obtain an appeal before Caesar (Acts 22:22–29).

6. Note that there are many possible ways of organizing legal discussions. This division into four quadrants is simple, yet effective for the purposes of this chapter.

7. See *Brannon v. Commissioner,* T.C. Memo. 1999-370 (U.S. Tax Court).

8. Due to the space available, we will not deal with any specific issues of school or educational law. Should a ministry be looking into formal education programs, it would be wise to investigate these specialized issues further.

9. The Fourteenth Amendment was adopted in 1868 to ensure that the Bill of Rights and other constitutional protections were fully applicable to newly freed slaves. Later, it was held that the due process clause of that amendment effectively required that the Bill of Rights be honored by the states as well as the federal government. See *Cantwell v. Connecticut,* 310 U.S. 296 (1940).

10. This clause simply and succinctly states that "Congress shall make no law respecting an establishment of religion."

11. Concerning religion, the free exercise clause of the First Amendment provides that "Congress shall make no law . . . prohibiting the free exercise thereof."

12. 330 U.S. 1 (1947).

13. This is generally referred to as the "Lemon Test" and is derived from *Lemon v. Kurtzman,* 403 U.S. 602 (1971) at 614.

14. *Engle v. Vitale,* 370 U.S. 421 (1962).

15. *Abington v. Schemp,* 374 U.S. 203 (1963).

16. *Epperson v. Arkansas,* 393 U.S. 97 (1968). (A 1929 Arkansas statute prohibiting the teaching of evolution was struck down.)

17. *Roemer v. Maryland Board of Public Works,* 425 U.S. 736 (1976).

18. See *Watson v. Jones,* 80 U.S. 679 (1871), where the court handed down a general rule of nonjudicial intervention into clergy employment decisions. This was due not only to First Amendment government entanglement issues,

but also due to the special expertise in these matters provided by the church's ecclesiastical government and the congregation's "implied consent" to the exclusive jurisdiction of the church. However, recent courts have indicated a willingness to review these matters if it can be done solely on secular grounds (i.e., contract or civil rights grounds) and without delving into religious doctrine. See *Jones v. Wolf,* 443 U.S. 595 (1979).

19. The case of *Sherbert v. Verner,* 374 U.S. 398 (1963) dealt with a Seventh Day Adventist who was denied unemployment compensation because of her refusal to accept jobs requiring work on Saturdays. Here, the court awarded unemployment benefits.

20. In *Wisconsin v. Yoder,* 406 U.S. 205 (1972), an Amish parent removed his eighth-grader from the public school and commenced an unaccredited and unlicensed Amish vocational program. Here, the court held that the state's interest in providing appropriate education and avoiding "wards of the state" was not as strong since the purpose could arguably be accomplished by the Amish program.

21. The court has held that it may not inquire into the rationality or the truth or falsity of one's claimed religious beliefs, nor is the protection of these beliefs dependent upon community acceptance or practice. *Thomas v. Review Board,* 450 U.S. 707 (1981).

22. In *Pierce v. Society of Sisters,* 268 U.S. 510 (1925), the state of Oregon attempted to require attendance at public rather than parochial schools. The Supreme Court held that parents had a constitutional right to select comparable yet religious education if they so desired.

23. Note that this issue also touches on freedom of speech issues within the First Amendment.

24. In *Young v. Northern Illinois Conference of the United Methodist Church,* 21 F.3d 184 (7th Cir. 1994), the court rejected a claim of sex and race discrimination while stating that "religious bodies may make apparently arbitrary decisions affecting the employment status of their clergy members and be free from civil review having done so." However, this First Amendment protection only applies to positions that are "ministerial" or "ecclesiastical" in nature.

25. *Employment Division v. Smith,* 494 U.S. 872 (1990). Here, a drug rehabilitation counselor was fired and denied unemployment due to his use of sacramental peyote at a Native American church. The court upheld the denial of unemployment benefits.

26. See *Muhlenberg Hospital v. Patterson,* 320 A.2d 518 (1974), where a New Jersey court stated that "it does not follow that parents who wish to be martyrs for their religious beliefs have a right to impose such martyrdom upon their offspring."

27. Nor may an individual deduct his payments to a homeowner's association as a charitable contribution.

28. Despite common belief, there is no constitutional provision exempting churches from real estate and sales taxes. This is simply a matter of public policy that has a long history and is determined by the state. While all states exempted houses of worship from real estate tax at one time, many states are

attempting to change this. Nonprofit organizations are exempt from sales taxes in a majority of states, but are not in a significant number (e.g., California). The real question here is whether the granting of an exemption to a religious institution constitutes an "establishment" of religion. However, in *Walz v. Tax Commission of the State of New York*, 397 U.S. 664 (1970), the U.S. Supreme Court upheld such an exemption where the exemption covered a broad spectrum of nonreligious, nonprofit, and charitable organizations as well.

29. This is a major source of conflict with tax-exempt organizations that wish to meaningfully participate in grassroots political issues, lobbying, or legislative efforts. Recently, this has become the largest source of IRS-initiated tax-exempt litigation and has resulted in the denial or revocation of tax-exempt status. See *Regan v. Taxation with Representation of Washington*, 461 U.S. 540 (1983), where the Supreme Court rejected the contention that this requirement violated the First Amendment rights of an organization.

30. See *Walz v. Tax Commission of the State of New York*, 397 U.S. 664 (1970).

31. This list was composed over a variety of cases and regulatory actions conducted by the IRS. It arguably originated from a 1959 ruling finding that the Salvation Army was a church. However, these 14 points were specifically listed by the U.S. Tax Court in *Spiritual Outreach Society v. Commissioner*, Tax Court Memo 1990-41 and affirmed 927 F.2d 335 (8th Cir. 1991). Here, the Spiritual Outreach Society was found to not meet the definition of a church.

32. For example, see Richard R. Hammar, *Pastor, Church and Law*, 3rd ed. (Matthews, N.C.: Christian Ministry Resource Press, 2000), 227.

33. For a good general overview of tax issues affecting churches and religious organizations, see IRS Publication 1828, *Tax Guide for Churches and Religious Organizations* (Revised 7/2002) which may be accessed at *http://www.irs.gov/pub/irs-pdf/p1828.pdf*.

34. Nonprofit organizations are exempted from FUTA [26 U.S.C. 3306(c)(8)].

35. For example, the state of Colorado follows the federal example [Colo. Rev. Stat. 8-70-140(1)(a)].

36. This exemption of income is for federal income tax purposes only and does not apply to Social Security taxes or other state taxes that do not specifically include such an exemption.

37. In *Richard D. Warren and Elizabeth K. Warren v. Commissioner of Internal Revenue*, 9th Circuit Court of Appeals, Case No. 00-71217, the court had indicated that it intended to rule on constitutional grounds to hold the exemption as a violation of the Establishment Clause of the U.S. Constitution. After passage of the Clergy Housing Allowance Clarification Act of 2002, both the Warrens and the IRS agreed to dismiss the case. Neither had petitioned the court to determine the case on constitutional grounds. However, this does not mean that the constitutional issue has been resolved, and it is anticipated that a new case may soon be litigated requesting a ruling on the constitutional issues.

38. See IRS Publication 517, *Social Security and Other Information for Members of the Clergy and Religious Workers* (Revised 2002), which can be accessed at http://www.irs.gov/pub/irs-pdf/p517.pdf.

39. For example, the Federal Fair Labor Standards Act requires annual gross income of $500,000 or more, although it specifically applies to schools of any size. Obviously, for many churches that would otherwise fit under this limitation, the definition of a "school" might be important. Other examples include the Age Discrimination in Employment Act, which requires at least twenty employees, and the Family and Medical Leave Act, which requires fifty or more employees. Yet, a warning is in order. Many states have enacted their own complementary statutes which have different applicability requirements. In addition, any time an organization is involved in interstate commerce or with grants or contracts with the federal or state government, it is important to consult the terms of these agreements. They may require participation in certain programs where the employer would be otherwise exempt.

40. Yet, a minority of states specifically excludes churches and charitable organizations from its provisions. As with unemployment compensation, if the organization and its employees are exempted, they also cannot participate or claim benefits from the program.

41. The Fair Labor Standards Act exempts persons employed in bona fide executive, administrative, and professional capacities, thus including most pastors and directors. Note that the federal statutes and many state statutes also exempt religious camps and summer programs utilizing students and interns.

42. This includes discrimination only based upon religious preference (regardless of whether or not the job is specifically religious in orientation). While the statutes do not exempt churches for the purpose of sex, race, national origin, or disability, these areas may have constitutional ramifications if they infringe on one's religious or moral requirements. For example, it has been held that a church may discriminate on the basis of sex, sexual preference, or marital status when hiring ministers. This exemption does not apply to nonpastoral positions or to sexual harassment claims among current employees. However, see *Bryce v. Episcopal Church in the Diocese of Colorado*, 121 F.Supp.2d. 1327 (2000), where the court ruled that it was barred from hearing a discrimination claim brought by a nonordained youth pastor.

43. In *Kathy v. Catholic Diocese*, 206 F.3d 651 (6th Cir. 2000), the court held that a dismissal based upon moral standards (pregnancy outside of wedlock) could not be a proper basis where the evidence showed that the standards were not clearly communicated and where it appeared that moral issues were only a subterfuge for other discriminatory reasons.

44. Note that some states may permit nonclergy religious personnel to officiate at weddings. For example, California not only allows "a priest, minister, or rabbi of any religious denomination" to perform marriages, but they also permit Ph.D.'s who are officials of a nonprofit religious organization and who regularly perform services and religious rites to perform marriages (Cal. Family Code §400 & §402).

45. This is a complex area of the law, and several publications are listed in the Bibliography that specifically deal with this issue. The Copyright Act does include a specific exemption for the performance of dramatic or musical works in the course of a regular worship service. However, this does not include reproducing the lyrics (as in bulletins or on PowerPoint slides) or the transmission of the service by tape or broadcast to those not physically present.

46. Churches are generally exempt from federal and the majority of state law provisions requiring the registration of securities, the registration of those soliciting the contributions, and the filing and approval of sales materials. However, arguably this is not a significant benefit as these registrations and disclosures are often prudent in avoiding the appearance of impropriety and in ensuring that federal regulators have reviewed the material with an eye toward the mitigation of possible, yet unintentional, misrepresentation.

47. This is known as the avoidable preference section of the U.S. Bankruptcy Code [11 U.S.C §548(a)].

48. *In re Tucker*, 102 B.R. 219 (D.N.M., 1989).

49. As in many areas, there are exceptions. For example, the creditor must be aware that the corporation is the creditor and that he is relying solely on the corporation for payment. In addition, the payment of certain required withholding and trust taxes may become the personal obligation of the officers or directors who participate in the decision not to make these payments.

50. Arguably, no employer authorizes his employee to make mistakes, whether understandable or not. Yet, the failure to authorize a mistake will not insulate an employer from liability. Clearly, mistakes are an unavoidable part of employment, and the employer is deemed to expect and anticipate them.

51. The definition of "personal participation" may vary under the circumstances. Participation has been held by some courts to include permitting the act to occur, authorizing its occurrence, turning one's back when the act could have been averted, or even ratifying an act after it has occurred.

52. For example, see *Abramson v. Reiss*, 638 A.2d 743 (Md. 1994), where the Maryland Court affirmed the doctrine of charitable immunity where an adult participant in a Jewish Community Center basketball game was denied recovery based on a theory of negligent supervision.

53. 42 U.S.C. §14501 (Public Law 105-19 signed on June 18, 1997).

54. State statutes are still effective if they provide additional protection over and above the terms of the federal act.

55. See *Subchapter C – Standards of Conduct*, Section 8.30 of the Revised Model Nonprofit Corporation Act. Be advised that this act has not been passed in all states, and the version passed in each state may contain modifications.

56. Even if the culpable individual (who often has no assets) remains personally liable, the organization is often claimed to be secondarily liable under theories of negligent hiring, retention, or supervision. However, most insurance will cover the organization's liability under such a negligence theory. Many cases have held that despite broad insurance exclusions for intentional and criminal acts such as sexual misconduct, an organization remains covered

against any allegations of negligence (such as negligent hiring or supervision). See *Doe v. Shaffer*, 738 N.E.2d 1248 (Ohio 2000).

57. Many of these cases are the direct result of sexual misconduct with minors. Such cases clearly do not violate any First Amendment establishment or free exercise provisions. For example, see *Smith v. O'Connell*, 986 F. Supp 73 (D.R.I. 1997).

58. See *Wallace v. Boy's Club of Albany, Georgia, Inc.*, 439 S.E.2d 746 (Ga. App. 1993), where the court remarked that "such a person is not an insurer of the safety of the child. He is required only to use reasonable care commensurate with the reasonably foreseeable risk of harm."

59. See *Sanders v. Casa View Baptist Church*, 134 F.3d 331 (5th Cir. 1998).

60. See *Handley v. Richards*, 518 S.2d 682 (Ala. 1987), where the court failed to recognize a claim of clergy malpractice. But see also *Nally v. Grace Community Church*, 763 P.2d 948 (Cal. 1988), where the California courts recognized a possible malpractice claim where unlicensed spiritual counselors failed to prevent a suicide. Not only was the theory not used as a basis of the court's final decision, but it was partially rescinded in a later opinion by the California Supreme Court concerning the same case.

61. This policy should define when it is applicable and to whom it applies. Normally only licensed and ordained clergy and psychologists should be covered. Avoid any suggestion that conversations with other employees or volunteers are confidential, as this may create a contractual duty to maintain confidence, while legally such confidentiality cannot be enforced or guaranteed.

62. A recent New Jersey decision held that a conversation with a deacon was not privileged or otherwise protected from compelled disclosure. *State v. Cary*, 751 A.2d 620 (N.J. Super. 2000).

63. This communication need not be spoken or in writing. It includes body language, actions during the conference, and even the internal assessment, thoughts, and intuition of the pastor. *Commonwealth v. Zezima*, 310 N.E.2d 590 (Mass. 1974).

64. Note that the existence of a valid privilege does not excuse the pastor from being subpoenaed or otherwise required to show at the court hearing. Normally, the court will decide the validity of the privilege only after the pastor has taken the witness stand.

65. Some states, such as California and Colorado, specifically provide that the privilege is available to both the clergyman and the penitent. Cal. Evid. Code §§1030 – §1034 and Colo.Rev.Stat. §13-90-107.

66. It is important to review the statute for your particular state. For example, in the state of Washington, two religious counselors who were not licensed or ordained ministers were held to be with the statute's definition of a "social worker" for reporting purposes. *State of Washington v. Motherwell*, 788 P.2d 1066 (Wash. 1990). This also points out the reason why religious counseling should not be done by employees who are not ordained ministers or licensed psychologists.

Part 4: Directing

1. Warren R. Plunkett and Raymond F. Attner, *Introduction to Management* (Boston: PWS-Kent Publishing, 1992), 12.

Chapter 17

1. James F. Bolt, "Developing Three-Dimensional Leaders," in *The Leader of the Future: New Visions, Strategies, and Practices for the Next Era,* ed. Francis Hesselbein, Marshall Goldsmith, and Richard Beckhard (New York: The Peter F. Drucker Foundation for Nonprofit Management, 1996), 163.

2. J. Robert Clinton, *The Making of a Leader* (Colorado Springs, Colo.: Navpress, 1988), 15.

3. Myron Rush, *Managing to Be the Best* (Wheaton, Ill.: Victor Books, 1989), 140.

4. Bill Hybels, *Courageous Leadership* (Grand Rapids: Zondervan, 2002), 122.

5. J. Robert Clinton, "Learning How God Develops Leaders over a Lifetime," in *Lessons in Leadership: Fifty Respected Evangelical Leaders Share Their Wisdom on Ministry,* ed. Randal Roberts (Grand Rapids: Kregel Publications, 1999), 73.

6. John C. Maxwell, *The 21 Irrefutable Laws of Leadership* (Nashville: Thomas Nelson Publishers, 1998), 133.

7. Hybels, 122–132.

8. Max De Pree, *Leadership Is an Art* (New York: Doubleday, 1989), 12.

9. Maxwell, *The 21 Irrefutable Laws,* 221.

10. Ken Blanchard, "Following the *Real* Leader," in *The Transparent Leader,* ed. Dwight Johnson (Eugene, Ore.: Harvest House Publishers, 2001), 31.

11. Jay A. Conger, *Learning to Lead: The Art of Transforming Managers into Leaders* (San Francisco: Jossey-Bass, 1992), 33.

12. Aubrey Malphurs, *Being Leaders: The Nature of Authentic Christian Leadership* (Grand Rapids: Baker Books, 2003), 75.

13. Clinton, *The Making of a Leader,* 15–16.

14. J. Clinton, "Learning How God Develops Leaders," 72.

15. Conger, 31–32.

16. James M. Kouzes and Barry Z. Posner, "Bringing Leadership Lessons from the Past into the Future," in *The Future of Leadership,* ed. Warren Bennis, Gretchen M. Spreitzer, and Thomas G. Cummings (San Francisco: Jossey-Bass, 2001), 87.

17. J. Oswald Sanders, *Spiritual Leadership,* 2nd rev. (Chicago: Moody Press, 1994), 79.

18. Jay A. Conger and Beth Benjamin, *Building Leaders: How Successful Companies Develop the Next Generation* (San Francisco: Jossey-Bass, 1999), 21–22.

19. Reggie McNeal, *A Work of Heart: Understanding How God Shapes Spiritual Leaders* (San Francisco: Jossey-Bass, 2000), 131.

20. Malphurs, 76–80.

21. Rick Warren, _The Purpose-Driven Life_ (Grand Rapids: Zondervan, 2002), 241–248.

22. Malphurs.

23. Malphurs, 80–86.

24. Peter G. Northhouse, _Leadership: Theory and Practice_, 3rd ed. (Thousand Oaks, Calif.: Sage Publications, 2004), 36–39.

25. Conger, 180.

26. Clinton, _The Making of a Leader_, 25.

27. Conger, 180.

28. Clinton, _The Making of a Leader._

29. Hybels, 124–126.

30. Carl F. George and Robert E. Logan, _Leading and Managing Your Church_ (Old Tappan, N.J.: Fleming H. Revell, 1987), 106.

31. Roy B. Zuck, _Teaching as Paul Taught_ (Grand Rapids: Baker Books, 1998), 121.

32. George and Logan, 117.

33. John P. Kotter, "What Leaders Really Do," in _Harvard Business Review on Leadership_ (Boston: Harvard Business School Publishing, 1998), 50.

34. Sanders, 145.

35. Conger, 9.

36. Conger and Benjamin, 211–212.

37. Lorin Woolfe, _The Bible on Leadership: From Moses to Matthew: Management Lessons for Contemporary Leaders_ (New York: American Management Association, 2002), 217.

38. John C. Maxwell, _Develop the Leaders Around You_ (Nashville: Thomas Nelson Publishers, 1995), 93–94.

39. Fred Smith, _Learning to Lead_ (Carol Stream, Ill.: Christianity Today, Inc., 1986), 114–115.

40. George and Logan, 106–113.

41. Maxwell, _Develop the Leaders_, 96–98.

42. Myron Rush, _Management: A Biblical Approach_ (Wheaton, Ill.: Victor Books, 1983), 132.

43. James M. Kouzes and Barry Z. Posner, _Credibility: How Leaders Lose and Gain It, Why People Demand It_ (San Francisco: Jossey-Bass, 1993), 153–182.

Chapter 18

1. Michael J. Anthony, "Mentoring," in _The Evangelical Dictionary of Christian Education_ (Grand Rapids: Baker Books, 2003), 459.

2. Howard Hendricks and William Hendricks, _As Iron Sharpens Iron_ (Chicago: Moody Press, 1995), 160.

3. Paul D. Stanley and J. Robert Clinton, _Connecting: The Mentoring Relationship You Need to Succeed in Life_ (Colorado Springs: Navpress, 1992), 40.

4. Marcia A. McMullen and Patricia M. Miller, *Because You Believed in Me: Mentors and Protégés Who Shaped Our World* (Kansas City: Andrews McMeel Publishing, 2002), 4–5.

5. Ibid., 12–13.

6. Ibid., 8.

7. Ibid., 68.

8. Chip R. Bell, *Managers as Mentors* (San Francisco: Berrett-Koehler Publishers, 1996), 6.

9. J. Robert Clinton and Richard W. Clinton, *The Mentor Handbook* (Altadena: Barnabas Publishers, 1991), 13–6.

10. Ibid., 13.

11. Ibid., 193.

12. Ibid., 195.

13. Maxwell, *Developing the Leaders Around You*, 11.

14. Gordon F. Shea, *Mentoring* (Menlo Park: Crisp Publications, 2002), 9.

15. Hendricks and Hendricks, *As Iron Sharpens Iron*, 98.

16. Clinton and Clinton, *The Mentor Handbook*, 2–23, 2–24.

17. Stanley and Clinton, *Connecting*, 65.

18. James M. Houston, *The Mentored Life* (Colorado Springs: Navpress, 2002), 86.

19. Larry Ambrose, *A Mentor's Companion* (Chicago: Perrone-Ambrose Associates, 1998), 12–13.

20. Chip R. Bell, *Managers as Mentors* (San Francisco: Berrett-Koehler Publishers, 1996), 75.

21. Ibid., 60.

22. Shea, 65.

23. Hendricks and Hendricks, 113.

24. Margo Murray, *Beyond the Myths and Magic of Mentoring* (San Francisco: Jossey-Bass, 2001), 34.

25. Bobb Biehl, *Mentoring: Confidence in Finding a Mentor and Becoming One* (San Francisco: Berrett-Koehler Publishers, 1996), 73.

26. Hendricks and Hendricks, 147.

27. Stanley and Clinton, 205.

28. Hendricks and Hendricks, 218–219.

29. Lois J. Zachary, *The Mentor's Guide* (San Francisco: John Wiley and Sons, 2000), 50.

30. Ibid., 52.

31. Hendricks and Hendricks, 219.

Chapter 19

1. Stephen C. Lundin, Harry Paul, and John Christensen, *Fish!* (New York: Hyperion, 1996). Cf. also *Fishtales and Fish Sticks*.

2. In this chapter the term *unit* will serve as a generic term for any grouping of people, and hence may refer to a mass, crowd, group, team, or clique, depending on the dynamics governing the unit.

3. Cf. Lee G. Bolman and Terrence E. Deal, *Reframing Organizations* (San Francisco: Jossey-Bass, 1997), 92–94. Their comments are based on Katzenbach and Smith's *The Wisdom of Teams* (1993).

4. Kenneth Gangel, *Feeding and Leading* (Chicago: Victor Books, 1989), 229–230, 232.

5. Olan Hendrix, *Management for the Christian Leader* (Milford, Mich.: Mott Media, 1981), 74–76.

6. Adapted from Robert Maddux, *Team Building: An Exercise in Leadership,* 3rd ed. (Los Altos, Calif.: Crisp Publications, 1992), 5.

7. Myron Rush, *Management: A Biblical Approach* (Chicago: Victor Books, 1983), 57.

8. Hersey and Blanchard, *Management of Organizational Behavior,* 348.

9. Maddux, 45.

10. Cf. Robert Heller and Tim Hindle, *Essential Manager's Manual* (New York: D. K. Publishing, 1998), 365 for a discussion of various team formats.

11. Based on diagram in Jeff Story, "Team Building and Lay Leadership," *Church Administration* 39 (1997): 31.

12. Robert G. Owens, *Organizational Behavior in Education,* 4th ed. (Boston: Allyn and Bacon, 1991), 135.

13. Karen Marie Yust, *Attentive to God* (St. Louis: Chalice Press, 2001), 7.

14. Ibid., 11–13.

15. Cf. Stephen R. Covey, *The 7 Habits of Highly Effective People* (New York: Simon and Schuster, 1989), 145–182; Stephen R. Covey, *First Things First* (New York: Simon and Schuster, 1994).

16. Covey, *First Things First,* 37.

17. Ibid., 205, 218.

18. Gangel, *Team Leadership in Christian Ministry.*

19. Cf. Heller and Hindle, 372–375.

20. Lyman D. Ketchum and Eric Trist, *All Teams Are Not Created Equal: How Employee Empowerment Really Works* (Newbury Parks, N.J.: Sage Publications, 1992), 154.

21. Cf. Lloyd S. Baird, James E. Post, and John F. Mahon, *Management: Function and Responsibility* (New York: Harper Collins, 1990), 429, for a discussion on these four roles.

22. Diagram adapted from Heller and Hindle, 379.

23. Cf. Rush, 59–60; Heller and Hindle, 368–369; Deborah Harrington-Mackin, *The Team Building Tool Kit* (New York: Amacon, 1994), 13–22, 58–61; Gary A. Yukl, *Leadership in Organization,* 2nd ed. (Englewood Cliffs, N.J.: Prentice Hall, 1989), 241; Hersey and Blanchard, 352–362.

24. Yukl, 235–236.

Chapter 20

1. Leighton Ford, *Transformational Leadership* (Downers Grove, Ill.: IVP, 1991), 251.

2. Lee G. Bolman and Terrence E. Deal, *Reframing Organizations* (San Francisco: Jossey-Bass, 1997), 297.

3. Joseph C. Rost, *Leadership for the 21ˢᵗ Century* (Westport, Conn.: Praeger, 1993), 102.

4. Ibid., 145.

5. Ibid., 149.

6. James M. Kouzes and Barry Z. Posner, *The Leadership Challenge* (San Francisco: Jossey-Bass Publishers, 1987), 27.

7. Warren Bennis and B. Nannis, *Leaders: Strategies for Taking Charge* (New York: HarperCollins, 1985), 21.

8. Covey, *First Things First*, 206.

9. Carl George, "To Expand Your Outreach, Be a Rancher," *Servant Life* (March 1995), 7.

10. Hersey and Blanchard, 186.

11. Ibid., 206.

12. Adapted from Bolman and Deal, 15.

13. "Facilitating: A New Kind of Management," *Ministry Advantage* (March/April 1994), 8.

14. This is *partially* based on an interpretation of Dave Anderson, "When 'Good' Isn't Enough: How to Overcome the 6 Temptations of Successful Organizations," *Arrivals* (January/February 2004), 39–41. This article was an excerpt from his book, *Up Your Business: Seven Steps to Fix, Build, or Stretch Your Organization* (New York: John Wiley & Sons).

Chapter 21

1. Thomas Holland and David Hester, eds., *Building Effective Boards for Religious Organizations* (San Francisco: Jossey-Bass Publishers, 2000), 24–25.

2. Maureen K. Robinson, *Nonprofit Boards That Work: The End of One-Size-Fits-All Governance* (New York: John Wiley & Sons, Inc., 2001), 55.

3. John Carver, *Boards That Make a Difference: A New Design for Leadership in Nonprofit and Public Organizations* (San Francisco: Jossey-Bass Publishers, 1997), 205.

4. John Carver and Miriam M. Carver, *Reinventing Your Board: A Step-by-Step Guide to Implementing Policy Governance* (San Francisco: Jossey-Bass Publishers, 1997), 182.

5. Robinson, 57.

6. Diane J. Duca, *Nonprofit Boards: Roles, Responsibilities, and Performance* (New York: John Wiley & Sons, Inc., 1996), 102.

7. Duca, 109–110.

8. Howe, 30.

9. Howe, 31–32.

10. Duca, 75.

11. Duca, 125–126.

12. Richard P. Chait, Thomas P. Holland, and Barbara E. Taylor, *Improving the Performance of Governing Boards* (Phoenix: The American Council on Education and the Oryx Press, 1996), 112–113.

13. Mark Light, *The Strategic Board* (New York: John Wiley & Sons, 2001), ix.

Part 6: Evaluating

1. Ann Louden, "This Won't Hurt a Bit," *Case Currents* (July-August, 2001): 13.

2. Ibid., 13–14.

3. Daniel Brown, "When You Need to Confront," *Leadership* (Spring 1995): 92.

4. Stanley M. Widrick, Erhan Mergen, and Delvin Grant, "Measuring Dimenions of Quality in Higher Education," *Total Quality Management* (vol. 13, No. 1, 2002): 130.

5. Robert D. Herman and Associates, *The Jossey-Bass Handbook of Nonprofit Leadership and Management* (San Francisco: Jossey-Bass Publishers, 1994), 298.

Chapter 22

1. Lee G. Bolman and Terrence E. Deal, *Reframing Organizations,* 2nd ed. (San Francisco: Jossey-Bass, 1997), 244.

2. Michael Woodruff, "Managing Your Ministry," *Youthworker* (Winter 1994 10.3): 38.

3. Much of this material was developed in conjunction with John Castelein, professor of contemporary theology, at Lincoln Christian Seminary (Lincoln, Illinois) and Dr. Robert Kurka, professor of Bible and theology, at Lincoln Christian College, Lincoln, Illinois.

4. John Castelein, "Lincoln Christian College and Seminary Assessment Plan," Lincoln, Ill., 2003, 6.

5. Robert Kurka, "Lincoln Christian College and Seminary Assessment Plan," Lincoln, Ill., 2003, 7.

6. Bolman and Deal, 245.

7. Robert J. Wicks, "Spirituality and Ministry," *The Princeton Theological Bulletin* 12 (1991): 24.

8. Kenneth Gangel, *Team Leadership in Christian Ministry* (Chicago: Moody Press, 1997), 383.

9. Jim Ryan, "Rewarding Good Performance," *Church Administration,* 40 (1997): 28.

10. Adapted from Patrick J. Montana and Bruce H. Charnov, *Management* (Hauppauge, N.Y.: Barron's Educational Series, 2000), 285.

11. William Savage, "Conducting a Performance Review," *Church Administration* 40 (1997): 24.

12. Cf. Larry Osborne, "How to Get a Healthy Performance Review," *Leadership* 15 (1994): 120—123.

13. Alvin Jackson, "Honesty and Honor," Case Study: The Entrenched and Ineffective Worker, *Leadership* 14 (1993): 70.

14. Richard M. Hodgetts, *Modern Human Relations at Work,* 2nd ed. (New York: Dryden Press, 1980), 332.

15. Hodgetts, 332–333.

16. Larry W. Osborne, "Assessing and Improving Effectiveness," *Leadership Handbook of Management and Administration* (Grand Rapids: Baker Book House, 1994), 249.

17. Cf. Keith Keeran, "The Under-Performing Employee," *Christian Standard* (Feb. 22, 1992), 6–7.

18. Ryan, 27.

19. Kennon L. Callahan, *Effective Church Leadership* (San Francisco: Jossey-Bass, 1990), 200.

20. *Performance targets*, or job targets, refer to assigning a very specific set of tasks or measurable expectations with completion deadlines to a staff member in order to set a definitive level of expectation to maintain his or her position within the organization.

21. Paul Borthwick, "To Fire or Not to Fire" *Leadership* 6 (1985): 82–86.

22. Savage, 25.

23. Keeran, 6.

24. Osborne, "How to Get a Healthy Performance Review," 119.

25. Cf. ibid., 119–120.

26. Montana and Charnov, *Management*, 173.

27. Leroy Lawson, "Firm and Fair," Case Study: The Entrenched and Ineffective Worker, *Leadership* (Summer 1993), 71.

28. Adapted from Mike Woodruff, "Confronting a Volunteer," *Group* (May-June 1995), 21.

29. Cf. Osborne, 20–23.

30. Adele Margrave and Robert Gorden, *The Complete Idiot's Guide to Performance Appraisals* (Indianapolis, Ind.: Alpha Books, 2001), cover insert.

Chapter 23

1. Kenneth O. Gangel, *Team Leadership in Christian Ministry*, revised (Chicago: Moody Press, 1997), 373.

2. Ibid.

3. Aubrey Malphurs, *Advanced Strategic Planning: A New Model for Church and Ministry Leaders* (Grand Rapids: Baker Books, 1999), 200.

4. Ibid., 201.

5. Ibid., 202–204.

6. Ibid., 208.

7. Bob I. Johnson, "How to Plan and Evaluate," 56–57.

8. Fairbank and Prue, "Developing Performance Feedback Systems," 337.

9. Malphurs, *Advanced Strategic Planning*, 208.

10. Johnson, "How to Plan and Evaluate," 52–57.

11. Fairbank and Prue, "Developing Performance Feedback Systems," 337.

12. Ibid.

13. Norman Shawchuck and Roger Heuser, *Leading the Congregation: Caring for Yourself While Serving the People* (Nashville: Abingdon Press, 1993), 215.

14. Ibid., 214.

15. Fairbank and Prue, "Developing Performance Feedback Systems," 338–40.

16. Gangel, *Team Leadership in Christian Ministry*, 375.

17. Johnson, "How to Plan and Evaluate," 49.

18. William L. Johnson and Annabel M. Johnson, *Planning for University Faculty Assessment: Development of a Brief Summative-Evaluation Instrument* (Big Sandy, Tex.: Ambassador College, 1990), ERIC, ED 325 059, 6–9.

19. Ibid.

20. Robert F. DeVellis, *Scale Development: Theory and Applications*, Applied Social Research Methods Series, vol. 26 (Newbury Park, England: Sage Publications, 1991), 68–70.

21. Ibid.

22. Johnson, "How to Plan and Evaluate," 57.

23. Ibid.

24. Ibid., 47.

Index

Accountability 18, 29, 47, 54, 72, 79,
116, 148, 151, 152, 168, 177,
180, 181, 261, 262, 264, 310,
316, 318, 319, 321, 322, 331,
363, 367
Administration 1, 2, 4, 9–13, 35, 52,
76, 78, 103, 109, 118, 125–126,
130, 172, 201, 204, 207, 212,
241, 248–249, 266, 274, 301,
354, 356, 358, 362, 365, 366,
377, 401, 405
Agenda 48, 57, 69, 71, 89, 98,
132–133, 142, 156, 160, 168,
177, 196, 197, 239, 341, 344,
347, 348, 358, 364, 369,
372–376, 404, 406, 408
Assessment 6, 16, 90, 115, 123, 135,
142, 143, 148, 179, 192, 200,
210, 218, 229, 233, 236, 262,
269, 309, 344, 358, 360, 363,
383, 387–397, 399–402, 404,
407, 412–413, 415, 417–418,
422, 426
Association 23, 162, 281, 307, 392
Authority 35, 39, 40–42, 46, 60, 88,
138, 147, 151, 155, 159–160,
166–167, 170, 172, 176–181,
184, 187, 292, 306, 310, 343,
350, 355, 358, 368, 375, 390,
392, 402
Background Check 253–254
Bible/Biblical 1, 2, 4, 9–14, 18, 21,
24, 27–29, 32, 37, 38, 41, 51,
59, 61–64, 66, 88, 95–99, 103,
109, 110, 112, 126, 137, 162,
166, 170, 172–173, 177, 188,
204, 212, 222–24, 241, 245–47,
255, 258, 260, 261, 266–267,
271, 274, 279–280, 288, 298,
305–308, 316, 341, 348–349,
356, 365–366, 385, 388–389
Boards 110, 136, 144, 163, 165, 190,
222, 250, 260, 264, 295
Brianstorming 146, 228–229, 347

Budget 6, 14, 28, 55, 69–70, 78–79,
105, 111, 115–132, 137,
145–147, 153, 168, 174, 189,
192, 228, 248, 262, 264, 293,
304, 371, 378, 381, 411, 412,
422
Business 1, 2, 10, 13, 21, 32, 37–38,
43, 45, 49–50, 78–80, 99, 103,
106, 118–119, 123, 134, 150,
165, 166, 168–169, 176–177,
186, 196–197, 212, 244, 246,
254, 277, 281, 284, 291, 297,
308, 327, 334, 340, 353, 365,
372, 374, 387–388, 426
Calling 6, 64, 77, 318, 344, 349,
352–354, 369
Capital Fund 120
Centralization 116
Change 1, 6, 23–24, 27–28, 41, 59,
61, 65–66, 69–70, 73–74, 79, 86,
89, 94, 97–98, 100, 103, 107,
110, 112, 118, 122–125, 129,
130, 136, 139, 143, 145–147,
153, 156–157, 161–162, 165,
168, 172–173, 182–183, 188,
192, 195, 198, 201, chapter 12,
224, 228, 230, 232, 247,
249–251, 263–266, 269–270,
272, 275, 278, 285, 291, 198,
297, 305, 313, 325–326,
330–332, 334, 335, 352, 355,
357, 361, 370, 371, 377, 378,
381, 389, 398, 407, 414, 415,
417, 423
Committees 10, 104, 110, 143, 147,
172, 190, 222, 295, chapter 21
Communication 30, 72, 78, 102, 105,
106, 155, 159, 160, 163, 166,
172, 178, 179, 189, 196, 198,
200, 209, 210, 213, chapter 13,
270, 289, 290, 311, 321, 329,
347, 358, 376, 398
Conflict 6, 21, 28, 54, 71, 73, 89,
102, 105, 106, 107, 109, 110,

111, 114, 124, 132, 133, 165,
177, 189, 201, 201, 204, 214,
218–221, 260, 262, 266, 269,
270, 273, 279, 288, 293, 295,
304, 331, 335, 342, 347, 357,
369, 374, 380
Control 28, 34, 70, 105, 106, 110,
111, 131, 133, 134, 150,
152–154, 156, 160, 165, 168,
169, 176, 197, 253, 272,
280–282, 284–286, 295, 305,
311, 327, 328, 356, 358, 360,
370, 371, 373
Core Values 41, 67, 90, 92, 208, 214,
247, 262, 263, 363, 367, 370,
371, 377, 378
Debt 131, 214, 282, 285,
Decentralization 116
Decisions 10, 29, 36, 38, 41, 42, 90,
91, 96, 99, 107, 116, 130, 135,
136, 141, 157, 162, 165, 168,
170, 193, 196, 198, 200, 208,
222–228, 231, 232, 239, 265,
279, 281, 286–288, 311, 321,
325, 341, 345, 347, 348, 361,
368, 377–381, 385, 386, 402,
404, 405
Education 1, 2, 6, 22, 37–41, 49, 50,
52, 62, 67, 74, 75, 78, 103, 109,
112, 115, 121–123, 127, 134,
137, 148, 152, 161, 163, 170,
171, 172, 175, 176, 178, 181,
184, 187, 189, 196207, 216, 227,
239, 240, 248, 252, 274, 276,
278, 279, 281, 284, 295, 300,
308, 312, 320, 334, 335, 362,
387, 388, 392, 395
Evaluation 4, 28, 54, 73, 90, 92,
96–98, 112, 180, 195, 197, 207,
216, 227, 239, 240, 248, 252,
274, 276, 278, 279, 281, 284,
295, 300, 309, 312, 317, 331,
345, 358, 363, 379, 380,
383–386, 390–392, 394–410,
chapter 23
Finance/Financial 9, 13, 28, 54, 55,
66, 70, 73, 93, 111, 112, chapter
7, 136, 140, 141, 145, 153, 157,

165, 176, 179, 214, 228, 278,
317, 368–370, 411
Goals 4, 21, 54, 55, 69, 75–89, 92,
94, 9–9, 125, 128, 129, 131,
133, 134, 137–148, 150–153,
155, 160, 165, 186, 192, 195,
196, 198, 231, 241, 258–266,
273, 278, 293, 294, 299, 304,
309, 310, 315, 331, 334, 338,
339, 343, 357, 358, 368, 370,
371, 373, 374, 378, 380, 381,
384, 390, 414–416, 418
Group 6, 11, 17, 20, 23, 36, 57, 64,
66, 67, 76, 78, 81, 83, 84, 91,
93, 94, 99, 111, 112, 123, 124,
126, 130, 131, 137, 147, 159,
162, 163, 170–173, 190,
192–200, 204, 205, 210, 222,
223, 225, 226, 229–233, 239,
241, 247, 250–252, 254, 261,
262, 294, 295, 302–304, 310,
311, 324, chapter 19, 358, 359,
361, 365, 366, 368–374, 379,
385, 394, 398, 404, 416, 418
Leaders/Leadership 1, 2, 4, 6, 7, 10,
12, 14, 17, 19–51, 55, 56,
60–93, 98, 99, 103–105,
107–112, 115–122, 125–133,
135–139, 148, 149, 153, 154,
156, 158–163, 165, 167–169,
171–181, 195, 198, 200, 201,
chapter 12, 223, 224, 231, 232,
237–241, 245–255, 259, 261,
263–266, 268, 270, 271, 294,
295, chapter 17, 315–319, 321,
323, 324, 326, 327, 329,
332–335, 340–343, 348, chapter
20, 366, 369, 370, 372, 382,
383, 385, 387, 389, 392, 395,
396, 403, 412–416, 425
Leadership styles 295, 342, 349, 356
Learning 34, 76, 119, 157, 190, 207,
210, 233, 271, 294, 301, 302,
306–312, 314, 318, 324, 329,
330, 370, 373, 416
Liability 119, 276, 278, 280–283,
285–287, 291, 414
Litigation 30, 275, 283, 371
Malpractice 289

Management 1–4, 6, 10–13, chapter
1, 36, 37, 56, 68, 77, 79, 94,
119, 123, 130, 134, 144,
145–148, 150, 152, 155, 165,
176, 180, 201, 201, 219, 224,
242, 258, 261, 262, 264, 269,
273–275, 287, 293, 299, 349,
354–357, 360, 361, 363, 395,
416, 423
Ministry 1, 2, 4, 6, 9–13, 16, 17,
20–34, 36–52, 54–83, chapter 5,
119, 123, 130, chapter 8, 165,
176, 180, chapter 12, 237,
240–243, 245–248, 250, 253,
255, 258, 260–266, 268–273,
chapter 16–18, 333–335, 337,
338, 341, 350–352, 356–359,
361, 363, 403, 409, 412–418,
422–426
Mission 4, 9, 11, 14, 16, 17, 23, 25,
36, 33, 36, 39, 41, 43, 48, 49,
52–56, chapter 3, 78, 79, 84, 85,
88–92, 96, 99, 100, 103, 105,
108, 116, 120, 126, 128, 129,
133, 136, 137, 142, 148, 150,
151, 152, 155, 172, 180, 187,
189204, 208, 212, 214, 215, 220,
224, 226, 228, 233, 235–238,
241, 245, 246, 254, 255,
258–263, 265, 271, 274, 275,
284, 293, 294, 297–299, 365,
366, 377–381, 383–387,
389–391, 395, 409, 414, 415,
418
Negotiate 110, 151, 273, 405
Objectives 6, 13, 21, 24, 28, 54, 55,
56, chapter 4, 87, 89, 90, 92, 96,
95, 96, 98, 99, 123, 125, 128,
129, chapter 8, 168, 186, 192,
202, 212, 213, 224, 233, 260,
262–264, 271, 281, 282, 293,
294, 319, 332, 334, 335, 357,
368, 371, 374, 378, 380, 381,
384, 405
Organization/Organizational 2, 4, 6,
10, 11, 13, 18–21, 24, 28, 33,
36, 38, 41–44, 49–51, 53–55, 57,
63, 65, 69, 70, 71, 73, 75–81,
83–85, 87, 89, 90, 92, 93, 94,

96, 97, 99, 103–112, 115–128,
131, 132, 134, 137, 138, 140,
142, 148, 149, 152, 153, 155,
chapter 9, chapter 10, 190, 193,
201, 201–221, chapter 13,
240–242, 245, 248, 249,
251–253, 258, 260–264,
267–273, 275–289, 291–295,
297–299, 302, 304, 305, 309,
311, 319–322, 324328, 329,
331335, 338, 339, 348–350,
352–357, 359–364, 366–374,
376–379, 381, 382, 385–389,
391–393, 395–397, 402, 403,
404, 406–409, 412, 415–418,
422, 423
Outcomes 54, 73, 76, 78, 79, 80, 88,
97, 104, 123, 178, 183, 198,
220, 226, 227, 229, 230, 244,
273, 315, 321, 325, 326, 393,
415, 416, 418, 422, 426
Performance 138–140, 142, 145, 146,
148, 150–152, 171, 176, 177,
179–183, 189, 200, 239, 341,
342, 364, 267, 294, 317, 329,
341, 346, 352, 363, 369, 371,
372, 377–381, 383, 384, chapter
22, 415–417
Planning 4, 6, 11, 13–17, 21, 32, 33,
37, 53–58, 86, chapter 5–8, 177,
196, 197, 200, 202, 204, 207,
212, 228, 248, 250, 252, 255,
266, 304, 319, 329, 341, 357,
369, 371, 374, 376–381, 396,
417, 422, 426
Policies 6, 14, 19, 21, 30, 42, 5455,
chapter 6, 115, 124, 159, 167,
170, 212, 214, 228, 231,
253–255, 266, 355, 367, 368,
371, 374, 375, 412
Procedures 6, 14, 19, 30, 42, 53–55,
79, chapter 6, 115, 124, 159,
167, 170, 212, 214, 215, 231,
261, 281, 343, 349, 355, 369,
371, 373, 388, 407, 412, 416
Professional 50, 55, 62, 125, 171,
219, 245, 255, 264, 266, 268,
271, 278, 284, 289–292, 305,
315, 323, 330, 362, 363, 367,
372, 387, 395, 416

Records 14, 19, 29, 112, 131, 253,
    288, 407, 411, 412, 418, 423
Relationships 18, 49, 50–52, 138,
    150, 155, 159, 160, 165, 172,
    178, 184, 187, 188, 201, 201,
    215, 218, 219, 244, 266, 268,
    271, 273, 300, 313–321, 324,
    326, 327, 329, 331, 332, 335,
    341, 344, 380, 387, 398
Recruitment 178, 182, 241, 246, 249,
    255, 352, 379
Reviews 140, 142, 143, 151, 380,
    383, 385, chapter 22
Rules/Regulations 63, 95, 105, 108,
    126, 168, 276, 278331, 343, 367,
    373, 416, 423
Servant/Servanthood 9, 23, 25, 33,
    34, 40, 45–48, 50, 62, 64, 168,
    246, 297, 298, 376, 393
Spiritual Gifts 21, 47, 103, 158, 248,
    250, 255
Structures 42, 73, 116, 124, 157,
    chapter 9, 207, 248, 261, 302,
    415, 416
Stewardship 1, 9, 10, 17, 20, 25, 28,
    47, 48, 97, 132, 135, 148, 153,
    172, 264, 275, 314, 320, 333,
    357, 381
Supervision 10, 23, 133, 150, 241,
    258, 266, 287, 288, 314, 320,
    333, 357, 381
S.W.A.T. Team/Teamwork 6, 11, 23,
    57, 58, 68, 69, 71, 77–79, 82,
    83, 93–97, 100–102, 124, 125,
    129, 132–134, 138, 141–145,
    147, 149, 152, 157, 167, 168,
    171, 175–177, 179, 181, 182,
    189, 191, 192, 194, 200, 210,
    212, 214, 222, 225, 237, 239,
    242, 243, 249, 250–252,
    258–260, 262–266, 269, 272,
    293–295, 303, 308, 309, 311,
    329, chapter 19, 357–361365,
    378, 381, 388, 411, 412
Testing 214
Theology/Theological 1, 2, 4, 10, 12,
    13, 31, 32, 35, 37–51, 42, 44,
    60, 62, 75, 103, 109, 158, 167,
    207, 212, 214, 222, 225–227,
    236, 245, 307, 309, 341, 348,

    353, 361, 362, 370, 374, 387,
    389, 390, 393, 404
Time/Time Management 6, 10, 12–14,
    16, 17, 20, 22, 24, 25, 27, 31,
    41, 47, 49, 50, 56, 57, 59,
    63–74, 77–85, 88, 91–94, 96, 98,
    101, 102, 104–114, 117, 118,
    121, 124–127, 129, 131–148,
    150–153, 156, 161, 165, 168,
    171, 173, 175, 177–183,
    188–200, 202–204, 209, 212,
    213, 224, 237, 241, 242, 244,
    245, 247–250, 252, 258,
    260–264, 268–273, 275, 276,
    278, 279, 281–283, 290, 291,
    295, 299, 303, 304, 306, 307,
    313–317, 320, 322, 324, 325,
    328, 329, 331, 332, 341, 358,
    361, 364, 369–385387, 393, 394
Training 6, 7, 20–24, 62, 67, 68, 97,
    119, 134, 137, 152, 167, 184,
    187, 189, 240, 242, 244, 247,
    248, 250–252, 255, 272, 287–
    289, 295, 297–300, 302–305,
    307–312, 315, 370, 372, 384,
    387, 393, 401–403
Vision 4, 6, 10, 14, 23, 26, 27, 41, 51,
    53–55, chapter 3, 79, 82–85,
    88–92, 94, 96, 98, 99, 107–109,
    125, 126, 131, 133, 134, 136–
    139, 142, 148, 150, 151, 155,
    159, 170, 171, 183, 184, 188,
    189, 202, 201, 208, 212, 214,
    224, 228, 232, 241, 245, 248,
    249, 252, 255, 258, 260, 261,
    262, 263, 265, 266, 274, 278,
    280, 281, 284, 287, 288, 293,
    297, 299, 302, 304, 309, 314,
    320, 330, 352, 355, 364, 370,
    377, 378, 391, 396
Voting/Consensus 36, 128, 163, 170,
    188, 198, 231, 343, 347, 348,
    361, 392, 407